For Mary Leamy
and in memory of
Morty and Eileen Broderick,
and Michael Leamy

THOMAS MEAGHER

THOMAS MEAGHER

FORGOTTEN FATHER OF
THOMAS FRANCIS MEAGHER

Eugene Broderick

IRISH ACADEMIC PRESS

First published in 2022 by
Irish Academic Press
10 George's Street
Newbridge
Co. Kildare
Ireland
www.iap.ie

978 1 78855 219 6 (Cloth)
978 1 78855 023 9 (Ebook)

A CIP catalogue record for this book
is available from the British Library.

Typeset in Minion Pro 11/15 pt

Front cover image: Portrait of Thomas Meagher as Mayor of Waterford,
courtesy of the Waterford Museum of Treasures
Back cover image: 'The Mall, Waterford, 1812', by Samuel Frederick Brocas,
courtesy of the Waterford Museum of Treasures

Cover design: riverdesignbooks.com

Irish Academic Press is a member of Publishing Ireland.

Contents

Foreword

I am glad to see that Thomas Meagher, prominent Waterford merchant, city mayor and member of parliament has found his biographer in the accomplished Waterford historian Eugene Broderick.

There are a number of reasons why I see Meagher as deserving of biographical attention. He was representative of the Catholic middle class that emerged as a factor in Irish public life in the first half of the nineteenth century, its major accomplishment being the achievement of Catholic Emancipation in 1829 under Daniel O'Connell's charismatic leadership.

Meagher is an ideal case study of O'Connellite nationalism, which was, despite its failure to deliver the repeal of the Act of Union, to my mind the outstanding political phenomenon of Ireland's nineteenth century. He was an important O'Connell loyalist in a city that played a significant role in O'Connell's ascent and durability.

The strained father-son relationship within the Meagher clan offers an irresistible dramatisation of the split between Repealers and Young Irelanders that preceded the rebellion of 1848 and Thomas Francis Meagher's deportation and permanent exile from Ireland. That divide between parliamentary nationalism and more advanced expressions of nationalism, even if not always an absolute one, was a permanent feature of the Irish experience throughout the nineteenth century and beyond.

There is a degree of irony in the fact that in the Meagher case the son's reputation has well and truly eclipsed that of the father. For while 'Meagher of the Sword' had a brief flourish as a patriotic orator and made one unsuccessful bid for elected office, his father had a decades-long record in Waterford's local government and a ten-year stint representing the city at Westminster. Meagher senior's quieter service has been drowned out by the swashbuckling character of his son's life on three continents, but that is often the way history pans out.

Another notable feature of Thomas Meagher's life was his unstinting devotion to the Catholic Church and to the cause of equal rights for the Catholic community. Meagher's parliamentary career (1847–57) coincided with the emergence of Cardinal Paul Cullen and the ensuing transformation of Irish Catholicism, which had long-lasting effects. Like most prominent Catholics of his day, Meagher was a staunch opponent of the Queen's Colleges, insisting that Catholics ought to have a university of their own, hence his decision to send Thomas Francis to Stonyhurst, the Jesuit institution in Lancashire, in preference to Trinity College Dublin.

Another notable feature of Meagher's life is that he held local public office during and after the Great Famine of the 1840s, and Eugene Broderick throws valuable light on the thankless task of trying to cope with the tsunami of misery unleashed during those catastrophic years. He does not spare his subject criticism for his role as a Poor Law Guardian, thus overseeing a cruel and heartless regime for dealing with the expanding ranks of the poor.

I am glad that this book pays due attention to Thomas Meagher's ten years as a Westminster MP. While, as his biographer freely acknowledges, Meagher was not a figure of the first rank, he was part of a significant Irish political coterie. It is important to recognise the labours of generations of Irish parliamentarians in London who, in supremely difficult circumstances, strove to represent and secure improvements for their constituents. While the careers of titans like O'Connell, Isaac Butt, Charles Stewart Parnell, John Dillon and John Redmond have all attracted significant attention, there are hundreds of other parliamentarians like Meagher whose reputations rest in obscurity. Across those decades, Irish MPs were required to wade into the shifting currents of British parliamentary politics to find niches where Irish interests could be accommodated. One such arrangement was O'Connell's deal with Lord Melbourne which produced, among other measures, the Municipal Corporations Act of 1840. This was an important reform of local government in Ireland which, in turn, led to Thomas Meagher becoming the first Catholic mayor of Waterford since the seventeenth century. By such unheralded increments is history – and biography – made.

Daniel Mulhall
Ambassador of Ireland to the United States
Washington DC, January 2022

Preface

I welcome this book on one of the most distinguished citizens of nineteenth-century Waterford, Thomas Meagher (1783–1874). As Mayor of Waterford City and County, I am especially gratified that the life and career of one of my most illustrious predecessors has been recorded by Eugene Broderick. Thomas Meagher was Mayor of Waterford in 1843 and 1844, the first mayor elected under the terms of the Municipal Corporations Act 1840, which heralded the beginning of a process that laid the foundations of our present system of democratic and representative local government.

Thomas Meagher served in other public offices, as MP for Waterford City from 1847–57 and as a poor law guardian over many years. He was active in the latter role during the Great Famine, seeking to alleviate the sufferings and deprivations experienced by so many in the city and county. Throughout his life, he was noted for his philanthropy and generosity towards his less advantaged fellow citizens, being a founder member of the Society of St Vincent de Paul in the city. He also advocated and supported in Parliament the extension of the franchise and the secret ballot, a reform which would politically empower a greater number of people.

Thomas Meagher was also the father of Thomas Francis Meagher and this book sheds much new light on one of Waterford's most famous figures, the young man who gave Ireland its national flag and who achieved fame in his adopted country of the United States. The exploration of the relationship between father and son is one of the most interesting and satisfying parts of this publication.

I am delighted that the life and career of Thomas Meagher has been researched and documented, and I congratulate Eugene Broderick on contributing to our knowledge of Waterford's, and Ireland's, history.

Councillor Joe Kelly
Mayor of Waterford City and County
March 2022

Introduction

Writing in 1929, the distinguished Waterford historian, Matthew Butler, asserted with conviction that 'the only claim of Thomas Meagher to remembrance is that he was the father and active opponent of [his son] Thomas Francis Meagher'.[1] This assessment is in stark contrast to that of the younger Meagher by Patrick Egan, who lauded him in near-hagiographical terms as 'the pride of Waterford, the day-star of its political heaven … the military hero who carried the sword of honour and chivalry … bringing fame and glory upon the Irish sword and Irish heroism'.[2] It is understandable that Thomas Meagher has been overshadowed by his son, whose dramatic and colourful life 'suggests a fiction from the quintessential era of European Romanticism, perhaps a novel by Victor Hugo or even an opera by Berlioz'.[3] Thus, while the younger Meagher has earned a 'luminous immortality',[4] his elder languishes in Lethean obscurity, notwithstanding the fact that he was a figure of some substance in his own right.

Thomas Francis Meagher himself contributed to the relative silence attendant on his father. John Mannion has noted that 'he makes little mention in his speeches, reminiscences and other writings to his ancestry and extended family'.[5] In his 'Recollections of Waterford', a piece of nearly thirty pages, his father scarcely features: there is a brief reference to the fact that he was Mayor of Waterford.[6] In his more lengthy 'A Personal Narrative of 1848', he mentions his father twice, highlighting his disapproval of his son's admiration for the French Revolution of 1848 and his participation in the Young Ireland rising of the same year.[7] For whatever reason, 'details on personal family background rarely entered [his] public discourse'.[8]

Accordingly, Thomas Francis's various biographers have accorded his father a 'walk-on' part.

In an introduction to his biography of Thomas Francis Meagher, Captain W.F. Lyons declared: 'Why the life of Thomas Francis Meagher should be written requires no explanation.'[9] However, it is necessary, perhaps, to explain why his heretofore ignored father deserves to be the subject of a biographical study. Three reasons may be offered.

Most obvious, a study of the life of Thomas Meagher contributes to a greater understanding of his son, described by Arthur Griffith as 'the most picturesque and gallant figure of Young Ireland',[10] whose historical persona continues to attract attention, interest and even admiration in Ireland and the United States. A biography of his father illuminates the paternal formative influences that helped shape the ideas and actions of the younger man. A focus on their respective political views highlights the conflict between constitutional and physical-force nationalism, which emerged in 1848, with Thomas Meagher rejecting his son's espousal of violence during the Young Ireland rebellion of that year. However, in terms of their politics, the two men had much in common, and the beliefs of the son were closer to those of his father than is appreciated, a fact obscured by the younger Meagher's rhetoric and participation in the abortive rising.

Second, according to Roy Foster, Thomas Meagher 'represents exactly the *couche sociale* politically empowered by the O'Connellite revolution.'[11] His life, therefore, may be regarded as a case study of a relatively neglected figure in Irish history: the Catholic middle-class O'Connellite nationalist. It was persons such as Meagher who gave local and national leadership to the campaigns of the 'Liberator' for Catholic emancipation, reform of municipal corporations and repeal of the Act of Union. This resurgent group, empowered by O'Connell, was to have a very significant impact on shaping the character of Irish politics and society during the nineteenth century. Thomas Meagher has a particular value as a candidate for this historical case study because Waterford was recognised as a stronghold of support for Daniel O'Connell.[12]

Third, a biography of Thomas Meagher gives a valuable insight into the matters which concerned and influenced the lives of people in the corner of Ireland that was Waterford and, in fact, in many other parts of the country. David Gorman has argued that biography is the ideal framework for historians to assess 'the ideas which contemporaries recorded, argued and propagated'.[13] Examining historical issues through the lens of an individual may facilitate a greater understanding and appreciation of the political and social context in which he or she operated.[14] And Thomas Meagher is an especially promising candidate for a biographical study because of his involvement in so many aspects of political and social life over a period of four decades, from 1820 to 1860.

He was born in Newfoundland *c*.1789, a fact which is a reminder of the close commercial links between Waterford, the south-east of Ireland and the far-flung Atlantic island. Relocating to Ireland in 1819, Meagher was a prominent leader in Waterford of the campaign for Catholic emancipation during the 1820s. The following decade saw him supporting O'Connell's first tentative steps in calling for repeal and reform of municipal government, and his election as a poor law guardian. The 1840s were busy and dramatic years for him: in 1842 he was elected a member of Waterford Corporation, as reformed under the terms of the Municipal Corporations Act 1840, and he was selected by that body as the first Catholic Mayor of Waterford since the seventeenth century, in which position he served for two years, from 1843 to 1845. In his mayoral capacity he became the effective local leader of O'Connell's repeal campaign, which was at its most intense in 1843. He was also a staunch advocate of the cause of temperance, as promoted by Father Mathew. At the height of the Great Famine (1845–48), he was active in voluntary measures to relieve distress, while also acting in an official capacity as a poor law guardian. He opposed the establishment of the non-denominational Queen's Colleges, as announced by Prime Minister Robert Peel in 1845, favouring a Catholic university instead. In 1847 he was elected an MP for Waterford city and was its parliamentary representative for ten years. In 1848 his son, Thomas Francis, was one of the leaders of the Young Ireland rebellion. Throughout the 1850s, Thomas Meagher was an active supporter of the cause of independent opposition and of the Independent Irish Party. He also served for a period during this decade as a member of the national committee seeking to establish a Catholic university.

Throughout his life in Waterford, Thomas Meagher was a noted philanthropist and benefactor of those less socially and economically advantaged than he was. He was an active supporter of many charities and a generous financial donor to them. His beneficence to Catholic religious orders is noteworthy, and indicative of his deep commitment to his religion and Church. He is an excellent example of the middle-class representative who contributed to the progress and development of the Catholic Church before and after the Famine. Indeed, Meagher's long career in political activism was characterised by his determined and prolonged campaigning for equality of treatment of his co-religionists and his defence of Catholic interests. However, it is this centrality of religion and religious issues that may present his biographer with a particular difficulty.

Given the social and cultural environment of the third decade of the twenty-first century, it may be difficult for many to appreciate how, in the nineteenth century, religion played a decisive role in the way in which individuals and nations saw themselves.[15] It is fundamental to an understanding of the world in which Meagher lived to realise that religious beliefs and values were normative, informing most aspects of a person's life. Meagher saw himself as a Roman Catholic Christian and this self-perception influenced, to a very significant degree, his thoughts and actions. His world view was religio-centric.

It is precisely because Great Britain defined itself in Protestant terms that the struggle for Catholic equality in Ireland was intense and lengthy. There was enormous resistance by the Protestant political establishment to admit Catholics to the benefits of a constitution founded on the principles of Protestantism. To enable the modern reader to appreciate the passions and emotions engendered by the issue of Catholic rights in the nineteenth century, it can be compared to the ongoing struggle in this century for women's rights, racial equality, climate justice and gay rights, the last of these described by former Tánaiste Eamon Gilmore as the civil rights issue of his generation.[16] Catholic rights was one of the principal civil rights issues of Meagher's generation. The concession of the Catholic Emancipation Act in 1829 did not mean a cessation of the struggle: its practical implementation was frustrated by Protestant obstructionism for many years after its enactment.

The biographer of Meagher faces yet another difficulty: the absence of known private papers belonging to him. As historian Senia Paseta has remarked, 'the re-construction of mentalities is notoriously difficult, especially when few records of intimate thoughts and aspirations such as those which sometimes appear in diaries and personal letters are available.'[17] This shortcoming certainly presents problems when discussing his personal relationship with his family, and especially with Thomas Francis Meagher. In terms of his public life, however, the difficulty is greatly mitigated by the fact that his political speeches and activities were reported in the Waterford and, at times, in the national press. Fortunately, some very important letters he wrote on issues relating to politics were published in newspapers. The local press is also an invaluable source, in the absence of official records which are no longer extant, of some of his time as a poor law guardian.

Thomas Meagher was not a leader of the first rank: he was never a major political or social actor, cast in an epic mould. But few members of any generation are. Rather, he is a significant representative of the Catholic middle class, who in their own localities and occasionally at national level gave purpose and direction to the various political and social campaigns of the nineteenth century. Thus, Meagher becomes a figure of historic interest, offering an insight into the mindset, values and attitudes of a loyal supporter of Daniel O'Connell and devoted adherent of one of the most influential and formative institutions of nineteenth-century Ireland, the Roman Catholic Church. And his life is of interest because he was the father of Thomas Francis Meagher, though he was much more than that. He deserves remembrance for the fact that he, too, was a patriot, though his patriotism was not attended by high drama. Rather, he was a patriot in the O'Connellite constitutional tradition, like hundreds of thousands, if not millions, of his contemporaries, who have been enveloped by the mists of historical oblivion. A biography of Thomas Meagher will help illuminate this aspect of our past.

CHAPTER ONE

The Meaghers of Newfoundland, c.1780–1819

Thomas Meagher was born far away from Ireland and Waterford, in St John's, Newfoundland. Relatively little is known about his life there, a place he was to leave when he was about thirty years of age. Much more information is available on the life of his father, also called Thomas, and an examination and consideration of his life offers an important insight into the economic, social, religious and ethnic milieu in which his son lived during his formative years. In the light of Thomas Jr's later career, it is significant that the years he spent in St John's were characterised by strong economic, cultural and personal ties between Newfoundland and Waterford. In fact, so expansive and deep was the relationship between the two places that Henry Winton wrote in 1859 that Newfoundland 'is merely Waterford parted from the sea'.[1]

TALAMH AN ÉISC: 'THE LAND OF FISH'

The Meagher family was wealthy and it owed its wealth to Newfoundland. The foundation of that wealth was the simple cod fish. Early explorers confirmed that the coast of North America was churning with cod of a size never before seen and in schools of unprecedented density.[2] Europeans began exploiting the fisheries of Newfoundland with 'the enthusiasm of a gold rush'.[3] Cod was prized for the whiteness of its flesh, the large flakes of which almost glow on the plate. The meat has virtually no fat (0.3 per cent) and is more than 18 per cent protein. When cod is dried, the more than 80 per cent of its flesh that is water evaporates and it becomes concentrated protein. And it is a fish that is easy to catch. Once caught, it does not fight for freedom – it simply has to be hauled up – and it is often large and heavy.[4] The early economy of Newfoundland came to be based on Europeans arriving, catching fish for a few months, drying them, then taking them back to Europe as a source of relatively cheap nutritious food.[5] The Irish were involved in the efforts to share in the bounty of these rich fisheries from the fifteenth century, and there was an Irish presence in Newfoundland by the end of the sixteenth century.[6] The name in the Irish language for the island – *Talamh an Éisc*: the 'Land of Fish' or 'The Fishing Ground' – reflects an early appreciation of its natural maritime wealth and that the sea around it was regarded as 'a garden of cod'.[7]

Initially, the Newfoundland fishery was controlled by merchants from England's West Country. Beginning around 1670, it became customary in the spring for their ships to call to Irish ports, and especially Waterford, to take on provisions to feed the fishermen working in Newfoundland. These ships also took on migrant labourers. By the mid eighteenth century, Waterford's merchants began to enter this trade in provisions and the transport of persons.[8] Certainly, by the 1760s the connection between Waterford and Newfoundland was very significant, with a local newspaper listing the fifty vessels that had departed the city in 1765 and noting that 'several more [are] expected this season … Waterford harbour is full of Newfoundland ships'.[9] Later in the century, Arthur Young, in his *Tour of Ireland* published in 1780, wrote:

> I was informed that the trade of the place [Waterford] had increased considerably in ten years … That the staple trade of the place is the Newfoundland trade; this is very much increased, there is more of it here than anywhere. The number of people who go as passengers in the Newfoundland ships is amazing; from sixty to eighty ships, and from 3,000 to 5,000 [passengers] annually.[10]

Vessels from Waterford arrived in Newfoundland in late April and through the month of May. Most were employed in bringing fish to the lucrative south European markets. The fishing season was over by late November and ships bound for Waterford were loaded with cod, cod oil, timber and passengers.[11]

THOMAS MEAGHER SR MIGRATES TO NEWFOUNDLAND

Among those who left Ireland for Newfoundland was the father of Thomas Meagher, also called Thomas. The time and place of Meagher Sr's birth are uncertain, as indeed are any particulars of his early life. John Mannion has suggested 1759 and 1764 as possible birth dates.[12] Various places have been identified for this birth. While Tipperary was named as the county of his birth by his grandson, Thomas Francis Meagher, the exact location therein is more problematic. Fethard has been advanced as a possibility, though Thomas Francis Meagher recorded 'Nine Mile Hill' as the place. 'Nine Mile Hill' may refer to the village of Ninemilehouse, situated between Kilkenny and Clonmel. Research by Mannion confirms the likelihood of this general location.[13]

According to Thomas Francis, his grandfather was a 'respectable farmer',[14] suggesting that he was the son of a fairly prosperous farmer. Meagher Sr's early career path, eschewing the family farm, suggests that he was not in line to inherit a portion of the land, which would be the natural expectation of an eldest son. In the late 1770s he may have moved to Clonmel and worked as a shop boy (perhaps in a drapery) or as an apprentice tailor, cloth production being a significant enterprise in that part of south-east Tipperary.[15] In the 1780s he decided to seek his fortune in Newfoundland.

Meagher had much in common with most migrants and immigrants. He was male, between eighteen and twenty-five years of age, the age at which the majority of migrants left for Newfoundland.[16] Like most of them, he left Ireland seeking to improve his economic prospects. However, in important respects, Meagher was not an average migrant. Most were poor – disproportionately so.[17] He was not; he was, after all, the son of a fairly prosperous farmer and he had probably been gainfully employed before his departure. Moreover, most migrants were unskilled workers. He was likely not; he may have acquired some skills as a tailor. Critically, as suggested by his subsequent career, Meagher was very ambitious and determined to achieve success beyond the modest ambitions of most Irish people who found themselves in Newfoundland. 'The big island of broken rock and blistering winds off the coast of the North American mainland' was to offer him 'a degree of respect' unknown in his native land.[18]

On his arrival in St John's, Meagher became apprenticed to a tailor, a Mr Crotty, whose first name is not known, but who, apparently, was the owner of a large tailoring and clothing business. 'Meagher soon established himself as a favourite in the household of his boss, whose wife found the strong Irishman especially charming.'[19] When Crotty died, Meagher married his widow, Mary, who was a number of years older than he was, and whose maiden name and place of birth are unknown. Whatever romantic element there may have been in the marriage, it was definitely advantageous to the ambitious Meagher, who now found himself in charge of a tailoring business. Tailoring was a craft still in its infancy in St John's when he arrived, and it was dominated by the Irish. All but one of the nineteen tailors recorded in 1795, for example, were of Irish birth or descent. It was a craft which attracted them because it required little start-up capital for premises, equipment or raw materials. Success depended on individual skill, reputation and cultural connections. Meagher's subsequent achievements suggest that he was very successful as a tailor, and the rising number of Irish settling in St John's likely contributed to this prosperity.[20]

COMMERCIAL SUCCESS

Driven by ambition, Meagher was one of a number of tailors who progressed to the status of merchant. The accumulation of the requisite capital was a slow process; as late as May 1808, he was still listed as a tailor. Later that same year, however, he acquired a sixty-ton brig for deep-sea trading. This was a major step in his career, which was further advanced by the replacement of the brig by a much larger vessel the following year.[21]

The well-established Waterford–Newfoundland trade route contributed significantly to the commercial success of the Meagher enterprise. John Mannion has reconstructed much of Meagher's trade at Waterford from the ledgers of his agent, Richard Fogarty. Each autumn he received Meagher's Newfoundland goods for disposal in Waterford. In addition to cod and oil, the shipments included salmon, capelin, herring, ox hides, barrel staves and some timber. During the winter Fogarty assembled supplies from Waterford merchants, which were then transported across the Atlantic on board Meagher's or some other vessel on which space had been secured. Between 1 November 1810 and 1 November 1813, over £12,000 worth of goods were shipped on Meagher's account.[22]

The timing of Meagher's entry into the mercantile world of maritime trading was fortuitous. The cod economy was experiencing a boom due to the Napoleonic Wars (1803–15), when there was a rising demand for Newfoundland fish in Europe. Moreover, the demand for cod in Waterford and its hinterland also increased because of a rising population, with imports of the fish trebling between 1794 and 1813. Finally, the traffic in passengers from Waterford to St John's rose dramatically in the years 1809–15.[23]

Like most successful merchants, Meagher invested in property. His house and shop were on the north side of Water Street, with his store and counting house on the south side. In 1816 he relocated his premises to Codner's Cove, and his former premises were advertised in terms which suggest his material prosperity: 'that well-known valuable premises formerly occupied by Mr Thomas Meagher'. This property included a house, shop, counting house and store located in what was described as 'the most eligible part of town for business'.[24] After he returned to Ireland in 1817, the contents of his house were offered for sale by public auction, the advertisement conveying his affluence and wealth: 'mahogany dining and card tables, mahogany and oak chairs, knife cases, dinner, china and glassware, silver tea spoons and an eight-day clock'. A gig and sleigh, with complete harness, and a pleasure boat were also to be auctioned.[25]

INCREASING SOCIAL PROMINENCE: THE BENEVOLENT IRISH SOCIETY

With commercial success came a more prominent role in the public life of St John's, a clear indication of Meagher's growing social status. He was selected as a petty juror on a number of occasions; for example, on

21 August 1804 and 1 September 1807. On 2 September 1811 he was appointed a member of the grand jury, only the twelfth Irishman to serve on it since 1789. On 16 October of the same year, the grand jury nominated him to serve on a committee to manage a local hospital.[26]

Unquestionably, Thomas Meagher's most notable public role was as a founder member of the Benevolent Irish Society, inaugurated on 17 February 1806 by gentlemen actuated by a desire to relieve the great misery and poverty which prevailed among many of St John's inhabitants, most of whom were of Irish descent.[27] Membership was limited to 'natives of Ireland, sons of Irish parents and descendants of any present or future members'.[28] It was non-denominational in character[29] and while over 90 per cent of its original 286 members were Catholics, the founding committee, except for one Catholic, was composed of Protestants. Meagher, however, was one of a handful of Catholics chosen in 1806 as a member of the 'committee of review and correspondence', the purpose of which was to keep the nature and object of the society before the public and whose office it was 'to interest the benevolent and humane who were in a position to assist it in its work'.[30] In modern parlance, it was a public relations and fundraising committee, an essential body in any charitable society.

The Benevolent Irish Society was to acquire an acknowledged position in St John's because of its philanthropic and charitable endeavours. During its early years, it combatted, with great success, the economic and social distress which prevailed throughout the city.[31] The society's centenary record names a number of businessmen who contributed to its funds, including Thomas Meagher.[32] In 1814 he became its treasurer, a position he was to hold for four years.[33] His appointment reflected the fact that within a decade of its establishment, Catholics had come to dominate the running of the organisation. Meagher Sr played a prominent role in one of Newfoundland's most influential institutions, a clear indication that he was regarded as a person of significance and substance in his adopted home.

INFLUX OF IRISH IMMIGRANTS

During the thirty years or so that Meagher Sr resided in St John's, both the town and Newfoundland generally were to witness a significant increase in population. There was a rapid rise in the number of permanent inhabitants between 1785 and 1815.[34] When Meagher first arrived in the 1780s, the population of the island was possibly 10,000; by 1815 it was nearly 40,000.[35] St John's reflected these demographic changes. On Meagher's arrival it was little more than a frontier fishery station with around 2,000 residents;[36] the number in 1815 was 10,000.[37] This rapid increase in the population occurred during the last ten years of the Napoleonic Wars, between 1805 and 1815, a consequence of the continued expansion in the fisheries in response to European demands for fish. This same decade marked the beginnings of a massive influx of Irish to Newfoundland.[38] Seasonal migration was replaced by emigration – the peopling of south-east Newfoundland from south-east Ireland had begun.[39] No other part of Canada or America was to draw so many of its immigrants from so compact a region within the island of Ireland; 90 per cent came from Waterford city and some twenty-five miles around it.[40]

The Irish immigrants swelled the ranks of adherents to the Roman Catholic Church. In July 1784 forty-seven-year-old Fr James Louis O'Donel, a native of County Tipperary, had arrived in St John's from Waterford as prefect apostolic of Newfoundland, to establish the formal and institutional foundations of Catholicism there.[41] There had been Irish Catholic settlers and migrants in Newfoundland a century before O'Donel's arrival; in fact, by 1735 they were almost as numerous as English Protestants.[42] However, these Catholics experienced the suspicion and intolerance which characterised British official and popular attitudes to them throughout the colonies of the expanding empire. The instructions given to Henry Osborne in 1729, on the occasion of his appointment as Governor of Newfoundland, contained the clause: 'You are to permit a liberty of conscience to all persons, except papists.'[43] This direction was routinely repeated to his gubernatorial successors.[44] Government policy was deeply rooted in the Irish and British experience, which found expression in the various penal enactments against Catholics in the eighteenth century. While Catholics in Newfoundland could not become governors, admirals or magistrates, the most significant impediment was the total ban on Catholic worship. Priests did travel there prior to O'Donel, but their presence was illegal. The activities of an Augustinian priest in Conception Bay in 1755 led to the prosecution, at the behest of Governor Richard Dorrill, of a number of Catholics for attending Mass.[45]

Shortly after O'Donel's arrival, Governor John Campbell issued, on 24 October 1784, a proclamation of liberty of conscience, thereby removing the worst restrictions on Catholics. Notwithstanding this proclamation, there persisted a deep-seated resistance among many Protestants to any concessions to Catholics, the increasing numbers of Catholic immigrants from Ireland being regarded as a threat to Anglican hegemony. Subordinate officials adopted an obstructionist stance and some of Campbell's immediate successors did not share his tolerant attitudes.[46] Perhaps the most dramatic and public example of the hostility experienced by Catholics involved Prince William Henry (later King William IV, 1830–37), who was a naval surrogate in Placentia in the 1780s. He became embroiled in a feud with Fr Edmund Burke, sent there as parish priest by O'Donel in 1785. The prince vented his anger against O'Donel, threatening to kill him and burn down his chapel. He even committed an assault, albeit a minor one, on the prefect apostolic.[47]

In 1796 James Louis O'Donel was to become the third Catholic bishop in North America. In spite of many obstacles, he was successful in laying the foundations of a strong and vibrant church: 'By the time he retired to Ireland in 1807, Newfoundland Catholics had ten clergy, which meant that in less than twenty-five years the Catholic Church had been able to provide more clergy to serve Newfoundland than the Church of England had been able to do in more than a hundred years.'[48]

Thomas Meagher Sr's arrival in Newfoundland broadly coincided with that of O'Donel's. Meagher, therefore, witnessed the embryonic origins of the institutional Catholic Church on the island and was present for its progressive development and expansion during his more than thirty years' residency. He would have been conscious of the discrimination directed against Catholics before his arrival, when the practice of their faith had been 'formally proscribed, intermittently persecuted [and] frequently harassed'.[49] It is almost certain that he was aware of the persecution of his co-religionists in 1755 by Dorrill: 'What is important is that Governor Dorrill's edicts entered the Irish-Newfoundland collective consciousness and cultural memory.'[50] The resistance to Campbell's proclamation of liberty of conscience or, at the very least, the publicised incident with Prince William Henry, is also something with which he was likely familiar. He could have had few illusions about the obstacles confronting Catholics in their struggle for religious equality in a colony that was certainly not immune to the anti-Irish and anti-Catholic bigotry widespread in the British empire at that time, a bigotry which was often intensified when Protestant authority felt itself threatened.[51]

CATHOLIC MIDDLE-CLASS SUPPORT FOR THEIR CHURCH

Meagher Sr typified the emerging middle-class support for the maturing Catholic mission in Newfoundland: 'For a decade or more the Irish merchants, traders, artisans and planters, particularly those with families in Newfoundland, provided the essential financial and moral support for priest and chapel.'[52] It is virtually certain that Meagher was active in his support during the O'Donel mission and the episcopate of his successor, Bishop Patrick Lambert, who governed the Diocese of St John's from 1807 to 1816.[53] It was during the latter's term of office that Meagher reached the status of merchant and it is consequently easier to identify his contribution to the welfare and development of the Catholic Church in Newfoundland. For example, in 1812 he presented a 'very liberal gift of books' to a newly established Sunday school in St John's and on 22 December 1814 he was appointed chairman of a committee to build a house for priests.[54]

Demonstrably, his religion was important to Meagher Sr and his strong Christian faith inspired his attitudes and charitable actions towards the less fortunate. The sentiments of the motto of the Benevolent Irish Society, 'He that gives to the poor lends to the Lord', appear to have been taken seriously by this committed Catholic, as he engaged in philanthropic deeds, many of them being in addition to those associated with his membership of the society.[55] On 10 January 1817, at a meeting of merchants to raise subscriptions to relieve the poor, he contributed £10, the third largest donation.[56] In the same year, on 22 February, he was appointed to a committee to alleviate distress caused by a fire in St John's.[57]

RELIGION AND ETHNIC IDENTITY

For Irish settlers in Newfoundland, their religion was to become the salient symbol of ethnic identity, even when they were subject to the restrictions imposed by discriminatory legislation.[58] Arrivals from Ireland naturally gravitated towards fellow migrants and immigrants. 'The most distinctive and enduring element of Irish tradition carried across the Atlantic was religion'[59] and St John's was like any Irish parish, albeit separated by 2,000 miles of ocean, especially as this parish grew with the influx of immigrants from Ireland's south-east. Notwithstanding the granting of religious toleration, Catholic and Protestants remained apart; a striking feature of the religious landscape on the island was the prevalence of denominationalism.[60] Religious adherence distinguished the Irish from the English settlers in the eighteenth and nineteenth centuries. 'Catholicism and Irishness, closely associated in the homeland, came to be perceived as virtually synonymous in Newfoundland.'[61]

Thomas Meagher Sr lived his life in St John's mainly within a world defined by ethnicity and religion. The clientele of his shop and the growing retail community was primarily Irish and Catholic. Social and economic links were reinforced and articulated through the Catholic Church.[62] He and his wife, Mary, acted as witnesses to marriages and godparents at baptisms between 1803 and 1817. Mary figures prominently in baptisms in St John's Old Catholic Chapel, being godmother to children born to members of the shopkeeping mercantile Irish of the town.[63] Her husband is recorded as godfather to seventeen children, all of whom were Irish by birth or descent.[64]

SPREAD OF REVOLUTIONARY IDEAS FROM IRELAND

Sections of this same Irish immigrant community were not immune to the revolutionary upheaval which gripped parts of south-east Ireland in 1798, the place from whence so many of Newfoundland's Irish hailed. The Society of United Irishmen was active in St John's, organising cells among townspeople and troops in the local army regiment. In the spring of 1800 a rebellion was planned, the objective of which is unclear – perhaps the proclamation of a republic. Bishop O'Donel made the conspiracy known to the government, an action consistent with the Catholic Church's hostility to revolution.[65] It is likely, even certain, that Thomas Meagher Sr was unsympathetic to any politically motivated violence, with its consequent social dislocation. He was gradually achieving merchant status, an ambition that did not encompass sedition. A devout Catholic, he was also likely to have been influenced by the teachings of his Church and the leadership of O'Donel. His acceptance, nearly fifteen years later, of an appointment as a special constable in St John's, on 17 January 1815,[66] suggests a cautious, if not conservative, disposition to political and social change.

THOMAS MEAGHER JR

Thomas Jr was the first of three children born to Thomas and Mary Meagher, all of them boys. Their dates of birth are uncertain: Thomas Jr may have been born in 1789, Henry in 1791 and Patrick in 1799.[67] The biographers of Thomas Francis Meagher virtually ignore his father and certainly make no reference to his Newfoundland roots, with the exception of Timothy Egan, in his book *Immortal Irishman*.[68] In 1816 Thomas Sr accepted Thomas Jr and Henry as full partners in his firm.[69] Nothing is known of the sons prior to that date, in particular their education and mercantile training. Mannion speculates that Thomas may have been educated abroad, at Stonyhurst, a Jesuit College in England, which he entered, possibly, in 1804.[70] More is known about the education of the youngest son, Patrick. He was sent to Stonyhurst in 1813, leaving in 1820. He began studying law but quitted this profession to enter the Society of Jesus on 24 February 1828.[71] According to Michael Howley, Archbishop of St John's (1894–1914), this son of Meagher Sr was the first native of Newfoundland to be ordained a Catholic priest.[72]

The firm of Meagher and Sons is recorded in 1816 as pursuing clients for payment of debts.[73] It also took advantage of bankrupt concerns to expand its clientele. For example, the Meaghers secured part of the custom of the insolvent Koughs, a New Ross company long established in St John's. They were also appointed joint trustees for notable estates, such as that of Luke Maddock of Waterford. All these estates were in considerable debt to Meagher Sr, an indication of his economic prowess in Newfoundland.[74]

In the autumn of 1817 Thomas Meagher Sr decided to return to Ireland with his wife and perhaps his son, Henry, settling in Waterford, long the focus of his family firm's engagement in transatlantic trade.

Most Irish emigrants never returned to the land of their birth; a wealthy merchant such as Meagher had the financial means to do so. It would appear that this move was more a continuation and extension of a successful mercantile shipping system already in place rather than a new beginning. He simply assumed the role of his Waterford-based agent, Richard Fogarty. In the spring of 1818 Meagher organised, in Waterford, his first cargo for shipment to St John's. This included provisions, salt and passengers. A second shipment was sent in September.[75]

Thomas Meagher Jr remained in St John's to manage affairs there. In the summer of 1818 the Meaghers recruited Thomas Beck as a partner to assist Thomas Jr. The latter 'continued his father's dealings in St John's land market, paying rents and collecting rents from under-tenants, acting as an administrator or trustee for clients' estates, issuing writs and settling accounts'.[76] In July 1819 the firm suffered a serious setback when fire destroyed its main waterfront premises in St John's. Meagher Jr had to oversee the reconstruction, but this was likely a drain on resources at a time when considerable capital was being directed to enterprises in Waterford. That December the property was put up for sale.[77]

A significant indication of his growing status was his election as treasurer of the Benevolent Irish Society in February 1819.[78] Of this event Mannion writes: 'It was a seminal appointment in a public career that spanned almost half a century in Waterford politics.'[79]

In the summer of 1819 Thomas Jr joined his family in Waterford. He never again returned to Newfoundland.

INFLUENCES OF NEWFOUNDLAND ON THOMAS MEAGHER JR

As will be seen later in this book, Thomas Meagher Jr's life in Ireland and Waterford was to be one of many achievements and successes. He was to make his mark on his adopted city, and in so doing he was influenced, profoundly and significantly, by his experiences in Newfoundland. He was born into, and came to maturity, in a community in St John's that was formed and shaped by Irish migrants and immigrants. His father's business, in which he became a full partner, was centred on a clientele composed primarily of representatives of the Irish diaspora. Meagher Jr was acutely aware of his ethnic origins. The pre-eminent badge of identity of the Newfoundland Irish was their shared Catholicism. Social and communal solidarity was articulated through the Catholic Church. Religion played a central and vital role in the Meagher family. They were active in their support of the Church, participating in its solemn rituals and contributing to it out of their considerable wealth. The Catholicism to which he was exposed in his formative years was to be a defining, animating and normative force throughout the life of Thomas Meagher Jr.

It was the vitality of their faith which inspired the acts of charity and philanthropy with which the Meaghers were associated in St John's. These acts were given expression primarily through the Benevolent Irish Society, of which both Thomas Meagher Jr and his father served as treasurers. The values promoted and fostered by this society remained with Meagher Jr throughout his adult life; in Waterford he was to receive public acknowledgement for his beneficence to the poor.

Meagher Jr would have been aware, through personal experience and that of his father, of the discrimination practised against the adherents of his Church and the resistance to according equality of treatment to Catholics by those, primarily Protestants, whose social and political ascendancy was threatened. The discrimination he was later to experience in Waterford he had first experienced in Newfoundland. His deep commitment to the struggle for equality of treatment of Catholics in Ireland had its genesis in St John's. Throughout this struggle, he adhered to constitutional and peaceful means; his father's rejection of violence as an engine of political change in Newfoundland in 1800 was reiterated by the younger Meagher during a long career of political activism in Ireland.

Thomas Meagher Jr, as he left St John's, was conscious that he was the scion of a family of consequence. An appreciation of this fact gave him an assured sense of confidence of what he regarded as his rightful place in society. He was not going to accept anything less, be it in St John's or Waterford. The transition to life in another country was probably not as difficult as it could have been. His experiences – commercial, cultural, social and religious – in St John's had prepared him for life in Waterford. In many ways, Newfoundland was Ireland in miniature, with a pronounced Waterford accent.

CHAPTER TWO

Waterford: The Early Years, 1819–1825

Thomas Meagher began a new stage in his life in Waterford in 1819, where his father, mother and perhaps his brother, Henry, were already settled, having moved there nearly two years before. What is noteworthy is how quickly he established himself as a figure of significance in the commercial, political, social and religious life of his adopted city. The 1820s were to be dominated by the campaign for Catholic emancipation and Meagher was to emerge as a champion of the rights of his co-religionists, a cause with which he was to associate himself for over forty years. The years 1819–25 were to be formative ones for the man from Newfoundland: the values, beliefs and principles which were to influence his subsequent public and political career were nurtured and strengthened during this period.

THE EARLY YEARS IN WATERFORD

Thomas Meagher Jr's father laid the foundations of his son's rise to social and political prominence in Waterford, in which city Meagher Sr was described as 'a gentleman who, among the many respectable merchants concerned with the Newfoundland trade, stands in the foremost class'.[1] There were few known analogues in south-east Irish ports to the spectacular ascent from apprentice tailor to shipowning merchant exemplified by him.[2] The considerable capital he had accumulated in St John's was transferred to Ireland. It exceeded £20,000 and was placed on deposit in Newport's Bank, Waterford.[3] He leased an imposing Georgian villa at Ballycanavan:

> Located four miles downstream from Waterford, on the south bank of the Suir, with a commanding view of the river and its traffic, it was the ideal location for a shipowning merchant. The estate comprised of sixty Irish acres, with an elegant tree-lined avenue, walled gardens, a coach house and out buildings. The Meaghers had been living in some style in St John's ... but there was nothing in St John's or elsewhere in Newfoundland in 1818 to equal the elegance of this commodious abode.[4]

Ballycanavan proclaimed the wealth and status of the Meaghers, and the confident sense of their position in society.

As was noted in Chapter 1, the decision of the Meagher family to relocate to Waterford represented more a continuation and extension of the family's shipping system that was already in place than a new beginning. Meagher Sr and his sons – his business partners – intended to assume the duties of their Waterford agent, Richard Fogarty, and to use their connections to continue their transatlantic trade.[5] The company's supply and marketing base was to be situated in Waterford, not St John's. Therefore, extensive trading premises were acquired on the Quay. However, just as the Meaghers seemed ready to begin their trading in accordance with a modified commercial dispensation, they abandoned the Newfoundland connection. In August 1820 the family dissolved the partnership with Thomas Beck in St John's.[6] This decision reflected a rapid decline in the transatlantic provision trade from Waterford and a recession in the cod fishery; in fact, fewer than a dozen mercantile houses remained active in this trade in 1820, one-quarter of the number in 1770. By the late 1820s, the firm of Meagher and Sons was no longer involved, to a significant extent, in commercial activity. The pursuit of profit in the urban property market became the focus of endeavour.[7]

Thomas Meagher Jr quickly emerged as the most active member of his family's firm. It was this association that propelled him into a high-profile role in Waterford's commercial life in 1820. On 6 June of that year one of the city's most revered institutions, Newport's Bank, went bankrupt, having a devastating impact on the lives of many people.[8] The Meaghers had £7,600 deposited in the bank at the time of the crash.[9] On 28 June Thomas Meagher Jr and John Harris, a bacon merchant, were appointed principal assignees:

> In the pages of the Waterford newspapers for the next dozen years may be found occasionally legal notices headed, 'In the matter of William Newport, a bankrupt', and ending, 'John Harris and Thomas Meagher'. Sometimes it was a summons for creditors to meet, sometimes an advertisement of certain property for sale … Thus the assignees pursued their dreary way, fighting contentious debtors, determining the respective rights of joint and separate creditors, and carrying on all manner of legal warfare.[10]

As Waterford's leading bank, it had had a large clientele, including landowners, merchants, retailers and artisans. Numerous meetings with many creditors 'extended over two years, exposing Thomas Jr not only to the local commercial community, but also to the complexities of financial exchange in an Old World port'.[11]

Thus, his partnership in the Meagher family business and the Newport bankruptcy helped establish Thomas Meagher Jr's public profile. In particular, his family's and his own involvement in the Newfoundland trade facilitated his entrée into the heart of the city's commercial community. His rising stature was reflected in his election, on 2 December 1822, as treasurer of the Chamber of Commerce.[12] There was a corresponding recognition of his social status: in 1824 and 1825 he was appointed a member of the city's grand jury.[13]

MARRIAGE TO ALICIA QUAN

If Meagher Jr's family associations contributed to his increasing prominence in the life of his adopted city, his marriage, in October 1821, to Alicia Quan, was of pivotal significance in that regard. The Quans came originally from Islandkane, a townland on the south coast of County

Waterford, near Tramore. They were big farmers and tenants of the Wyse family, of the manor of St John's, one of Waterford's most prominent families since the Reformation. Alicia's father, Thomas Quan (1756–1822) and his brother, James (1761–1832), were taken on as apprentices by James Wyse in his mercantile concern, and by 1775 had graduated to a partnership, together with one of Wyse's brothers-in-law, Roger Cashin. Wyse, Cashin and Quan was to become one of the great Catholic merchant houses of Waterford.[14]

Thomas Quan was active in the campaign for Catholic rights. In 1792 he was a member of the Catholic Convention which met in Dublin to adopt a petition to the king requesting relief from penal legislation. The 231 delegates were mainly businessmen and country gentlemen. This evidence of Catholic organisation and determination prompted the government to grant a substantial Catholic Relief Act in 1793, by which middle-class Catholics were granted the right to vote and to hold most civil and military offices.[15] A year later, he was one of the first Catholics appointed to the grand jury of Waterford.[16] As a prominent citizen, he supported the work of Edmund Ignatius Rice, founder of the Irish Christian Brothers, contributing £14 in 1818 towards Rice's charitable activities.[17]

Alicia Quan's mother was Christina Forstall (1766–1819), who had a distinguished ancestry, with deep middle-class roots in rural Kilkenny. She could trace her lineage back six generations to the castle at Carrickcloney, by the River Barrow. Though the Forstalls lost much of their land holdings in the confiscations of the seventeenth century, some branches of the family managed to retain leasehold interests in large farms.[18]

The marriage contracted between Thomas Meagher and Alicia Quan united two families of substantial wealth. In return for a bond of £4,000 from the Meaghers, the Quans assigned Meagher Jr their leasehold interests in three properties.[19] This union was a public proclamation of the status and ambitions of the recently arrived Meaghers: the 'outsiders' had married into one of Waterford's most prestigious 'insider' families. This gave Thomas Meagher Jr access to the considerable social and political capital of the Quans, and this was to prove invaluable in his ascent to the pinnacle of Waterford society.

CATHOLIC EMANCIPATION

The 'Catholic question' or Catholic emancipation – the right of Roman Catholics to be admitted to certain offices of state and membership of Parliament from which they were excluded on religious grounds – was the major issue in the politics of Great Britain in the first three decades of the nineteenth century. It led to the collapse of governments and much parliamentary time being expended on the matter. From 1805 to 1823, only six passed without a debate on emancipation.[20] That so much time was spent on the consideration of Catholic grievances was due to the endeavours of aristocratic and, in particular, middle-class Irish Catholics, who were campaigning for the repeal of the remaining penal laws. By the early 1820s, the leader of the cause was Daniel O'Connell.

The first public speech made by Thomas Meagher Jr was in St Patrick's Church on 1 April 1821 and it related to the issue of emancipation. The occasion was a meeting of Catholics from the city and county, who had come together to express their opposition to a bill before the House of Commons, which had been introduced by William Plunket, a Protestant supporter of Catholic rights. This legislative proposal, while removing penal disabilities, included provisions aimed at appeasing opponents of religious equality. Under the terms of the bill, a commission was to be established to certify the loyalty of all newly appointed Catholic bishops and to examine all communications between Catholic prelates in the United Kingdom and Rome. In effect, the British government was given the right of veto over episcopal appointments and sight of confidential ecclesiastical correspondence.

In his address to the assembled Catholics, Meagher declared his rejection of Plunket's proposals. While expressing his appreciation of the provisions removing penal disabilities, he believed it was necessary

> to announce firmly, though temperately, our determination never to consent to give to his Majesty's government an undue influence in the appointment of our bishops or an arbitrary control over the communication of our clergy with the see of Rome. Such an influence in the appointment of our bishops would soon leave every diocese in Ireland without a spiritual head, except such as no

one would approve of but the secretary of state; and such a control over the intercourse of our clergy with the pope would be highly prejudicial to the discipline of our Church and the purity of our faith.[21]

He presented, for the consideration of those in attendance, five resolutions he had drawn up to express disapproval and rejection of Plunket's proposals. The meeting decided to appoint a committee to consider the resolutions. Seven gentlemen were elected, including Meagher, and they withdrew to deliberate. On their return, it was announced that Meagher's resolutions had been accepted and were recommended for adoption.[22]

Meagher's contribution to this gathering of Catholics is noteworthy for a number of reasons – it was a contribution which prefigured, in many respects, his later career in public life. He revealed himself as an articulate, effective and persuasive public speaker. He marshalled his arguments in a logical and coherent manner. And he was more concise than other contributors, a quality that characterised his future addresses. His draft resolutions further confirm him as an intelligent and accomplished man, capable of summarising and encapsulating his thoughts with impressive clarity and force. In future years he was often to be appointed secretary of various committees, and these resolutions go some way towards explaining why he was selected for this role.

Meagher, in his speech and resolutions, articulated ideas and concerns which informed, to a significant degree, a political creed which was to be the foundation of his beliefs and actions over the next four decades of political activity. First, by rejecting the right of the British government to exercise a veto over the appointment of Catholic bishops, he was declaring for unqualified emancipation. The matter of the veto had divided the Catholic movement for nearly two decades, thus dissipating its effectiveness. Opposition to it was led by Daniel O'Connell. By taking this stance, Meagher was identifying himself, openly and unequivocally, with O'Connell's position and leadership, an identification which was to define his politics.

Second, his speech and resolutions were those of a man deeply committed to his Catholic faith and concerned about its welfare. His sentiments evinced a deep respect for the clergy of his Church. In his fourth resolution he rejected the veto on the basis that it would 'repress their zeal in securing to posterity the purity of our religion, of which hitherto they [the clergy] have been the faithful guardians'. The fifth resolution described the clergy as being 'endeared' to their flocks 'by a communion of sufferings and privations … during which they have sacrificed every proffered advantage and have sought no earthly consideration for their spiritual ministry'. The defence of the Catholic Church, its clergy and its teachings was to be an important and central theme of Meagher's actions and utterances during his public life.

Finally, Meagher highlighted what he evidently regarded as the important role of the Catholic clergy in contributing to peace and order in Ireland. He referred in his resolutions to their 'disinterested zeal in teaching an unconditional subordination to the law', to which 'we chiefly attribute the tranquil state of the country'. It was his considered and definite opinion that the granting of emancipation with the conditions attached to it by Plunket would 'deprive the clergy of the confidence of their flocks and break the invaluable bond of peace and order'. Clearly, he valued this 'peace and order'; he was deeply committed to constitutionalism and the rule of law, beliefs which were to inform his political attitudes throughout his public career.

The formative influence of Meagher's Newfoundland years is evident in this, the first public speech delivered by him in Waterford. He appears to have been remarkably at ease and confident. On the island of his birth, he lived his life in a community shaped by Irish migrants and immigrants, primarily from the south-east of Ireland. He gained an understanding of and empathy for them, which he was able to transfer to his Waterford audience – he had met the likes of his listeners in Newfoundland. He understood discrimination as practised against Catholics; he had learned about it from his father and likely had personal experience of anti-Catholic attitudes in St John's. He was able to speak forcefully and with conviction in St Patrick's Church because he had learned to detest the consignment of Catholics to second-class status in his younger years. In St John's he had grown to maturity in a home which had accorded a deep respect for the Catholic faith and its ministers, a fact which shone through the words he spoke and the resolutions he composed. Meagher, now nearly two years in Waterford, was really beginning to appreciate the similarities between the place of his birth and his adopted home.

MEAGHER AND WATERFORD CORPORATION

Nine months later, in the same year of 1821, Thomas Meagher again addressed a public meeting. The occasion was a protest against the dismissal in November of the recorder of Waterford, the city's chief judicial officer, by the corporation.[23] Twenty-four persons, including Meagher, signed a requisition asking the mayor to convene a meeting of citizens to consider the circumstances of the dismissal, the reasons for which were surrounded by a wall of secrecy. When the mayor refused, these same persons called a meeting for 17 December.[24] One of the local newspapers reported that, 'Thomas Meagher Jr rose and spoke at considerable length and with much ability.'[25] In his speech he impressed on his listeners the importance of knowing why the corporation had acted as it did. It appeared to him that it was an arbitrary exercise of power. He presented, for the consideration of the meeting, five resolutions he had prepared detailing his concerns. According to him, the recordership of Waterford was 'an office of great trust and confidence ... essentially necessary for the due administration of public justice'. The right of appointment was a 'trust' reposed in the corporation and should not be regarded as 'a source of patronage'. He argued that this trust had been breached and this fact could 'prove in many instances detrimental to the liberties and interests of the inhabitants at large'. The resolutions were adopted by those in attendance.[26] It was again an impressive display of eloquence and composition (of resolutions) by Meagher.

More significant was the fact that his concern about the corporation went deeper than its treatment of the recorder. This was the proximate cause of his concern, but at a more fundamental level, and informing his essential attitude to that body, was his belief that it was a profoundly unrepresentative institution which could never enjoy his trust nor that of the Catholics of Waterford. Its very existence, in fact, was an affront to them, a symbol of religious and social domination, because it was a Protestant preserve which excluded from its membership and the benefits of its patronage the representatives of the majority Catholic faith.[27]

Meagher's attitude to the veto and the corporation should be seen in the context of the wider campaign for Catholic emancipation. This campaign was led, nationally and locally, by members of the Catholic middle class, of which Meagher was a notable representative. One of the consequences of the penal laws, particularly in relation to their adverse impact on Catholic land ownership, had been the increasing involvement of the ambitious Catholic middle class in commerce. Its wealth and confidence had grown throughout the eighteenth century. By the 1790s, its members were adopting a more assertive attitude, realising they were of considerable consequence in the kingdom because of their wealth.[28] In the 1820s their leadership of the Catholic struggle for equality 'was motivated by an aspiration for social and political influence, by a wish to end religious discrimination, [and] by a powerful drive to advance Catholics in general in public life'.[29] What was especially galling was the fact that the position of members of this Catholic middle class in society and their political influence were not commensurate with their wealth. Their exclusion from a meaningful role in municipal government caused particular offence and resentment. The Catholic middle class was at least the financial equal of its Protestant counterpart, and yet Protestants controlled the country's corporations.[30]

WATERFORD'S CATHOLICS AND SIR JOHN NEWPORT

In Waterford, proponents of Catholic emancipation valued the support of John Newport. This liberal Protestant supporter of emancipation had held the Waterford city parliamentary seat since 1802; of the six general elections between that year and 1820, he had been returned unopposed in four of them.[31] In 1824, however, there were rumours that he would face an opponent in the forthcoming general election.[32] On 24 March there was a meeting of his friends and supporters, at which Meagher spoke on behalf of the Catholics of the city, praising Newport's 'long continued and eminent services' to the cause of emancipation. He made clear the sentiments of Catholics when he rejected the notion of any opposition to Newport's return at the next general election, while promising their support and influence in the event of an electoral contest.[33]

FOUNDATION OF THE CATHOLIC ASSOCIATION, 1823

In the spring of 1823 Daniel O'Connell founded the Catholic Association, the object of which was the achievement of emancipation by constitutional means. The annual subscription was one guinea, a fact which precluded a wide membership base. Consequently, Thomas Wyse, a prominent Waterford-born Catholic and first historian of the association, observed that its 'first seeds were scarcely perceptible'.[34] In fact, it hardly survived, 'being a caucus of Dublin-based members of the professional, commercial and landed elite'.[35]

A turning point came in January and February 1824, when O'Connell made a number of proposals with the purpose of transforming the association into a mass movement. The means to effect this was the enrolment of associate members at a subscription of a penny a month. Moreover, the scope of the association's concerns was broadened to embrace all grievances affecting all Irish Catholics, and not simply exclusion from Parliament. Thus, the grievances of the poor and less well-off peasants were to be joined to the aspirations and concerns of the more privileged Catholic upper and middle classes; in Wyse's words: 'In Ireland Catholic grievance was a Proteus; it took the shape of education, charity, agriculture, commerce, amusement; … whatever was social or civil was more or less infected by the sour taint of the general oppression.'[36] O'Connell had come to appreciate that the most effective way of engaging the Catholic masses in the campaign for equality was to deal with their practical concerns and their sense of victimisation by a Protestant state and ascendancy. Thus, the Catholic Association ceased to be a mere pressure group and became a kind of parliament which took cognisance of all political and social grievances.[37]

There was an almost immediate response in Waterford to O'Connell's plans, a fact revealed in a letter dated 1 March 1824 from a Catholic activist in the city, John Fitzpatrick, and read out at a meeting of the Catholic Association in Dublin. The letter stated that a Catholic Association had been established in Waterford; it had resolved to cooperate with the Dublin association; and the penny a month subscription had been adopted.[38] The Waterford association confirmed the middle-class leadership of the movement at this critical juncture in the campaign for emancipation. Fergus O'Ferrall, in his magisterial study of this campaign, describes its leadership as 'landed, professional and commercial men', and they included John Leonard, who chaired meetings of Waterford Chamber of Commerce; Roger Hayes, a barrister; and Thomas Meagher Jr.[39] In 1825 the aforementioned Thomas Wyse was to emerge as a very influential and significant leader, on his return to his native city, having spent ten years in Europe.

These and other key figures constituted a small and closely knit group. Using data from the 1841 census, it has been calculated that the Irish middle class, Catholic and Protestant, formed only about 12 per cent of the national population.[40] Therefore, the middle class comprised, nationally and locally in Waterford, a compact social group 'that went to school, intermarried, prayed, ate and had leisure together'.[41] In addition to being closely integrated socially, they were also integrated ideologically, sharing the political values of their class. The members of Waterford's middle class were in constant touch with each other, in organisations such as the Chamber of Commerce and the Catholic Association. In many respects, they lived in an atmosphere bordering on claustrophobia.[42] A shared sense of common religious identity underscored their sense of political purpose and endeavour, especially at a time of struggle and conflict that was the campaign for emancipation during the years 1823–29.

Having organised themselves in an association, the Catholics of Waterford were intent on signalling their determination in respect of emancipation. On 18 March 1824 there was a meeting in the cathedral at which a number of resolutions were adopted. Regret was expressed that 'the penal laws still exclude us from the enjoyment of our rights and privileges as British subjects'. One resolution was redolent of the Catholic middle class's confidence in its social position, declaring that 'the rapid increase of wealth, intelligence, and public spirit in the Roman Catholic population affords ground for confident expectation of our liberation from the dishonourable incapacities under which we labour'. It was decided that a petition be presented to both Houses of Parliament seeking the removal of the legal disabilities to which Catholics were subject. The meeting agreed to entrust its preparation to 'Counsellors Sheil and Hayes and Thomas Meagher Jr.'[43]

RELIGIOUS CONTROVERSY

Seven months later, in October 1824, there was a meeting held, once again in the Catholic cathedral, and it was an event of particular significance for the Catholic Association in Waterford. It is important to understand and appreciate the context in which this gathering convened. The 1820s were to witness a sharp resurgence of sectarianism, affecting all sections of Irish society.[44] The distinguished historian Donald Akenson has cautioned against 'the danger of permitting the dominant political narrative to shove the religious conflict aside'.[45] To do this is to seriously distort the character of Irish society and politics during that tumultuous decade and to ignore seminal forces which shaped the decisions and actions of the Catholic Association, and also influenced the outlook and attitudes of its leaders, including those of the subject of this book, Thomas Meagher.

During the first two decades of the nineteenth century, Irish Protestantism was imbued with the spirit of evangelicalism, the consequences of which became apparent in the 1820s.[46] It was the deeply held conviction of many evangelicals that the main source of Ireland's economic, social and political problems was the Catholic religion. *The Waterford Mail*, an organ of Protestant opinion, articulated this view with forceful brevity when it pronounced in 1826 that, 'Popery was the root of all the evils which afflict this country'.[47] Roman Catholicism was regarded by ardent evangelicals as a pernicious faith, based on superstitions and heresies, these being perpetuated by a priesthood steeped in ignorance and obscurantism, the members of which held a tyrannical sway over their congregations, reducing them (the congregations) to a state of servile thraldom.[48] Following the Act of Union, it became the firm belief of many evangelicals that if the Catholic Irish could be converted to the reformed faith, a transformation of the country would be effected.[49] It became their religious duty to free Irish Catholics from 'Popish superstition' and the authority of the 'Anti-Christ in Rome' [the pope]. By the 1820s, a movement – often called the 'Second Reformation' – to promote the conversion of the Catholic population to Protestantism was under way. For the next four decades and more, a religious war was fought.

Education became a battleground, the control of the minds of the young being contested by the rival faiths. Some evangelicals put enormous effort into establishing schools to effect the conversion of Catholic children. Those of the Kildare Place Society became objects of special revulsion for Catholics. Founded in 1811, this body was genuinely undenominational throughout its early years, but by the 1820s it was being accused of proselytism.[50] O'Connell resigned as a director in February 1820, and his attacks on the society and the consequent withdrawal of the leading Catholic patrons 'was a turning point in the history of Protestant–Catholic relations in Ireland'.[51]

The combined pressures of the Second Reformation and the attendant controversies surrounding education had a transformational effect on the struggle for Catholic emancipation. Catholic bishops and priests, increasingly alarmed by the activities of Protestant proselytisers, were brought 'openly into the world of popular politics, where they acted as a unifying force behind the campaign for emancipation'.[52] Thomas Wyse wrote that 'The cause of education became identified with the cause of emancipation,'[53] and this issue resulted in the Catholic clergy becoming 'deeply politicised by the summer of 1824'.[54]

While Waterford was not a centre of the Second Reformation, it did not escape the religious convulsions disturbing the country. The efforts of Protestant evangelicals to bring about the conversion of Ireland had its supporters in the county.[55] *The Waterford Mail* was one of the most vocal, hailing the Second Reformation as 'the brightest day that ever beamed upon the moral regeneration of Ireland'.[56] Commencing on 13 November 1824, it began publishing a series of articles, under the general title *Vindication of the Principles of the Reformation*, denouncing the principal teachings of Catholicism, which attracted a dedicated readership.[57] The issue of education was the subject of particularly bitter controversy. The parish priest of Passage East, a village lying nearly eight miles from Waterford city, informed the secretaries of the Kildare Place Society in 1822 that a proposal to open a school in his parish had been successfully opposed. The society's method of education he described as 'a snare for the faith of the child' and as 'an undisguised system of proselytism'.[58] Wyse denounced its schools, of which there were sixteen in the county in 1825, as 'sectarian decoys'.[59] Thus, it was in a cauldron of increasing tensions that a plan to establish a school in Waterford according to the system pursued by the London Hibernian Society caused such concern among Catholics, culminating in a public meeting in October 1824.[60]

The London Hibernian Society held the dubious honour of being the most aggressive of the Protestant proselytising bodies, having been founded in 1806 on strident anti-Catholic principles.[61] The prospect of its involvement in the provision of educational facilities alarmed middle-class Catholic opinion. A meeting was called to consider the matter on 28 October, and it attracted a large attendance.[62] Thomas Meagher played a prominent role in its proceedings, acting as secretary in addition to proposing a resolution and seconding another. The resolution he seconded was a proclamation of the fidelity and loyalty of the Catholics of the city to the hierarchy of their Church: 'We take this opportunity to express our firm and unshaken attachment to the hierarchy, the faithful guardians and divinely constituted interpreters of the sacred truths of revealed religion.'

Speaking in support of this resolution, Meagher gave expression to opinions which elucidated his convinced Catholicism and his uncompromising loyalty to the clergy. On previous occasions the Catholics of Waterford had assembled to petition for the restoration of their rights; they were now gathered, according to him, for a higher purpose, namely, 'to preserve inviolate the purity of their true and ancient faith'. The intentions and actions of Protestant proselytisers had stirred them to action: 'If, deprived of their civil rights, they had for ages of persecution adhered to their religion and stood by their pastors, was it to be wondered at that they rallied to oppose this new attack.' He dismissed as futile all efforts 'to weaken the attachment in which they gloried, to their ancient faith and its exemplary ministers'. However much Catholics regretted the reasons for calling this meeting, Meagher hailed the occasion as one 'of great rejoicing', because 'the clergy and the laity had been brought together, to act in unison for the recovery of the rights of all'. Despite the public protestations, three London Hibernian schools were eventually founded in the county, at Dungarvan, Stradbally and Tallow.[63]

This meeting was of real significance because it publicly heralded and formalised an alliance between the Catholic Church and the Catholic Association in the city and county. The Waterford Mail, recognising this circumstance, commented that between 'Mother Church' and the association 'the liaison is now complete'.[64] This was to be a 'liaison' that was to have profound implications for the course of the emancipation struggle in Waterford, as was to be apparent during the 1826 general election. Moreover, it was a meeting in which Meagher played a conspicuous and significant role and established his profile as an increasingly consequential figure in the public life of the city. As with his first public speech in 1821, he expressed his deep attachment to his Catholic faith and its clergy. This attachment had been formed in Newfoundland, confirmed in Waterford and strengthened by his involvement in the campaign for emancipation. There was emerging, in the public persona of Meagher, an uncompromising champion of Catholicism.

THE CATHOLIC RENT

Before the October 1824 meeting, the Catholic clergy had been playing an important role in the collection of the one penny a month subscription of associate members of the Catholic Association, more popularly known as the 'Catholic rent'. It has been noted that Waterford was quick to adopt this rent scheme. At a meeting of Catholics of the city and county held on 18 March 1824, and referred to earlier, warm support was expressed for the proposal 'of raising money by a small but general collection'. It was agreed to appoint a committee of twenty-one to carry the plan into effect.[65] Thomas Meagher was one of those appointed to it. Clerical support was essential to the success of this collection, both in Waterford and nationally.[66] Throughout the country priests publicised the rent from their pulpits.

The collection of the rent by Meagher and his colleagues required sustained hard work, meticulous organisation and dedicated commitment on the part of all those involved. Wyse has left a description of this effort; he was an active participant in Waterford and his account was likely influenced by his experiences there:

> The rent was first organised in the towns; it then spread, though slowly, to the neighbouring parishes; and from thence, by degrees, to the most remote parts of the country. The collectors at first

volunteered; formed a committee; divided the town into walks for collection, and transmitted their funds, through their secretary, to the association [in Dublin]. As they increased, and improved their system, they enlarged considerably its objects. They took rooms; held their meetings weekly; not only received reports of rent and remittances to the association etc., but discussed every subject of public policy connected with the general question.[67]

On 11 August Daniel O'Connell attended a dinner in his honour hosted by the Waterford Catholic Association, at which Meagher acted as a steward. In the course of O'Connell's address, he expressed his pride that the rent 'had been so readily adopted and so liberally paid in the city'.[68] Waterford city and county, in fact, was one of the key centres of support for the rent.[69] Between 1824 and March 1825, when the Catholic Association was disbanded (see below), £739 was remitted to Dublin. This figure was the sixth highest in the country.[70]

The rent did more than fund the activities of the Catholic Association, important as that was. It was also pivotal in the development of political consciousness among the Catholic masses.[71] O'Connell observed that through the channel of the rent, the association nationally would be informed of every grievance that occurred in every part of Ireland.[72] Dealing with such matters became an essential element of the association's activities. Local concerns became an integral part of the national struggle for emancipation; the common grievances of Ireland's Catholics animated the association. Thus, the collection of rent and the 'collection' of grievances operated in tandem. Wyse noted that 'the rent proceeded rapidly and with it a corresponding passion for political discussion, which pervaded everybody and every class of society ... The Catholic peasant was taught by it to think *daily* on his grievances'.[73] It was to this heightened political consciousness that Meagher referred in a letter to Sir John Newport in March 1825:

The Catholic rent committee of this city has been one of the earliest, most active and most successful in supporting and forwarding the measures adopted and hitherto pursued so steadily, temperately and effectively by the Catholic Association, to obtain the equalisation of civil rights for all his Majesty's subjects, and to secure on a solid foundation the peace and welfare of the people of the country.[74]

The essential effect of the Catholic rent was to transform the Catholic Association into 'a colossus of democratic power unprecedented in the annals of political organisation in the British Isles'.[75]

DISSOLUTION OF THE CATHOLIC ASSOCIATION, MARCH 1825

It was this 'colossus' which alarmed the authorities in Dublin and the government in London. Their response was the Unlawful Societies in Ireland Bill, introduced into the House of Commons on 10 February 1825 by Henry Goulburn, Chief Secretary for Ireland. It proposed to make it illegal for an organisation such as the Catholic Association to exist.[76] Prompted by this development, a requisition was signed by nineteen activists and supporters of emancipation in Waterford, including Meagher, requesting a meeting of Catholics of the city and county to express opposition to the bill.[77] The meeting took place on 15 February and attracted a large attendance. Meagher was appointed secretary and member of a committee selected to draw up a petition to Parliament. A number of resolutions were adopted which gave expression to the middle-class credo of the Catholic leadership, locally and nationally. It was the view of the participants that the agitation for emancipation alarmed its opponents 'lest Catholics, by their prudence, firmness and talents may be put on an equality with their more favoured fellow subjects and share that patronage which they have long monopolised'. The constitutional means favoured by the Catholic Association were highlighted and the fact that 'our peasantry … have been taught to seek for redress by peaceful and legal modes' was referred to approvingly. Moreover, the association embraced 'many of the Protestant nobility and gentry' and 'all the Catholic nobility and gentry, and men of prosperity in the country, who never could be so infatuated as to lend themselves to any measures tending to exasperate animosities or endanger the peace of society'. The petition adopted at the meeting called on Parliament to pause before adopting measures calculated to 'spread discontent through the land'. It stated, very forcefully, the constitutional principles underpinning the actions of the Catholic Association, and its rejection of contrary methods: 'It is monstrous to suppose that all the Catholic nobility, men of the most ancient rank in the land and every Catholic of property or influence in the country would countenance proceedings so inconsistent with their interests and their status in life'. The petition certainly expressed rejection of government policy; it was also something of a manifesto of the middle-class values informing the association.[78]

In spite of vigorous opposition in Parliament from Protestant supporters of emancipation, the Unlawful Societies Bill received the royal assent on 9 March 1825.[79] Nine days later the Catholic Association dissolved itself. The last meeting of the Waterford Catholic rent committee took place on the evening of the same day, 18 March. It was agreed that a letter be sent to Sir John Newport, expressing appreciation of his 'persevering and important services in the cause of Catholic emancipation'. Meagher was entrusted with this task.[80]

TENSIONS IN THE CATHOLIC ASSOCIATION

Even before the Unlawful Societies Bill became law, the Catholic Association found itself embroiled in a divisive internal controversy. On 28 February Sir Francis Burdett introduced a Catholic Relief Bill in the House of Commons. It contained two provisions intended to placate Protestant opposition: state payment of Catholic clergy and the disenfranchisement of a category of voters known as the forty-shilling freeholders (see below for a more detailed discussion of the freeholders). O'Connell, perhaps anxious for a settlement of the emancipation issue, accepted the bill. This acceptance released a torrent of abuse directed at him because of his attitude to the freeholders. While the bill passed the Commons, it was defeated in the House of Lords.[81] A deflated O'Connell faced a most difficult situation: his movement internally divided and then legally suppressed. On 13 July he launched the New Catholic Association, which kept strictly within the law. This new body acted with more restraint than its predecessor; in fact, its proceedings in general 'were cautious to the point of timidity'.[82] For example, the collection of the Catholic rent was not resumed immediately. Despite these changes, divisions continued to fester within the organisation throughout 1825.

Waterford was not immune to the problems visited on the Catholic movement in 1825. Evidence of this comes from a meeting held on 4 January 1826. A requisition signed by some of the most prominent Catholics in the city and county – including, once again, Meagher – called for a meeting to be held to petition for emancipation.[83] *The Waterford Mirror*, reporting on the occasion, noted that 'the assemblage was by no means so numerous as custom … would have led us to expect'. The newspaper continued:

> But the most palpable absence was that of the substantial middle classes, the independent farmers, traders and shopkeepers, those whom Mr O'Connell, at the zenith of his popularity, designated in Waterford with emphatic propriety as 'practical patriots'. We think we never before, upon any similar occasion, witnessed so thin an attendance of those truly valuable and independent members of society.

However, while the emancipation movement in the city and county had been affected by the suppression of the Catholic Association and its divisions over Burdett's bill, one resolution adopted at the January 1826 meeting indicated that 1825 had not been a complete political washout in Waterford. The resolution in question pledged support for two liberal Protestant candidates, who were supporters of emancipation, for the representation of the county at the next general election.[84]

In early April 1825, a few weeks after the dissolution of the Catholic Association, its leaders in Waterford, including Meagher, hosted a public dinner in honour of one of the luminaries of the defunct organisation, Richard Lalor Sheil.[85] Perhaps the occasion was motivated by a desire to proclaim the justice of their cause and their right and determination to campaign for it. The resolve of the Waterford champions of emancipation was confirmed in July, when it was widely indicated that Henry Villiers Stuart, a liberal Protestant who favoured Catholic rights, would be a candidate for the representation of Waterford county in the general election, in opposition to Lord George Beresford, a sitting MP and an opponent of emancipation. On 3 November Stuart was the guest of honour at a public dinner in Waterford city. The organisers were a veritable 'who's who' of the Catholic gentry and middle class. The *Mail*, a strident supporter of Beresford, mocked the event in a (truly bad) satirical poem. Meagher's inclusion in one of the verses is testament to the fact that he was regarded, by 1825, as a pillar of the local Catholic establishment:

> Next Waterford musters House-keeper and Lodger –
> Hunt, Ivie and Hayes – (not the Friar, but Roger)
> John Archbold, James Birnie, John Leonard, Tom Scott –
> And Tom Meagher, Junior, Esquire (why not!).[86]

Between 1819 and 1825, Meagher became an acknowledged leader of Waterford's Catholic community. In his pursuit of religious equality through the campaign for Catholic emancipation, he was committed to constitutional and legal methods, and the leadership of Daniel O'Connell. He was confident in his assertion of the rights of his co-religionists to equal treatment under the law, and became a vocal defender of his faith and Church. These years were formative ones for him, during which he established the principles and beliefs which informed his attitudes and actions for the next three decades and more. And the prominent position the man born in Newfoundland had achieved in his adopted home became apparent in the 1826 general election.

CHAPTER THREE

Towards Catholic Emancipation, 1826–1829

The 1826 general election in Waterford was, in many respects, something of a titanic struggle between entrenched opponents of Catholic emancipation and the increasingly assertive and confident Catholic Association in the city and county. In this electoral joust, the religious and political establishment was to be represented by Lord George Beresford, and Henry Villiers Stuart was the representative of those who sought to supplant it.

STUART AND BERESFORD

Villiers Stuart was the grandson of the last Earl of Grandison, who had vast estates in Waterford, and in 1824 Stuart, having attained his majority, decided to make Dromana, located in Waterford county, his principal residence. By August 1825, he had commenced an active canvass and on 8 August he issued his election address.[1] In it he asserted that Catholic emancipation would uphold and strengthen the British constitution and declared his belief in the justice of Catholic claims.

While Stuart was the embodiment of a liberal candidate, Lord George Beresford represented Protestant conservatism on the issue of emancipation. He was a member of an ascendancy family remarkable for its resistance to Catholic claims.[2] Lord George was markedly antirelief, as his voting record in the Commons reveals.[3] His family was very powerful, locally and nationally, and had many critics:

> During the period of the Protestant ascendancy the Beresford family had become the real rulers of the Irish kingdom. Their influence permeated every government department; their relatives occupied every key position. Whether in church or state, their dependents were found to be battening upon the Irish people in every walk of life. Their tentacles, like those of a gigantic octopus, were everywhere, and embraced everyone and everything, and in no county was this more true than in that of Waterford.[4]

It was claimed in 1812 that one-quarter of the positions of patronage in the kingdom were filled by their connections.[5] The County Waterford seat had been held since 1806 by George Beresford and there had been no electoral contest in the seven subsequent general elections. Prior to 1806 the seat had been held for forty-five years by the Right Honourable John Beresford.[6] Accordingly, to their opponents the Beresfords were the quintessential representatives of an unredeemed Protestant ascendancy and a challenge to them was a challenge to those who believed in Protestant hegemony. In Wyse's words: 'In striking at the Beresfords, they [the Catholic Association] struck at the very heart of the ascendancy.'[7]

'INCURSION INTO THE ENEMY'S TERRITORY'

In order to defeat Beresford, the supporters of Stuart found it necessary to adopt a high-risk strategy. Devised largely by Thomas Wyse, it entailed an appeal to the predominantly Catholic electorate to vote for him. This electorate was composed, for the most part, of those possessing the forty-shilling freehold franchise, granted under the terms of the 1793 Relief Act. According to a parliamentary return of 1825, 2,199 such freeholders were entitled to vote in the county of Waterford.[8] However, these voters were generally regarded as the political property of their mainly Protestant landlords and expected to exercise their vote in a manner determined by, and pleasing to, these same landlords. To defy the electoral wishes of a landlord could mean eviction in an age when voting was a public rather than a private affair. Therefore, the forty-shilling freeholders were not seen as having any political independence. Wyse described their condition thus: 'They *still belonged* to their respective landlords and did not even conceive the idea of acting out of the range of this dependence, for themselves. They were, as far as their franchise or its exercise was concerned, mere serfs.'[9] Wyse's proposed appeal to the freeholders was indeed a daring plan; in his words it was 'an incursion into the enemy's territory'.[10]

Wyse was able to contemplate this strategy because the political groundwork had already been laid by Catholic activists, such as Meagher, while he was still on the continent. As was noted earlier, the collection of the Catholic rent in Waterford had heightened popular political consciousness. Wyse was aware of this fact in relation to his electoral strategy: 'The "Catholic rent" … had already prepared the mind of the people for any appeal which might be made to it.'[11] Moreover, when it came to addressing what he called 'their first care', the provision of a proper organisation to manage Stuart's election campaign,[12] the existing structures of the Catholic Association and those established for the collection of the Catholic rent were employed. Parochial branches of the Catholic Association were transformed into election committees. These met as required; association representatives from city and county met every Saturday.[13] And the alliance between the Catholic Church and the Catholic Association forged during the controversy in October 1824 over the planned London Hibernian Society school ensured the critical support of the priests. Thus, the Catholics of Waterford were organised and conscious of a wide range of issues upon which they could contest the general election– in truth they had been so since 1824.[14]

1826 WATERFORD ELECTION

When the long anticipated general election was eventually called in 1826, much national attention was focused on Waterford, described by *The Dublin Evening Post* 'as the most important contest in Ireland'.[15] That election was to prove a truly momentous one in the campaign for religious equality in Waterford and throughout the country. And in the words of Roy Foster, 'The famous Waterford election of 1826 was steered by propertied local Catholics (Wyses, Gallweys, Meaghers, Hayses) …'[16] It was to be a fiercely fought encounter between Stuart and Beresford, with sectarian bitterness being all too evident.[17] This was inevitable, given that the fundamental issue separating the candidates was the divisive and contested matter of religious equality between Catholics and Protestants. The sectarianism was further fuelled and intensified by the divisions caused by the Second Reformation.

Stuart's campaign was well organised and disciplined. There was a notable absence of the rioting and drunkenness which so often characterised Irish elections. Major Richard Wilcocks, a police commander in Waterford, reported to Dublin Castle that 'the profoundest peace prevailed, in spite of the fact that he had never witnessed in all his experience such party spirit, with the Catholics all wearing green handkerchiefs, sashes, cockades and ribbons, flying green flags in all parts of the city'.[18] Stuart enjoyed a dramatic and comprehensive victory: 1,357 votes to Beresford's 257. The result sent shockwaves through the country: it was the 'most remarkable popular triumph since the Union and a crushing demonstration of Catholic electoral power'.[19] No parliamentary seat was safe if this achievement were to be repeated in future elections.

This achievement was a testimony to the vision, hard work and commitment of Wyse. Recognition must also be given to those other leaders of the Catholic movement in Waterford who espoused this vision and contributed significantly to its realisation by their hard work and commitment. In particular, many of these same leaders had laid down the foundations of the Catholic Association and structures for the collection of the Catholic rent upon which Stuart's victorious election machine was built. This success was achieved with little encouragement from the Catholic Association in Dublin. O'Connell did not believe in the capacity or potential of the freeholders for independent political action, hence his willingness to countenance the disenfranchisement of this class of voter in his support for Burdett's ill-fated bill in 1825. He did, however, canvass for Stuart, accepting an invitation from him to visit Dromana before the election.[20] Once in Waterford, O'Connell came to appreciate the ambition of Wyse and his local fellow leaders, and he threw himself into the election campaign with energy and enthusiasm.[21] What happened in Waterford in the summer of 1826 was significant and remarkable:

A Catholic democracy was emerging with the power to undermine Protestant control in Ireland. In 1826 the Catholic Association, for the first time, provided a national framework for local electoral contests. What was being slowly grasped by the Catholic leaders was the fact that they had created the first mass Irish political party which focused primarily on parliamentary and constitutional objectives. The Waterford leaders, inspired by Wyse, were in the forefront of this development.[22]

Thomas Meagher was one of those leaders.

Waterford was the most dramatic of the 1826 election victories, but it was not the only one. In other counties – Louth, Monaghan and Westmeath – revolts of the forty-shilling freeholders also resulted in the return of pro-emancipation candidates. The fortunes of the Catholic Association were rejuvenated after the debilitating effects of suppression and divisions in 1825. In a letter to the Catholics of Ireland on 10 July 1826, an exultant, even ecstatic, O'Connell declared: 'The spirit of liberty is abroad. It flits on the wild winds of heaven ...' He hailed a 'new day dawning upon Ireland'. For Waterford or, to use his words, 'beloved Waterford', he had special praise: it had 'annihilated the proud, but tasteless and talentless Beresfords'.[23]

AFTERMATH OF THE ELECTION

In the aftermath of Stuart's victory there was a palpable sense of excitement in Waterford among members and supporters of the Catholic Association. The sentiments of an editorial in *The Waterford Chronicle* reflected their mood: 'Ireland is emancipated ... the Beresfords are down. The citadel of the ascendancy has been levelled to the ground.'[24] Such optimism and enthusiasm inspired a period of intense political activity. *The Waterford Mirror* observed on 7 October 1826 that 'the county is alive with Catholic meetings'. The activities of the local Catholic Association attested to the accuracy of this comment. It was reported that its 'meetings were formerly held twice a week, but by a recent regulation, in consequence of an extraordinary pressure of business, they are now held every night'. From 100 to 200 people could be in attendance.[25] An examination of local newspapers confirms a demanding schedule of meetings.[26] Parish meetings were also held, such as the one in Trinity Without on 20 August, over which Thomas Meagher presided. A petition to Parliament was adopted, stating that 'Emancipation ought to be granted, as tending to the stability of the empire and consolidating the people into a common interest.'[27] In recognition of Waterford's contribution to the Catholic Association's successes in the general election, the city was the venue for the Munster Provincial Meeting on 28 August. Meagher was a member of the organising committee and the event attracted a large attendance of representatives.[28]

In a letter to the Catholics of Ireland in July 1826, O'Connell advised the revival of the Catholic rent, under the title of the 'New Catholic Rent'.[29] As with the previous version of the rent, Waterford was very active in its collection. Meagher, in his capacity as secretary of the Waterford Catholic Association,[30] was responsible for remitting moneys to the national association in Dublin. This he did: for example, on 9 August he remitted £50; on 18 August, £24; and later in the same month, £26.[31] On 31 August he informed Dublin that 'the collection of the new rent will be general throughout the county in the course of the next week'.[32] By the end of November, Waterford's total of £513 made it the second largest contribution after Dublin's £590.[33]

A critical factor in explaining the high levels of contributions to the new Catholic rent in Waterford was the reprisals endured by the forty-shilling freeholders in the aftermath of the 1826 election. Tenants suffered the retributions of their landlords for defying their wishes and voting for Stuart. The circumstances of many of the forty-shilling freeholders in the county were certainly very difficult. At a meeting of the Catholic Association in Waterford city in September 1826, it was reported that 500 eviction notices had been served on Beresford estates.[34] In early October Richard Sheil read a petition at an association meeting in Dublin from tenants in Kilmacthomas, a Waterford village sixteen miles from Waterford city, detailing the miseries they were enduring for defying Lord George Beresford and imploring assistance to alleviate their plight.[35] A month later, Fr John Sheehan wrote to Daniel O'Connell: 'The gentry and the aristocracy here have resolved to wage a war *usque ad internecionem* [of extermination] against the forty-shilling freeholders who overturned their power at the last election. The Marquis of Waterford's trustees have adopted a most harassing system towards them.'[36]

Thus, while the Catholic Association in Waterford city and county had witnessed a revival of activity after the 1826 election, nevertheless the local leadership was facing a major crisis. The need to combat the economic reprisals of the landlords was of critical importance. A key local activist, James M. Galwey, began to express fears to Wyse in early September that the priests and freeholders would never support the association 'in the same way as the time past' because they were feeling let down by the agitators for emancipation.[37] The reality was that the freeholders, in spite of the ever-present threat of eviction, had voted for Stuart, and to ignore this fact was to politically imperil the future effectiveness of the emancipation cause in Waterford. The crisis facing the Waterford association demanded an urgent, meaningful and coherent response.

WATERFORD PROTECTING ASSOCIATION

On 7 August 1826 a meeting was convened in the city to establish the County of Waterford Protecting Association. Thomas Wyse stated that the association was a response to all acts of oppression directed at forty-shilling freeholders. The situation demanded energetic and decisive action: funds were to be made available to protect their fellow Catholics suffering for their 'meritorious exertion' at the general election in support of Stuart. He explained that a committee was to be appointed to undertake the management and control of any money that was collected. Moreover, it would inquire into any applications for financial assistance made by freeholders. It was resolved at the meeting to elect a committee of twenty-one gentlemen, two-thirds of whom were to be from the county (where the suffering freeholders resided) and the remaining third from the city. In the subsequent election, Thomas Meagher was selected as a city representative and was also appointed treasurer.[38] According to Fergus O'Ferrall, the brunt of the work of the Protecting Association was taken on by Wyse (chairman), Roger Hayes (secretary), Fr John Sheehan and Meagher.[39]

An insight into the crisis facing the committee of the Protecting Association is afforded in a report sent by that body to the Catholic Association in Dublin. On Thursday, 21 December 1826, representatives of fifty families of former freeholders on Beresford estates at Curraghmore and Portlaw attended a Protecting Association meeting 'to claim or rather beg assistance, to save from starvation themselves and their families'. According to the report, 'Their votes at the late election caused them to be abandoned, and in this inclement season of the year they are exposed to all wants and miseries incident upon their destitute condition'. The report continued: 'There is an extensive factory establishment at Portlaw, but such is the extent of persecution that no employment can be had there without a recommendation from the Curraghmore [the Beresfords' estate] steward, who has instructions not to suffer work to be afforded to *any* of those *marked* individuals who had the temerity to vote against Lord George Beresford'. One pound to each head of family was all the association could afford to give and this response 'leaves us without the means of administering one other pound to meet the many other calls which are daily pouring in upon us'.[40]

The purpose of the report, apart from informing the national association about the situation in Waterford, was to seek financial assistance for the freeholders. Much of the work of the Protecting Association involved making requests to Dublin for such assistance. Meagher, in his capacity as secretary of the Catholic Association in Waterford, was instructed by its committee to apply for £400 in early September and £200 a month later.[41] In late August Wyse applied for £250.[42] The national response was sympathetic; speaking at a meeting of the association in Dublin, Richard Sheil stated that as much money as possible should be sent to Waterford.[43]

All money sent to the county had to be disbursed by Meagher, as treasurer of the Protecting Association, and his colleagues on the organisation's committee. A report of the Catholic Association in Dublin detailed the money remitted to Waterford in 1826 'for the relief of the persecuted freeholders':[44]

September 4	£300
October 3	£300
November 3	£300
November 14	£150
November 27	£150

At a meeting of the Waterford Catholic Association, held on 7 April 1827, it was announced that the Protecting Association had been dissolved.[45] It would appear that it had, to the best of its ability, fulfilled its purpose. The significance of the establishment of this association cannot be overstated. Its activities represented a public and practical response to the sufferings of the forty-shilling freeholders who had answered the calls of Waterford's Catholic leaders to defy the landlords in 1826. On a humanitarian level, it was imperative to alleviate their sufferings. On a political level, it was essential to render such assistance to retain their support in any future elections. The activities of the Protecting Association in aid of the freeholders also had the effect of increasing subscriptions to the Catholic rent. Subscribers were attracted by the prospect of being able to assist the sufferings of victimised tenants. Remitting £50 collected for the rent in the parish of Trinity Within in Waterford to the national association, Thomas Meagher noted:

> You will be pleased to observe that the entire of this sum is exclusively from the city and that the citizens who have contributed are impressed with a conviction that its application is at this moment necessary for the relief of their countrymen, who are now suffering in this county for a conscientious discharge of their public duty at the late election.[46]

Failure by Catholic activists in Waterford to respond to the distressing plight facing some freeholders for voting against their landlords – an act encouraged by the local Catholic Association – would have done the emancipation cause irreparable damage in one of the strongholds of its support. Inactivity would have appeared callous and indifferent; indeed such inactivity could have been characterised as an act of betrayal. Those who responded to the plight of the freeholders understood this.

However, there is evidence that influential sections of the Catholic community may have been indifferent. At the meeting on 7 April, at which it was announced that the Protecting Association was dissolved, a report was read from the Waterford Catholic rent committee complaining of apathy in the 'higher classes'.[47] This apathy probably extended to the situation facing freeholders. The members of the Protecting Association, and particularly Wyse, Hayes, Sheehan and Meagher, who acted to assist them in a time of crisis, did the Catholic cause great service in challenging circumstances.

DEATH OF ALICIA QUAN

While Meagher's political works continued apace, in his private life he was to suffer a significant loss. On Saturday, 28 February 1827, his wife, Alicia, died. An obituary was published in *The Waterford Mirror* on 3 March:

> Wednesday evening, at eight o'clock, at the house of her husband, on the Quay, in her 28th year, Mrs Alicia Meagher, wife of Thomas Meagher Jun. Esq., and daughter of the late Thomas Quan, Esq. This amiable and excellent lady (who was lately delivered of twin daughters, one of whom has since died) was an object of the warmest regard to all who knew her, being as much and as justly admired for her numerous and sterling virtues, as she was universally loved for her kind, benevolent and truly charitable disposition. To her respected relatives and connections, who had the best opportunity of appreciating her worth and goodness, and particularly to her tenderly attached partner, her premature dissolution is a source of the most poignant affliction – an affliction in which all classes of the public sincerely sympathise. By the poor, to whom she was a constant and generous, though unostentatious benefactor, her loss will be most sincerely felt and deplored.[48]

Very little is known about Alicia Quan and her married life with Thomas Meagher. In fact, there is a dearth of documentary evidence and scholarship on the experiences of women of any rank, religion or era.[49] Alicia is usually described in relational terms: as the mother of Thomas Francis Meagher; the wife of Thomas Meagher; the daughter of Thomas Quan. She scarcely has an existence or historic memory independent of the three Thomases.

From the late seventeenth century, among wealthy merchant families, negotiations for marriage normally included the drawing up of a formal, legally binding marriage settlement. This provided for exchange of money and property between the families of the bride and groom.[50] A marriage between wealthy middle-class families involved the careful negotiation of a bargain, as marriage was an important social institution which merged property as much as people.[51] The personal preferences of the individuals who were the subjects of such agreements were usually – or, at least, often – subordinated to economic considerations and the social interests of their families.[52] Money, after all, was at the centre of the world of the middle class.[53] However, it should not be assumed that this meant an unhappy married life for the couple. The fathers, who negotiated marriage settlements, and their respective sons and daughters, were all products of the same culture. Children accepted the same system of priorities as their parents, who worked out the terms of a settlement.[54] Happiness in such a marriage was possible or, at least, a mutually satisfactory marital accommodation.

Alicia and Thomas began their married life at No. 57, King Street, Waterford. It was here that Alicia gave birth to two children: Thomas, on 1 August 1821, who died in infancy; and Christina Mary, born in August 1822. The family moved to a mansion on the Quay (the present Granville Hotel) and it was there that a son, Thomas Francis, was born on 3 August 1823. Nearly two years later the couple had another son, Henry, on 23 January 1825. A daughter, Mary Josephine, followed, but she too died in infancy. It was on 3 February 1827 that Alicia had two daughters: Christianna and Alicia Catherine. Christianna died shortly after birth; Alicia Catherine died, aged seven years, on 28 July 1834.[55]

Infant mortality and childhood deaths were a real threat in the nineteenth century: the experience of Alicia and Thomas was not unusual. Their reaction to these events is not available. Erin Bishop writes: 'Some historians argue that this high rate of infant mortality kept parents from forming emotional attachments to their children. Recent studies, however, suggest that parents did indeed forge bonds of love and affection with their offspring from the time of birth.'[56] On the evidence of his relationship with his children, to be discussed in later chapters, Thomas Meagher was a caring and loving father, and there is nothing to suggest that his wife was any less a caring and loving mother.

Childbearing and child-rearing were Alicia Quan's main pre-occupations as a married woman. In fact, from early childhood girls were prepared for future roles as wives and mothers. Central to society's perception of a woman's place in the social order was the concept of public and private spheres.[57] The public sphere was the domain of men, a world which included politics, business, law and medicine. The private sphere was the world of domesticity, assigned to women in the patriarchal society that was nineteenth-century Ireland. This domestic sphere was the only one where a woman had a defined and accepted role, where she could exercise influence and authority in her maternal and uxorial capacity.[58] In this private world she could express, in keeping with prevailing social norms, her female virtues and qualities in caring for her husband and children.

In lauding Alicia Quan, the author of her obituary was influenced by this view of the domestic sphere being the proper place for women. 'Her kind, benevolent and truly charitable disposition' was highlighted; she displayed attributes that were regarded as quintessentially feminine, and desirable and necessary in a good wife and mother. Moreover, the privacy of her world in the family home was underscored: only those who had access to it – 'her respected relatives and connections' and her 'tenderly attached partner' – had 'the best opportunity of appreciating her worth and goodness'. Alicia could give expression to her finer qualities in the domestic realm, the proper place assigned to women by the norms of society.

LIBERAL CLUBS

In the aftermath of the 1826 general election, Thomas Wyse conceived the idea of a permanent electoral organisation to co-ordinate the political forces unleashed by that event. He envisaged a national system of city and county Liberal Clubs and a network of parochial associations under the control of the county club.[59] However, while such clubs were established, for example in Louth[60] and Clare,[61] progress was delayed in Waterford due to the crisis facing the forty-shilling freeholders. At a meeting of Catholics in the city on 7 April 1827, it was resolved to form a city Liberal Club,[62] but it was not until 5 July 1828 that this happened. Thomas

Meagher was in attendance at this July meeting, together with his father and brother, Henry, and they subscribed £5 towards its formation.[63] The aim of the club was to 'consolidate the good work which we have begun' and to oppose the election of 'illiberal and anti-popular' candidates to Parliament.[64] The evidence would suggest that the club was active after its foundation.[65]

TOWARDS EMANCIPATION

While Meagher mourned the loss of his wife and sought to comfort his children, the struggle for emancipation continued. After a period of relative calm in 1827, Daniel O'Connell renewed popular agitation in 1828. The appointment of the Duke of Wellington, widely regarded as an opponent of religious equality, as prime minister in 1828, provoked a hostile reaction in Ireland. The country seemed destined for an explosion of social and religious warfare, and an election in Clare 'lit a fuse that led to a bomb'.[66] The Catholic Association had decided to oppose at an election any candidate who supported the Wellington government. In June 1828 O'Connell was selected to stand against William Vesey Fitzgerald. The ensuing Clare election was one of the most exciting, dramatic and significant in modern Irish history. The Catholic Association's organisation of the forty-shilling freeholders into a disciplined electoral force secured O'Connell's victory.[67]

After this result there was enormous pressure on the Wellington administration: no parliamentary seat could be regarded as safe in light of these events and this outcome could be replicated in most constituencies at the next general election. Moreover, there was a real fear in London that O'Connell would be unable to control the passions of his followers in the face of a continuing refusal to concede emancipation. Britain faced the real prospect of the situation in Ireland spiralling out of control. The government surrendered to the inevitable and by April 1829 the Catholic Emancipation Act had received the royal assent.[68]

By the terms of the Emancipation Act, Catholics could at last enter Parliament. All civil and military offices, except the monarchy and the lord chancellorships of England and Ireland, were opened to them. As a sop to Protestant militants and popular opinion in Britain, Catholics were forbidden to hold religious celebrations outside their houses or churches; and the Jesuits and religious orders were forbidden from entering the country. From the outset these restrictive clauses were ignored. However, accompanying the act was one disenfranchising the forty-shilling freeholders; this measure was 'a counter-attack on those who, it was held, were most dangerous to the political stability of Ireland'.[69]

MEAGHER'S CATHOLIC ACTIVISM CONTINUES

In February 1829 the Catholic Association dissolved itself in anticipation of the enactment of the Emancipation Bill. This did not mean, however, that Catholic activists were now redundant. In Waterford, on 23 March, a meeting was held in the schoolroom of the Irish Christian Brothers at Mount Sion for the purpose of petitioning the House of Commons regarding the clauses affecting the Jesuits in the bill before it for debate. Thomas Meagher played a prominent role, revealing himself, yet again, to be a determined defender of the interests of the Catholic Church. He proposed the adoption of a petition which he probably authored himself.[70] While welcoming emancipation, the document regretted the inclusion of the provisions relating to the Jesuits. The petition also expressed concerns about any implications the bill might have for 'the no less useful societies for the diffusion of gratuitous instruction amongst the poor'. This was a reference to the Christian Brothers, with mention being made of the more than 700 poor boys being educated by them in the city. The meeting adopted the petition.

On 25 March 1829 close associates of O'Connell proposed a testi-monial in his honour, in order to raise money to enable him to support his family as an MP, then an unpaid position which restricted his practice of law, thus obliging him to forgo most of his earnings.[71] In response to this proposal, a meeting was convened in Waterford on 1 May by thirty-three prominent citizens, including Meagher, to consider measures 'to mark our high sense of the important and valuable benefits conferred by Daniel O'Connell upon our common country'. A decision was made to contribute to the proposed 'patriotic fund' and a committee comprising the citizens responsible for calling the meeting was appointed to give effect to this decision.[72]

The 'patriotic fund' evolved into the annual 'O'Connell Tribute'. This became an important means of affirming loyalty to the 'Liberator' (as O'Connell was commonly styled after the achievement of emancipation). Moreover, its collection allowed for the retention, albeit in attenuated form, of structures established to collect the Catholic rent – structures which had contributed significantly to the formation and mobilisation of Catholic opinion during the campaign for religious equality.

AFTERMATH OF EMANCIPATION

In the aftermath of its achievement, Irish Catholics were initially optimistic about the significance of emancipation. Soon, however, a deep sense of disappointment set in. For the great majority of people, the Emancipation Act made very little difference in their lives. The popular understanding was that its achievement would represent liberation from injustices which the peasantry was forced to endure in a society dominated by a Protestant ascendancy. The campaign for religious equality exploited the power of common grievance – the implication was that emancipation would remedy such grievances. This did not happen. For the vast majority of Catholic peasants, life continued as before, irrespective of their emancipated or unemancipated state.[73]

Middle-class Catholics were also to be disappointed. With the enactment of emancipation, Richard Sheil looked forward to 'a great moral and political change', affecting every part of Irish life. This change, according to him, had to 'be diffused and dispersed into every department of state … it must be worked into the essence and being of the government. It must be found everywhere …'[74] This change did not happen as quickly as expected. The Protestant establishment which had long wielded power and influence, proved tenaciously resistant to surrendering its privileges. The ambitious middle class could certainly aspire to all but the highest offices in the land. Aspirations, however, were all very well; actual achievement was another matter: the Catholic middle class gradually came to understand this reality.

While the Catholic middle class's progress towards its much desired social and political Elysium encountered the obstacle of Protestant obstructionism, nevertheless the concession of emancipation by

Wellington's government represented a significant achievement by that same class. As has been noted several times in this chapter, its members provided the leadership of the Catholic Association, at local and national level. It was during the campaign for religious equality that the middle class emerged as a significant political force; in fact, the era of its predominance in society was dawning.[75] 'A Catholic middle-class "ascendancy", already in the making, was given a vital psychological boost'.[76] This class had informed the policy and strategy of the association. It had ensured adherence to constitutional and legal methods, supporting a policy by which Ireland was 'constitutionally insurgent', that is, 'agitated but not rebellious'.[77] Merchants, lawyers and gentry were inimical to revolution. Catholic emancipation was never regarded by them as a precursor of a new social order. It was essentially about the accommodation of demands for religious equality within the framework of the British constitution, such an accommodation being necessary to permit middle-class Catholics to obtain the political influence and status to which they felt entitled by their position in society.

Fergus O'Ferrall, indeed, has commented that 'as far as middle and upper class Catholics were concerned, emancipation had allowed them to escape their alliance with the peasantry'.[78] Certainly, the dissolution of the Catholic Association in February 1829, in advance of the enactment of the Emancipation Bill, ensured the proposed disenfranchisement of the forty-shilling freeholders never became a significant issue during the debate on that measure. This dissolution, possibly, 'revealed the conservative, and perhaps cynical, nature of the Catholic Association leadership in relation to their poorer and more exposed followers'.[79] As was noted earlier, the freeholders' plight in Waterford in 1826 was ignored by important sections of the Catholic higher classes. Meagher did not ignore their sufferings; however, notwithstanding his sympathetic and supportive reaction on that occasion, it is not possible to adduce his attitude to their disenfranchisement in 1829, in the absence of specific evidence.

OVERVIEW OF 1819–1829: A FORMATIVE DECADE FOR MEAGHER

On 10 October 1829 Thomas Meagher attended a meeting in the Catholic cathedral for the purpose of raising subscriptions to erect a monument to

Bishop Patrick Kelly, who had died two days previously. Wyse described Kelly as 'a remarkable man'.[80] Appointed Bishop of Waterford and Lismore in February 1822, he was 'a churchman of strong views and character', who had given leadership and support to the emancipation campaign.[81] Meagher was requested to act as treasurer and secretary of the committee charged with oversight of the memorial project.[82] By then he had been ten years in Waterford and his involvement in this committee may be regarded as emblematic of what had been a formative decade for him in terms of establishing himself as a figure of consequence and stature in the life of the city. Kelly had been a champion of the Catholic faith and Catholic rights, two causes which had consumed Meagher's time and energy since his arrival in his adopted city. His selection as secretary and treasurer was again an affirmation of the perception of him as an honest, reliable and committed person. His contribution to the various causes with which he was associated is best summarised in the exhortatory words of Wyse: 'exertions must be constant and systematic ... it is not by poetry, but by prose, that we are to succeed – by the common-place, plodding, persevering habit of every day'.[83] His next twelve years in Waterford were, in many respects, less dramatic than his first decade, but they were to be for him personally very significant. Thomas Meagher, the administrative factotum and committee leader and stalwart, was to be elected to public office, as a poor law guardian and a member of Waterford Corporation.

CHAPTER FOUR

Politics, Philanthropy and Public Office, 1830–1842

At the conclusion of the campaign for Catholic emancipation, Daniel O'Connell – 'The Liberator' – was unquestionably the greatest single political force in Ireland, a position he was to retain, despite occasional slumps in popularity, for most of the next two decades.[1] During the 1830s, however, there was no mass movement under his leadership engaging in a struggle for a popular cause. His attention and energy, for much of this time, were focused on the House of Commons. Consequently, the politics of this decade, lacking, as it does, the excitement and drama of the preceding one, can appear dull and uninteresting. This characterisation, however, is to ignore developments which had a significant political impact on Ireland generally, in particular the enactment of a poor law in 1838 and the reform of municipal corporations in 1840. For Thomas Meagher, personally, the period 1830–42 was critical in his emergence as a figure of consequence in Waterford. He was to be active in charitable and philanthropic endeavours. He was to be elected a poor law guardian and a member of the city's corporation, events which were to inaugurate a career in public life that was to last almost two decades.

DANIEL O'CONNELL AND REPEAL

Daniel O'Connell hoped that emancipation would herald sweeping political changes in Ireland by the admission to positions of power of ambitious Catholics hitherto excluded from them. This is what he had in mind when in late 1829 he announced that the government should 'give the Emancipation Act its natural effect'.[2] When it became apparent that ministers had no intention of committing to such a course of action, in early 1830 he founded the Society for the Repeal of the Union. Its stated aim was the removal of the Act of Union from the statute book and the restoration of the separate Irish Parliament which had existed until its abolition under that act in 1801. In response to O'Connell's initiative, a meeting of citizens was held in Waterford on 15 October 1830 to petition Parliament in support of repeal.[3] Reflecting O'Connell's popularity, there was another meeting on 20 December regarding the national fund to support him.[4] A collection was begun in January 1831 and Thomas Meagher was one of the subscribers to the O'Connell tribute.[5]

At the 1832 general election, thirty-nine repealers were elected, though some may have been only nominal supporters of O'Connell on the issue.[6] Two were returned in Waterford, one each for the city and county.[7] The electoral successes throughout the country were built on the foundations of the former Catholic Association and Liberal Clubs.[8] In Waterford the political organisation, which had its roots in the Catholic rent and the 1826 election, had survived the dissolution of the Catholic Association and the disenfranchisement of the forty-shilling freeholders.[9] The Catholic rent, for example, was supplanted by the O'Connell tribute, thereby ensuring a measure of organisational continuity, pre- and post-emancipation. Thus, structures, in whose establishment Meagher had played an important role, continued to serve the political cause and interests of Catholic and Liberal activists.

In April 1834 O'Connell raised the issue of repeal in the House of Commons. His motion was not one demanding repeal: it was merely asking for the establishment of a committee to inquire into the effects of the Union. On 29 April it was defeated by 523 votes to twenty-eight, with only one English member supporting it. The unconcealed hostility of the Commons to any alteration in the constitutional arrangements governing Ireland and Great Britain was apparent in this rout. This was the one and only time O'Connell was to bring a repeal motion before Parliament.[10] The issue was to be quietly withdrawn from public attention for the next few years, as he embarked on forging an alliance with the Whigs.

This alliance took shape in the spring of 1835 and is known as the Lichfield House Compact. O'Connell pledged support for the Whig government of Lord Melbourne, in return for a settlement of the tithe question, municipal reform and an informal veto on Irish bills and appointments. This compact, which was to last six years, was a pragmatic response by O'Connell in the face of the inescapable reality of a parliamentary arithmetic implacable in its opposition to repeal. The agreement, however, was more than this.

A key concern for O'Connell was the actual realisation of the terms of the Emancipation Act: the achievement of parity between Catholics and Protestants in terms of appointments to state and local offices. A hand on the levers of power was necessary to effect this and required cooperation with the party in power. Thus, with the Lichfield House Compact 'the prospect of sharing power and equal standing in their native land was unfolding before Irish Catholics, of the middle class, at least'.[11]

This prospect pleased the middle class. The fact was that a section of this class, whose leadership had been crucial to the success of the emancipation campaign, had been reluctant to engage in one for repeal. Their immediate objective was the translation of their newly won political status into tangible achievements: preferment, government appointments and state contracts.[12] One of the great successes of the Lichfield House Compact was to be in the area of Irish patronage and administration. Almost all judges, magistrates, law officers and other officials appointed during 1835–41 were either Catholics or liberal Protestants (who favoured emancipation). These were good years for the ambitious Catholic middle class, and for its members such years were 'a Saint Martin's summer in the long winter of the Union'.[13]

THE POOR LAW

On 31 July 1838 the 'Act for the Effectual Relief of the Destitute Poor in Ireland' passed into law. More popularly known as the 'Irish Poor Law', it was one of a number of measures introduced by the Whig government of Lord Melbourne, which sought to address grievances in Ireland. However, unlike the legislation relating to tithes and municipal corporations, the poor law had been opposed by practically every group in the country, 'by Protestant-Irish, Catholic-Irish, landlords, tenants, smallholders, shopkeepers and industrialists', the general contention being that Ireland was too poor to afford such a system.[14] Whatever the reaction to it, the poor law was to affect 'every stratum of Irish society, whether indirectly through taxation or directly through workhouse experience or outdoor relief'.[15]

The scale of Ireland's poverty was highlighted by a commission of inquiry, chaired by Dr Richard Whately, Church of Ireland Archbishop of Dublin, established in 1833 and which issued its final report in 1836.[16] The report found that 2,385,000 people, more than 30 per cent of the 1831 population of 7.7 million, were in distress during thirty weeks of the year.[17] Such findings confirmed the prevailing contemporary sense of the scale of poverty in the country. A few years earlier, in 1831, a report on sanitary conditions in Waterford's streets and lanes noted that 'much filth and human misery may be witnessed ... in any part of the city':

> At the rear of Summerland, coming from Morris's Road, are several stagnant pools and fetid sewers with filthy houses and most obnoxious back premises, which require constant attention. Every cabin on the Lower Yellow Road is in a frightful condition and scarcely can be entered ... Proceeded to Olave's Lane, and penetrated to the very attics of the houses in the lower part of that lane; witnessed extremes of poverty with its concomitant filth; some of the poor room-keepers were actually in a state of nudity, and scarcely a particle of furniture to be seen in their apartments; the end of the lane is a reservoir of filth.[18]

The Whig government's response to the problem of poverty was the Poor Law Act. Under its terms, the country was divided into poor law unions; by 1840 there were 130. A workhouse was situated in each union, financed by a poor rate, half of which was levied on the owners and half on the occupiers of land. A board of guardians was responsible for the building, maintenance and administration of each workhouse. Two-thirds of the guardians were elected by the ratepayers of a union; one-third was composed of local magistrates appointed ex-officio. Elections were held annually. In Ireland, unlike England, there was no legal right to relief; it was granted at the discretion of the local board of guardians. This relief had to be provided within the workhouse. Only the truly destitute were eligible for admission. The system operated under the direction and supervision of a central Poor Law Commission.[19]

MEAGHER'S ELECTION TO BOARD OF GUARDIANS

In early May 1839 meetings were held in the city hall, Waterford, to nominate candidates for the first election of members to the board of guardians of Waterford city union. One of those nominated for the Tower ward was Thomas Meagher. It is significant that he was nominated by Fr John Sheehan, parish priest of St Patrick's parish in the city.[20] According to Fergus O'Ferrall, he had been 'the most active priest in the local Catholic Association' during the emancipation campaign.[21] He was a trusted confidant of the Liberator on matters pertaining to Waterford.[22] It is improbable that Sheehan would have given Meagher a nomination unless he considered his O'Connellite credentials impeccable. Meagher was to be a candidate at the subsequent election and was returned unopposed.[23]

The first meeting of the newly elected board of guardians took place on Saturday, 8 June 1839.[24] Meagher was unanimously elected deputy vice-chairman. The meeting was not open to the press, in accordance with an order of the Poor Law Commissioners. Meagher challenged the validity of this order, but was overruled by a Mr O'Donoghue, the assistant commissioner of the district, who was in attendance. Meagher then gave notice of his intention of bringing forward a motion at a later meeting to allow members of the public to be admitted to meetings of the board. A motion to this effect was introduced at a meeting on 1 July, though by another guardian, William Aylward. While it was passed, the Poor Law Commissioners continued to prohibit the admission of the public. The matter of the admission of the press was, in fact, a source of contention throughout the country. Despite the strenuous efforts of the commissioners to enforce its directive, it was eventually obliged to concede on this issue.[25]

The most important issue for decision at the first meeting was the election of a chairman. There were two candidates: Alderman Henry

Alcock and William Christmas. The voting of guardians seems to have been informed by political considerations. Christmas was a Conservative and an opponent of repeal. He had been a successful candidate in the city constituency in the 1832 general election, standing on a platform of total opposition to repeal.[26] Meagher and a majority of his colleagues were supporters of O'Connell and this ensured the defeat of Christmas, with eleven votes for him and twenty-nine for Alcock.[27]

The board of guardians had to establish the structures of the poor law in the Waterford city union. The first meeting decided to proceed with the appointment of a clerk to the board, with a successful motion proposed by Meagher requiring that the position be advertised in the newspapers.[28] At the second meeting, arrangements were considered for the important task of valuing the rateable property of the union, which valuation would provide the basis for the striking of a poor rate.[29] By 1 July a clerk was appointed, together with valuators of rateable property.[30] On 8 November the members of the board gathered for the laying of the foundation stone of the Waterford union workhouse at John's Hill, in the city. In attendance was George Wilkinson, architect of the Poor Law Commissioners, whose standard design was the basis of the construction of workhouses throughout the country. In accordance with the prevailing ethos of the poor law, he was directed to make them 'uniform and cheap, durable and unattractive'.[31] Designed to accommodate 900 persons, the John's Hill complex covered an area of just over six acres. It was opened on 15 March 1841, at the cost of £7,850, with an additional £1,577 for fitments.[32]

Thomas Meagher did not seek re-election as a guardian in March 1840. He was, however, to resume his membership of the board at the height of the Great Famine. During his period of office, he was not involved in the practical administration of relief: the board, of which he was a member, was concerned with setting up the mechanisms and structures of the poor law in Waterford city. It was, nevertheless, a significant milestone in his career, not least because it marked his first election to public office. Moreover, the introduction of the poor law was a major innovation in the Irish body politic and represented a radical departure in terms of Irish local government. By 1842, with nearly one million registered ratepayers, the new boards of guardians were the most representative bodies in the country,[33] and Meagher played his part at the inception of this new, promising and exciting departure in Irish politics.

The elections of the boards did cause excitement, especially in the early years, in a country as intensely politicised as Ireland was by the 1830s. The new bodies offered supporters of O'Connell a representative public forum for the first time and by the 1840s they (the new bodies) were themselves to become highly politicised. Several boards came under the control of repealers.[34] The rejection of Christmas as chairman of the Waterford city board of guardians was a portent of this. Membership of boards of guardians gave middle-class Catholics a role in local government denied to them heretofore. The election of the first guardians marked a new era for them in Waterford city and throughout the country. It may be regarded as their first '"flowering" on the coat-tail of Daniel O'Connell's leadership and achievements'.[35]

MEAGHER'S PHILANTHROPY AND CHARITY

When nominating Thomas Meagher as a candidate in the poor law elections, Fr John Sheehan said that he was 'influenced by a long acquaintance with the gentleman in question and with his charitable disposition'. He continued, however, that 'this was not the place to speak of or particularise the gentleman's numerous acts of charity and beneficence'.[36] A future colleague on Waterford Corporation referred to Meagher's 'great exertion and watchfulness over the interests of the city and the comforts of the poor'.[37] In fact, Meagher was widely acclaimed for his philanthropic and charitable work in Waterford during his long residency there.[38] As was noted earlier, poverty was pervasive and his concern for his less fortunate fellow citizens was manifested in a number of ways.

Meagher was an active supporter of the Trinitarian Orphan Society, a charitable body founded in 1811, to 'rescue' orphans from 'the dreadful calamities of famine, ignorance and vice'. It managed an orphanage on John Street, receiving as many orphans as the available funds permitted. These children were 'trained in the path of religion and morality, instructed in the duties which were owed to God and man and finally apprenticed to correct and approved persons'.[39] A report issued in

1829 stated that 225 orphans had been received into the orphan house since its foundation; 115 had been apprenticed and in 1829 care was being given to sixty-five children.[40] Meagher was listed as treasurer of the society in 1823[41] and he served as a vice-president and trustee for the year 1830.[42]

In 1789 a distinguished physician, Dr Francis Barker, acquired a house on John's Hill, which he converted into the Waterford Fever Hospital. This is regarded as the first of its kind in Ireland and only the second such institution in the then British empire.[43] Meagher was a subscriber to the hospital and served as a member of the management committee for 1839–40.[44] It was a demanding and responsible position. In 1838, for example, 663 patients were admitted; 592 were dismissed cured; sixty-six died and five remained in the hospital at the end of that year.[45] This institution provided a crucial service to poor citizens at a time when epidemic fevers were common. Richard Ryland wrote in his history of Waterford, published in 1824: 'Previous to the existence of this charity, the poor, residing in crowded and confined parts of the city, suffered severely from fever and it is well ascertained that many streets, lanes and lodging houses were, for many years, never entirely free from it.'[46] Meagher was also a subscriber to the Fanning Institute, which aided natives of the city, who through indigence, old age or infirmity, were unable to support themselves.[47]

MENDICITY SOCIETY

In the aftermath of the Napoleonic Wars (1803–15) there was widespread poverty, social distress and demographic dislocation. Beggars became ubiquitous figures and begging a very visible aspect of life in pre-Famine Irish cities and towns.[48] These mendicants became associated with the propagation of diseases and all manner of moral evils in the community.[49] In response to this social problem, mendicity societies were established in the early nineteenth century. These charities were committed to the suppression of begging in a given city or town.[50] One such society was established in Waterford city in 1821 and Meagher was an active supporter.[51] This society, like others throughout the country, offered food and work, by means of a mendicant asylum, to those who would otherwise probably have had to resort to mendicancy for their sustenance:

> The general practice [in mendicant asylums] was that applicants were admitted in the morning, provided with food at stipulated times and discharged in the evening, when they returned to their place of residence or found shelter on the streets. During the day, the able-bodied were put to labour ... while the infirm and elderly were given succour and occasionally allocated basic work.[52]

The asylum in Waterford gave the street on which it was located its name – Mendicity Lane.

The near-total dependence of mendicity societies on voluntary contributions meant that financial uncertainty appears to have been their universal experience.[53] The Waterford society was no exception. In November 1825 there was a meeting of citizens to discuss the financial situation of the local society. It was decided to establish a committee to solicit subscriptions and Meagher was appointed to it.[54] On 3 December *The Waterford Mail* reported that he, together with two colleagues, had raised £86. Meagher was also a subscriber to the society.[55]

Fourteen years later there was still a problem with finances. In January 1839 a public meeting was convened 'to consider the best mode of preventing a large number of persons, the present inmates of the mendicity institution, amounting to 184, from being thrown on the streets from want of means to support them'. Thomas Meagher was in attendance. It was decided to form a committee to seek funds and Meagher was again appointed a member.[56] It met the next day and divided the city into districts to facilitate a more effective collection. Meagher and another member called on the Catholic bishop, Nicholas Foran, to seek his assistance. He agreed to act as a collector.[57]

In September 1839 there was yet another meeting to consider the finances of the mendicant asylum. According to *The Waterford Chronicle*, the attendance, though not 'numerically great, consisted for the greater part, of those useful and excellent citizens, who always take a prominent part in the glorious work of charity'. Meagher was again in attendance and was nominated a member of the society's managing committee.

He was also selected to serve on another committee charged with the collection of funds.[58] Waterford's mendicant asylum was never put on a sound financial footing; it ceased to operate with the opening of the workhouse in 1841.[59]

GENEROSITY TO CATHOLIC RELIGIOUS

Meagher's charity and philanthropy also found expression in his beneficence to the Catholic Church. He was especially generous to a number of female religious congregations in Waterford. He represented the Ursuline community in business matters. In the 1830s the nuns incurred a debt of £700 for extension works to their convent. Meagher, on hearing of their financial difficulties, offered a loan of the required sum, for as long a time as needed, without interest. He later made a gift of the money.[60] He also assisted the Presentation Order, acting as a trustee and adviser on matters relating to property and the leasing of land.[61] Meagher was a major benefactor of the Sisters of Charity and played a significant role in their foundation, in 1842, of a convent in Waterford city, one of the nuns being his sister-in-law, Christiana Quan.[62] The foundress of the congregation, Mother Mary Aikenhead, described him as 'our munificent patron' and wrote: 'Nothing can exceed Mr Meagher's thoughtful care and charity towards the community.'[63] His generosity included gifting a chalice and paten to the convent.[64]

MAGDALEN ASYLUM

Thomas Meagher was also involved in the management of Waterford's first Magdalen asylum. In 1848 a public appeal was launched for funds to support its work. It had been six years in existence and Meagher, who was then MP for Waterford city, was the asylum's treasurer. A circular published in *The Waterford Chronicle* in January 1848 gave an account of its foundation and purpose:

> For many years, all classes of the community felt and admitted the
> necessity of an asylum, where those erring beings, whose lives have
> been a profession of sin, but who sincerely desire to abandon the evil

of their ways, should have an opportunity of flying from the occasion and commission of crime, and of entering on paths of rectitude and morality. It is a melancholy fact that many of those helpless victims of crime and despair have been cast upon the world, and deprived of a parent to guide the steps of their youth, have fallen an easy prey to the wiles of the heartless seducer, who first corrupted and then abandoned them to the nameless horrors of a career of vice. It is no less certain that poverty is one, perhaps the greatest, cause of the infamy and degradation of these daughters of misfortune.

The circular noted that since its foundation fifty-nine women had been received into the asylum, located in a house on Barrack Street. Only six had again lapsed 'into vice'. Of the remaining fifty-three, six had gone into service with respectable families; three had gone to America; five were married; two had died and twenty-eight were now resident in the asylum.[65]

The governors of the Magdalen asylum (Meagher and three Catholic priests) were appealing for funds to support and enlarge the home for the women. The terraced house, it was claimed in the circular, was too small, and consequently was unhealthy. The dormitory and the rooms for washing, mangling, drying and ironing clothes for the laundry attached to the asylum were all under one roof. In the twenty-first century such institutions are, understandably, viewed with deep suspicion and revulsion. However, Dr Frances Finnegan, a historian and strident critic of the Magdalen system, has described the circular published in *The Chronicle* as 'balanced and kindly, citing seduction and poverty as contributory, if not determining factors, in the women's downfall' and was in marked contrast to the language often used by contemporaries in relation to such women.[66] In the 1850s the management of the Magdalen asylum was transferred to the Sisters of the Good Shepherd.[67] With this transfer the character of the institution was changed, and not always for the better.[68]

MEAGHER'S CHARITABLENESS AND PHILANTHROPY CONSIDERED

Meagher's charitable and philanthropic endeavours were influenced by a number of factors. The pre-eminent influence was his Catholic faith. As a devout Catholic, he would have understood, appreciated and practised the teachings of his Church's theology that Christ manifested himself in the poor and to relieve the poor person was to relieve Christ. 'The poor possessed a spiritual significance, given that they presented the prospective giver with the opportunity to provide alms and to sanctify oneself.'[69]

Second, his association with the Benevolent Irish Society in St John's, Newfoundland, informed his attitudes and actions. His father was a founding member; he himself served for a period as treasurer of an institution which, as was noted in Chapter 1, acquired an acknowledged position in St John's for its efforts at alleviating distress among the poor. Its motto, 'He that gives to the poor lends to the Lord', was resonant of the Christian teaching that alms-giving was a sacred duty of the Christian. Undoubtedly, it was the philosophy and ethos of this society which were the greatest personal legacy of Thomas Meagher's years in Newfoundland.

A third factor was the influence of middle-class social attitudes, which were considerations in the establishment of charitable bodies such as mendicity societies:

> The visibility of ragged and dirty mendicants offended the sensitivities of the middle classes who increasingly esteemed and expected respectability in one's conduct and appearance. The removal of these eyesores from public spaces frequented by the respectable classes was an important motivating factor behind initiatives to suppress street begging ... it was the visibility of such persons that led to public concern ...[70]

Mendicity societies, such as the one in Waterford, were founded, run and supported largely by middle-class men drawn mainly from the professional and commercial classes, men who were prominent figures in their local communities.[71] By voluntarily supporting these local societies, these individuals emphasised the civic duty which contributed to the formation of middle-class identity. Meagher epitomised the type of person who involved himself in the mendicity movement.

Of course, such middle-class attitudes did not necessarily negate genuine feelings of humane and religious benevolence towards the poor, and Meagher does appear to have had such genuine feelings and his association with the Irish Sisters of Charity may be a significant indicator of this. The presence of his sister-in-law in the community may go some way to explaining this, but a deeply religious and charitable man such as Meagher was likely motivated by other, perhaps more substantial considerations.

While numerous female congregations and orders were established in Ireland in the eighteenth and nineteenth centuries, the foundation of the Religious Sisters of Charity by Mary Aikenhead in 1815 marked a new departure in Irish religious history, as these sisters pioneered social work by female religious in the wider community.[72] Concern for the poor was central to the foundress's vision and the sisters took a fourth vow of 'perpetual service of the poor' in addition to the three standard vows of poverty, chastity and obedience.[73] Aikenhead believed that poverty was caused by external factors, and not by some moral flaw in the poor themselves, a popular view in the nineteenth century. They were not the idle, improvident and wicked poor of the public discourse of many members of the middle class.[74] It is reasonable to suggest that Meagher was aware of Mary Aikenhead's outlook and expressed his approval of it and of the work of her religious sisterhood by his support for the establishment of a convent of this congregation in Waterford. His charitable and philanthropic acts certainly resonate with Aikenhead's views.

REPEAL REVIVED

By the end of the 1830s, Daniel O'Connell was becoming disillusioned with the Whig alliance and the amount of reform that had been achieved. Moreover, he realised that the Conservatives were likely to be returned to power after the next general election. Accordingly, he turned back to repeal and began laying the political foundations for a renewal of that campaign. In 1838 he founded the Precursor Society; this became the Loyal National Repeal Association in July 1840.[75]

There is evidence of renewed activity by supporters of O'Connell in Waterford city, with Thomas Meagher playing a prominent role. In May 1838 subscriptions were raised towards sustaining the Liberal interest in the city, to which Meagher contributed £10.[76] In that same year £238 was raised locally in a collection for the O'Connell tribute, with Meagher acting as treasurer of the fund.[77] A branch of the Precursor Society was established, of which he was chair. At a meeting held on 10 January 1839, he urged that 'there was no time to be lost, as every man ought to now come forward to manifest to Mr O'Connell his unbounded confidence in his integrity and wisdom'.[78] This local society, however, did not enjoy success, reflecting the fact that the repeal cause at national level was failing to attract popular support.[79] Waterford's Precursor Society was dissolved on 21 November.[80]

In late April 1839 a requisition signed by a large number of prominent citizens, including Meagher, requested a meeting to consider 'the necessity of establishing an association under the title "The Waterford County and City Liberal Club", for the purpose of registering voters sympathetic to the Liberal interest'.[81] This meeting was held on 2 May and an association was formed. Meagher was appointed to its general committee and was also chosen as one of the two 'inspectors-general' for the city, charged with the responsibility of overseeing the effective operation of the new body.[82]

At the general election of 1841, however, the two Conservative candidates, William Christmas and William Reade, were elected to represent the city constituency in Parliament.[83] Alleging irregularities, the supporters of the defeated Liberal candidates held a meeting in the city hall on 17 July to petition the House of Commons against the return of the recently elected Tory members. Meagher was in attendance and was chosen, by acclaim, to act as secretary for the occasion.[84] The petition was subsequently upheld and the Liberal candidates deemed elected.

REFORM OF MUNICIPAL CORPORATIONS

The bitter resentment felt by middle-class Catholics at their exclusion from any role in municipal government has already been noted. Meagher was no exception: he was vocal in his criticisms of Waterford Corporation at one of the first public meetings he addressed. The country's corporations were bastions of Anglican privilege and exclusiveness. They were a symbol of the political and social order Daniel O'Connell was seeking to supplant in favour of a system of governance which reflected the reality of Ireland's majority Catholic population. For him, reform in this area was a crucial step in completing the process begun by Catholic emancipation: 'There remains this corporate monopoly and it is the only thing remaining that prevents justice being done. This, and this alone, shuts the inhabitants out from participation in the advantages of British institutions ...'[85] A detailed consideration of the issue of municipal reform illustrates the extent of Protestant privilege in Ireland and the determined resolve of those possessing such privileges to thwart any efforts to change the system. Quite simply, municipal politics highlight the Herculean task facing Meagher and his colleagues in their quest for equality, as they attempted to wrest control from the clenched fist of obdurate Anglican resistance.

Under the Lichfield House Compact of 1835, the Whigs had indicated their support for municipal reform in return for O'Connell's support in Parliament. Two years before this compact, the Whig government had established a royal commission to inquire into Ireland's municipal corporations. The report, issued in 1835, described them as being 'in many instances, of no service to the community; in others injurious; in all, insufficient and inadequate to the proper purposes and ends of such institutions'.[86] Furthermore, the commissioners concluded that 'the unpopular character of municipal bodies is, in too many cases, aggravated by their being considered inimical, on the ground of sectarian feelings, to a great majority of the resident population'.[87] These descriptions were certainly apposite in relation to the Corporation of Waterford.[88] Evidence given to the commissioners when they visited Waterford in December 1833, together with the 1835 report, exposed Waterford Corporation as a bastion of Anglican privilege.

The extent to which the corporation was an exclusive body was underscored when the report revealed that its affairs had been regulated by a compact which had been entered into in 1818 by John Newport and Henry Alcock, by the terms of which these two members became the effective leaders of the council. This agreement divided up the offices and patronage of the corporation between the two men. The effect of the compact was to reduce aldermen and councillors to 'mere puppets' doing the will of Newport and Alcock. While the compact ended in June 1830, its effects were still evident when the commissioners visited the city in 1833.[89]

Their report also revealed that the city council was a self-perpetuating clique composed of forty members: a mayor, two sheriffs, eighteen aldermen and nineteen assistants or common councilmen. The mayor was elected annually by the council from among the aldermen, who, in turn, were elected by this same council from among the assistants. This latter group was elected, again by the council, from among the freemen. Aldermen and assistants held office for life. The city council was overwhelmingly Anglican: only two Catholics had been elected to that body, Thomas Wyse and John Archbold.[90]

The commissioners' report found that no office under the corporation was held by a Catholic, except some of the petty and market constables, though a Catholic had served as sheriff since emancipation and another had been offered the office.[91] Offices of emolument in the gift of the council were being used as forms of economic and political patronage, to the advantage of the city's Anglican population. Some of the offices were quite lucrative, others less so,[92] but there were ones to suit Protestants of every social class.

The prevalence of such obvious discrimination angered Catholics. At the first meeting of the Waterford City Liberal Club on 10 July 1828, it was reported that:

> A very strong and decided feeling of indignation pervaded the meeting, when it was stated that there were persons in the city, whose ancestors held the highest offices in the civic government, but who were then overlooked and excluded even from the humblest situation in the corporation, to make way for pig-jobbers and men whose qualifications in any other way were almost wholly overlooked, provided they were not Catholics.[93]

A resolution adopted at the meeting acknowledged the just complaint of Catholics who were 'excluded [from the corporation], by the mere circumstance of adherence to the religion of their fathers'.[94]

RESTRICTED ADMISSION TO THE FREEDOM OF THE CITY

Admission to the freedom of the city was in the gift of the corporation. This freedom was sought because it conferred on the recipient the right to vote in parliamentary elections. It was also from among the freemen that common councilmen were elected. There is evidence that the corporation adopted a very restrictive approach to granting freedoms. An examination of an official corporation document, 'Applications for Freedoms, 1824', reveals this.[95] For example, on 14 April 1824, thirty-seven applications were considered by the relevant corporation committee. Only three persons were admitted to freedom; twenty-three were rejected and the other applications were postponed. On 20 April 1824, of the thirty-seven applications, only six were granted; twenty-six were rejected and the remainder postponed. Moreover, the right of admission was confined, for the most part to Anglicans. In spite of Catholics forming the majority of the city's population, only 305 had been admitted as freemen between 1790 and 1826, against 1,009 Protestants.[96] In evidence given to the municipal commissioners in 1833, the mayor stated that many respectable Catholics had applied in vain to the council for freedom, though he later modified his evidence to the effect that rather than excluding persons on account of their religion, the council threw obstacles in their way.[97] Thus, it was difficult for Waterford Corporation not to appear as a citadel of Anglicanism.

The words of a witness before the commissioners serves to highlight the degree to which the council alienated the majority of the city's population: 'Did not the custom of excluding persons differing from them in religion diffuse doubt and suspicion over all their acts, even when they might have been right?'[98]

PROTESTANT RESISTANCE TO MUNICIPAL REFORM

During the 1830s, Waterford Corporation became a shrill voice, defying the political causes espoused by most Catholics. As the adherents of the majority faith became more assertive in their political demands, the majority of Waterford's Anglicans, increasingly fearful of the emerging Catholic democracy, retreated behind the entrenched and exclusive bastion that was the city's system of municipal governance. The prospect of repeal of the Act of Union alarmed Protestant opinion in Ireland, and Protestants in Waterford articulated their concerns and attitudes by means of the corporation's deliberations. For example, on 18 February 1831 the council resolved to address the Lord Lieutenant, Lord Anglesey, on the matter. The language used was very strong in its denunciation of the agitation, which was 'exciting the worst passions of the lower orders of the people, fomenting commotion, engendering animosity against Great Britain and endangering the very foundation of civil society'. Repeal, the address stated, would lead to the separation of Ireland and Great Britain, a consequence which would mean 'desolation and utter ruin' for the country.[99]

The Waterford Mail, the organ of Waterford Protestant opinion, in its opposition to municipal reform articulated views which reflected those of most members of the city's corporation and the majority of its readers. The newspaper conducted its debate on the issue in sectarian terms, with no real concern being shown for the efficiency or otherwise of corporate institutions.[100] It defined the purpose of corporations as 'the maintenance and promotion of the English or what is more properly termed the Protestant interest in Ireland'.[101] Reform threatened to subvert this purpose, having the effect of handing corporations over to Catholics, who would use them to promote repeal. O'Connell himself had stated that reformed corporations would be like schools 'for teaching the science of peaceful political agitation'.[102] Crucially, for many Protestants municipal reform was held to have a constitutional aspect, in that the weakening of the 'Protestant interest' would weaken the Union itself.

The *Mail* rejected any reform initiatives which impaired the 'essential Protestantism' of municipal institutions.[103] It was better to abolish corporations altogether than have them fall under Catholic control. Under a reformed regime, the town hall would become a school of agitation: 'Better suppress them than suffer them to be so remodelled as to afford papists and an anti-British spirit the protection and encouragement which may enable the new possessors to cope with and conquer the religion and interest which they were originally created to protect.'[104] In its opinion, since corporations were given to Protestants for the express purpose of giving them the 'upper hand', it was vital not to transfer this advantage to Catholics.[105]

THE MUNICIPAL REVOLUTION

In 1835 the Whig government introduced a municipal reform bill, but it was not until 1840 that the measure was enacted. Six times the House of

Commons passed a bill, only to have it amended out of all recognition by the ultra-Tory House of Lords. Finally, a compromise emerged. This compromise restricted the powers of corporations and confined the municipal franchise to £10 householders.[106] Daniel O'Connell had a deep belief in the importance of reforming corporations and that was why he was willing to accept a greatly watered-down version of the legislation, with a much higher franchise qualification than his preferred £5 one. For him, municipal reform represented 'the commencement of the reign of justice'.[107]

Waterford Corporation itself was not, hardly surprisingly, enthusiastic about the proposals for municipal reform. In 1835 it petitioned the House of Lords to postpone the bill, offering various technical reasons for doing so.[108] A motion proposing a petition to the legislature praying for municipal reform failed at a meeting in 1839, for want of a seconder.[109] Another petition was sent to the Lords in 1840 seeking the omission of the clause extending the municipal franchise, a feature of the bill which alarmed conservatives because of its democratic tendencies.[110] This action reflected a common view that every increase in the rating qualification automatically meant fewer Catholics being entitled to vote.

Throughout Ireland, the position of corporations as strongholds of the Protestant interest made them far more difficult to dislodge than had been anticipated.[111] This was certainly true of Waterford – in fact, the 1840 Municipal Corporations Act was to come into operation later in Waterford than in most other cities or towns.[112] Supporters of reform believed the city's corporation was engaged in deliberate efforts 'to retard' its introduction. In response, seventy-three prominent citizens, including Meagher, sought a public meeting in May 1842 to consider the matter.[113] At this meeting, a committee of thirteen, which included Meagher, was appointed to draw up a memorial to the lord lieutenant to counteract one sent by the corporation to him, which was regarded by reformers as simply another delaying ploy.[114]

Notwithstanding the die-hard resistance of Waterford's Anglican-dominated corporation, elections for a new council, to be constituted under the terms of the 1840 Municipal Corporations Act, were held in October 1842. The main issue was to be repeal, a reflection of the fact that O'Connell's campaign was beginning to gain some traction. Early in the month, at a meeting of the Waterford Loyal Repeal Association, it was declared that the election results would give the city 'a repeal corporation'.[115] Similar sentiments were expressed at a meeting of citizens convened for the purpose of making 'preliminary arrangements for nominating fit and proper persons to form a council under the Municipal Act'. One speaker stated that 'there was one object alone that demands the attention of Ireland – and that is to make Ireland an independent nation. The municipal body has advantages to advance that purpose as part and parcel of this great nation.' He concluded by asserting that, 'Repeal feeling was so strong in Waterford that no persons but repealers would be admitted to the corporation.'[116]

The reformed corporations brought about a municipal revolution. Matthew Potter has written: 'All over the country, a paradigm shift occurred, which altered the urban areas permanently.'[117] The Catholic middle class gained control of a significant aspect of the country's administrative machine for the first time. All corporations, except those of Belfast and Derry, came under Catholic control.[118] This achievement proclaimed, in a dramatic and unequivocal fashion, the continuing rise of the Catholic bourgeoisie.

The newly elected Corporation of Waterford was composed of thirty-five Catholics, a singular transformation in terms of religious affiliations.[119] It was also transformed politically: it had a clear majority of members favouring repeal. In social terms, however, little had changed: of the forty councillors, seventeen were merchants, eleven commercial employers, eight professionals and four from the 'squirearchy'.[120] To qualify for membership, under the terms of the 1840 Municipal Corporations Act, a man had to have property valued at £1,000 over and above his debt, or occupy a house rated at £25 or more per annum.[121] This precluded the overwhelming majority of the city's inhabitants. The electorate, confined to men holding valuations of £10 or more per annum, was about 700 voters,[122] in a city recording a population, according to the 1841 census, of 23,216.[123] Thus, the reformed corporation remained under the control of a small and wealthy elite, this time one professing the Roman Catholic rather than the Protestant variety of Christianity. Catholics had emerged victorious from a contest in the 1820s and 1830s between politico-religious rivals and translated their social and economic position into a political one. The new corporation was to come to serve the same purpose for Waterford's Catholic middle-class elite as the old one had for Protestants, in that it legitimised what they regarded as their rightful roles as leaders of society.[124]

Among those elected to the reformed corporation was Thomas Meagher. Representing the Tower ward, he received fifty-six votes.[125] He and Sir Benjamin Morris, being the two candidates with the highest votes in the eight-seat ward, were returned as aldermen. It was a significant personal achievement for the man from St John's: his membership of the corporation was recognition of the prominent role he had played in the political, social and economic life of his adopted city for two decades and of his stature within the Catholic bourgeoisie. Alderman Meagher was now a member of the small elite that managed the affairs of Waterford city. His successful venture into municipal politics in 1842 was to herald the beginning of a career in public life which was to last fifteen years.

CHAPTER FIVE

Mayor of Waterford, 1843, 1844

When Thomas Meagher took his seat on the corporation of Waterford in 1842, he can hardly have imagined the vista that was to open before him. He was to serve successively as alderman, mayor and member of parliament, confirming his position of eminence in the civic, political and social life of Waterford. He was to establish himself as one of the premier leaders of the Catholic middle class and of the inhabitants of the city in general. He was to offer leadership at times of great political turbulence and was to display uncompromising loyalty to Daniel O'Connell.

The first duty of the new corporation was the election of a mayor, and this it did on 1 November 1842. According to *The Waterford Chronicle*, this caused great excitement in the city, with large crowds around the city hall, 'all engaged in a conversation on one topic, namely, the extraordinary change about to take place in having a Roman Catholic mayor placed over them.'[1] It had been expected that Alexander Sherlock would have this honour. He was proposed but declined the nomination due to the pressure of other commitments. In turn, he proposed Thomas Meagher, the motion being seconded by Sir Benjamin Morris, a member of the Church of Ireland.[2] Meagher was duly elected.[3] In his first speech as mayor, he referred to his election as 'the first time there was a chosen officer of the people to fill the high office.'[4] He clearly appreciated the historical significance of the event: he was the first chief magistrate of the city chosen under a more democratic (though still severely limited) system. Consequently, he was more representative of the citizens of the city than his Protestant predecessors, these having been selected by an exclusive and grossly undemocratic council. And he was the first Catholic mayor since the seventeenth century.[5] His period in office was to be dominated by three issues: reform of the corporation; temperance; and Daniel O'Connell's campaign for repeal of the Act of Union.

One of the first official duties undertaken by the new mayor was to attend mass on the Sunday after his election. The occasion resonated with symbolism and was a public expression of the significant changes which Meagher's assumption of the mayoralty presaged. It was a tangible and visible manifestation of a new political dispensation, a demonstration of the fact that Catholics were progressing towards the achievement of religious equality. The mayor's attendance at mass was an event which captured the popular imagination: the city's Catholic citizenry could identify with this act as a clear signal that the old order was in the process of being swept away. Accordingly, thousands of people assembled opposite the city hall, in festive mood. Shortly before noon, Meagher, accompanied by all members of the corporation and civic officers, and led by the John Street Band, walked in a dignified and impressive procession to the Cathedral of the Holy Trinity, in Barronstrand Street. The preacher at the religious service alluded to the extraordinary events taking place in Waterford's social and political life. After the ceremony, Meagher processed to the city hall, accompanied by a crowd of at least 10,000, highlighting the significance with which the Catholics of Waterford regarded the election of a Catholic mayor.[6]

WORK OF THE CORPORATION UNDER MAYOR MEAGHER

The corporation, under Meagher's leadership, was determined to distinguish itself from its predecessor. The unreformed institution had been condemned for its corruption, inefficiency, peculation and indifference to the people of the city. Its successor was intent on showing that it was more responsible, more competent and more honest. At one of its first meetings, it was resolved 'that all applications for offices and employment under the town council shall be made in open council ... the usage of giving pledges or promises shall be discouraged'.[7] This resolution was a clear acknowledgement that the old corporation operated a system of secret patronage and the decision represented an attempt to remedy this situation. The same meeting appointed a committee 'to inquire into the nature of the duties and emoluments of all offices under or connected with the council ... and to take into consideration the utility or advantage of abolishing all useless offices'.[8] Acting on its report, the corporation abolished the offices of inspector of markets[9] and inspector of streets and works.[10] Moreover, it proposed the revocation of some previous appointments.[11] In keeping with the corporation's determination to purge the malfeasance of officials associated with its predecessor, it was decided that 'it be a fixed principle that the duties of officers be discharged in person, not by deputy'.[12]

During Meagher's mayoralty, the corporation embarked on a series of civic improvements which were intended to highlight and confirm a determination to present the council as an institution working for the welfare of the citizens of Waterford – unlike its predecessor. For example, £100 was allocated for the flagging of John Street and Michael Street.[13] A decision was made to construct a sewer at Ballybricken and from there to Thomas Street and adjoining lanes,[14] which were parts of the city with a relatively high population density. Funds were assigned to the Streets' Commissioners for repairs of city streets[15] and 'improvements in the borough'.[16] Members of the corporation were determined that the inhabitants of the city would benefit from corporate expenditure in the area of employment. Therefore, in November 1842 it was resolved: 'That it be an instruction to the Streets' Commissioners that residents of this city for some years and of good character be employed in all public works in their department and strangers only to be employed when such residents are unable to be procured.'[17]

The old corporation had mismanaged the financial affairs of Waterford city and it was imperative that the reformed version address this problem. As early as 29 November 1842, it was resolved that 'negotiations be opened with capitalists in London or elsewhere with a view to diminish the high interest payable on the city's debt'.[18] Councillors learned the extent of the financial crisis in April 1843, when they were informed that the corporation's debt stood at £66,000, at an annual interest rate of 5 per cent. The borough income for the previous year was £6,207, while expenditure totalled £8,337.[19] On 6 February 1844 a memorial was sent to the Treasury seeking permission to borrow £70,000 at an interest rate of between 3 and 4 per cent, by mortgaging corporate property to pay its debts. The lower interest rate payable to the new lenders would result in a saving of around £700, which could be expended on municipal improvements. The seriousness of the situation was impressed on the Treasury by stating that the corporation faced legal action from its creditors.[20] In November of the same year the sale of some property and the borrowing of £40,000 were sanctioned.[21]

The newly elected corporation expended much time and effort in cleansing the Augean Stable that was its much-reviled predecessor. Such remedial action was consistent with the essence and principles of good corporate governance, to which ideal the newly elected corporation declared its commitment. There was another motive, however, for this action. The majority of councillors were repealers. There was a desire, on their part, to show that by the effective management of civic affairs, Ireland was capable of governing itself through an Irish parliament, to be restored by the repeal of the Act of Union. Speaking at a meeting in Waterford on 10 November 1842, the recently elected mayor, Thomas Meagher, was reported as saying: 'They would, he hoped, show a proof in miniature, among their civic body, how the affairs of the people can be managed by themselves ... They (the municipal body) shall manage their own affairs, responsible to those who had chosen them.'[22]

REPEAL CAMPAIGN

It was after a debate on repeal from 28 February to 2 March 1843 in Dublin Corporation that the campaign for this measure began to gain momentum.[23] It was re-energised. 'Sections of the middle class, which had previously remained aloof, conceded the merits of an Irish parliament, and more "men of social or political rank" joined the association in three weeks than had in the preceding three years.'[24] The campaign was at its most intense during the period of Meagher's mayoralty. Waterford Corporation was to play a central part in the struggle, becoming a focus of local support and a vehicle for the articulation of the city's adherence to O'Connell's crusade. By virtue of his position, Meagher became, in many ways, the public face of the movement in the city. At various times he had to offer decisive leadership, as the political reverberations of the repeal campaign convulsed Waterford.

The importance accorded to repeal by Waterford Corporation was apparent at its first meeting on 1 November 1842. It resolved that Thomas Meagher, as mayor, should write to O'Connell and invite him to visit the city, at his earliest convenience.[25] O'Connell replied on 3 November, accepting the invitation. In his letter he wrote that he was only beginning the repeal agitation,[26] and his prompt response was indicative of the significance he attached to the support he was receiving in the city and county. Doubtless, he was mindful of the key part Waterford had played in the emancipation campaign, the memory of which he hoped to exploit in his quest for repeal.

He made his visit on 10 November. Meagher and fellow councillors met O'Connell at the outskirts of the city and walked in procession, together with a huge crowd, behind his carriage. The place was in festive mood. A contemporary account recognised the pivotal role the corporation would play in the forthcoming political struggle: 'The cortege moved onwards to the town hall, thus consecrating to purposes of national independence a spot hitherto sacred to public rapine, plundering monopoly and the withering influence of a foul, corrupt and bigoted ascendancy.' O'Connell addressed a public meeting of nearly 50,000 from the building. That evening he was the principal guest at a dinner presided over by Meagher. In his address the mayor reminded his audience of the Liberator's triumphal achievement of emancipation and of Waterford's decisive role in the 1826 election. He referred to his own election as mayor, something inconceivable in 1826. Finally, he declared himself a committed repealer, because of his conviction that it was for the benefit of Ireland that 'she enjoy the fostering protection of a domestic legislature.'[27]

On 21 March 1843 the corporation resolved to petition Parliament for the repeal of the Act of Union and the restoration of an Irish legislature.[28] This meeting was probably inspired by the aforementioned one held by Dublin Corporation the previous month. Addressing the assembly of councillors, Meagher declared that 'the people of Ireland cannot be raised from their present state of suffering and destitution, unless by the fostering care of a parliament chosen by themselves, and solely devoted to the improvement of the country and the advancement of her true interests'. Destitution and suffering were widespread: 'The people, in thousands, he might say millions, are in distress and in such distress as was never witnessed before ... after nearly fifty years of united British legislation ... the poor [are] dying of want in our streets'. This would not have occurred, argued Meagher, 'under a legislature devoted, as it ought to be, to the improvement of the conditions of the people'. Such an improvement demanded the restoration of a native parliament: 'Ireland's prosperity depends on her being legislated for by men who understand her wants and feel for her people'.[29] Meagher was giving expression to 'a declensionist historical narrative of economic stagnation', which had been quickly established in the aftermath of the Union to describe Ireland's experience of rule from Westminster. In this narrative, description and prescription were fused to furnish incontrovertible reasons for the restoration of an Irish parliament.[30] Unsurprisingly, the petition adopted by the corporation was a litany of the misfortunes, economic, social and political, attributable to the Union, which was described as 'a national calamity': 'the necessary consequences of this intolerable injustice have overspread the entire kingdom with helpless misery and with unavoidable ruin; and your petitioners are constrained to avow their distressing conviction, that its continuance must be inevitably followed by still more affecting disasters'.[31]

1843: 'YEAR OF REPEAL' AND 'MONSTER' MEETINGS

Daniel O'Connell declared that 1843 would be the 'Year of Repeal'. His intention was to achieve victory in the same way he had won emancipation: by the engagement of the masses in his campaign. However, because of the absence of any significant body of support from MPs in the House of Commons, he had to make his extra-parliamentary agitation more imposing and dramatic than anything he had done before. What he was trying to do was to translate his successful Clare election campaign of 1828 into a national campaign and terrify the British government into conceding repeal by showing his control and mastery of the people of Ireland.[32] Thus, O'Connell began organising a series of huge gatherings around the country, which quickly became known as 'monster meetings', such were the crowds in attendance. Between March and October 1843, thirty-one major outdoor meetings were held.[33] The actual numbers of those who attended were disputed by O'Connell's supporters and the government, but even a conservative figure of one-and-a-half million people – one-quarter of the population of the three southern provinces in which these meetings were organised – is impressive.[34] This constituted an unparalleled achievement in political mobilisation,[35] and these occasions became 'demonstrations of the massiveness of organised democracy' and 'hedge schools in which the masses were educated in the nationalist politics of repeal'.[36]

Repeal fever swept the country in the summer of 1843.[37] And it was on 9 July that Waterford city was the venue for a monster meeting. This gathering, at Ballybricken, is probably the largest that has ever been witnessed in the city's long history. The event attracted over 300,000 people, the occasion capturing the popular imagination, especially the dramatic procession which preceded the meeting. This left the city early in the morning to meet O'Connell. The vast concourse was led by groups of tradesmen, each marching behind a banner with an inscription supporting repeal. On meeting O'Connell, the procession returned to the city, accompanied by over thirty bands. It was not until 5 p.m. that the actual meeting began, such was the throng on the route of the procession.

The first speaker was Thomas Meagher, who delivered an admirably brief address. He began by stating that it would be 'an act of injustice' to detain the crowd by any lengthened observations at that late hour. All he intended to do was to read a resolution, and any comments were unnecessary. The resolution was simply a reiteration of the oft repeated theme of repealers: such was the 'unexampled pitch of poverty and degradation' to which Ireland had been reduced that the only solution lay in the restoration of a native parliament. That evening a banquet was held in the city hall with 800 in attendance. Once again, it was Meagher who commenced proceedings by proposing a toast to the Liberator and repeal.[38]

By means of these monster meetings, O'Connell had worked the country into a fever pitch of excitement by the autumn of 1843. The repeal cause, however, suffered a severe setback when the government banned the meeting scheduled for Clontarf on 8 October. Then, on 14 October,

O'Connell was arrested and charged with conspiring to cause disaffection. His supporters in Waterford assembled a few days later in the city hall to 'record their unflinching and unalterable determination to stand firmly by the cause of native freedom and to proclaim their unbounded confidence in the fidelity and wisdom of Daniel O'Connell'. The building was thronged and thousands failed to gain admission. Meagher, addressing the crowd, declared that he was not surprised to see such a gathering, 'knowing that nothing had occurred to change your opinion upon the subject which has brought you together … to change your mind … [and] disturb your confidence or weaken your affection towards the illustrious man who is leading on the peaceful warfare for the restoration of your liberties'. He affirmed his conviction in repeal as the only means of righting Ireland's many wrongs and grievances.[39] A meeting of the corporation on 20 October passed a resolution expressing 'its unalterable confidence in Mr O'Connell and a firm determination to support him'.[40]

MEAGHER'S RE-ELECTION AS MAYOR

In late November 1843 a requisition, signed by many of the city's most prominent citizens, Catholic and Protestant, called on Meagher to allow his name to be put in nomination for re-election as mayor for the coming year. The signatories made this request as an expression of their 'admiration' of the 'strict impartiality, unceasing efficiency and unexampled disinterestedness' with which he had discharged his duties during the past year.[41] The matter was discussed at a meeting of the corporation on 22 November and it was resolved that Meagher be re-elected because of 'his most efficient and virtuous fulfilment' of his duties and 'his zealous support of the vital question to Ireland of repeal'.[42] His second term as mayor of Waterford, like his first, was dominated by the issue of repeal. The year 1844 was a very difficult one for O'Connell, but Meagher never faltered in his loyal support of the Liberator.

WATERFORD'S LOYALTY TO O'CONNELL

On 15 January 1844 O'Connell was put on trial for conspiracy; a month later, he was found guilty, with sentencing being deferred until May. A dinner in Cork in his honour in April was seen by Waterford Corporation as 'a suitable occasion to manifest towards that distinguished individual our unabated confidence'. It was resolved that councillors would attend in their official capacity.[43] A steamer, *The Mermaid*, was chartered to convey 200 repeal supporters to Cork. Many corporation members travelled on this vessel, although Meagher went by coach. Once there, accompanied by a number of Waterford representatives, he presented an address to O'Connell, in which loyalty to the repeal cause was affirmed.[44]

On 30 May O'Connell was sentenced to twelve months' imprisonment. The next day, at a meeting of Waterford Corporation, it was decided to convene a special meeting to consider the best means of expressing 'its unalterable sentiments of respect, confidence and attachment' to O'Connell during what was described as 'his present unremitted suffering'.[45] This meeting took place on 4 June. Meagher, once again, attested to his personal commitment to repeal, urging all councillors to 'labour more than ever for legislative independence'.[46] A resolution was adopted declaring the 'imperative duty to renew in the most unqualified terms the expression of entire confidence in the great leader of the repeal cause'.[47]

On 5 June there was a public meeting in the city hall to adopt an address to the incarcerated O'Connell. According to *The Waterford Chronicle*, the venue was 'crowded to inconvenience' and 'repeated plaudits' greeted the arrival of Meagher, who presided at the event. He deplored the fact that O'Connell, 'the Father, the Liberator of his country is immured in prison'. Again he reiterated a familiar theme: the need to persevere in the struggle for repeal. It was agreed that the mayor would present the address to O'Connell in Richmond Prison, and this he did on 13 June.[48]

Daniel O'Connell's conviction was overturned on appeal by the House of Lords on 4 September 1844 and he was released from prison. On 11 September Waterford Corporation met to express its delight and to adopt another formal address to him.[49] On 12 September there was a public meeting in the city hall, this assembly being described as 'a powerful demonstration of joyful patriotism'.[50] Presided over by Meagher, the occasion was one to express gladness at O'Connell's release, and fidelity to him as Ireland's national leader and to the repeal cause. The mayor called on his listeners to 'promise that you will now, with more zeal, with more energy and with more determination than ever, sustain his [O'Connell's] constitutional and peaceful efforts to obtain for Ireland her legislative independence'.[51] A formal address to O'Connell was adopted and this address was presented to him by Meagher on 19 September, the day before a great banquet was held in Dublin in honour of the Liberator.[52]

THOMAS MEAGHER: O'CONNELL'S POLITICAL ACOLYTE

As mayor, Thomas Meagher promoted the cause of repeal in Waterford with vigour and was unfailingly loyal to O'Connell's beliefs. He was very much the Liberator's political acolyte. In keeping with his leader's deeply held convictions, Meagher repeated many times that only non-violent methods were to be used in the repeal campaign, no matter what the circumstances and difficulties facing the cause. Addressing the audience at the dinner honouring O'Connell during his visit to the city in November 1842, he referred to the Liberator's triumphant achievement of emancipation, reminding his listeners: 'All that had been accomplished without the shedding of one drop of blood, without the commission of a single crime or scarcely the slightest infraction of the peace of the country'.[53] At a repeal meeting in February 1843, he had called on his audience to persevere in their 'judicious and temperate cause' and to exhibit to the English government 'the example of a people remarkable for their legal, constitutional and peaceable conduct'.[54] This attitude was given trenchant expression in relation to the preparations for the monster meeting in Waterford in July of that year: 'The mayor is determined to prosecute vigorously any person firing cannon in the river or small arms from houses, as the very smell or smoke of gun powder would be quite inconsistent with the temperate and strictly constitutional display of moral force, the only weapon repealers will use in the peaceful battle'.[55]

In the aftermath of the banning by the government of the Clontarf monster meeting in October 1843, Meagher addressed a repeal gathering in Waterford and urged his listeners to remain peaceful, declaring that they were 'seeking to injure no person in their endeavour to restore our parliament'.[56] Speaking at a meeting of the corporation in June 1844, shortly after O'Connell's imprisonment, Meagher associated himself unequivocally with the Liberator's appeal for no violence in response to the government's actions:

> I fully agree with the view taken by his [O'Connell's] master mind … that we should stringently pursue a peaceful course. It is not necessary to impress on you the necessity of carrying fully into effect his wishes. Every individual here will inculcate peace and tranquillity; and not only endeavour to prevent a breach of the peace, but to abstain from all expression of animosity towards those who differ from us.[57]

Addressing a public meeting a few days later, he repeated his plea to avoid giving any offence to those who opposed repeal: 'Let not even a word be uttered or an expression be used, that would tend to excite bad feeling or give the slightest offence even to an enemy.' Such actions would 'stain the holy cause' in which they were engaged.[58] When O'Connell was released from prison, Meagher told a meeting in Waterford that supporters of repeal had 'refrained from crime, from violence, from insult or offence to anyone'. He urged a continuation of this 'peaceable and honourable course'.[59] Thus, Meagher played a pivotal role in disseminating O'Connell's message of political non-violence. But he was doing more than relaying the opinions of the Liberator – he was also giving expression to his own conviction in peaceful, legal and constitutional means of agitation. As was noted in Chapter 1, during his first public speech in Waterford in April 1821, he expressed such views. Thomas Meagher, Mayor of Waterford, was demonstrably a committed constitutionalist.

LOYALTY TO THE CROWN

Daniel O'Connell was adamant in rejecting the charge that repeal would lead to the separation of Ireland and England. Launching the Repeal Association in July 1840, he asserted that he 'would rather perish than see the connection between the two countries broken or allegiance to the throne in the slightest degree lessened by our demand'.[60] One of the most important means adopted by him to counter allegations of promoting separatism was to emphasise the Irish sense of loyalty to the crown. At the Repeal Association launch, he proclaimed his respect for 'the golden link of the crown which binds forever Ireland and England together'.[61] Joining the Repeal Association involved an oath of allegiance to the queen and wearing a button with the harp and crown and the slogans 'God Save the Queen' and 'Repeal of the Union'.[62] Fervent, and sometimes even servile, expressions of adherence to the crown were from first to last a leading feature of O'Connell's repeal campaign.[63]

In his advocacy of repeal, Meagher reiterated O'Connell's contention that it would not result in Irish independence. At a meeting of Waterford Corporation to petition Parliament for repeal, held on 21 March 1843,[64] he stated in his address to councillors: 'We do not seek to dim the jewel of Ireland in the crown of their beloved sovereign, but that it should shine forth the brightest ornament of the imperial diadem.' In its account of these proceedings, *The Waterford Chronicle* reported that 'the meeting ended with cheers for the queen, O'Connell, the mayor and repeal'.[65]

During a dinner organised in honour of O'Connell's visit to Waterford in November 1842, Meagher proposed a series of toasts which reflected the professed loyalty of repealers to the crown. In proposing the first toast, he told his audience that 'he felt actuated by feelings far above the ordinary sense of duty: he offered to their notice the health of their most gracious queen in all the outpouring spirit of a grateful Irish heart'. Continuing, Meagher said that the happiness of those who were near and dear to the queen 'should be particularly so to them'. Therefore, he proposed a toast to Prince Albert, the Prince of Wales and the princess royal. Not yet finished, his third toast was to the Duchess of Kent (Queen Victoria's mother), the Duke of Sussex and 'the rest of the royal family resident in England'.[66]

Such toasts were unexceptional and an accepted element of any public event. Indeed, public bodies, such as educational institutions and corporations, were expected to furnish loyal addresses to the crown on occasions such as royal visits or the birth or death of members of the royal family.[67] The city council, over which Meagher presided, discharged its duties in this regard. On 2 May 1843 an address of condolence was sent to Queen Victoria on the death of the Duke of Sussex. The same meeting also resolved to congratulate the queen on the birth of a daughter.[68]

The practice of presenting the monarch with a formal address should also be seen in the context of wider Irish society, where royal events were acknowledged and celebrated. Accordingly, the actions of Waterford Corporation were consonant with public opinion. The coronation of Queen Victoria at the end of June 1838 united the country in enthusiastic celebration.[69] The event received extensive coverage in Waterford's newspapers.[70] The queen's wedding to Prince Albert in 1840 also generated a real sense of excitement, with *The Waterford Chronicle* reporting: 'The auspicious event of our most gracious queen's marriage to Prince Albert was celebrated in this city and the neighbouring towns of Carrick, Dungarvan, Clonmel, Cappoquin, Lismore and New Ross on yesterday with a degree of enthusiasm and devotional loyalty never paralleled on any former occasion when manifestation in favour of royalty was made by the Irish people.'[71]

When Meagher expressed his fidelity for the queen, he was not simply repeating the views of his party leader, O'Connell. Certainly, 'as a figure of central authority for the nationalist people of Ireland, O'Connell established loyalty to the throne as a core element of the Irish constitutional tradition.'[72] Meagher, however, was a monarchist in his own right and his actions and words with regard to the occupant of the English throne reflected this fact. This ought not to come as a surprise:

> Most Irish nationalists were monarchists ... In the nineteenth century the vast majority of countries were monarchies of one form or another. International relations were relations between monarchs ... Monarchy seemed the natural form of government and it had the blessing of the Catholic Church – a fact of great significance in Ireland, where the overwhelming majority of nationalists were Catholics.[73]

MEAGHER, REPEAL AND TEMPERANCE

In pursuit of his objectives, O'Connell enlisted Fr Theobald Mathew's temperance movement, convinced that it would provide the manpower and moral force that might transform his political campaign into an irresistible crusade.[74] He succeeded in channelling the inherent political energy of the temperance movement in the direction of repeal agitation. Sobriety contributed to the discipline of monster meetings and this orderliness made them all the more intimidating for the government. Such was the appreciation by O'Connell of the political significance of Fr Mathew's activities, that he told a meeting in Kilkenny that temperance would bring repeal.[75] Limerick and Waterford, vibrant centres of temperance, were also strongholds of support for O'Connell.[76] It has been observed that practically every town had local leaders who endorsed both crusades and bore witness to the case argued by O'Connell, that temperance societies and repeal associations were two sides of the same coin.[77] Meagher was one such leader and, in his service to the repeal cause, he played a very important and significant role in encouraging cooperation between the repeal and temperance campaigns in Waterford.

At a repeal meeting held in October 1843, he addressed special words to the teetotallers in the audience:

> There is one class of repealers, in particular, the most important and influential, on whom depends in great measure the success of the present movement, to whom I will address a few words – the teetotallers. On you depends the destiny of your country. Mr O'Connell himself has declared that but for the influence of temperance he could not have advanced the [repeal] cause to its present position.[78]

After O'Connell's imprisonment, Meagher again directed particular remarks to teetotallers:

> As I see many teetotallers here, I wish to address a few words to them. Mr O'Connell has often declared that he could never, with safety to the public peace, have raised the people to a just sense of their rights and of their wrongs but for the establishment and diffusion of temperance. Teetotallers, do you want another motive to persevere in your holy career? Continue to be guardians of the public peace, by your fidelity to the pledge, for the love of O'Connell and your country.[79]

The sense of public order and obedience to the law associated with the temperance movement won the strong approval and endorsement of Meagher, a constitutionalist, who abhorred any association between politics and violence, and a prominent member of the middle class, a section of society that sacralised social stability.

MEAGHER, TEMPERANCE AND POVERTY

While Thomas Meagher was happy to associate the temperance movement with repeal for political reasons, he, unlike Daniel O'Connell, had a genuine interest in promoting Fr Mathew's cause. The temperance crusade was the single most extraordinary social movement that occurred in pre-Famine Ireland.[80] After O'Connell, the Cork-based Capuchin friar was the most popular figure in the country in the early 1840s, *The Waterford Chronicle* opining: 'No one has done more for his country than Fr Mathew – we scarcely except the Liberator himself. One has been the great moral regenerator, the other the political.'[81] Over the five years beginning in 1838, between three and five million people – at least half the population – took the pledge to abstain from alcoholic drink for life.[82] The movement's most striking feature was the enthusiasm, emotion and eagerness with which people embraced it,[83] and across most of Ireland public life became marked by a fiercely determined temperance ethic.[84] One historian has observed that the crusade against intoxicating drink 'set its face not merely against private habit, but against a very public and practically universal way of life'.[85] That it was successful for a time is beyond question. There is evidence which indicates a decline in drinking during the early 1840s approaching 60 per cent or more.[86]

Meagher's interest in temperance reflected the influence of Fr Mathew on Irish life, and his belief that he should support the friar's activities in his capacity as mayor. He was motivated, moreover, by a real concern for the poorer classes of Waterford. On the occasion of his election as mayor, he was reported as saying that 'the industrious poor, although no sharers, directly or individually, in the proceedings of the day, shall be the peculiar objects of his solicitude'. The newspaper report continued:

Their [the poorer working classes] uniform good conduct, especially since the introduction and happy influence of temperance rendered his duty with respect to them one of comparative ease. He only begged of them to cooperate with him in preserving the present peaceable state of the city and to continue in the good course of tranquillity and sobriety which they had long persevered in ...[87]

The importance of the temperance crusade to him is apparent: he chose to highlight it on the day of his election as mayor. Meagher clearly appreciated that the abuse of alcohol was having a debilitating effect on the city's economic and social life, and causing widespread suffering. In 1833 the then mayor had commented to the commissioners inquiring into the corporation that a considerable portion of the inhabitants were in a state of poverty. Among the reasons he ascribed to this situation was the excessive consumption of alcohol.[88] According to a witness to the Poor Inquiry of 1836, drunkenness was a factor in contributing to the impoverished condition of many in the city.[89] In the same year it was estimated that 6,000 gallons of legal whiskey were consumed in Waterford every year.[90] This would only account for a fraction of alcohol consumption, as poteen, at half the price, was widely available.[91] The problems caused by excessive drinking were to be seen in the fact that 60 per cent of those tried before the mayor's court in September 1838 were charged with drunkenness.[92] Abuse of alcohol was having an impact on the prosperity of the city: there was a leakage of at least £300,000 out of the circular flow of income of the local economy and one-third of this figure was attributable to expenditure on drink.[93] There is evidence to suggest that a reduction in alcohol consumption had a positive impact. Brother Murphy, of Mount Sion, Waterford, a temperance campaigner, estimated in 1841 that the property of the labouring class in the city had increased by more than £100,000 in the past two years in the form of clothes, furniture and other domestic comforts, a consequence of the thrift with which teetotallers were becoming associated.[94]

The Christian Brothers at Mount Sion had, with the cooperation of the Catholic bishop, Dr Nicholas Foran, established teetotal societies in the summer of 1839 to cater for those who could not travel to Cork to take the pledge to abstain from alcoholic drink from Fr Mathew. The friar was invited to visit the city and did so in December 1839. This visit, and an earlier one to Limerick, marked a significant stage in the development of the Cork Total Abstinence Society as a national movement.[95] The December visit popularised the temperance cause in Waterford, with between 70,000 and 90,000 people from the city, county and adjoining areas taking the pledge.[96]

MEAGHER AND FR MATHEW

Thomas Meagher certainly identified himself very closely with Fr Mathew's crusade. In January 1843, when the friar visited the city, the mayor's carriage met him. He was taken to Meagher's house where he was entertained. The next day, accompanied by the mayor, Fr Mathew administered the pledge to a large number of people.[97] In May of the same year, Fr Mathew visited Mount Sion, again in the company of Meagher. The pledge was administered to over 1,000 children. A comment in *The Waterford Chronicle* serves as a reminder that for Meagher his support for temperance was inspired by a desire to improve the conditions of some of the city's poorer inhabitants: 'The general appearance of the children, in point of dress and cleanliness, furnished a powerful attestation to the sober and orderly habits of their parents, notwithstanding the lamentable state of poverty that now prevails amongst the working classes.'[98] That same evening there was a temperance meeting at the school and Meagher presided over the proceedings. In the course of a short address, he referred to the orderly conduct of the city's teetotallers and the significant reduction in crime since the progress of teetotalism. The next day Fr Mathew went to the courthouse, accompanied by Meagher, to administer pledges. The mayor used the occasion to present an address to the priest, on behalf of the citizens of Waterford, extolling his achievements.[99]

In September 1843 Meagher attended the general meeting of the city's temperance societies, once again at Mount Sion. In a speech he referred to the fact that he had been absent from Waterford for a number of months in 1839 and 1840, when Fr Mathew first visited the city. When he left the country it was 'sunk to the lowest state of degradation, owing to the intemperance of the people'. On his return, he noted what he termed 'a happy and extraordinary change': 'His ears, as he walked the streets, were no longer assailed with horrid blasphemy – no longer the spectacles of drunkenness, which but a few months before were familiar to the public, presented their hideous forms in the public way – in their stead tranquillity, sobriety and increased comfort were manifest.' He stated that his object was to give 'permanence and consistency' to the temperance cause.

At this same meeting, Meagher declared that 'his anxious wish was that it [temperance] should extend, not only over the city, not only to the country, but to the whole world'.[100] These sentiments reveal a certain zealot-like enthusiasm for the cause; in fact, at times, he did not so much engage in the promotion of teetotalism, as in quasi-evangelisation. Speaking at a meeting in 1843, he fulminated against the harm drunkenness did to the repeal movement:

> Recollect that the drunkard cannot be relied upon; he is capable, at all times, of being converted into the willing instrument of dangerous persons. I, therefore, most earnestly entreat of you to be on your guard, to be more zealous and assiduous than ever in the observance of the pledge, to let nothing tempt you from the paths of sobriety … The success of the cause we are seeking to advance depends on your sobriety …[101]

Addressing another meeting in June 1844, shortly after O'Connell's imprisonment, he directed words at those who had not taken the pledge:

> A word now to such as are not teetotallers. From my experience, I am convinced that intemperance in drink is the chief cause of all the disorder that occurs in this country. To you, therefore, who have not yet become teetotallers, I would say, if no other motive will influence you, will you not for O'Connell's sake abstain from all intoxicating drink, at least while he is suffering imprisonment for you. For my part, if I were not a teetotaller – if I was not aware of the benefits and blessings of which temperance is the abundant source, I would become one now, that I might more faithfully obey O'Connell's injunction to peace and order. If you have money to spend, spend it not on intoxicating drink – give it to liberate O'Connell from prison.[102]

The level of support for temperance offered by Thomas Meagher was appreciated by Fr Mathew. During his visit to Waterford in May 1843, he thanked the mayor, whom he described as 'his esteemed friend', for all the assistance and encouragement he had given his mission.[103] The association of a person of Meagher's social position with the temperance cause was especially valued because there was a general reluctance among the Catholic middle classes to involve themselves in the advocacy of the abstinence movement.[104] Due to the fact that the temperance movement recruited from the nation at large and placed no financial barriers to membership, it possessed a decidedly plebeian profile which discouraged class-conscious persons from becoming members.[105] This was a matter of concern for the leadership and attempts were made to induce the wealthier elements of Catholic society to become involved. During a visit to Dublin in March–April 1840, Fr Mathew concentrated much of his energy on trying to attract such support.[106] Even when some joined, they did not want to be associated with the mass pledge-taking that was an important feature of Fr Mathew's campaign. During his first visit to Waterford in December 1839, 'respectable men above the working class' took the pledge at Bishop Foran's house in the evening, not wishing, it would appear, to join the masses assembled in front of the courthouse during the day.[107]

The temperance movement, however, was in decline by 1843 and in the middle of that year there were reports of an increase nationally in public drunkenness.[108] Comments made by Meagher in his address at Mount Sion in September of the same year confirm this. He stated that he regretted to inform his audience of teetotallers that for the last month there were more cases of drunkenness brought before him 'than during all the rest of the time he had held office'. He feared that 'inebriety' was beginning to creep into the city once again. Deploring such behaviour, Meagher called on sober and decent people to assert themselves in the face of such developments.[109] He would remain deeply committed to the temperance ideal and as late as 1847, in the course of a speech in support of his parliamentary candidature in the general election, he announced:

I am a teetotaller myself, and I do not like to see any man drunk. Oh! They are not my friends or supporters who would be drunk; I repudiate them. Let them vote, if they have a vote, for whoever they please, but not for me. I am a strict follower of O'Connell's doctrine that 'the man who commits a crime gives strength to the enemy'. I ask you what greater crime can there be than drunkenness. For by it a man lowers himself to the condition of the brute and, in that condition, not knowing what he does, he is capable of committing any crime.[110]

DIFFICULTIES FACING THE REPEAL MOVEMENT

Daniel O'Connell's release from Richmond Prison in September 1844 was an occasion of national celebration, an 'unexampled spectacle of a whole people, in a delirium of triumph'.[111] He was still, unquestionably, the most popular political figure in Ireland. In Waterford arrangements were made in November for the collection of the O'Connell testimonial tribute, with one local repeal activist articulating thoughts which resonated with O'Connell's supporters: 'After his enemies doing everything in their power to find him guilty – after his being placed within the walls of a prison for our sake – is there anything that would deter us from supporting him who battled for our liberty?'[112] The following year, 1845, though no longer mayor, Thomas Meagher was a signatory to a requisition to convene a public meeting to organise the effective collection of the tribute,[113] at which meeting he was nominated to act as one of the collectors in the parish of Trinity Within.[114] He himself contributed £10.[115]

In December 1844 O'Connell himself visited Waterford, and it was an occasion for what *The Chronicle* described as a 'powerful demonstration' of loyalty to him. He told a very large crowd gathered outside the city hall that repeal would be won by 'peace' and 'perseverance', and he observed that he had enjoyed the 'popular confidence' of the Irish people for nearly fifty years. Mayor Meagher, in his address, repeated sentiments that had featured in some of his earlier speeches. For example, he categorically rejected the charge that repeal meant separation from Great Britain: 'Now it is the first article of our political creed, as promulgated by our illustrious master, that our undivided allegiance is due to the sovereign of these realms; and in looking for the restoration of our native parliament we do not but seek to secure more firmly the golden link of the crown.'[116]

Such sentiments from O'Connell and Meagher would seem to suggest that it was business as usual for the repeal campaign after the Liberator's release from Richmond Prison. This, however, was most certainly not the case: the reality was that repeal, as a viable political cause, was dead. When O'Connell told his supporters in Waterford that agitation would be renewed in January, he was simply telling them what they expected to hear. More significant was a speech he delivered to the Repeal Association in Dublin shortly after he left prison. He did not utter a word on the matter of fresh agitation and it was evident that he had no intention of trying to revive or repeat the monster meetings of 1843.[117] Rather, he used the occasion of this address to praise the Whigs.[118] Clearly, he regarded the possibility of a renewed alliance with them as offering the prospect of an escape from the political cul-de-sac in which he found himself.

Nor did O'Connell possess the mental and physical resources necessary, even essential, to embark on another phase of the repeal campaign. In 1844 he was sixty-nine years of age, and creeping old age and ill health were beginning to weaken him. He underwent an operation for haemorrhoids, but a doctor who performed a post-mortem on him in 1847 was of the opinion that this surgical procedure had caused 'a bacteraemia [bacteria in the blood], whereupon organisms lodged in the frontal lobe of his brain.'[119] Subsequently, his health began to go into decline. And it was at the very time that this was happening that the repeal movement began experiencing severe external and internal challenges.

CHAPTER SIX

Thomas Meagher: 'Old Irelander', 1845–1847

The years from 1845 to 1847 were to be very difficult ones for Daniel O'Connell. The Tory prime minister, Robert Peel, was determined to weaken and undermine the repeal movement by introducing a series of reforms in Ireland. These same reforms brought to the surface policy differences and tensions within the Repeal Association, with a group known as 'Young Ireland' questioning and challenging the Liberator's leadership and authority. Thomas Meagher, however, remained an ardent 'Old Irelander'.

PEEL'S REFORM MEASURES

The British political elite regarded 'the repeal agitation as a crypto-revolutionary movement whose goal, if achieved, would lead ultimately to the disintegration of the British empire.'[1] Peel and his ministers, with the near-unanimous support of MPs, were determined to resist O'Connell's demands: the very notion of conceding repeal was anathema to them. With monster meetings convulsing Ireland, on 9 May 1843 Peel stated in the House of Commons that he was authorised on behalf of the queen to say that 'she would do all in her power to uphold the Union and that the government would, if necessary, prefer civil war to the dismemberment of the empire.'[2] This was not oratorical hyperbole – Peel meant what he said. The repeal campaign, however, did put the government and British political establishment under enormous pressure,[3] and it was not until the autumn of 1843 that Peel decided on his response: suppression of Irish agitation and an extensive programme of reforms to conciliate Ireland. The planned Clontarf meeting gave him the opportunity to suppress the repeal movement: given the attitude towards repeal in Britain and O'Connell's deeply rooted aversion to violence, the outcome was predictable. When O'Connell cancelled the meeting, Peel decided to crush Ireland's agitators by having O'Connell arrested and prosecuted for sedition.

After Clontarf, O'Connell's repeal campaign faced a crisis as to how to respond to the actions of the government.[4] His trial and imprisonment, however, obscured the fact and extent of this crisis. Attention was focused on the Liberator's plight, and the sympathy and indignation it caused in Ireland. The substantive issue of repeal was eclipsed for nearly a year, a most fortuitous circumstance for O'Connell, who needed to devise an urgent strategy to extricate himself from the bleak political circumstances which faced him.

It was during this time of political trial that O'Connell was confronted with the additional challenge of Peel's policy of conciliation towards Ireland. In February 1844 the prime minister presented his cabinet with his proposed programme of Irish reforms. It was his intention to kill off repeal by kindness, by addressing matters which were sources of grievances in Ireland. By this means he hoped to detach moderate Catholics from the repeal movement. Some of the reforms were specifically directed at the Catholic clergy; by hiving off clerical support from O'Connell, the repeal campaign would be weakened.[5] Therefore, Peel proposed the establishment of a new legal mechanism to supervise the law on bequests and donations, with a view to safeguarding Catholic charities.[6] His second proposal entailed raising the annual grant to Maynooth College from £9,000 to £26,000.[7] Finally, he sought a solution to the problem of providing university education acceptable to Catholics, without the endowment of a Catholic denominational university.[8] Peel's policy was to generate much controversy in Ireland and England, with the proposals pertaining to university education, in particular, contributing to internal divisions in the repeal movement.

These divisions were to centre on a conflict between Daniel O'Connell and his supporters and an advanced nationalist grouping within the Repeal Association, which became popularly known as Young Ireland.[9] It was a conflict which was to have a very particular significance for Thomas Meagher – his son, Thomas Francis Meagher, was to become a luminary in the Young Ireland movement, while he himself remained steadfast in his loyalty to O'Connell. The details of the clash between Old and Young Ireland, and particularly the clash between the older and younger Meagher, will be the focus of Chapter 9. For the purposes of the present chapter, it is sufficient to note that it was Peel's programme of reforms and, especially, his proposals on university education, that brought the simmering tensions and recriminations between the Liberator and the Young Irelanders to the surface. These same tensions and recriminations were present from the early 1840s, but had been sublimated and dissipated while the repeal campaign had momentum and purpose. After Clontarf, however, it was a political cause devoid of direction and it 'had nowhere to go except in on itself'.[10]

CHARITABLE BEQUESTS ACT, 1844

The first reforming piece of legislation introduced by Peel's government was a bill to establish legal mechanisms to safeguard bequests and donations to Catholic charities.[11] This was to become the Charitable Bequests Act, 1844 and it represented a great improvement on the existing law, not least the inclusion of Catholic members on the commission nominated to oversee the operation of the new statute.[12] However, it was greeted with hostility and deep suspicion by many Catholics, lay and clerical. Archbishop John MacHale of Tuam led the clerical opposition,[13] while Daniel O'Connell rejected the proposed measure from Richmond Prison, asserting that it would injure 'the doctrine, discipline and constitution of the [Catholic] Church'.[14] Opponents trumpeted their many concerns, including a continued prohibition on legacies to religious orders. Nevertheless, three Catholic bishops agreed to act as members of the commission, thus sowing some disunity in Catholic opinion.[15]

On 13 December 1844 there was a meeting in the Catholic cathedral in Waterford, at which, according to *The Chronicle*, 'a magnificent protest was effected against the vile and destructive act of a foreign legislature against the religion, peace and nationality of Ireland'.[16] Presided over by Mayor Meagher, it was addressed by O'Connell. At the conclusion of proceedings, Meagher referred to a meeting held on 23 March 1829, in which he played a prominent role, to protest against provisions relating to religious orders contained in the Emancipation Bill; to quote *The Chronicle*: 'The mayor stated that he recalled with satisfaction the circumstances of his uniting with his fellow citizens before the passing of the Emancipation Act against its clause which was opposed to the regular clergy ... This proved that Waterford remained an unstained city'.[17]

In his comment Meagher was making a comparative connection between the Emancipation and Bequest Acts, as they pertained, especially, to religious orders (regular clergy), and in so doing was rejecting the latter act as a conciliatory measure. He was taking a linear perspective: assessing the law on bequests in the context of its representing a continuing and progressive step in the achievement of true equality for Catholics. He did not believe that progress had been satisfactorily advanced between the concession of emancipation and the most recent legislation on bequests: what he regarded as the ongoing unfair treatment of Catholic religious orders attested to this fact. Meagher's reference to the 1829 meeting contained the implication that Catholics would continue to agitate for equal treatment. His description of Waterford as the 'unstained city', a description which echoed the city's motto of 'Urbs Intacta' (the untaken city), was an emotional, if perhaps overly subtle statement of his pride in Waterford's history of resistance to injustice against Catholics and its determination to persevere in such resistance.

Meagher's attitude to the Bequests Act was also likely to have been influenced by the general rejection of it by Catholic opinion. Critically, Peel's recent humiliation of O'Connell did not create a favourable atmosphere for the acceptance of any conciliatory initiatives by his government.[18] *The Pilot*, an organ of O'Connellite opinion, asserted in July 1844 that 'the imprisonment of O'Connell had infused into the hearts of the Irish ... a deep brooding hatred of England'.[19] Furthermore, there was a widespread distrust of the government's intentions, which were correctly viewed by repeal supporters as an attempt to break up their movement. In fact, in the course of his speech in Waterford in

December 1844, O'Connell stated that the act had been 'thrown on us by the ministry ... with a kind of foregone knowledge that it would create dissension'.[20]

However, Peel's efforts to detach moderates from the repeal movement would have failed, utterly and completely, in Meagher's case, for the very simple reason that he was not a moderate. On the contrary, he was an ardent supporter of the Liberator, a determined advocate of repeal, and an uncompromising champion of Catholic equality. These attributes were to become very apparent in his response to Peel's policy on university education and the attendant controversy which convulsed the Repeal Association.

THE QUEEN'S COLLEGES BILL, 1845

On 9 May 1845 the Academic Colleges Bill, which provided for the foundation of university colleges at Cork, Galway and Belfast, received its first reading. A capital grant of £100,000 was provided for the buildings and each institution was given an annual grant of £7,000.[21] The colleges were to be non-denominational. Almost immediately a dispute broke out in the Repeal Association regarding these proposals and, in particular, the non-denominational character of the colleges. *The Freeman's Journal* and *The Pilot*, journals supportive of O'Connell, denounced the bill. The organ of Young Ireland, however, *The Nation,* welcomed the measure and lauded the principle of mixed education contained in it.

O'Connell described the bill as an unacceptable attack on the Catholic religion due to the exclusion of religion from the proposed colleges. He regarded the university system being promoted by Peel as anti-Catholic and anti-national, and demanded equal rights for Catholics in the matter of university education; they were entitled to a Catholic university, just as Protestants had one in Trinity College.[22] He was confirmed in his opinion by the condemnation of the government's plan by the Catholic bishops, who demanded significant amendments to the bill to protect the faith and morals of any future Catholic students.[23] He also, correctly, saw the bill as representing another attempt to undermine his support in Ireland by yet again seeking to lure moderate opinion away from the repeal cause. The leader of Young Ireland, Thomas Davis, argued a contrary position. He viewed a non-denominational system as a means of bringing the youth of Ireland together and alleged that the reasons adduced in support of separate education were the reasons 'for religious animosity, for penal laws and for religious wars'.[24]

The tensions which were simmering between the Liberator and the Young Ireland group exploded during a debate on the bill in the Repeal Association on 26 May 1845. O'Connell used the occasion to launch a philippic on Davis and his supporters:

> The section of politicians styling themselves the Young Ireland party, anxious to rule the destinies of this country, start up and support this measure. There is no such party as that styled 'Young Ireland'. There may be a few individuals who take that denomination on themselves. I am for Old Ireland. 'Tis time that this delusion should be put an end to. Young Ireland may play what pranks they please. I do not envy them the name they rejoice in. I shall stand by Old Ireland, and I have some slight notion that Old Ireland will stand by me.[25]

While the meeting ended with a reconciliation of sorts, the damage had been done. There was no ignoring or forgetting what had transpired: the genie of discord had been released and could not be returned to its bottle. Within a year the Repeal Association was to split – Peel was to achieve his objective of weakening O'Connell's movement.

THOMAS MEAGHER AND THE QUEEN'S COLLEGES

When O'Connell declared that he enjoyed the support of 'Old Ireland', by which he meant the support he traditionally enjoyed among the majority of the Irish people, he was asserting a demonstrable fact. For example, most of the middle class followed his lead on the issue of the Queen's Colleges.[26] Thomas Meagher approved of the Liberator's position on the university question and proved himself then, and in subsequent years, to be an unrepentant Old Irelander. At a meeting in November 1845 to consider the national tribute to O'Connell, he proposed the following motion which was unanimously approved:

That the indomitable exertions of our illustrious leader in promoting the national independence of Ireland call once more for the assurance of our full confidence in his wisdom and ability, and that gratefully appreciating the eminent services he has conferred on our country, and especially those in opposition to the Academical [sic] Colleges Bill in which we all agree, we deem it our bounden duty to adopt the necessary measures to secure the effective collection of the 'O'Connell tribute'...[27]

A number of factors may be adduced to explain Meagher's attitude to the proposed Queen's Colleges. His deep commitment to the Catholic Church has already been noted. He was, indeed, unquestionably religious and possessed the fervour to give public expression to his beliefs. On the occasion of his election as mayor of Waterford, it was reported that:

He said they were called on to elect a chief magistrate for the borough of Waterford – it was a good old custom to commence all proceedings in the name of God, and though they would not then use any form of prayer, they should recollect they were in the presence of God, to whom they were accountable for all their acts and they should, therefore, beg his blessing.[28]

Addressing a temperance meeting at Mount Sion in September 1843, he commented that drunkards, who could not be 'corrected by law' or influenced by the good example of teetotallers, could only be 'reached by religious influence'. He asked those assembled 'to pray for them and to do all in their power to induce them to return to their religious duties, as the only means of reclaiming them'.[29] In the course of a speech in the city hall after the debacle at Clontarf, he declared to his listeners that they had to rely 'upon that Divine Providence which orders and directs events as they occur here below'.[30] When O'Connell visited Waterford in December 1844, Meagher attributed 'to the kind interposition of Divine Providence ... the pleasure of having him among them instead of being still immured within the walls of a dungeon'.[31] Interestingly, when his two terms as mayor ended, The Chronicle observed in an editorial on his period in office that 'intemperance and vice fled before the pure morality and religion of the chief civic functionary'.[32] A deeply religious person, he would have regarded it as a conscientious imperative to come to the defence of his Church, if he believed that it was threatened in any way. And Meagher regarded the Queen's Colleges as a threat.

For many Catholics, the non-denominational character of the proposed colleges constituted a threat to the faith and morals of prospective students. One reason for this was the danger of proselytism through education, fear of which haunted the Irish bishops.[33] It was because of such apprehension that the only university in the country, Trinity College, Dublin, was viewed with suspicion and hostility by a significant section of the Catholic population, it being alleged that pressure was brought to bear on Catholics attending there to conform to the Church of Ireland.[34] These fears were confirmed by a list drawn up in the 1840s, which named seventy-four students who had abandoned the Catholic faith during the period 1801 to 1831.[35] This reputation informed Meagher's attitude to Trinity College when it came to deciding on the education of his son, Thomas Francis. According to the latter's biographer, Michael Kavanagh, his father 'saw no necessity for his gifted son being beholden for intellectual advantages to a university founded and supported by the spoils plundered from the National Church and its faithful defenders, and which was known to be a hot-bed of bigotry and intolerance ...'[36]

Meagher was of the decided opinion that only a Catholic university could safeguard against proselytising activities. He was likely to have been strengthened in his conclusion during the years of the Great Famine, when allegations of proselytism were to poison relations between Protestants and Catholics.[37] It should also be remembered that in 1824 Meagher had played a significant role in opposing the establishment in Waterford of a school associated with the London Hibernian Society, an aggressive proselytising body.

Almost certainly, Meagher's opinion of the Queen's Colleges was also informed by the negative reaction of the Catholic bishops at a meeting held on 23 May 1845. His opposition was probably strengthened by resolutions adopted by the Roman Catholic clergy of the Diocese of Waterford and Lismore at a meeting presided over by Bishop Nicholas Foran on 7 July 1845. The bishop and his priests expressed their support for denominational education and a Catholic university for Ireland, and described the bill before Parliament as 'dangerous to the faith and morals of the rising and future generation'. The Catholics of the diocese were exhorted 'to continue firm in the opposition which they had already manifested to the bill'.[38] A subsequent declaration was adopted by this same body of clergy in October: it affirmed their convinced opinion that Peel's proposals constituted a danger to the Catholic faith.[39] The importance of these pronouncements was that Meagher regarded the clergy and, in particular, the hierarchy as the authentic teachers and interpreters of the truths of the Catholic faith. For him, therefore, these various assessments of the Queen's Colleges were authoritative: for this orthodox Catholic, the voice of the bishops was akin to the voice of God. Meagher was utterly convinced of the need for a Catholic university and this conviction motivated his later involvement in Archbishop Paul Cullen's endeavours to establish such an institution in the 1850s (See Chapter 14).

In considering Meagher's attitude to the Queen's Colleges, it is essential to situate it within the wider context of his demands for equal rights for Catholics, a cause for which he had advocated since his arrival in Waterford. For him, true equality of treatment meant Catholics enjoying the same benefits as Protestants: consequently, Catholics should have a university, as Protestants had. Meagher would have concurred, unreservedly, with these sentiments expressed by the Liberator in May 1845:

> While I ask for education for Catholics, I freely and gladly concede it to the Protestants and Dissenters ... Let the Protestants of the Establishment have the free use of Trinity College ... Let the Presbyterians have the complete control over the education of their children in the Belfast institution, but for the purposes of Catholic instruction, let two more colleges be instituted.[40]

Meagher's was an uncompromising conviction in the right of Catholics to full equality of treatment. In April 1846 he presented a petition to Waterford Corporation 'for the removal of the pains and penalties still imposed on Catholics'. He highlighted the disabilities (consequent on the Emancipation Act, 1829) applied to members of Catholic religious orders. In this regard, he referred, as he had done on previous occasions, to the Christian Brothers at Mount Sion, described by him as 'exemplary' men who were 'restricted from the rights and privileges of free subjects'. He ended his address with an enunciation of his deeply held political credo: 'Protestants and Catholics ought to know no difference.'[41] It was this view which ultimately shaped his reaction to the proposed Queen's Colleges.

A CATHOLIC UNIVERSITY: AN UNREALISTIC DEMAND

O'Connell's insistence on a Catholic university, while popular in Ireland was, however, wholly unrealistic. Peel and his ministers would certainly have preferred a system based on religion.[42] However, 'the combined difficulty of pleasing the different parties in Ireland where religious divisions ran deep and of extracting more money from the English Treasury to subsidise purely Irish and Catholic education appeared to them to constitute unsurmountable obstacles'.[43] The home secretary, Sir James Graham, acknowledged as much when he told the House of Commons that 'religious differences constitute the great difficulty in the way of a satisfactory adjustment of a general system of education'.[44]

In 1845 Peel's government had already secured parliamentary approval for an increased grant to Maynooth College, from £9,000 to £26,000. This proposal had engendered a paroxysm of rage and hostility among English Protestants, who were resolutely opposed to any state endowment of a seminary producing 'popish' priests. These same priests were regarded as fomenters and instigators of violent political agitation by their support for repeal. Anglicans and Nonconformists united in their opposition; at the second reading of the bill on 11 April 1845, 2,400 petitions opposing the grant were presented to Parliament.[45] The anti-Maynooth campaign was a salutary reminder of the difficulties faced by an English government seeking to make concessions to Catholic opinion in Ireland because, as diarist Charles Greville observed, 'the good people of England have, for the most part, sucked in with their mothers' milk a dislike of the Catholic religion'.[46] After the Maynooth grant, the establishment of a Catholic university would have been a step too far. O'Connell and Meagher, by their stance on the matter, displayed a certain wilful unwillingness to face political reality. Don Quixote-like, they fruitlessly pursued the windmill of the Catholic university. Meagher was to continue to chase this dream throughout the 1850s.

THOMAS MEAGHER: SELECTION AS REPEAL PARLIAMENTARY CANDIDATE

Within the Repeal Association, O'Connell had emerged triumphant from the battle with Young Ireland on the issue of the Queen's Colleges. The association, however, was politically adrift in relation to progressing the repeal cause or formulating an alternative strategy in the absence of such progress. O'Connell may have still been leader, but he was not offering purposeful leadership; 'during the third quarter of 1845 the Repeal Association began to suffer badly from the malaise of weakening central power'.[47] There was a failure of morale in the movement and this manifested itself in organisational conflicts in various parts of the country.[48] One such conflict occurred in Waterford city, involving a dispute between repeal activist, Alderman James Delahunty, and some clerical supporters of the cause.[49] A number of priests alleged that Delahunty had offended Bishop Foran in the course of an intemperate speech. Given the importance of Waterford in the repeal campaign, O'Connell felt it was his duty to visit the city and restore harmony. This he did and resolved matters to the satisfaction of all parties.[50]

While O'Connell was in Waterford, the question of the future parliamentary representation of the city was considered. He informed the Dublin association in December that the two sitting members, Thomas Wyse and Sir Henry Winston Barron, were not members of the Repeal Association and were not, in his opinion, true repealers.[51] The Liberator was pleased to tell the meeting that 'influential repealers' in the city had nominated the current mayor, Sir Benjamin Morris Wall, and Thomas Meagher, 'two real and Conciliation Hall repealers', as their preferred candidates at the next general election.[52] He described Meagher as 'one of the best men that ever lived', who was 'from his high character twice elected Mayor of Waterford'.[53] O'Connell moved that the Repeal Association 'highly approve' of the selection of Meagher and

Wall. Moreover, he proposed that they be requested to accept positions of 'inspectors of the repeal cause in Waterford'.[54]

At a time of political tensions in the repeal movement, apparent in O'Connell's use of such terms as 'real and Conciliation Hall repealers', as opposed to Young Irelanders, Meagher was evidently regarded by O'Connell as the most loyal of supporters. In July 1846 he confirmed this loyalty by remaining in the Repeal Association when Young Ireland seceded from it, and continued his staunch support for O'Connell and his policies. His decision was a significant one, not only politically, but also personally, because his son, Thomas Francis Meagher, by then a member of Young Ireland, played a leading role in the events culminating in the secession, the details of which will be examined in Chapter 9.

THE DEATH OF O'CONNELL: THOMAS MEAGHER'S TRIBUTE

Daniel O'Connell died on 15 May 1847. There was a meeting of citizens in Waterford city on 4 June to express sorrow and respect on this sad occasion. In the course of an address, Thomas Meagher referred to his services for Ireland. Significantly and interestingly, he also chose to highlight O'Connell's 'services for mankind'. 'His heart was truly Irish and his labours, as should be, were principally directed for the welfare of his native land – yet his heart was large enough to extend its sympathies to the grievances of mankind.'[55] Probably unknown to himself, he was echoing words spoken by the prominent French liberal Catholic, Charles de Montalembert, to O'Connell on his way through Paris in May 1847, while en route to Rome: 'But you are not only a man of one nation, but you are a man of all Christendom.'[56] There was an acknowledgement by Meagher that O'Connell's concerns were not confined to the shores of Ireland; they transcended race and nation and, as a champion of the liberty of the individual, in the words of J.J. Lee:

> [H]e detested any system that placed one people, one race, one religion, one class, above another … If he championed Catholic emancipation in Ireland, he denounced Spanish persecution of Protestants. He opposed slavery, even to the extent of alienating some of his support among Irish Americans, anxious to insist on

their own [racial] superiority ... He was a powerful advocate of the emancipation of the Jews, and of Latin American independence, the main 'colonial' issue of the day. He was, too, in the context of his time, an advanced advocate of women's emancipation. 'Mind', he liked to say, 'has no sex'.[57]

Meagher was an ardent supporter and admirer of O'Connell, and loyal to him and his memory, because for Meagher, the Liberator was greater than the sum of his achievements. He regarded him as the undoubted leader of the Irish people. In the absence of his own words, Oliver MacDonagh's modern assessment would almost certainly have gained his approval: 'It is rare in the history of any country ... for an individual to leave so deep an impress on its organisations and opinions as O'Connell did on the Ireland of his day.'[58] For Meagher, Daniel O'Connell was a political colossus and he rejoiced in, and was inspired by, the political shadow he cast.

GENERAL ELECTION, 1847

In August 1847, almost three months after O'Connell's death, the general election for which he had endorsed Meagher took place. A confluence of three circumstances gave this contest a peculiar character. It was enacted against the backdrop of the Great Famine, with its attendant misery and suffering casting a dark shadow over events; the repeal cause had lost its leader; and, finally, the Repeal Association itself was split.

On 21 June there was a meeting of electors in the city hall for the stated purpose of selecting 'two undoubted and uncompromising repealers' to represent Waterford city in Parliament.[59] The occasion was charged with emotion and was used to rededicate those in attendance to the cause of repeal as a means of honouring O'Connell's memory. The invocation of the memory of the dead Liberator and the bitterness caused by the divisions in the Repeal Association suffused the atmosphere of the proceedings. The mayor, Councillor Owen Carroll, declared that they were there to 'do their duty to Old Ireland and follow in the footsteps of Mr O'Connell'. A resolution was adopted stating 'That our opinions on the question of repeal are unaltered and unalterable; ... we hereby declare our determination to persevere in the peaceable policy laid down by our dead leader, and to struggle by every peaceable, constitutional and legal means to accomplish the independence of our native land.'

It was inevitable that reference was made to the Queen's Colleges, an issue which had contributed significantly to the animosity between Old and Young Ireland, with one speaker declaiming: 'Of all the means of poisoning the young and rising mind of a country, nothing can be worse or more insidious than the plan hit upon by the concoctors of the Colleges' Bill.' This scheme propagated 'infidelity' and 'education without religion'. The Rev. Dr Dominic O'Brien, a future bishop of the diocese, proposed that 'Sir Benjamin Morris Wall and Alderman Thomas Meagher be selected as two uncompromising and undoubted repealers'. In his address he stated that 'for the last several years the interests of our most holy religion ... had been insidiously invaded' and he instanced the Colleges' Bill. O'Brien reminded his listeners that these same colleges had been denounced by the bishop and priests of Waterford and Lismore and it was in 'conformity' with the spirit of that denunciation that he proposed two candidates, who would continue to oppose the colleges, if elected.[60] Morris Wall declined to stand, but Meagher accepted.

On 7 July he issued his election address.[61] He began by announcing that he was a reluctant candidate: 'Since the period when the lamented Liberator of Ireland first announced my name in connection with the representation of your city, I have on more than one occasion publicly declared my intention not to be a candidate for it.' This reluctance was to be a recurrent theme of his parliamentary career. Under pressure, however, he had agreed to enter the electoral contest.

The remainder of his address expressed sentiments consistent with those of the meeting at which his candidacy had been proposed and with those of a faithful and loyal follower of O'Connell. He declared himself a repealer. The independence he sought for Ireland, he explained, was not 'incompatible with the union of Great Britain and Ireland with the golden link of the crown'. Such independence could 'be best attained by the peaceful, legal and constitutional course devised by the Liberator for the guidance of the Repeal Association'. To that policy he 'avowed' himself 'an undeviating adherent'. He also stated that as a Roman Catholic, 'no parliamentary measure affecting the interests of my religion should have my support until it has received the approbation of at least the majority of the bishops of the church'.

The sentiments contained in this address reflected the views expressed at the meeting of 23 June, during which the terms of the nomination being offered to him were elucidated and defined. These sentiments were also in keeping with those of O'Connell. It was certainly expedient for Meagher to hold such views if he wished to be selected as a candidate. His election address, however, was not an exercise in calculated political expediency, not least because he was a reluctant candidate. This address was, in fact, consistent with views he had previously expressed, on several occasions, during his period of political and public activism. He was a convinced repealer, constitutionalist, O'Connellite and Old Irelander. He was a fervent Catholic, for whom the guidance of the bishops was an accepted norm. This election address, therefore, was a true and accurate summary of the political opinions of Thomas Meagher.

What is noteworthy about Meagher's election address is the absence of any reference to the Famine. Brian Walker has observed that from the evidence of such addresses nationally, it was not 'the dominant subject of discussion' during the election campaign of August 1847.[62] However, Kevin Nowlan has written that the election speeches (as against election addresses) of 1847 'show that in all sections of the [repeal] movement people were becoming increasingly aware of the importance of social issues'.[63] An examination of Meagher's speeches confirms this observation. At a meeting in July, he condemned the fact that upwards of 12,000 people in the city were in receipt of food assistance. That so many were existing on charity was a scandal in a country he described 'as teeming with abundance of rich produce'. He attributed this situation to the mismanagement of Irish affairs by the English government. Overcome emotionally, he declared in words unusually passionate for him: 'I love Ireland. My heart beats with ardour for her welfare – it bleeds for her sufferings. And oh! would it were in my power, by pouring out the last drop of that heart's blood, to rescue the country from her misery and degradation.'[64] Addressing a meeting of citizens in early August, he proclaimed that his listeners were not content 'that famine should periodically sweep millions of your fellow countrymen from the face of the earth'. Ireland had been degraded to a land 'fit for nothing but the erection of poor houses, outdoor relief and the distribution of yellow meal whenever you are starving'.[65]

In a speech delivered a few days later, he denounced the haemorrhaging of rents from the country to absentee landlords. He highlighted the increase in pauperism among the population, deplored the insecurity of tenants and declared himself an advocate of tenant rights.[66] In his speech at the nomination of candidates on election day, he accused the Act of Union of creating a state of affairs in Ireland which reduced the population to dependency on 'the most perishable of crops, the potato'.[67]

On election day Thomas Meagher headed the poll, being elected with 521 votes. The other successful candidate was Daniel O'Connell Junior, the Liberator's youngest son, who received 499 votes.[68] Before the election, *The Chronicle* had asserted that Waterford was committed to repeal and was bound by 'an eternal tie to Daniel O'Connell'.[69] The results seemed to confirm this.

The Chronicle's comment only served to underscore the surreal aspect of the election, both locally in Waterford and nationally. An effectively dead cause, which had been championed by a now dead leader, was being promoted at a time when hundreds of thousands were dead by hunger and disease. The election witnessed the triumph of (understandable) emotion over political rationalism. The result was a good one for the Repeal Association – it won thirty-nine seats[70] and showed more spirit than might have been expected in the circumstances.[71] The reality, however, was that the repeal movement was in terminal decline and had been so since the abortive Clontarf meeting, its final obsequies only being delayed by O'Connell's continuing leadership. The results of the 1847 general election were nothing more than a temporary fillip. Thomas Meagher, newly elected MP for the city of Waterford, was a member of a parliamentary party associated with a movement that was teetering on the brink of political oblivion.

MEAGHER AND PROTESTANTS

As was noted earlier, Sir Benjamin Morris Wall, a prominent Protestant supporter of repeal, declined nomination as a parliamentary candidate in the general election. Meagher commented at some length on this in the course of a speech he delivered in July 1847. He lamented that 'circumstances have occurred to deprive us of the gratification of returning to Parliament one of the best citizens of Waterford'. Continuing, he made the following important observation:

> I regret that you [supporters of repeal] have not an opportunity of proclaiming to the world that the repeal movement is not an exclusive one; that it is not intended for the sole benefit of Catholics alone ... [It] might satisfy the most sceptical that when an honest Protestant is to be found, who will come forward and manfully join the people, you are ready to confer upon him the highest honour you can bestow.[72]

In August he told another meeting: 'We are not repealers for the benefit of a class; we are not repealers for a section of the people; no, we are repealers for the benefit of all Ireland.' He affirmed that it was their wish 'to invite conservatives [who were mainly Protestants] and men of all parties, to come and join us in the battle for the independence of Ireland'.[73]

Meagher fully appreciated that few Protestants supported the repeal movement.[74] Morris Wall had seconded his nomination on the occasion of his election as mayor of Waterford, prompting Meagher to comment that by his support for the repeal cause, Sir Benjamin 'had separated himself from his class' among his own religious community.[75] The members of this Protestant community feared that repeal of the Union would herald the establishment of a Catholic ascendancy, thus consigning them to an inferior social and political status. Most Protestants were convinced that the fulfilment of the politics of the Liberator meant the erosion of their power and the triumph of Catholicism.

Thomas Davis had attempted to voice his concerns at 'the apparent Catholicising of repeal'[76] and his fears of what he regarded as priestly domination of the national movement.[77] The controversy over the Queen's Colleges served to confirm these fears, as O'Connell cast himself as 'the political guardian of the interests of the Catholic Church'.[78] Davis's response to this growing identification of Catholicism with repeal was to promote, through the Young Ireland movement, a supra-sectarian and non-denominational nationalism.[79] His ideal found expression in the line of one of his verses: 'What matter that at different shrines we pray unto our God.'[80]

Meagher, of course, was aware of the controversy over the Queen's Colleges and was certainly familiar with the views of Davis. He would not, however, have aligned himself with the opinion of Young Ireland. Davis was foreshadowing what is generally regarded as 'liberalism' in contemporary Ireland. The conclusion of his views could lead to a secular state.[81] The deeply religious Meagher would have deplored the implications of secularism. The shrine at which he prayed was of central importance in his life – his religious beliefs informed his world view. Meagher wanted true equality of treatment between Protestants and Catholics, but this was not to be achieved at the price of religious indifferentism.

Meagher regarded the prospect of Benjamin Morris Wall's parliamentary candidacy as an expression of the religious equality he (Meagher) championed with conviction and determination. He deplored the practice of religious exclusiveness by virtue of denominational affiliation. Meagher believed that Catholics were discriminated against because of the application of Protestant exclusiveness; Wall's candidacy would have proclaimed that the Repeal Association did not engage in such a practice when there were Protestants willing to associate themselves with the repeal campaign. On a personal level, he likely valued his friendship and relationship with Wall and other Protestants as an expression of his ideal of mutual religious toleration and mutual respect.

Meagher had experienced the respect of his fellow Protestant citizens and it was the kind of experience he would have wished to characterise interdenominational relations. Reference has already been made to the requisition of November 1843, signed by prominent citizens, requesting Meagher to allow his name to be put forward for re-election as mayor. There were 202 signatories, of whom at least forty were Protestants.[82] After he left mayoral office, at a meeting of citizens, it was decided to organise a testimonial honouring his mayoralty. Addressing those in attendance, Fr John Sheehan said that while Meagher did not compromise his opinion on the matter of repeal, those who differed from him on the issue (and these were mainly Protestants) were pleased to express approbation of the manner in which he had discharged the duties of his office.[83] In effect, Sheehan was claiming that Meagher, despite his being a convinced repealer, was not a divisive figure.

The composition of the committee selected to organise the testimonial would seem to confirm that Sheehan's views had a basis in fact. Of the twenty-seven members, at least ten were Protestants.[84] Sheehan would later highlight that the list of 131 subscribers to the testimonial included the names of radicals, repealers and conservatives (who were generally Protestants).[85] An examination of this list suggests that at least thirty-eight (nearly 30 per cent) were Protestants.[86] The text of the testimonial referred to 'the good feeling entertained towards you by your fellow citizens of all ranks and religious persuasions'.[87] One of those who presented Meagher with this testimonial was a retired Anglican naval officer, Captain Thomas Roberts, who, in letters to his brother, wrote of Meagher's 'proper conduct (during the two years he served as mayor) in every respect',[88] and how his conduct had won him general approval.[89] Most of the Protestants associated with this testimonial were conservatives. Interestingly, *The Chronicle*, in its analysis of the results of the 1847 election, expressed the view that Meagher had headed the poll because he attracted the votes of some conservatives, described as his 'personal friends', by the newspaper.[90]

The years 1846 and 1847 were dramatic and turbulent years for the repeal cause, marked by a split in the movement in July 1846 and the death of O'Connell in May 1847. For Meagher these years were fraught and significant in political terms. However, the upheaval in the repeal movement was as nothing in comparison to the social turmoil of the Great Famine. Meagher was to witness the sufferings associated with this cataclysmic event in his capacity as a member of various relief committees, and, more especially, as a member of the board of guardians of Waterford union workhouse.

CHAPTER SEVEN

Famine, 1845–1848

Cities and towns were to play a central role in the human and social catastrophe that was Ireland's Great Famine, 1845–50.[1] This was due to their employment, market and administrative functions, together with their roles as workhouse and poor law union centres. They were to be inundated by desperate men, women and children seeking relief from starvation. 'Heart-rending scenes, involving destitution, disease and death were to be enacted and witnessed on [their] streets.'[2] Thomas Meagher witnessed the plight of the hungry and sick who, in their desperation, gravitated to Waterford city in search of relief. He was to be actively involved in various efforts to alleviate the mass suffering visited on so many of his fellow citizens during the years of the Great Hunger.

On 10 September 1845 *The Cork Examiner* carried a report on the appearance of potato blight in County Waterford. While it has been estimated that nationally the total loss of the crop was slightly less than one-third of the entire crop of 1844,[3] the incidence of blight in 1845 varied considerably in different parts of the country. The most severely affected counties appear to have been Waterford, Antrim, Monaghan and Clare.[4] The local newspapers fully appreciated the seriousness of potato failure when so much of the population was dependent on this crop as their staple food, and in the words of *The Waterford Mail*: 'To about six million it is the chief, if not only, article of diet.'[5] *The Waterford Freeman* overstated the gravity of the situation in 1845; its words, however, were to prove prophetic in subsequent years: 'Great famine threatens the land.'[6]

RELIEF COMMITTEE

The British prime minister, Sir Robert Peel, acted promptly to address the possible problems associated with the partial failure of the potato crop.[7] In November he authorised the purchase of £100,000 worth of maize (Indian meal). By January 1846, these supplies had been secretly stored in depots around the country, and between March and June they began operation. The Waterford city depot opened on 20 May. Though such food could act as a last line of defence against starvation, its primary purpose was to dampen down the threat of rising food prices and thereby provide a guarantee against profiteering by local traders. The government also sought to ensure that those affected by famine would have the means to purchase food. Legislation was enacted to finance public works to provide employment to the needy. Such schemes were to be organised by either the Board of Works or grand juries, the forerunners of county councils. In both cases funding was advanced by the government, though grand juries were required to repay half of the costs of Board of Works projects and all of the costs of those initiated by grand juries themselves.[8]

A Relief Commission was established to co-ordinate relief measures throughout the country. The formation of unpaid local relief committees, which were intended to play a central role in the alleviation of distress, was encouraged by the government. The main burden of providing for the destitute was to be borne by them. Their principal function was to raise funds with which to purchase and distribute the food imported by the government to those in need. The committees were entitled to purchase this food at cost price from the local depots established by the government. The money raised by local subscriptions could be matched by equal amounts from funds at the disposal of the lord lieutenant. Committees were also permitted to instigate and supervise their own public works, though these were expected to be on a smaller scale than works organised by the government. In relation to government works, relief committees, using local knowledge, were to identify those who were most deserving of employment on public works.[9]

It was not until February 1846 that the Relief Commission published rules for local relief committees and these were formed throughout the country in March and April.[10] On 6 April there was a meeting in the city hall, Waterford, to form such a committee for the city, and Thomas Meagher was in attendance.[11] These committees encompassed a wide spectrum of respectable society, including Catholic and Protestant clergymen, businessmen, landowners and prominent citizens.[12] Meagher would become a member of the Waterford city committee.[13] One of its initial tasks was to raise subscriptions for a relief fund. A decision was made to form a 'begging committee', with Meagher proposing that a committee be formed to collect money in each corporation ward. This proposal was accepted and five were formed, one for each ward. Meagher himself was appointed to the group responsible for the Tower ward.[14] A list of subscribers was subsequently published in the local press,[15] in accordance with the instructions of the Relief Commission.[16] The highest amount subscribed was £50, from the Malcolmson Brothers, wealthy ship owners, with Meagher contributing £10. The vast majority of subscriptions ranged between twelve shillings and £5.[17]

A meeting of the relief committee on 24 April heard a report from Meagher and Dr Nicholas Foran, Catholic Bishop of Waterford and Lismore, who had been deputed to seek financial aid from the government. The two men had met with the lord lieutenant in Dublin and argued the 'strong claims which Waterford had to the best consideration of the government', on the basis that in a few days a sum in excess of £1,100 had been raised by voluntary subscriptions. The result of this meeting was that on receipt of the subscription list by the government, a recommendation would be immediately made to the Relief Commission to grant financial assistance to the city.[18] By May, £750 had been received by the relief committee.[19]

At a meeting on 27 April, this committee gave consideration to various schemes which would provide employment to labourers and skilled workers. Meagher reported that the corporation had allocated £1,000 for the repair of streets and footpaths.[20] On 17 June, at a meeting of subscribers to the relief fund, which was managed by the relief committee, information was given to those in attendance on the numbers employed as a consequence of voluntary subscriptions and government assistance. The previous week £157 had been expended to provide work for 220 labourers, twenty-two carmen, twenty-two masons, fifteen quarrymen and ten smiths.[21] In September the secretary of the relief committee informed members that forty-seven tons of Indian meal, purchased at the government depot by means of public subscriptions, had been given gratuitously to destitute persons.[22]

CITIZENS' RELIEF COMMITTEE

The relief committee was not the only body established to respond to the needs of those affected by the privations resulting from the partial failure of the potato crop. On 13 April 1846 a meeting of citizens was held to consider 'the wants and destitution of the unemployed population'. The city's MP, Sir Henry Winston Barron, observed that the high price of provisions, combined with the lack of work, had created conditions of real hardship for many of Waterford's inhabitants. Meagher proposed that a committee be formed to cooperate with the city's relief committee in raising subscriptions, devising means of employment and providing cheap food. His proposal was adopted and he was appointed one of the three treasurers to oversee the finances of this new committee.[23] At a meeting of it on 1 May, he gave an account of fundraising efforts, and was reported as being anxious that the public understand that its money was not being wasted. The meeting was concerned, for the most part, with a discussion on the progress of the construction of sewers, towards which, it would appear, the citizens' committee had contributed financially.[24]

RELIEF EFFORTS OF RUSSELL'S GOVERNMENT

The potato blight returned with virulence in the summer of 1846 and was to destroy upwards of 90 per cent of the crop nationally. By late August, *The Waterford Mail* reported that the failure of the crop was evident throughout Waterford county,[25] with other newspapers presenting an equally dismal assessment.[26] The county, as distinct from the city, was to bear the brunt of the ensuing humanitarian crisis, with the winter of 1846–7 witnessing scenes of unimaginable suffering and distress.[27] The government of Robert Peel, which has been generally credited by historians with reacting promptly to the partial potato failure of 1845,[28] lost office in June 1846. It was a Whig government, led by Lord John Russell, that had the task of responding to the unfolding catastrophe which was to befall Ireland. And it was to approach the crisis in a significantly different manner to its predecessor.

The policy of the government of Lord John Russell in relation to the famine was heavily influenced by a deep commitment to the economic doctrine of *laissez-faire*.[29] This proscribed state intervention in economic affairs in favour of free trade and private enterprise. The response of Russell's government to the situation in Ireland, therefore, was to be characterised by a number of fundamental considerations. There was to be no intervention in the grain trade: market forces were to operate in terms of supply and demand, and these would determine prices. The focus of government attention was to be on the provision of employment through a revised scheme of public works, not on the direct provision of food. If those in need were given the means of purchasing food, the government believed, in accordance with the principles of *laissez-faire*, the normal operations of trade and commerce would supply this food.

To give practical expression to its policy, a number of key decisions were taken by the government. Peel's Relief Commission was stood down and public works under its auspices were discontinued; food depots were closed; and any planned future public works schemes were placed under the direct control of the Board of Works, which was answerable to the Treasury. This was intended to ensure efficiency and economy. All charges pertaining to public works were to be met out of local taxation. While the Treasury advanced the necessary funding, it had to be repaid in full – Irish property had to support Irish poverty. Local relief committees, however, were to continue in existence and, under the supervision of a newly formed Relief Commission, their primary task was to be the preparation of lists of those in need of employment on public works.[30]

The Waterford food depot closed on 15 August, while the public works schemes associated with Peel's government began to be closed from the second week of that month. In late September the Waterford relief committee received formal notification of the government's decision that no more maize was to be imported for the purpose of relief.[31] With the total failure of the potato crop in the autumn, there was a remorseless rise in Irish food prices between September and the end of the year, and 'as each succeeding month brought higher prices, malnourishment increased, eventually to the point of starvation'.[32]

At a meeting of the relief committee in early October, Meagher raised the matter of the high price of provisions in the city. He favoured the opening of depots by the government for the sale of such provisions at a reasonable price. He suggested that a letter to this effect be sent to the government. The following resolution was adopted: 'That considering the present very high prices of the food of the people, and having no reasonable expectation of any immediate reduction in those prices by the ordinary commercial resources, our chairman be respectfully requested to communicate with the government for the purpose of having depots for provisions established as speedily as possible in this city.'[33]

A reply was received to this communication in late October stating that it was not the government's intention to open such a depot.[34] In December the relief office in Dublin rejected an inquiry from the Waterford relief committee as to whether £50 from the relief fund could be used to provide cheap food. The reply was terse and definitive: 'It is presumed the intention of the committee is to provide food for sale under cost; and as this involves partial gratuitous relief, it cannot be sanctioned.'[35] Clearly, the principles of *laissez-faire* were to prevail.

PUBLIC WORKS

The public works schemes, the centrepiece of Whig policy, experienced great difficulties and were the subject of much contemporary criticism. There were long delays before some works were operational, a fact that was frequently highlighted in the Waterford newspapers.[36] It was reported at a relief committee meeting in December 1846 that 706 persons were on the list seeking employment. However, the clerk of the committee observed that there was a great number seeking work who were not on the list. The committee resolved that 'the Office of the Board of Works be called to commence forthwith some of those works which have been approved of ...'[37]

Complaints about delays in the payment of wages owed to those engaged on public works became commonplace.[38] This had the effect of impairing the efficiency of the schemes, the purpose of which, after all, was to enable the destitute to earn the wherewithal to purchase food. In the course of a public meeting in December, called to consider the plight of the poor, Meagher highlighted these delays and called on the Board of Works:

> to get rid of the cumbersome machinery which prevented the labourers from being paid their wages at the close of the week; for there was such mystery about the payment of men at present that some of them did not receive their week's wages until Monday, Tuesday or Wednesday; and he believed in some cases that it was allowed to go as far as Thursday. It cannot be doubted but that such arrangements caused great inconvenience to poor labourers.

Replying to Meagher, Henry Winston Barron said that he had been informed by the Board of Works that because of the demands made on it by so many relief committees, it was impossible for the board to depart from their present arrangements. This comment provoked an angry response from Meagher: 'They should endeavour to simplify the management of their machinery, so as not to leave poor creatures starving for two or three days together. I wonder would they (the officials of the Board of Works) like to be left in such a state themselves.' At the conclusion of the meeting, subscriptions were opened to help alleviate the sufferings of the destitute and the sum of £120 pounds was collected, Meagher contributing £10.[39]

The rate of payment to labourers on public works also received much contemporary negative attention and criticism.[40] The inadequacy of wages proved to be a fundamental weakness of the scheme,[41] this small sum condemning labourers and their families to malnutrition and disease.[42] Thus, the economics of survival were virtually impossible in the winter of 1846–7.

HARDSHIP AND SUFFERING INCREASE

The hardships visited on those labouring on public works throughout the country are beyond imagining and description, especially during the winter of 1846–7, which was bitterly cold.[43] 'Heavy outdoor labour, especially in the cold and snowy winter conditions of 1846–7, placed extreme stresses on the bodies of the malnourished, who began to die in large numbers on the works in early 1847.[44] In addition to remorseless hunger and bitter cold, the destitute congregating at worksites were exposed to the dangers of contagious fevers, which were reaching epidemic proportions. It was the plight of the victims of fever which Meagher highlighted at a meeting of the relief committee on 8 January 1847. He instanced the case of a married man, the father of two children, who had succumbed to fever while employed on a work's scheme. According to Meagher, the Board of Works paid wages to persons who met with accidents until they were fit to return to work. He argued that in the case of fever it would be equally humane to pay labourers their wages until they recovered their health. He proposed a motion to that effect, which was adopted.[45]

The public works were as unattractive and uninviting as they could possibly be for the starving destitute: low levels of remuneration for physically demanding work, in the most inclement of weather, on sites infected by pestilential fevers. Desperation, however, forced hundreds of thousands to apply for such employment. The alternative was starvation. The numbers employed nationally soared from 114,000 in October 1846 to 714,390 by March 1847.[46] The situation in Waterford reflected this trend, as is evident in the table below, which records the numbers of able-bodied persons employed in public works in the city and county during December 1846:[47]

Date	Waterford city	Waterford county
12 December	170	7,890
19 December	245	7,362
26 December	255	8,555

The public works policy of Russell's government failed to alleviate the widespread distress prevalent in Ireland during the winter of 1846–7, the mass mortality of these months trumpeting this failure. The fundamental reason why the policy failed was that public works could not cope with the shivering, diseased and starving mass of humanity seeking relief. The scale of the crisis simply overwhelmed the official response. Those in charge of the Board of Works felt equipped to manage about 100,000 persons at a maximum,[48] but the actual figure of nearly 720,000 in the spring of 1847 was a stratospheric amount. The indisputable fact is that 'not even the herculean efforts of the Board of Works' 12,000 strong establishment could supervise effectively the employment of three quarters of a million people.[49] The government decided, therefore, to wind up the relief works, a process which began in March 1847.

SOUP KITCHENS

Russell and his ministers realised that a policy to halt starvation and disease was necessary, even if this meant departing from the principles of *laissez-faire*. The chosen method was the soup kitchen, by which food could be distributed directly and gratuitously to the destitute. Meagher was again a member of the relief committee charged with implementing this policy in Waterford city. At a meeting on 6 April, he was especially vocal, even animated, in his contribution. He informed his colleagues that he had just come from a scene (he gave no details) which, had it been witnessed by the Lords of the Treasury, would have inclined them to think that their duty was to give immediate relief to the destitute. He insisted that 'the present state of the people could not admit of a moment's delay'. To underscore the sense of urgency he evidently felt, he told his colleagues, as reported in *The Waterford Mail*, 'that he knew a very decent and respectable family whose father took dysentery about a week since and was dead today. If relief had been afforded to that family one week ago, the poor man might now be living and preserved to his wife and her helpless children.' When a committee member observed that many of those seeking relief were not inhabitants of the city and should therefore be seeking assistance in their own localities, Meagher responded with the comment: 'We cannot stop giving them relief, as we cannot allow them starve.'[50] The committee met again on 9 April, to consider arrangements for the establishment of soup kitchens, Meagher commenting that 'we should at least commence operations for the setting up of our depots [kitchens]'.[51]

By the summer of 1847, soup kitchens were operational throughout the country and successfully feeding up to three million persons daily.[52] This policy, however, was only ever intended as a temporary emergency measure; a circular issued by the Relief Commission in early August stated that the kitchens were established 'solely to replace for one season the food of which the people were deprived'.[53] The government had already made the fateful decision to transfer responsibility for relief of distress to the poor law system. Accordingly, in June 1847 the Poor Law Extension Act was passed.

ASSESSMENT OF MEAGHER'S ROLE ON RELIEF COMMITTEES

Before this act is considered, it is appropriate to assess the role of Thomas Meagher on the Waterford city relief committee. Of such committees in general, Ciarán Ó Murchadha has written:

> Committees varied greatly in their levels of efficiency and commitment; where they were most effective, the work was carried on by a small core of active members ... At their best, the active membership was dedicated and painstaking in their duties, and equal to the task of challenging government bureaucracy ... [becoming] adept in discerning the needs of genuinely poor people ... At their worst, committees were negligent and lazy, failed to meet regularly or adequately collect subscriptions ...[54]

The relief committees of which Meagher was a member were certainly not negligent and lazy. Evidence suggests that he and his colleagues discharged their collective responsibilities, meeting reasonably frequently and collecting subscriptions. They were involved in the organisation of public works, distributed maize and established soup kitchens to feed the destitute. Meagher personally displayed genuine concern and humanity for the plight of the victims of the Famine; for example, he criticised delays in initiating public works and in the payment of wages, and emphasised the urgency in getting soup kitchens operational. He also subscribed to various appeals to assist those in need.

POOR LAW EXTENSION ACT, 1847

By the terms of the Poor Law Extension Act of June 1847, a separate Poor Law Commission was established for Ireland and the number of poor law unions increased from 130 to 163. The act contained a key provision that under certain conditions a board of guardians could grant relief outside the workhouse. This applied not only to the old and disabled, but also to the able-bodied poor.[55] With effect from 15 August 1847, the provision of relief was the responsibility of the poor law. Boards of guardians, therefore, found themselves at the centre of efforts to deal with the ongoing social catastrophe that was Ireland's famine. And Thomas Meagher was a member of the board of guardians of the Waterford city union during 1847–8.

In March 1847 Meagher was elected a poor law guardian, for the term of one year, representing the Tower ward.[56] He assumed office at a very difficult period in Ireland's, and Waterford's, history. The reoccurrence of the potato blight in 1846 and the consequent destruction of the entire crop transformed the food shortages of 1845 into 'a subsistence crisis of unique range and longevity'.[57] Hunger and the failure of the public works programme of the Whig government to alleviate the widespread distress forced people into the country's workhouses. The one in Waterford city had been built to accommodate 900, and its capacity quickly became a concern for the guardians.[58] The extent of the problem they faced is evident from the following table which records the number of inmates, as reported at guardians' meetings, on various dates over a period of six months in 1847:[59]

Date of meeting	Number of inmates
1 April 1847	1,144
24 June 1847	1,034
19 August 1847	812
23 September 1847	895
28 October 1847	1,088
25 November 1847	1,262

A meeting of the board on 29 April 1847 was attended by a Mr Crawford, representing the Poor Law Commissioners. He urged the necessity of limiting, in particular, the admission of women, due to the overcrowded state of their wards. There were at that point two women to a bed. The matron in charge of the female section confirmed the gravity of the situation. She informed the guardians that there were 400 female inmates and the admission of any more would result in three to a bed.[60]

CONTAGIOUS DISEASES

A consequence of this overcrowding was the spread of contagious diseases. Dr Joseph Mackesy, medical officer of the workhouse, stated categorically to the guardians that it was 'most dangerous to crowd the house with sickly persons ... it was making a complete pest hole of the poor house if you continue to admit females when you know the house to be so crowded'. He was of the decided opinion that it was better 'to leave the poor creatures to take their chances outside in the pure air and not put them into the vitiated atmosphere of this house'. According to him, there were seventy-six cases of fever in the institution on 29 April 1847. The guardians resolved not to admit any more females, but reversed this decision before the end of the meeting on humanitarian grounds.[61] Contagious diseases continued to be a problem. By May, Mackesy was reporting that typhus fever was becoming 'more malignant'.[62] A medical report on the state of the workhouse, dated 13 September 1847, noted: 'The type of fever that at present prevails is the mild typhoid, with great prostration, the general duration being fourteen days, with great tendency to relapse in all cases, and these occur three or four times ... Dysentery at present prevails to a great extent ...'[63]

An official report issued in 1852 observed that 'experience had shown that a scarcity of food in Ireland, of any considerable duration, had been invariably followed by an epidemic of fever'.[64] The Great Famine bore tragic testimony to the accuracy of this statement. Typhus, relapsing fever, dysentery and scurvy became widespread during 1845–50.[65] 'It was social dislocation and the disruption of normal living patterns caused by famine, which transformed the nation's epidemic fever into destructive, terrorising epidemics':[66]

> The advent and extension of famine and the consequent deterioration in the sanitary standards of the afflicted people provided a fertile soil to receive the seeds of fever. Those exhausted by hunger and struggling to keep body and soul together by what they could find of dock leaves and nettles or the handful of raw meal, were not likely to trouble greatly about personal cleanliness, even had they the strength to fetch water or firing to heat it. Such

of their clothing as had any market value had been sold to passing pedlars, and the rags that were left they wore night and day, huddling together for warmth.[67]

A report on the number of persons treated for fever in the principal cities of Ireland in 1847 and 1848 gave the following figures for Waterford:[68]

Year	Numbers treated	Number died	Percentage mortality
1847	2,446	236	9.6
1848	1,854	179	9.3

Many of those treated accessed medical assistance through the workhouse. Thomas Meagher, indeed, expressed the view at a guardians' meeting on 28 October 1847 that it should be the object of the Waterford workhouse to have medical assistance procured for diseased persons entering the establishment.[69] These institutions, however, were never intended to have to deal with epidemics consequent on a crisis such as the Great Famine. The report of the Poor Law Commission for 1846 commented that hospital wards in a workhouse 'were provided to meet the casual sickness arising in a number of inmates generally presumed to be healthy'.[70] During the years of the Famine, these same wards were obliged to manage a medical situation that bore no resemblance to casual sickness. In fact, close on one-third of a million died in workhouses in the Famine years of 1846–52.[71]

GUARDIANS' RESPONSE TO OVERCROWDING AND DISEASE

The crises of overcrowding and the outbreak of fever in the workhouse demanded urgent responses by the Waterford guardians. From December 1846, the Poor Law Commission recommended that boards should take steps to secure additional accommodation. It was suggested that this could be achieved in a number of ways, including renting suitable premises within the union.[72] This was the course of action adopted by the Waterford board. The Presentation Convent on Hennessy's Road was the first building rented in October 1847.[73] In December two more buildings were acquired: Mr White's malthouse[74] and Mr Grady's yard.[75] In spite of these initiatives, in early February 1848 the workhouse was described by one guardian, James Delahunty, as being 'crowded to suffocation'. He continued: 'Sixty-four had died during the last fortnight; they were dying like rotten sheep.'[76]

Due to the prevalence of infectious diseases in the workhouse, the guardians applied in March 1847 to the Poor Law Commissioners to erect an emergency fever hospital.[77] Permission was granted in May for such a building, in accordance with the standard plan approved by the Central Board of Health.[78] This 'temporary fever ward' was a wooden building, 100 feet long, capable of accommodating fifty persons. It was opened by the summer of 1847, but was full to capacity almost immediately.[79]

As a guardian, Thomas Meagher participated in the collective decisions regarding the critical issues of additional accommodation and the management of infectious diseases. (The manner in which the board performed its duties will be considered later in this chapter.) There were two matters, however, about which he was particularly vocal: money owed by the board of guardians to Waterford Fever Hospital and the collection of arrears of the poor rates.

FEVER HOSPITAL

Regarding the fever hospital, under the existing poor law arrangements, one method of dealing with workhouse inmates who contracted fever was to remove them to a fever hospital and reimburse that institution for its services.[80] The Waterford board of guardians availed of this mechanism: in 1846, for example, 181 inmates were sent to the city's fever hospital.[81] It has been noted that Meagher was an active supporter of this hospital; in 1847 he was a member of its 'regulatory committee'.[82] At a meeting of the board of guardians on 20 May, a deputation of representatives of the fever hospital was received. These representatives were seeking payment of some portion of the £1,000 owed for the treatment of workhouse inmates. It was explained to the guardians that great demands were being made on the resources of the hospital and that the institution did not have the means to pay its debts. A discussion ensued and Meagher asserted that it was simply unacceptable that the guardians incur financial responsibilities and not meet them. Judging by a newspaper report, he became somewhat agitated, declaring that as the hospital could not get the money owed to it by the workhouse, it (the hospital) would have no option but to close down. When asked what would happen to the patients in such circumstances, he replied that they would have to be 'let out on the town'. While this was a bald assessment of the situation, and perhaps not a particularly constructive contribution towards a resolution of the matter, it was nevertheless a possible scenario. The guardians decided to pay £100 in part payment of moneys owed.[83]

The finances of the hospital continued to be problematic: at a guardians' meeting on 9 September, Meagher announced that it would run out of funds by the end of that month and its 300 patients would have no place to go for treatment. He proposed, as a solution, that the board of guardians 'should take the hospital entirely under their protection', i.e. assume financial responsibility for it. The likely rationale for this proposal was that the board, notwithstanding the enormous pressures on its finances, had a more reliable source of income (i.e. the poor rates) than the hospital, which was very much dependent on voluntary subscriptions, donations and the occasional government grant. The meeting agreed that a committee of guardians would meet with representatives of the hospital to discuss the matter.[84] In late December Meagher was again reminding his fellow guardians that the debt owed to the fever hospital was still outstanding.[85] The matter was considered once more by the board in January 1848, when it received a deputation from the hospital seeking financial support.[86] As late as March, shortly before the dissolution of the board, Waterford union did not have the means to pay its debts to the institution.[87]

Meagher's concern in relation to the fever hospital may be explained by the fact that he had a long association with it and, as a member of its regulatory committee in 1847, understood the precarious nature of its financial situation.[88] Moreover, he appreciated the importance of an institution with a long history of caring for the poor of the city: according to the hospital committee's report for 1846, it had admitted 35,815 patients from its opening in 1799 to 1 January 1847.[89] He simply did not want it to be forced to close, especially in a year like 1847, when epidemics were rife and its services were vital to the welfare of so many of the inmates of the city's workhouse.

COLLECTION OF POOR RATES

A second issue on which Meagher was vocal was the failure of the board of guardians to collect arrears owed on the poor rates. It was a subject he raised at one of the earliest meetings of the board that he attended after his election in March. On 15 April he referred to the minutes of proceedings in January, when strong complaints were made against the rate collectors for 'remissness of their duties'. A resolution had been adopted at the January meeting giving the collectors one month from that date to collect and pay the whole amount of their warrants. Meagher noted that two months had elapsed since the date given in February and he asserted that the state of the collection was 'in as bad, if not a worse state'. He claimed that £2,300 was still owed in rates. By failing to act, he believed that the guardians were not only doing an injustice to those who had paid what they owed, but also to their creditors, as the failure to collect the rates meant they (the guardians) were unable to pay their lawful debts. Meagher explained that he felt so strongly about this matter because the workhouse could not be kept open if the rates were not collected. For him there was a solution to this situation: 'Now when they asked, "What would they do with the bread contractor and the fever hospital …?", he would say to them, "Make the [rate] collectors do their duty, and if they do not, get others who will."' He stated his intention of proposing a motion to dismiss the present collectors but, after some discussion, agreed to adjourn the motion until the next meeting, on 6 May, thus giving the collectors an opportunity to discharge their duties.[90]

At that May meeting, the clerk to the board reported that £1,016 and £778 were still outstanding for the city and county respectively. Meagher moved his motion to dismiss the collectors. When a proposal was made and adopted that the motion be postponed for another week, he announced that he was withdrawing it and would not be moving it again: 'Any other may take it up, I am done with it.'[91] This somewhat petulant reaction probably betrayed his frustration that his sense of urgency and desire to address the matter of the non-collection of arrears was not shared by a sufficient number of his fellow guardians. He may have concluded that he was wasting his time: no action had been taken in the past and there was no indication that this would change in the future. When, on the following week, the county collector, a Mr Phelan, appeared before the guardians to explain the difficulties he experienced in collecting the poor rate, Meagher made no contribution to the discussion.[92]

Meagher's silence, however, on the matter of collection of poor rates did not last long. Phelan was dismissed by the guardians in early July, and when he wrote a letter of protest to the board, Meagher defended the decision by highlighting the fact that the collector had not forwarded to the board any rates since April, a situation he described as 'unjust' to the union's creditors, to whom money was 'so long due'.[93] At a meeting on 19 August, Assistant Commissioner Burke of the Poor Law Commission, who was in attendance, observed that in relation to the collection of poor rates in the Waterford union, 'great irregularity had crept in' and a recently dismissed collector (Phelan) 'came and went as he pleased'. Moreover, Burke stated that Phelan had been embezzling the rates he was collecting.[94] The assistant commissioner's comments were a vindication of Meagher's concerns regarding the state of the poor rate in the union, concerns which were further underscored when it was revealed to the board in late November that Phelan had helped himself to £500.[95]

However, the guardians still did not formulate a concerted response to the problems of poor rate collection. By late October, only a fraction of the arrears had been collected, prompting Meagher to propose that the city collector be required to appear before the guardians in order to give an account of the manner in which he was discharging his duties.[96] A few days later the Poor Law Commissioners wrote to the union regarding the urgency of making arrangements to pay off the sum of £18,000 it owed in borrowings.[97] Yet on 27 January 1848 the clerk of the Waterford board reported that arrears in payments of rates totalled £4,845. Meagher, one suspects with grim determination, and more in hope than expectation, proposed a motion which was adopted:

> That it appears in some districts … considerable arrears are yet due of the collection of the last rate … notice is given to each of the collectors to proceed with some diligence in the collection, otherwise the board will feel bound to dismiss any collectors

continuing to be backward in his collection after this notice … as the board must expect the collection to be completed by the 25th March next.[98]

This notice had no effect. As late as 17 March 1848, an official of the Poor Law Commission noted in a report to the commissioners on the Waterford workhouse that about a quarter of the poor rate remained uncollected, 'and there seems to be no trouble taken by the guardians to have this large arrear got in'.[99] In the city a sum of £2,177 was outstanding.[100] Moreover, the official noted that 'for what cause I cannot learn', the money owed by Phelan had yet to be recouped.[101]

Meagher's tenacious attitude to the issue of collection of poor rates was motivated by a strong sense of moral principle. Defaulters had to be pursued in justice and fairness to those who had paid and to creditors owed money by the board of guardians. The proper, effective and sustainable operation of the union workhouse necessitated the payment of rates. The scriptural injunction, 'Render to Caesar the things that are Caesar's',[102] probably encapsulates the essence of the outlook of this most religious of men. As Meagher proclaimed to his colleagues, 'we owe a duty to the public'[103] – Caesar (or at least, Victoria) had to be paid and that was the heart of the matter for him. Meagher was also conscious of a new stridency apparent in the attitude of various officials of the Poor Law Commission regarding the collection of poor rates nationally.[104] When moving the resolution to dismiss one of the collectors, he referred to the fact that the 'commissioners had very frequently and very severely animadverted on the collection of the rate of this union'.[105] He apparently regarded such observations as demanding a response.

The problem of poor rate arrears was not unique to Waterford.[106] In their criticisms of boards of guardians, the Poor Law Commissioners were inclined to ignore or minimise the difficulties and obstacles faced by unions in their efforts to collect this impost. The same charge may be levelled at Meagher in respect of his complaints against the collectors of the Waterford union. Notwithstanding these qualifications, there evidently was an issue with the non-collection of rates in this union, which demanded a more proactive response from the guardians. Such a response was hampered, however, by a number of factors.

According to the official report to the commissioners, referred to earlier, two-fifths of the outstanding arrears of £2,177 in the city were owed 'by one hundred persons of a class well able to pay'.[107] This report included a list of the names and the amount of arrears due in each instance.[108] Allowing for some exaggeration on the official's part, his observation about 'a class well able to pay' is instructive. Perhaps some of the guardians were tardy and reluctant in taking action against persons with whom they were acquainted and who were, after all, members of the respectable middle class, like the guardians themselves. In the context of this argument, a comment made by Meagher at a meeting of guardians is interesting: 'There is, also, another feature, another evil, on the face of the present system of collecting rates and I must say it is an unjust one. I find that while the comparatively poor and miserable occupier is proceeded against and put, unmercifully, to all those expenses attendant upon law, the landlords are allowed get off "scot-free".'[109]

It should also be noted, however, that this comment was primarily directed at the collectors. In all Meagher's vociferous denunciations pertaining to the poor rates, there is no evidence that he uttered direct criticisms of his fellow guardians, who were ultimately responsible for the collection of this tax. While sympathetic to the plight of poorer rate payers, perhaps the bonds of middle-class brotherhood did not extend to criticisms of his colleagues?

Moreover, that some guardians could be accused of blatant double standards is evident from a newspaper report in April 1847 on the board that was elected the previous month: 'By the return of the list of elected guardians laid before the board by the returning officer, Mr Heney, it appeared that a few of the late guardians were disqualified for the non-payment of poor rate.'[110] Even some of those charged with overseeing the collection of poor rates were not paying them, and this was indicative of an attitude which infected the whole taxation system underpinning the operation of the poor law in Waterford union. By contrast, for example, when a rate was struck in the Killarney union, it was collected with 'vigour'. The guardians put pressure on the collectors, but more importantly they led by example: when a rate was struck in 1848, the board adopted a resolution instructing the collectors to call on the guardians first.[111] In another union in Kerry, that of Kenmare, a poor law inspector noted that it was difficult to pursue defaulters when ten of the guardians had failed to pay their rates.[112] This comment could also be applied to Waterford. It should be noted that there is no record of Meagher highlighting this circumstance in his campaign for a more vigorous response to collect the poor rates. Perhaps, this is another example of middle-class reluctance to confront the crimes of the bourgeoisie?

DAMNING REPORT ON WATERFORD GUARDIANS, MARCH 1848

There have been a number of references made already to an official report to the Poor Law Commissioners on the Waterford union. This report of March 1848 was the result of what has been described as 'a most intemperate letter' to the commissioners by one of the guardians, Sir Henry Winston Barron.[113] Dated 11 March 1848, in it he urged the 'absolute and pressing necessity of either dissolving the board or appointing an inspector' (a full-time official who would assume the board's functions). Barron alleged neglect of duties and corruption on the part of some guardians and relieving officers (paid officials of the union who assisted the guardians in organising relief).[114] An inspector, a Mr Burke, acting on behalf of the Poor Law Commissioners, arrived in Waterford to conduct an investigation.

Burke authored a report damning in its contents.[115] He found the master of the workhouse incapable of managing it; consequently, the institution was characterised by 'laxity of discipline' and 'idleness'. The bread and meat used to feed the inmates were of a very inferior quality. Burke reported that it was the opinion of Dr John Elliott, medical officer, that the broth made from the meat was 'so bad as to prove actually pernicious to many of those who partook of it, especially to children'.[116] There was no evidence of any contracts having been entered into for the supply of meat and bread, as required by regulations. The spectre of corruption was thereby raised. Burke also expressed concerns about the non-collection of arrears of poor rates. The union was effectively insolvent, with only £106 in the bank, a weekly expenditure of £296 and liabilities of £1,640. This was a report which charged the Waterford guardians with serious, even wilful, neglect in the exercise of their duties of supervision and government of the workhouse.

On the basis of the report furnished by Burke, the Poor Law Commissioners concluded that the duties of the board of guardians of Waterford union were not being 'effectively discharged according to the intentions of the Irish Poor Relief Acts' and, accordingly, it was decided to dissolve it, the relevant order being issued on 23 March 1848.[117] The enactment of the 1847 Poor Law Extension Act facilitated the process of dissolution, forty-two boards being dissolved for a variety of reasons, including, as in the case of the Waterford board, failure to implement the poor law as prescribed by the rules and regulations of the commissioners.[118]

ASSESSMENT OF MEAGHER'S ROLE AS A POOR LAW GUARDIAN

Meagher's concern for the plight of those affected by the Famine was genuine and heartfelt, and he involved himself in 'front-line' efforts to relieve distress by contributing his time and money. He was a member of the various relief committees established to organise and manage government relief initiatives. He also participated in voluntary relief endeavours, such as the citizens' relief committee and the regulatory committee of the fever hospital. It was his role in all these efforts which almost certainly influenced his decision to seek election as a poor law guardian. By this decision, however, he was associating himself with the operation of a system that was much reviled from its inception. Workhouses, the physical expressions of the poor law, were so regulated, in the words of an assistant poor law commissioner, William Voules, 'as not to hold out much inducement for those to enter who can avoid it'.[119] They were regarded in the popular consciousness as places of confinement, discipline and punishment, so much so that before the Famine 'the Irish poor preferred the freedom of their precarious trade to the dismal certainty within workhouse walls'.[120] However, the personal and social ravages wrought by the failure of the potato crop forced the starving destitute into them. These institutions, notwithstanding all their grave, even terrible deficiencies, were the principal, and at times, the only sources of assistance for truly desperate people. It was precisely because the workhouses and the poor law were central to the whole system of Famine relief that Meagher sought membership of the Waterford union board of guardians. He wanted to play his part in a time of unprecedented social crisis.

In attempting an assessment of his performance as a guardian, it is essential to appreciate the context in which Meagher and his colleagues strove to discharge their duties. The poor law, as originally conceived in 1838, was never intended as a mechanism to address a humanitarian crisis on the scale of the Great Famine. It was designed to deal with the 'normal' level of poverty and distress in Ireland. George Nicholls, on whose report the system was based, recommended that workhouses should be able to hold approximately 1 per cent of the total Irish population, or an estimated 100,000 paupers.[121] At the height of the Great Famine almost 50 per cent of the population was to require relief, and, unsurprisingly, the workhouses and the poor law system in general proved totally inadequate.

Ireland's workhouses were already under enormous stress when the government decided to extend the scope of the operation of the poor law in June 1847 and transfer primary responsibility for Famine relief to it from 15 August 1847. This decision was emblematic of the fact that assistance from the government was at an end and that Irish taxpayers were responsible for future relief, through the poor rates.[122] This policy of almost total reliance on the already over-stretched resources of the poor law was implemented 'in the midst of a social implosion … and appalling levels of excess mortality due to starvation and famine-related disease'.[123] The Relief Commission, in its report to the Treasury on the cessation of the soup kitchens, noted 'the awful amount of distress occasioned by the failure of the crop of potatoes' and commented: 'The discontinuance of this extensive system of relief … must be attended with distress and difficulty, and all the energy and public spirited expenditure that can be applied will be required to meet this emergency'.[124] There was to be no such 'public spirited expenditure'; rather ideological dogmas informed the response of the Russell government[125] and it was these ideological and financial concerns, rather than humanitarian ones, which shaped the administration of relief throughout the Famine crisis.[126]

The additional duties imposed by the Poor Law Extension Act of June 1847 made substantial extra demands on the Waterford guardians.

They were obliged to oversee the operation of an already seriously overburdened system as the principal source of relief. Over the six months of April to September 1847, there were twenty-seven meetings of the board; however, in the two months of January and February 1848 there were twenty-five, this dramatic increase being due to the provision of outdoor relief and attendant issues.[127] The consequence was that many of Waterford's guardians found the demands made on their time excessive. Burke acknowledged as much in his report to the commissioners: 'many of [the guardians] however well inclined, having their own affairs to attend to, cannot be expected to devote the time which the increased duties now devolving on boards of guardians require.'[128]

Burke's acknowledgement notwithstanding, the board had a serious problem of non-attendance at meetings by many of its members, a problem that was highlighted by the Poor Law Commissioners in their decision to dissolve it.[129] The commissioners' concern was based on a return of attendance furnished to Burke by the clerk of the Waterford union and included by him (Burke) as part of his report to the commissioners. The return recorded the attendance of the sixty-two guardians at seventy-eight meetings between 26 March 1847 and 16 March 1848.[130] Even the number of meetings at which the ten best attendees were present – and these included Meagher – appears unimpressive.

Name of guardian	Number of meetings attended
William Morris	49
Thomas L. Mackesy	43
John E. Feehan	38
Simon Newport	37
Thomas Meagher	36
John Bogan	34
Patrick Carrigan	32
John Hackett	30
P.A. Power	27
Sylvester Phelan	26

Thirty-one guardians attended ten meetings or less, including six who attended no meetings at all.

Clearly, there were guardians whose commitment to their duties was shamefully, even scandalously, derelict, on the basis of the evidence of their attendance (or more correctly, their non-attendance) at board meetings and the contents of Burke's report. By this dereliction, they abandoned the duties of governance and supervision enjoined upon them by their office – an office upon which they entered entirely of their own volition. Moreover, by the neglect of their responsibilities, guardians contributed to the perpetuation of grievous failings in the management of the workhouse, as revealed in Burke's report, and did nothing to mitigate or ameliorate such failings.

Burke's report was not the only evidence of the guardians' failings. By the time of the 1847 guardian elections, Waterford was suffering the effects of a complete failure of the potato crop. In their administration of the workhouse, the guardians were faced with problems of overcrowding and the spread of contagious diseases. As was noted earlier, they attempted to address both concerns. In relation to overcrowding, additional accommodation was acquired. However, their response appears to have been tardy and lacking a sense of urgency. It may be remembered that these acquisitions were not made until October and December 1847, although the workhouse was overcrowded for much of that year. In the matter of contagious diseases, inmates were sent to Waterford Fever Hospital, but the guardians were unable to fully reimburse that institution for services rendered. This inability to pay was due, in part, to inaction by the board of guardians in collecting outstanding poor rates. On the basis of this evidence, the Waterford guardians were inadequate, if not actually derelict, in the performance of their duties in relation to overcrowding and the management of contagious diseases.

While Meagher was among the more regular attendees at meetings of the guardians, his attendance rate of 46 per cent is hardly exemplary. The problem was that there were significant competing demands on his time: he was an alderman of Waterford Corporation and was elected an MP for the city in August 1847. The latter role certainly impacted his position as a guardian and accounts for many of his absences from meetings. Around the time of the general election he missed at least four,[131] and parliamentary duties at Westminster meant that he could not attend any of the nineteen meetings in February and March.[132] When he was present, he did contribute to collective decision-making and was vocal on a number of important issues, such as the non-collection of poor rates and the fever hospital.

Though Meagher was undoubtedly constrained, for good reasons, in his ability to participate fully in the activities of the guardians, he must, however, by virtue of his membership of the board, take his share of the responsibility for the grave defects in the workhouse. But however contributory his explained absences and the apparently more culpable absences of others in relation to the inadequacies of the workhouse in Waterford city in late 1847 and early 1848 – and such absences undoubtedly did contribute significantly to the manifold miseries of the impoverished, hungry and diseased victims of the Great Famine resident therein – they were not the fundamental cause of the relief system's failings. Rather, the problem lay with a government policy inherently and catastrophically flawed from its inception, and consequently lamentably incapable of addressing the grave humanitarian crisis that was Ireland's Great Famine.

FACTORS MOTIVATING MEAGHER AS A GUARDIAN

As one of the more conscientious guardians, Thomas Meagher's attitude to his membership of the board and its attendant duties were motivated by two fundamental considerations. The first, and principal one, was the obligation he felt as a Christian to help those in need. This charitableness had been nurtured in St John's, Newfoundland, especially by his membership of the Benevolent Irish Society, and was given determined expression in his adopted country and city during the cataclysm that was the Great Famine. He simply could not ignore what he witnessed on the streets of Waterford and read in the newspapers. These same newspapers became, 'after a fashion, the chroniclers of the poor and destitute',[133] exposing members of the privileged middle class to the horrors experienced by the more socially disadvantaged. A man such as Meagher could not help but be moved by accounts such as this published in The Chronicle in March 1847, describing conditions around Ring, Old Parish and Ardmore, all located in Waterford county:

Every house you enter (with the exception of the occasional strong farmer's) presents nothing but one black mass of the most deplorable wretchedness. Not a spark of fire on the hearths of nine out of every ten of the wretched houses. And where you do see a spark of fire little larger than a tea-cup, you will behold the squalid and misery-stricken creatures crouching round it, like spectres, with not a human lineament traceable upon their countenances. As to food, good or bad, they have none. In the districts I have enumerated ... there cannot be less than twenty or thirty deaths from starvation every day. Coffin-making is the staple trade of the country; every turn you take you see them in dozens being brought to the rural districts ...[134]

The second consideration which informed Meagher's response to the Famine was a sense of *bourgeois oblige*: the duty of philanthropic endeavour incumbent on conscientious members of the middle class. Meagher was a prominent civic and social figure in Waterford city and he believed that with this position came the duty to assume a leadership role in times of crisis. For him, a privileged place in society carried obligations to the wider community: hence, his membership of various official relief committees, a citizens' relief committee, the regulatory committee of the fever hospital and the board of guardians. In addition to giving of his time, he also gave of his money. Whatever criticisms may be levelled at Thomas Meagher, it must at least be acknowledged that he did try to help his less fortunate and less privileged fellow citizens during the social catastrophe that was the Great Hunger.

CHAPTER EIGHT

Father and Son, 1823–1844: A Common Purpose

In 1843 Thomas Francis Meagher returned to Waterford, having completed his formal education at Stonyhurst in England. His father was mayor of the city and a prominent figure in its public life. For the two years of Meagher's mayoralty, his son would gradually emerge from the shadow of his father, especially when Thomas Francis began to associate himself with the Young Ireland movement from 1845 onwards. It was this association with Young Ireland that secured the young Meagher's iconic status in the pantheon of republican and revolutionary nationalism, while his father was consigned to the shadows of near-historical oblivion.

However, it is very difficult for the historian to write with the desired detail and conviction about the private, familial relationship between father and son, as Thomas Meagher left no known private papers and Thomas Francis made little mention in his speeches and writings of his family.[1] References to the paternal–filial relationship are noteworthy precisely because they are so rare. It was as if Thomas Francis, a student of the classics, had drunk from the waters of the River Lethe when it came to that aspect of his life. Nevertheless, there are occasions mentioned by him, albeit tantalisingly brief and often perfunctory, which shed some light on his relationship with his father and the influences of the latter on his attitudes and actions. Other sources, in particular, contemporary newspapers, also enable us to gain an insight into this relationship.

THOMAS FRANCIS MEAGHER: THE EARLY YEARS

Thomas Francis Meagher was born on 3 August 1823 in his family home on the Quay, a building that is now the Granville Hotel. He was four years of age when his mother, Alicia Quan, died. In his memoir of Thomas Francis, Michael Cavanagh attempted to convey the profound sadness and impact of this event on the young boy:

> In early childhood Thomas Francis Meagher experienced the first and greatest misfortune of his life, in the death of his mother. What influence the loss had upon his future destiny 't were hard to tell; but to a nature so loving and susceptible as his, the desire to contribute to the happiness of a fond mother must, in a greater degree, tend to direct the current of his thoughts and control his actions, so as to merit her approbation and stimulate her maternal pride.[2]

His father found himself caring for four very young children: Thomas Francis; Christina Mary, aged five; Henry, aged two; and Alicia Catherine, aged one month. Two of his late wife's sisters, Johanna and Christina Quan, came to his assistance. Johanna was to be especially important in the children's young lives, judging by a comment of Cavanagh's: 'The boy's [Thomas Francis] irreparable loss was, however, mitigated by the affectionate care of his mother's maiden sister, Miss [Johanna] Quan, who devoted her life to his care and that of his younger brother, Henry.'[3] (There is no reference to the girls.) According to another biographer of Meagher, Captain W.F. Lyons, her 'heart was interwoven with the life of the boy'.[4] Thomas Meagher's parents also helped: Thomas Sr and his wife, Mary, sold their interest in their house at Ballycanavan and moved into the house on the Quay.[5] Following the death of his mother in 1831, Thomas Meagher moved the family to a house located in the fashionable William Street. From there they moved to the Mall, to a house beside that of the Quan sisters. The role played by these women in the rearing of his children was a decisive factor in Thomas's choice of residence. This was to be his home during his years in public life.[6] Appropriately, this most ardent of O'Connell's supporters named the house 'Derrynane', after the Liberator's residence in Kerry.

The domestic lives of middle-class children in general and of children of all classes in nineteenth-century Ireland are yet to be examined in detail by historians.[7] However, by 1750 'the evidence of representational art, material culture, and the correspondence and reading habits of the upper and middle classes suggest that childhood was viewed as a distinct period of life. Children were cherished as individuals with their own personalities … and not merely as imperfect adults, economic units or a means of ensuring the survival of families.'[8]

The high infant mortality rate of the nineteenth century meant that the health of their children was the principal and constant anxiety of parents. Thomas Meagher and Alicia Quan were no exception and the couple certainly experienced the distress caused by the loss of three children: Thomas in 1822; Mary Josephine; and Christianna in 1827. Their father would suffer further with the loss of Alicia Catherine on 28 July 1834, aged seven. 'Survival, therefore, was the main challenge posed to the Irish child.'[9] Having survived, its subsequent upbringing was determined by its parents' understanding of its future role in society.[10] Thomas Meagher wanted his son to receive an education befitting the scion of a middle-class family of status and consequence. His early education was likely attended to by his aunts, who ran a school for a time.[11] Then, in 1833, aged ten, Thomas Francis was sent away to boarding school at the Jesuit-run Clongowes Wood College in County Kildare.

CLONGOWES AND STONYHURST

Thomas Francis arrived in Clongowes with his younger brother, Henry.[12] The fees were a little over £45 for each boy,[13] and for his money their father hoped that this educational institution would supply his sons 'with the attainments and tastes of a nineteenth-century Catholic gentleman'.[14] The curriculum embraced 'the full classical course adapted for universities or learned professions: Hebrew (if required), Italian, French, English, with public speaking and composition, history, geography, writing, arithmetic, book-keeping, mathematics, philosophy and chemistry'.[15] Moreover, the college claimed that 'unceasing care is taken to convey to the minds of the pupils solid instructions on the principles of religion, and to engage their hearts to the observance of its precepts'.[16] Such sentiments would have been pleasing to that most devout of Catholics, Thomas Meagher.

Commenting on Thomas Francis's education at Clongowes, Michael Cavanagh wrote that 'it was not through his college education but, I may say, in spite of it, that he developed into the most brilliant exponent of Irish nationality of his generation'.[17] This observation was prompted by Meagher's account of his time at the school and his declaration that, 'They [the Jesuits] never spoke of Ireland. Never gave us, even what is left of it, her history to read'.[18] Meagher continued: 'It is an odd fiction that represents the Irish Jesuits as conspirators against the stability of the English empire in Ireland. With two or three exceptions, they were not even O'Connellites'.[19] Of this he was acutely aware because he was at this period of his life a great admirer of Daniel O'Connell:

> In the library at Clongowes – the one devoted to the boys – there was a copy of Sheil's and O'Connell's speeches. It was a shabby old book ... Beggarly as it looked, it was to me beyond all price. It was my favourite book. I loved it ... The very pleasantest hours I had in the old college of Clongowes, I spent with this indigent volume ... A rickety casket ... and threatening every minute to fall to pieces, it contained for me a heap of the rarest emeralds, the lustre of which, even in the hardest frost, made my eyes melt and water.[20]

This evident regard for the Liberator was due to the influence of his father and grandfather, both of whom were staunch O'Connellites. It is easy to imagine discussions between them at the dinner table in the family homes on the Quay and the Mall, in the course of which O'Connell was lionised, and to which the young Meagher was a most attentive and interested listener. Opinions formed in Waterford remained with him at Clongowes. Cavanagh regarded such opinions as in the nature of an antidote to the English and anti-national character of the education to which the young Meagher was subjected. In a comment on these years of his childhood, Cavanagh expressed the view that even before Meagher 'left his paternal home, the foundation of his patriotic education had been deeply laid and also that the lessons then learned were sacredly treasured by a loving heart and most retentive memory'.[21] Clearly, one of those responsible for this 'patriotic education' was his O'Connellite father.

On 17 October 1839 Meagher entered Stonyhurst, another Jesuit college, located in Lancashire, England.[22] It had a senior class of 'philosophers', and this was the nearest equivalent that young Irish Catholics could have at that time of a university education, unless they attended Trinity College, Dublin.[23] However, this was never going to be considered by Meagher's father, who, like many Catholics, regarded it as a 'hotbed of [Protestant] bigotry and intolerance'.[24] At Stonyhurst, the young Meagher's political views were obviously noted by his Jesuit educators. In its *Centenary Record*, published in 1894, there are a few lines about him and the fact that he 'made himself very conspicuous for his pronounced nationalism, which he paraded on all possible occasions'.[25] This nationalism was certainly O'Connellite in character and accordingly detested by influential sections of English society. An advocate of O'Connell's politics would have been viewed with deep reserve in the bastion of Englishness that was Stonyhurst.

There occurred a notable episode in which the young Thomas Francis gave public expression to his 'pronounced nationalism'. This happened on 15 June 1840 and was described by Richard O'Gorman, a Young Irelander, in a biographical sketch of Meagher:

> A few months after his arrival he gave the first public exhibition of that detestation of England which marked his career through life. It being the custom at the college to celebrate the anniversary of the battle of Waterloo by music and other recreations, the college band was, as usual, called upon to play. To the astonishment of all, masters and scholars, young Meagher, who was first clarinet player, positively refused to comply. He never would, he said, sound a note of praise for England's victory, and despite entreaties and threats, he adhered to his determination, and eventually compelled the band to disperse without having delivered the music.[26]

Why did Thomas Francis act as he did? His protest was informed by an amalgam of considerations, some of which had their genesis in attitudes and views espoused and articulated by his father. O'Connell was beginning the slow construction of his repeal campaign by 1838. Young Meagher's father, a committed repealer, expressed the accepted nationalist narrative that the Act of Union was primarily responsible for Ireland's social, economic and political problems and failures. Moreover, Thomas Francis would also have heard that Catholic emancipation had been extracted from an unwilling British government; it had not been conceded as of right, but in the face of irresistible popular agitation. As noted earlier, his father was unhappy with aspects of that legislation. And the prime minister associated with this act was none other than the Duke of Wellington, the victor at Waterloo. For Thomas Francis, the remembrance of Waterloo was a celebration of English superiority and achievement. He could not, and would not, honour this occasion in the history of a country which was denying Ireland its national rights, and thus condemning it, according to the repeal mantra, to social, economic and political under-development. Wellington's central role in this battle and in the flawed Emancipation Act probably reinforced his convictions – convictions shaped and influenced by Thomas Francis Meagher's father, a dedicated and committed political activist in the emancipation and repeal causes.

RETURN TO WATERFORD

Thomas Francis Meagher returned to Waterford on Easter Tuesday, 18 April 1843. In his recollections of his return, he noted that 'a great change' had taken place since he left the previous year.[27] 'The old corporation or city council had been displaced and a new one, installed in the ancient seats, had been talking and voting for the last six months.' Its predecessor he described as 'an irresponsible, self-elected, self-conceited, bigoted body'.[28] And one senses that it was with pride that he declared: 'My father was sitting in the curule chair. Chief magistrate of the city, he presided at the meetings of the city council and the bench of borough justice.'[29]

Thomas Francis sensed a mood of satisfaction among his fellow citizens in relation to these changes: 'It was a glorious thing, the people thought, to see some of their own sort in possession of the town hall; to see the mayor going to Mass; to see him presiding at a public dinner given to

Map of Newfoundland, *c.* 1747.
(Courtesy of Kurt Korneski and Newfoundland and Labrador Heritage Website)

Commins Commercial Hotel, once the former residence of Thomas Meagher and now part of the Granville Hotel. (Courtesy of the National Library of Ireland)

Daniel O'Connell, 1775–1847, whose emancipation and repeal campaigns were strongly supported by Thomas Meagher in Waterford.
(Courtesy of the Waterford Museum of Treasures)

Thomas Meagher as Mayor of Waterford, a position he filled from 1843 to 1845. He was the first Catholic mayor of the city since the seventeenth century.
(Courtesy of the Waterford Museum of Treasures)

Sir Benjamin Morris Wall, a close political colleague and supporter of Meagher.
(Courtesy of the Waterford Museum of Treasures)

Thomas Wyse, 1791–1862, a prominent leader of the emancipation movement in Waterford.
(Courtesy of the Waterford Museum of Treasures)

Fr Mathew administering the pledge.
(Courtesy of the National Library of Ireland)

Thomas Francis Meagher as a young man.
(Courtesy of the National Library of Ireland)

Chalice and paten (left) and monstrance (right) presented by Thomas Meagher to the
Sisters of Charity, Waterford.
(Courtesy of the Waterford Museum of Treasures)

Inscription on the base of the monstrance.
(Courtesy of the Waterford Museum of Treasures)

Nicholas Foran, Bishop of Waterford and
Lismore, 1837–1855.

(Courtesy of the Waterford Museum of Treasures)

Dominic O'Brien, Bishop of Waterford and
Lismore, 1855–1873.

(Courtesy of the Waterford Museum of Treasures)

John Sadleir (left) and William Keogh (right), leaders of the Irish Brigade and the
Independent Irish Party.

(Sadlier courtesy of the National Library of Ireland; Keogh courtesy of the Mary Evans Picture Library)

Catherine Bennett, wife of Thomas Francis
Meagher.
(Courtesy of the Tasmanian Archives, NS/23/3/13)

Brigadier General Thomas Francis
Meagher, in a uniform of the American
Union Army.
(Courtesy of the Waterford Museum of Treasures)

Paul Cullen, Archbishop of Dublin,
1852–1878.
(Courtesy of the National Library of Ireland)

The Meagher family vault in Faithlegg churchyard, County Waterford, and the inscription on grave.

(Courtesy of Ray Leahy)

The grave of Thomas Meagher, Glasnevin Cemetery, Dublin.
(Courtesy of Glasnevin Cemetery)

A photograph of
Thomas Meagher,
date unknown.
(Courtesy of the Waterford
Museum of Treasures)

O'Connell ... '[30] The displacement of Protestant ascendancy consequent on corporate reform was a source of particular pleasure: 'and sure they never thought they'd see Felix the basket maker, the bitterest Orangeman of them all, carrying the white wand before his Catholic Worship, as his Worship, with the gold chain around his neck, went up to Ballybricken to preside at petty sessions.'[31]

On his return, Thomas Francis had to effectively reacquaint himself with the city of his birth, having left it in 1833 to pursue his education, only returning for holidays during his school vacations. Little is known about this process of refamiliarisation. However, he did record the fact that he was a member of a gentleman's club, the County and City Club, and his memories of this association are strikingly warm and affectionate.[32] Its membership was predominantly Protestant; according to him, nearly three-fourths of the club were conservatives or Tories, 'who were loyalists to the marrow and never lost an opportunity to assert the fact'.[33] Meagher was very much in the minority, as a Catholic and a repealer; nevertheless, he respected the sincerity of their beliefs, while being unable to concur with them. He described himself as 'a staunch friend of the pleasant institution' and regarded the club as an example of 'that tolerant, genial, generous brotherhood among Irishmen' that he espoused and advocated.[34]

Thomas Francis's membership of this body may afford some insight into his father's influence on him. Thomas Meagher would certainly have approved of, and even encouraged, his decision to join, for three reasons. First, while the members were predominantly Protestants, they did not seek to apply a policy of Protestant exclusiveness. This was very important to Thomas Meagher – his public career was one of rejection of such exclusive attitudes and the promotion of equality between Catholics and Protestants. That membership was not prescribed by denominational affiliations was significant in terms of the equal interaction between the different faiths locally. Second, the Protestant members in the County and City Club were primarily composed of members of the middle class. Thomas Meagher most definitely considered himself and his family as their social equals; therefore, his son's club membership was a public acknowledgement of this fact. Third, and most significant, the attitudes of this club gave some measure of expression to Thomas Meagher's ideal of mutual religious toleration and mutual respect as the desired hallmark of relations between Catholics and Protestants.

The County and City Club may be regarded, therefore, as a practical and concrete expression of some of Thomas Meagher's principles and beliefs, ones to which he likely exposed his son and thus influenced Thomas Francis's generous and inclusive attitude to the Protestant members in the club and in the wider community, locally and nationally. In the final paragraph of his recollections of this association, he penned sentiments which would undoubtedly have pleased his father, and indeed some were likely redolent of sentiments he had expressed: 'may the social institutions flourish which bring Irishmen together, make them know each other, trust each other, love each other and, in convivial circles, teach them they are all brothers all! This done, there is a family. From a family comes a camp. From a camp a Nation.'[35]

TEMPERANCE CAMPAIGN

On the afternoon of 3 May 1843, Father Mathew visited Mount Sion school, together with Mayor Thomas Meagher,[36] who was a champion of temperance, as promoted by the Capuchin priest. Thomas Francis was also present and this was probably the first occasion on which he accompanied his father to a public event. That evening, at the same venue, the mayor presented an address, lauding his achievements, to Fr Mathew. *The Waterford Chronicle* recorded that this 'admirable address' was 'from the pen of Mr Thomas Meagher Jnr. and which does him very high honour'. The newspaper report continued: 'It was read by the mayor in a tone of feeling and emphasis which expressed fully his coincidence with the sentiments it spoke.' In his reply, Fr Mathew noted the authorship of Thomas Francis, describing him as 'a talented gentleman … the son of their respected mayor'.[37] Cavanagh, in his memoir of Thomas Francis, commented that it was at this event that 'the young man gave his fellow citizens the first public proof of his wonderful oratorical powers'.[38]

At a meeting in September 1843, at Mount Sion, Thomas Francis was again in the company of his father, thus associating himself, for a time, with the cause of temperance.[39] This fact has a certain irony, considering his later reputation, deserved or otherwise, for intemperance.[40]

CONTINENTAL TOUR

Sometime in May 1843, Thomas Francis went on a tour of parts of continental Europe, returning to Waterford in early July of the same year. According to Cavanagh, he 'spent some agreeable weeks among the medieval cities of the Low Countries, to which he was especially attracted'.[41] He was impressed by Belgium, which had won its independence from the Netherlands in 1830.[42] Cavanagh further noted that while Meagher's published writings make no reference to this event, he did, however, speak of it occasionally to close associates.[43] Moreover, he referred to this tour towards the end of his famous 'Sword Speech': 'I learned that it was the right of a nation to govern itself ... upon the ramparts of Antwerp'.[44] Meagher's continental tour was a truncated and modified version of the 'Grand Tour', a period of foreign travel undertaken by the sons of wealthy families in the eighteenth century to complete their education.[45] It was his father who funded this undertaking, clear evidence of his determination to give his son the best education possible in the absence of his attending university at Trinity College. This tour was also a statement of Thomas Meagher's sense of the status of his family and of his ambition to prepare Thomas Francis to play a role in society commensurate with his family's position of consequence in Waterford.

REPEAL CAMPAIGN

One of Thomas Francis Meagher's biographers, Robert Athearn, is correct when he wrote that, 'The youthful Meagher had followed O'Connell's campaign [for repeal of the Act of Union] with interest during his days at Stonyhurst and looked forward to his return home where he could be a witness or even a part of the exciting political scene'.[46] On his first returning to Waterford in 1843, Meagher recorded that he felt 'he had come home to an era of excitement and hopes'.[47] He described it as a 'stormy year':

> O'Connell had opened it with a shout for repeal. The repeal debate in Dublin Corporation had taken place ... The interest of the people was awakened – their enthusiasm excited. They had been inert, sluggish, listless. No people had been more so. But the true

chord once struck, everything was restored. Hope, delight, ecstasy, defiance – a tumultuous life leaped to the summons.[48]

Throughout 1843, christened by O'Connell the 'Year of Repeal', Thomas Francis revealed himself to be a confirmed repealer. He supported this cause with dedication and enthusiasm and associated himself, in particular, with the efforts and endeavours of one of the most important leaders of the political campaign in Waterford city, his father, Mayor Thomas Meagher. Back from his continental tour, Thomas Francis played a prominent role in the monster meeting held in Waterford on 9 July, an event in which his father was one of the main actors.[49] Thomas Francis and Councillor Roger Hayes collected O'Connell, using the mayor's carriage, in the village of Kilmacthomas, where the Liberator had spent the previous night. He was a member of the platform party at Ballybricken, the venue for the meeting. Later that evening, he acted as one of the three secretaries of the repeal banquet, his duties requiring him to read letters of apology and support to the assembled gathering. Later the same month, he addressed a monster meeting at Lismore, using the occasion to affirm the loyalty of Ireland to the British crown and rejecting ministerial imputations to the contrary.[50]

After the abandonment of the Clontarf meeting in October 1843 and the subsequent arrest of O'Connell, there was a meeting of repealers in Waterford to affirm their support for, and confidence in, their leader.[51] Mayor Meagher spoke, as did his son. Professor Denis Gwynn has noted that the latter's speeches were always written out in advance[52] and this address, one of his earliest, is testimony to deliberate and considered construction. It was especially powerful and was shaped by the fundamental principles which inspired the repeal movement. His words were an unequivocal declaration of loyalty to the Liberator. This declaration to O'Connell reflected Thomas Francis's appreciation of the difficulties facing the Liberator in the aftermath of Clontarf: it was an occasion demanding trenchant expressions of fidelity and admiration. O'Connell was described by him as 'the illustrious leader'; 'the incomparable man, by whose hand the destinies of Ireland in the hour of danger are fearlessly upheld'; and 'the man they will ever stand indebted to' because of his services to the nation.

Thomas Francis's address was also an eloquent appeal for, and defence of, constitutional and peaceful methods. He reminded his listeners that the Liberator 'at the present crisis, with more than ordinary anxiety, inculcates the precept of peace and solicitously recommends to the people the strict observance of the law'. He cautioned against being goaded into 'even one venal transgression' and delivered a forceful injunction for peaceful methods and an equally forceful rejection of violence: 'You lost your Parliament because of one senseless insurrection [in 1798]. Do not frustrate its restoration by another.' He continued:

> Do not dig up the broken pikes of '98 – let them rust and canker in the graves to which they have been consigned. A new weapon has been discovered since that fatal period, which is not only irresistible, but imperishable. The weapon is public opinion. By that weapon in modern times have factions adverse to popular rights been routed, have governments been dismembered, have thrones been shaken.

He reminded his audience that the power of public opinion had secured Catholic emancipation, the abolition of slavery, the extension of the elective franchise and corporate reform. He concluded by urging them all to continue to demand 'the [sic] repeal, the whole repeal, and nothing but repeal'.

The speech was well received. In fact, one of those in attendance, a Jeremiah O'Brien, declared himself so impressed that he was of the opinion that 'at the next election they should return that clever young gentleman as a repeal representative for the city'. He considered it 'nonsense' to talk about repeal 'unless we support an out and out repealer'.[53] Thomas Francis was clearly such a person in O'Brien's view.

The biographer of Thomas Meagher may be forgiven for speculating on his reaction to his son's speech. It was likely to have been one of real and deep satisfaction at an impressive exposition of the importance of constitutionalism, a forceful rejection of violence, and an unqualified endorsement of O'Connell's leadership. These were the very beliefs and ideals he had espoused and been advocating since the 1820s, and especially during his term as mayor. And another reason for satisfaction was that O'Brien's reaction was a definite indication that his son was beginning to take what his father would have considered as his desirable and rightful place in Waterford society: desirable and rightful in the sense of familial status, education and obvious natural ability. (One suspects also that the businessman in Thomas Meagher felt that the fees paid to the Jesuits were realising a dividend.) It is hard not to imagine that on Tuesday, 17 October 1843, father and son were never closer politically.

THOMAS FRANCIS MEAGHER: O'CONNELLITE

In his biography of Thomas Francis, Timothy Egan writes that 'the elder Meagher ... pressured the son of many words about his next step'.[54] While pressured may be somewhat of an overstatement, it is reasonable to assume that they spoke about his future career. In any case, Thomas Francis went to Dublin in 1844 to study at the Queen's Inns with a view to being called to the Irish bar. He arrived in January, during the state trial of O'Connell and others for sedition, which he attended occasionally.[55] As a confirmed repealer, he naturally attended the debates of the Repeal Association in Conciliation Hall, but only 'as a silent and interested spectator'.[56] Gradually, the excitement of nationalist politics came to occupy his time and by year's end he was no longer a student of law.

His father was likely disappointed at his son's decision to quit his studies, but Thomas Francis's increasing immersion in politics mitigated this reaction. A career in politics was a real prospect for his son and was suited to his status as the scion of a wealthy and influential family, his education and the promise he was displaying as an orator. Moreover, Robert Athearn, has noted: 'It is not strange that an Irish youth should consider politics as a field of endeavour during the forties, for it was during this decade that Ireland throbbed with a desire for legislative separation from England.'[57] In fact, the study of law may simply have been a preparation for such a career, Thomas Francis himself observing that the law 'was the main road to political preferment'.[58]

His biographers have focused their attention on his life in Dublin in 1844. What has been ignored was his engagement in the political and community life of Waterford city in that same year. His father was mayor, and 1844 may be viewed as a period during which his son was laying the foundations for his candidacy in the next parliamentary election for the Waterford city constituency. And he did this with the active support of his father.

There are two noteworthy aspects to the relationship between father and son during that year. First, Thomas Meagher was accompanied to many important public and political events by his son. In a previous chapter, reference was made to them, but only in relation to Mayor Meagher. Thomas Francis was also present. Such events included a dinner in honour of O'Connell in Cork in April;[59] a meeting of citizens in Waterford to prepare an address to the incarcerated repeal leader in June;[60] another such meeting in September to address him on his release from prison;[61] a banquet in Dublin to celebrate his release, also in September;[62] a meeting in Waterford to consider the erection of a monument in honour of Brother Edmund Ignatius Rice in October;[63] a demonstration and banquet in December to honour O'Connell in Waterford;[64] and a meeting in the city in the same month to oppose the Charitable Bequests Act.[65] The presence of both men suggests the closeness of their political relationship. These occasions also allowed Thomas Francis to establish a political and public profile, with a view to advancing his prospects as a candidate in any future parliamentary election. Equally important, their being together in each other's company suggests a closeness in their personal relationship. Clearly, there was a paternal–filial bond.

Second, these events confirm that Thomas Francis was a loyal O'Connellite. This fact has already been established in relation to the elder Meagher, but there is ample evidence in 1844 to support the same characterisation of his son. In the course of a meeting in Waterford on 5 June, he lauded O'Connell as 'the illustrious man who, from the bright spring of youth even to the glorious autumn of old age, has toiled for the freedom of his country through all the hard vicissitudes of a long political career'.[66] Addressing a repeal meeting at Tramore, County Waterford, in September, after the Liberator's release from prison, Thomas Francis declared O'Connell to be 'free, triumphant, invincible'. Continuing, he indulged in oratorical hyperbole: 'in vain, may we explore the histories to find a triumph equal in magnitude, comparable in glory, to that which the old patriarch of a captive people was rescued from his bondage'.[67] At another meeting, in Waterford city, a few days later, he again employed hyperbolical flourishes: 'Magnificent, enabled by his triumph, his name will stand out like one of the great pyramids in the wilderness of the future – illustrious, imperishable, amid the crash of sceptres and the fall of crowns.'[68]

Significantly, a testament to Thomas Francis's O'Connellite credentials may be found in his attack on the Charitable Bequests Act made at the Tramore repeal meeting in September:

> We must not forget that on 24 July a bill entitled 'the Charitable Bequests Bill, Ireland' was passed into law, in direct opposition to the earnest remonstrance of the clergy, the bishops and the people of Ireland, which bill (as the illustrious John [MacHale] of Tuam has fearlessly denounced it) surpasses, in the atrocity of its odious terms, the worst enactments of penal times and develops a refinement in legislation which the more clumsy artifices of the anti-Catholic code will in vain attempt to rival. No, not until the Irish House of Commons be re-opened and the Liberator stands upon its floor, shall that wrong be redressed ...[69]

In December he attended a meeting in Waterford's Catholic cathedral organised to express opposition to this statute.[70]

The political opinions of Thomas Meagher and those of his son were similar in 1844. They both subscribed to repeal of the Union, constitutionalism, the rejection of violence and loyalty to O'Connell. While these undoubtedly represented the views and beliefs of Thomas Francis, they were clearly influenced and shaped by those of his father. In an earlier chapter, the latter was described as the Liberator's 'political acolyte'; Thomas Francis may be accorded a similar appellation. However, during 1845 he was to fall increasingly under the influence of the ideals and teachings of the Young Ireland movement – thus beginning the sundering of his political relationship with his father.

CHAPTER NINE

Father and Son, 1845–1847: Political Divisions

Young Ireland, which became 'a party within a party',[1] had its origins in a number of recruits to the repeal cause, who were also associated with *The Nation* newspaper, which first appeared in October 1842. Thomas Davis, Charles Gavan Duffy, John Blake Dillon and their associates were, arguably, 'one of the most talented group of young men ever to combine in Irish politics'.[2] Through the pages of *The Nation*, it was argued that the Repeal Association 'should advance on a broader cultural front, with the demands for self-government bolstered by a strong assertion of Ireland's cultural distinctiveness and historical traditions'.[3] Irish claims for self-government were presented as that of a historic nation seeking to regain its independence.[4] For Young Irelanders, whose beliefs were informed by contemporary European ideas of romantic nationalism, nationality was a product of history, language and literature, and they had a mystical reverence for the very notion of the nation;[5] in Ó Tuathaigh's words: 'For the Young Irelanders the nation was a spiritual entity in itself.'[6]

YOUNG IRELAND VERSUS DANIEL O'CONNELL

When Daniel O'Connell emerged from Richmond Prison in September 1844, he had no clear idea of how the repeal movement should develop.[7] He came to regard the renewal of an alliance with the Whigs as a realistic and pragmatic alternative to repeal agitation and as a means of bolstering his flagging political influence. However, Michael Cavanagh observed: 'The Young Irelanders in Conciliation Hall determined to treat the rumour of any compromise with the Whigs as incredible and its consummation as treason to Ireland.'[8] For them repeal was a hallowed cause that could not be compromised, as such an act would constitute sacrilege against their belief in the sacred character of the nation. Any arrangement with any British political party hostile to granting an Irish parliament was a betrayal of the national movement to which Young Ireland had contributed such vitality. O'Connell's pragmatic attitude to politics, and to the Whigs, seemed to his Young Ireland critics to be nothing more than the worst manifestation of a grubby and base political opportunism that was all too ready to compromise high national ideals and principles for the filthy lucre of immediate advantage and gain at Westminster. In their eyes, Westminster was a veritable cesspool of political corruption, from which British politicians had despoiled Ireland of its independent nationhood and rich natural resources. For this 'purist elite',[9] the call of Thomas Davis 'for a nationality reified through righteousness provided a stirring antidote to the failure of late O'Connellism'.[10]

The reality is that 'the Irish national movement had taken shape on the basis of a personal leadership and command. The hero at the centre, O'Connell, acted as the focus, marshal and arbiter of aspirations, as champion, father-figure and vicarious achiever all in one'.[11] O'Connell's very dominance of the repeal movement meant that his failings were highlighted in relief for Young Irelanders. He was subjected by them to a level of microscopic examination applied to no other contemporary Irish politician. His every error, inconsistency and policy reversal were noted and commented upon by the younger men, who regarded themselves as the pure-hearted opponents of a leader whose political style and pragmatism they viewed as suspect, at the very least.[12] His Young Ireland critics began to express concern at a lack of accountability for his actions and management of the Repeal Association's funds. The Liberator had become accustomed to a certain docile servility in the repeal ranks. O'Connell resented criticism and those making it, in turn, resented his intolerant reactions. All of this had the effect of exacerbating unease and tensions.

These tensions also had an inevitable generational aspect – young, idealistic political neophytes bridling at and rebelling against what they regarded as the dictatorial leadership style of a gerontocrat – a man who had been dominating political life since the second decade of the century, even before some Young Irelanders had been born. Furthermore, the leader was now ageing (and looking even more aged through youthful eyes) and power seemed to be in the process of being transferred to his heir apparent, his son, John O'Connell, who commanded little or no respect among the Young Ireland group. Thus, the unease and recriminations between this section of the Repeal Association and the O'Connellites were intensified by 'a sublimated succession battle'.[13]

THOMAS FRANCIS MEAGHER: YOUNG IRELANDER

Like many Irish people of his class, Thomas Francis Meagher was 'an ardent admirer' of *The Nation* newspaper.[14] In its columns he was exposed, in particular, to the ideas of Thomas Davis, 'the principal ideologue' of Young Ireland.[15] John Mitchel, in a memoir of Meagher, commented on the influence Davis, 'that most puissant and imperial character', exerted on the young men of his day and how Thomas Francis had been 'inspired, possessed by him'.[16] Thus, 'in the lengthening light of spring, 1845, he became infatuated with the rarest kind of subversive: a poet with power'.[17] The premature death of Davis at the age of thirty, on 16 September 1845, was regarded by him as 'an unspeakable calamity'[18] and occasioned his first public appearance on the platform of Conciliation Hall, later in the same month, at a meeting to honour the dead man's memory.[19] He hastened from Waterford to be in attendance and declared in his address: 'His meteor genius has ceased to burn – his noble heart to beat. But there are thoughts of his generous sentiments, liberal views, enlightened principles of his which death could not strike down.'[20] He was to subscribe to a memorial to remember Davis.[21] In the months following his death, young writers and intellectuals became involved in *The Nation*, including Meagher. They were to revitalise the repeal movement, but more on the side of Young Ireland than Daniel O'Connell and Old Ireland.[22]

Thomas Francis Meagher's increasing gravitation towards Young Ireland was revealed in a letter published in newspapers in Waterford in November 1845. This letter followed a meeting held in the city on 7 November to organise the national tribute to O'Connell and at which Thomas Francis acted as secretary.[23] On this occasion his father proposed a motion lauding the Liberator's opposition to the Queen's Colleges. The next day Thomas Francis wrote a letter to the editor of *The Waterford Freeman*, which was also published in a number of other newspapers. In it he dissociated himself from the resolution relating to the Queen's Colleges. He stated unequivocally that he was 'an ardent advocate of the principles of "mixed education"'. He argued that such a system would be productive of advantage to the country: 'They who had been companions in their youth would be colleagues in their manhood. Thus, a sound union of parties would be gently, yet nobly, accomplished; and sectarianism, the most serious obstacle to the progress of the nation, would be forever removed.'[24] (This letter was to be cited in an effort to inflict damage on Meagher in the course of a bitter election campaign in February 1848.[25]) In a subsequent letter he reaffirmed his support for mixed education.[26]

In these two letters Thomas Francis made no reference to the fact that his father had proposed the motion from which he was now dissenting. This fact, however, would have been known in the city. A major point of difference, controversy and bitterness between Old and Young Ireland was being highlighted in Waterford's newspapers, introducing into the public domain the contrasting and conflicting views of Thomas Meagher and his son on this significant political issue. Their differences were to be further reinforced before the end of 1845, when Thomas Meagher was named by O'Connellite repealers as a potential candidate for Waterford city in the next general election.[27]

Throughout 1846, John Mitchel in *The Nation* newspaper and Thomas Francis Meagher in Conciliation Hall spearheaded an assault on the proposed alliance between O'Connell and the Whigs,[28] and affirmed the uncompromising conviction of Young Ireland in the repeal cause. On 16 March Meagher denounced the Whigs as the 'foes' of Irish freedom.[29] Speaking on 15 June, the day the Whigs assumed government office, he declared that 'whatever statesmen rule the empire … the principles of this [Repeal] Association are immutable.'[30] He called on true repealers to oppose the Whigs at the next election.[31] At later meetings, he reminded his listeners that they had made a vow to campaign for repeal,[32] and asserted that 'any repealer taking office under the present [Whig] government was an apostate from the cause'.[33]

EMERGING FROM HIS FATHER'S SHADOW

Meagher's increasing commitment to Young Ireland had consequences for his relationship with his father. On his return to Waterford in 1843, his position in society was very much defined by his being Thomas Meagher's son. His involvement in public events and his being invited to speak at political meetings was by virtue of the fact that he was the mayor's son. His oratorical prowess certainly confirmed his meriting an invitation, but his initial access to the public platform was because of his family's and, in particular, his father's status. In the newspapers he was generally mentioned in association with Thomas Meagher, e.g. 'our excellent mayor and his highly gifted son'.[34] Charles Gavan Duffy, after his release from Richmond Prison, where he had been incarcerated with O'Connell, went on a tour of Munster. He recounted that 'in Waterford … whilst we hastily visited the historic places, the "son of the mayor" was reported at various parts to be in search of us, but we exulted in escaping his pursuit; and only came to know him two years later as Thomas Francis Meagher …'.[35] When he first arrived in Dublin, he 'was well known to be the son of the Mayor of Waterford'.[36]

Thomas Francis did not make a particularly favourable initial impression on some of those he met in Dublin. Gavan Duffy described the lines of Meagher's face as 'so round as to give him a character of languor and indolence … To the common eyes the new recruit [to Young Ireland] was a dandified youngster with a languid air and a mincing accent, derived from his English education'.[37] John Mitchel's first impressions were equally underwhelming: 'To me, at first, he seemed merely a rather foppish young gentleman, with an accent decidedly English'.[38] He was, however, a young man looking for a meaningful role and purpose in life, the need of which was likely accentuated by an awareness of his father's success and position, and his family's status. The nationalist politics of Young Ireland satisfied this need. When Arthur Griffith wrote that 'Meagher found himself when he found his country', he was speaking a substantive truth.[39] Duffy noted the change which came over him: 'But after a little while, [Meagher] addressed the [Repeal] Association in language such as it had never heard, language not only of conviction, but of passion, poetry and imagination.'[40] His impact on Young Ireland clearly depended on his powerful oratory; to again quote Griffith:

> His eloquence at the public meetings in Conciliation Hall quickly made him celebrated in the capital, and any announcement that Meagher would speak crowded the hall; for his was an eloquence that before was not heard within its walls, where there was no lack of trained and accomplished speakers. Passion and poetry transfigured his words and he evoked for the first time in many breasts a manly consciousness of national right and dignity. As handsome and chivalrous as he was eloquent, he became something of a popular idol and [was] eagerly sought after in the social circles of Dublin.[41]

With his involvement in Young Ireland, Thomas Francis began emerging from his father's shadow and carving out an independent political and social role.

How did Thomas Meagher regard his son's progress? On balance, probably with qualified approval. This was perfect preparation, after all, for a career in politics, as a future MP for Waterford city. This satisfaction was likely tempered with some reservations about Thomas Francis's association with Young Irelanders, a group championing the establishment of the Queen's Colleges. It was Young Meagher's emergence as a spokesman for Young Ireland that would erect political barriers between him and his father: they were to find themselves on opposite sides when the Repeal Association split in July 1846.

DIVISIONS IN THE REPEAL ASSOCIATION

Thomas Francis Meagher's increasing prominence within Young Ireland and the Repeal Association was evident when he was selected to chair a meeting in Conciliation Hall on 8 June 1846.[42] By that time it was evident that the days of Robert Peel's Tory government were numbered because of internal divisions over the repeal of the Corn Laws. (Peel's government was to fall by the end of the month.) It was equally evident that O'Connell was determined to enter into an alliance with the Whigs, who seemed poised on the threshold of power. June proved to be a tense month in the relationship between the Young Irelanders and O'Connell, and Thomas Francis was regarded by the Liberator as contributing to this circumstance. In a speech delivered on 15 June, Meagher described Thomas Davis as 'our prophet and guide',[43] causing offence to O'Connell's supporters, who believed their leader alone deserved such an elevated title. O'Connell regarded Meagher's speech as 'a base attack on me', describing the oration as 'claptraps by juvenile orators'. [44] A by-election was imminent in Kilkenny and he revealed the depth of his antipathy to Young Ireland and Meagher by rejecting a proposal that the latter be considered as a suitable candidate. According to O'Connell:

> Kilkenny [county] must return a repealer, and I cannot possibly permit it to return either a Tory or a Whig or an animal more mischievous than either of the others, called a Young Irelander ... Nothing could afflict me more than any leaning to Meagher after his recent misconduct. I really think him more dangerous than that undermining fellow – [Michael] Doheny.[45]

He warned that Meagher and his colleagues 'are actually ruining the repeal cause. It will, I fear, become impossible to work the Repeal Association with them.'[46]

This conviction was amplified in the same month of June when the new Whig prime minister, Lord John Russell, denounced Young Ireland in the House of Commons as a revolutionary body intent upon the separation of Britain and Ireland by violent means.[47] O'Connell decided to act and drive Young Ireland from the Repeal Association to demonstrate to the Whigs that he was in complete control of the repeal movement and that it was free from any taint of unconstitutionality or illegality.[48] The 'peace resolutions' were to be his chosen method.

O'Connell decided to demand that all members of the Repeal Association adopt a pledge to repudiate the use of physical force in any and all circumstances.[49] The question of the use of physical force was an entirely abstract one: no one in the association, including the Young Irelanders, was advocating violent means in the pursuit of constitutional and political objectives. Young Ireland, however, could not accept the universal principle that the use of force was wrong in every circumstance. The issue was debated in Conciliation Hall on 27 and 28 July. Thomas Francis spoke on the latter day and his contribution was to enter the Irish nationalist lexicon as 'The Sword Speech'.[50] He clearly stated his reasons for opposing the resolutions: no member of the association, including himself, was suggesting recourse to arms, but he could not assent to an unqualified repudiation of physical force:

> I do not abhor the use of arms in the vindication of national rights. There are times when arms alone suffice, and when political ameliorations call for a drop of blood and many thousand drops of blood ... force must be used against force ... The man that will listen to reason – let him be reasoned with, but it is the weaponed arm of the patriot that can alone prevail against battalioned despotism ... I do not disclaim the use of arms as immoral, nor do I believe it is the truth to say that the God of Heaven withholds his sanction from the use of arms ... His almighty hand hath ever been stretched forth from His throne of light to consecrate the flag of freedom – to bless the patriot sword. Be it for defence or be it for the assertion of a nation's liberty, I look upon the sword as a sacred weapon ... Abhor the sword? Stigmatise the sword? No ... for at its blow, and in the quivering of its crimson light a giant nation sprang up from the waters of the Atlantic, and by its redeeming magic the fettered colony became a daring, free republic ...[51]

Meagher was interrupted by John O'Connell, who had been commissioned by his absent father to allow no concessions to the Young Irelanders. He accused Meagher of uttering sentiments completely at variance with the principles of the Repeal Association. When it became apparent to the Young Irelanders present that it was impossible for Meagher to continue, he, together with William Smith O'Brien, John Mitchel and Charles Gavan Duffy, led their supporters out of Conciliation Hall, never to return.[52] Daniel O'Connell had achieved his objective: the secession of his opponents by the manipulation of a spurious quarrel between Old and Young Ireland to facilitate a possible alliance with the Whigs.

The supporters of Young Ireland regarded Meagher's 'Sword Speech' as a tour de force. Michael Doheny recalled the reaction in Conciliation Hall to his 'most impassioned oration': 'The meeting yielded to the frankness, sincerity, enthusiasm and supreme eloquence of the young orator, and rewarded him by its uncontrollable and unanimous applause.'[53] Michael Cavanagh wrote that 'the enthusiasm it evoked is indescribable'. He noted that older people compared Meagher with Emmet: 'Reminiscences of Emmet were recalled, and loving comparisons instituted between the idol of their youthful prime and the hero who seemed destined by providence to be his heir and avenger.'[54] The speech secured for Meagher a position of leadership in the post-secession Young Ireland movement. However, the next year and a half were to be very difficult for this movement, as it struggled to establish itself in the Irish political landscape.[55]

IRISH CONFEDERATION

In the aftermath of their secession, Daniel O'Connell used every meeting of the Repeal Association to denounce the members of Young Ireland in the most vehement terms.[56] John Mitchel noted that, 'Meagher had his full share of the odium which many people attached to us for daring to differ in anything from the great Liberator.'[57] Indeed, Meagher himself was to comment in December 1846: 'Some say I have much to answer for. The guilt of the physical force debate has been exclusively attached to me.'[58] He and his colleagues had to forge a way in politics having been cut adrift from the Repeal Association. For much of the next eighteen months or so – up until February 1848 – they lacked a sense of coherent political direction. The seceders looked to the one person with something of a public profile and stature to lead them: William Smith O'Brien, MP for County Limerick and acting leader of the Repeal Association during O'Connell's incarceration. They looked in vain, and in the words of Smith O'Brien's biographer: 'The disarray into which Young Ireland later fell owed much to the abdication of their only natural leader. If Smith O'Brien had any claims to greatness, it was forfeited not in the tragic events of July 1848, but in his failure to give effective leadership during the preceding years.'[59]

In January 1847 Young Ireland configured itself into the Irish Confederation. Thomas Francis Meagher played a prominent role at its inaugural meeting and was elected to its governing council.[60] On the resignation of Charles Gavan Duffy, he was to replace him as one of the confederation's secretaries.[61] The political rudderlessness that was a defining characteristic of the organisation for most of its existence is apparent in the fact that by December 1847 it still had not developed a coherent policy statement.[62] Its weakness is further underscored by the fact that its most prominent members, such as Gavan Duffy and Meagher, did not contest a seat in the August 1847 general election. This was a clear recognition that their prospects against Repeal Association candidates were dismal in the emotive political climate fostered by O'Connell's death in May. A common trope of Old Ireland was the accusation that Young Irelanders had hastened the Liberator's death by their opposition to him.

The absence of the Irish Confederation from this electoral contest was a significant obstacle to its emergence as a political force in 1847. Further problems confronted the confederation in January 1847 when it was beset by internal dissension and divisions, as John Mitchel and his supporters advocated militant policies in place of constitutionalism. By February, the organisation was split.[63] Mitchel and some of his allies withdrew from the council of the confederation and founded a newspaper, *United Irishman*, to give expression to their militancy.

REPEAL ASSOCIATION AND IRISH CONFEDERATION COMPARED

The schism in the Repeal Association in July 1846 and the foundation of the Irish Confederation in January 1847 found Thomas Meagher and Thomas Francis Meagher on opposite sides, being representatives of Old Ireland and Young Ireland respectively. By February 1848, after more than eighteen months of political drama, recrimination and division, how exactly did Old Ireland differ from Young Ireland, O'Connellites from Young Irelanders and Thomas Meagher from Thomas Francis? Notwithstanding the existence of two organisations, in early 1848 the O'Connellite Repeal Association and the Young Ireland Irish Confederation still shared common objectives and political methods. Though they had seceded from O'Connell's association, Thomas Francis, addressing a meeting of Young Irelanders on 2 December 1846, declared: 'We insist upon repeal ...'[64] At the inaugural meeting of the Irish Confederation in January 1847, it was resolved 'That a society be now founded under the title "The Irish Confederation" for the purpose of protecting our national interests and obtaining the legislative independence of Ireland ...'[65] As with the Repeal Association, the Irish Confederation's main objective was repeal of the Union and members of the confederation continued to refer to themselves as repealers throughout 1847.[66]

Both the Irish Confederation and the Repeal Association were committed to constitutional and peaceful means in the pursuit of their objectives. Meagher's 'Sword Speech' must not be allowed to obscure this fact and was delivered in a particular context. To quote Meagher in his address to the meeting of 2 December: 'I fully concurred in his [John O'Connell's] condemnation of the sword as an instrument unfitted to achieve the independence of Ireland. I stated this distinctly. But, recollecting that it had been destructive of despotism in other lands, I refused to join in the sweeping condemnation he had made.'[67] Each speaker at the December meeting disavowed the use of physical force in the pursuit of an Irish parliament.[68] The Irish Confederation affirmed its espousal of peaceful means, seeking to achieve repeal 'by the force of opinion, by the combination of all classes of Irishmen, and by the exercise of all the political, social and moral influences within our reach'.[69] Confirming its adherence to legal and peaceful methods, the council of the confederation submitted its constitution to a queen's counsel to ensure its compliance with the law.[70] The first meeting of its governing council appointed a committee to prepare a petition to Parliament in favour of repeal.[71] In January 1848, when the confederation was confronted with John Mitchel's advocacy of more radical, non-constitutional politics, Meagher wrote to William Smith O'Brien: 'I am convinced that the only mode which we can adopt – the only policy we can successfully conduct – is the constitutional policy advised by Duffy.'[72] In February Meagher supported proposals put forward by Smith O'Brien in support of achieving repeal by constitutional means.[73]

Demonstrably, on the central matter of political objectives and methods, the newly formed repeal society – for that is what it was – calling itself the Irish Confederation, shared similar objectives and methods with O'Connell's Repeal Association. Thus, Thomas Meagher, a confirmed Old Irelander and his son, Thomas Francis, a confirmed Young Irelander, did not differ on these critical political issues.

The Repeal Association and the Irish Confederation were similar in another important respect: the leadership of both organisations was dominated by members of the middle class, of which Thomas Meagher and Thomas Francis Meagher were quintessential representatives. The bourgeois origins of the leaders of O'Connell's national movements had been well established since the 1820s. The Irish Confederation was no different: the majority of its forty-member council was drawn from this section of society.[74] This middle-class control of the leadership of the organisation explains its political and social conservatism, making it a mirror image of the Repeal Association in that regard. Both Young Ireland and O'Connell were anxious to win the landowners over to the repeal cause, regarding them as the natural leaders of an independent society. To achieve this, a cautious approach was adopted to policy formulation lest the landed classes be alarmed by any hint of radicalism.[75]

Thomas Francis Meagher, in the course of a speech in February 1848, criticising Mitchel's militant ideas, revealed himself a social conservative: 'Nor do I wish … that this movement should be a democratic movement. I desire that it should continue to be what it has been, a national movement, not of any one class, but of all classes … No, I am not for a democratic, but I am for a national movement.'[76]

The Young Irelanders believed the nation to be superior to all sectional interests and regarded nationality as a force which somehow would resolve the many conflicts in Irish society.[77] Thus, Meagher was urging the sublimation of social issues in the unifying spirit of nationalism. For him, the attention of the Irish Confederation was to be directed on national, and not on class or sectional concerns, as such issues could be politically divisive. Clearly, Thomas Francis Meagher did not envisage the Irish Confederation heralding a social revolution; repeal was about a radical change in the constitution, not in society.[78] Writing in 1847 he declared: 'I desire to see this country raised to the position of an independent nation … I would prefer, however, to have this done by the confederate power of the ARISTOCRACY and the PEOPLE, rather than the power of the

DEMOCRACY alone. In the former case, the social arrangements of the country would be less disturbed ...'[79]

These were opinions with which his father would have concurred, words spoken by Daniel O'Connell articulating the elder Meagher's outlook: 'I desire no social revolution, no social change ... In short, salutary restoration [of an Irish parliament] without revolution.'[80]

The substantive matter dividing the Irish Confederation and the Repeal Association was the issue of an alliance with the Whigs. William Smith O'Brien, one of the most influential members of the confederation, identified such an alliance as the principal obstacle to any reconciliation between the feuding organisations. What he described as 'Whig repealers' would have to renounce this political relationship before any serious discussion could begin on the restoration of a united repeal movement.[81] In 1847 the Irish Confederation declared 'that the basis and essence of the Irish Confederation shall be absolute independence of all English parties.'[82] Supporters of Young Ireland believed that there could be no alliance with the Whigs or any other English party because they were fundamentally hostile to repeal and the price of any such alliance would inevitably involve compromising the demand for repeal. Quite simply, for the Irish Confederation being independent of English politicians was a *sine qua non* of any movement demanding an Irish parliament. Thomas Francis Meagher gave expression to such sentiments at the inaugural meeting of the confederation:

> You cannot serve the minister who is pledged to maintain the Union and serve the people who are pledged to repeal it ... Will the repealers fight the Whigs upon the hustings with Whig favours in their pockets? Recollect the Union was carried by Irishmen receiving English gold. Depend upon it, the same system will not accelerate its repeal. The trappings of the Treasury will restrict them [repealers] more than the shackles of a prison.[83]

Repeal was an absolute demand: Ireland's parliamentary independence was non-negotiable. In truth, for Young Ireland purists, who regarded the Irish nation as a spiritual entity, a Whig alliance represented, on a fundamental level, an existential threat to the rights of this same nation.

For O'Connell this simply was not the case; repeal was not non-negotiable. The Liberator was very careful not to define exactly what he meant by it. He did not put forward a specific proposition when launching his political movement.[84] Roy Foster is correct when he commented that 'by "repeal" O'Connell probably meant, first, a recognition of the illegitimacy of the Union; and then negotiation of an alternative mechanism of government'.[85] While he delineated, in general terms, the outline form of this alternative form of government – 'an Irish parliament, British connection, one king, two legislatures'[86] – it would be necessary to engage in discussions and negotiations with the English government to construct a new constitutional architecture between the two countries. In his campaign the word 'repeal' became a popular rallying cry against the misgovernment of Ireland from Westminster, in a calculated attempt to rouse the Irish people to a fever pitch of opposition to the Union. Thus, he hoped to intimidate the government into making an offer to restore political calm. In effect, his repeal campaign was a prelude to negotiations.[87] Unlike Young Ireland, O'Connell did not recoil from the prospect of such negotiations, a fact to which the Lichfield House Compact of 1835–41 bore testimony. His willingness to consider another alliance with the Whigs in 1846 represented for him a realistic response to the political situation facing him: the urgency to devise an alternative strategy in the aftermath of the Clontarf debacle. The divisions and fissures which this prospective détente caused between O'Connell and Young Ireland was a consequence of a conflict between ideological purists and idealists, and a leader whose perspective on politics was pragmatic and utilitarian. Critically, O'Connell did not conceive the Irish nation as a spiritual entity; for him it simply meant all the inhabitants of Ireland as an aggregate.[88] Hence, negotiation and compromise with the Whigs were not anathemas.

In the matter of parliamentary tactics, such as negotiations with the Whigs, loyal O'Connellites like Thomas Meagher accepted the Liberator's leadership. This acceptance highlighted a factor which divided Old and Young Ireland, and contributed very significantly to the recrimination and bitterness of the split: contrasting perspectives on O'Connell's management of the national movement. Oliver MacDonagh has observed that, 'The type of leadership O'Connell exercised in the early 1840s was, in many respects, more dominating than that of ten or twelve years before. His organisational structures were more pyramidical, his associates more decidedly lieutenants, the nationalist newspapers more his instruments.'[89] He was very intolerant of criticism and unreceptive to new ideas. His final years of national leadership were 'surely not his best'.[90] His deteriorating health further undermined his undoubted erstwhile energy and ability. This was the O'Connell Young Ireland encountered and their perspective on him was shaped by their experience of a man who no longer was the political force he once had been.

Old Irelanders, such as Thomas Meagher, took a wider perspective, one informed by their knowledge and experience of his national leadership since the 1820s. For them he was dynamic and creative, a force of nature, whose achievements were many and impressive. In the 1820s he led the struggle which resulted in Catholic emancipation, an achievement that 'was meaningful because it was seen as a great civil rights issue, as a way of recognising in law that Catholics were equal to Protestants and an acknowledgement that the majority population on the island need no longer feel inferior'.[91] During the 1830s 'he sustained an endless succession of organisations, maintained a highly visible parliamentary presence, made endless speeches, supported numerous reforms and ... successfully affirmed his position as the undoubted leader of popular and Catholic opinion'.[92] The 1840s witnessed, after a long campaign led by O'Connell, a reform in municipal government and mobilisation of a vast section of the Irish population in pursuit of repeal. O'Connell's achievements were often imperfect, but were nonetheless regarded by his supporters as an improvement in conditions for Catholics. All this helps explain why Thomas Meagher and Old Ireland remained loyal to the Liberator – vistas of his political accomplishments opened before them.

In the course of a speech to the Repeal Association in June 1846, Thomas Francis Meagher identified, albeit unknowingly and unintentionally, this reason for the loyalty of Old Irelanders to O'Connell. Addressing the Liberator's dismissive description of Young Ireland as 'juvenile orators', he defended its contribution to the repeal cause. He continued: 'Youth is a season of promise more than of retrospect. We cannot rest upon the memory of past services – we cannot appeal to your gratitude'.[93] These words, though used in a different context, actually give a critical reason as to why his father remained an O'Connellite repealer. The Liberator, from the perspective of Thomas Meagher, could rest upon his achievements and appeal to the gratitude of his supporters because of his more than two decades of political campaigning in the cause of Ireland. He had a retrospect of twenty-five years; his son and his associates not much more than five.

There was a clear generational divide in the contrasting and conflicting perspectives on O'Connell's accomplishments; as Denis Gwynn has noted: 'But the younger men had no recollection of the fierce fight he had sustained to achieve even the right of free speech.'[94] Moreover, within months of their secession from the Repeal Association, *The Nation* was revising the historical record to play down O'Connell's achievement in winning Catholic emancipation. This 'signalled what would become a recurrent theme in Young Ireland accounts of these years, namely the disparagement of O'Connell and his contribution to Irish history'.[95] Thomas Meagher never abandoned O'Connell because of the difficulties he was experiencing in the 1840s: in the preceding twenty-five years, personal seeds of deep and abiding loyalty, admiration and gratitude were sown, and it was Old Ireland and O'Connell, and not Young Ireland and his son, that were to reap the harvest.

Whatever about the political reasons for the differences between Old and Young Ireland, the fissures were transformed into chasms by the near-collective animus of O'Connell and his followers towards those who challenged and rejected the Liberator's leadership of the repeal movement. For Conciliation Hall repealers, the actions and words of Young Ireland were akin to *lése majesté*. Any prospect of reconciliation foundered amidst recriminations, as the vitriolic language of the O'Connellites created a toxic relationship between the two repeal factions. The confederates were subjected to particular abuse because of their support for the Queen's Colleges, which allowed their opponents to represent them as enemies of the Catholic faith, an especially damaging charge. The death of Daniel O'Connell, within a year of the split in the Repeal Association, intensified passions.

Thomas Francis Meagher's role in the events inspired many personal attacks against him, such as the one in a letter published in *The Chronicle* in May 1847:

[He] has had the adamant impudence and audacious temerity to assail, belie and calumniate the character; misrepresent and suspect the motives; scoff at and denounce the prudence of the veteran patriot, through whose mighty exertions, profound wisdom and scrupulous honesty this *boy* has been emancipated from the corroding shackles of penal laws and persecution the most direful ... What has he [Thomas Francis Meagher] done for Ireland? What are his testimonials of service, his credentials of success? ... his success exists in his being the father, a youthful father of dissension, destruction, contention, confusion and everything disastrous in the heretofore united and invincible repeal body.[96]

Attitudes such as these strengthened and perpetuated hostilities between the two factions of the repeal movement.

IRRELEVANCE OF REPEAL ASSOCIATION AND IRISH CONFEDERATION

With all their differences, there was one very significant thing which the Repeal Association and the Irish Confederation had in common: their utter irrelevance in the lives (and in the deaths) of so many Irish people in 1846 and 1847, years when Ireland was being ravished by famine and disease. The peace resolutions, the speeches they elicited and the subsequent acrimony between O'Connell and Young Ireland are strikingly incongruous against the backdrop of the 3,020,712 people who were fed at soup kitchens on 3 July 1847[97] and 68,890 inmates of workhouses who died in the same year.[98] Politics were failing the people of Ireland at a time of cataclysmic crisis; the eloquence of the various parties on both sides of the divided repeal movement echoed across a desolate Irish landscape. The privations of the Famine exposed something that every nationalist movement disguises: 'the almost total irrelevance of constitutional questions to the basic things of life, such as the provision of food'.[99] The words of *The Waterford Freeman* describing the plight of John Sheehy and his family, of Abbeyside, Dungarvan, County Waterford, in May 1847, jar with the finest orations of Old and Young Ireland:

We found him on his knees offering up his privations and sufferings to his Creator; his poor wife was striving to console her famishing children by promising them that 'God would send them relief to-morrow.' They did not eat a morsel of food that day, and the mother said that herself and John, her husband, did not care about themselves, but the poor children. 'When they were asking for something to eat and when we have nothing to give them, their cries go through our hearts; they must (added the unfortunate woman in a subdued tone) go to bed supperless tonight; and 'tis long since they got anything like a supper or dinner before.' When she got up to open the door, she faltered and fell prostrate on the floor from exhaustion. This is but a faint idea of the condition of the poor of Abbeyside.[100]

While it is easy to be wise after the event, it is difficult not to agree with Mary Daly's observation that, 'O'Connell and the Young Irelanders could have devoted less time to squabbling over political issues and more attention to the condition of the people.'[101] Thus, the Meaghers, father and son, were united by the fact that the opposing organisations they supported were directionless and irrelevant by January 1848. However, membership of these same conflicting organisations was to bring the two men into personal political conflict in 1847 and 1848.

CHAPTER TEN

Two Elections, 1847, 1848

In the course of a speech on 15 June 1846, Thomas Francis Meagher called on repealers to vote for no man who was not a member of the Repeal Association. He continued:

> I know that to pursue this line of conduct manfully, a sacrifice of personal interest – more than all, a sacrifice of private feeling – may be required from some of us. But the cause is worthy of the most severe sacrifice which men could undergo. I tell you candidly, if my father was in Parliament, and had up to this period refused to join the association, were he at the next election to present himself to his constituency and ask their votes again, I would be the first to vote against him. It is better that the heart of a few should be pained than that the great heart of the nation should be broken.[1]

Meagher was essentially arguing that political principles were not to be compromised or discarded for personal considerations. As he uttered these words, he cannot have known that he and his father were each to face such a situation at elections in 1847 and 1848.

GENERAL ELECTION, 1847

Thomas Meagher was a successful candidate in the 1847 general election in the Waterford city constituency. In advance of this contest, however, there is evidence of some rumblings of discontent directed at him because of the activities of his son. A letter published in *The Chronicle* in May 1847 commented that 'the "star" of the Young Ireland farce is a native of this city and that he has been allowed – I will not say encouraged – to gratify his love of oratory at the expense of repeal without receiving any public admonition from his respected father [and] that he has indulged in this love to an enormous and extravagant extent'.[2] An editorial in the same journal in July on Thomas Meagher's election address also suggests certain reservations about him, which likely had their origins in his son's Young Ireland leanings.[3]

Thomas Francis Meagher, consistent with his statement that political principles could not be compromised for personal reasons, did not support his father's candidacy, on the basis that he was an O'Connellite, while his son was associated with Young Ireland. On the evidence of the coverage of the election in newspapers, the political differences between them do not appear to have featured during the campaign. Both were present in the courthouse during the nomination of candidates at the commencement of polling on 4 August 1847. However, considering the prevailing tensions between Young and Old Ireland, it was perhaps inevitable that some supporters of the Irish Confederation used the occasion to promote their cause and to cheer one of its most articulate advocates in the person of Thomas Francis. One of the most prominent O'Connellite repealers, Alderman James Delahunty, was interrupted while making a speech by a person, in the words of *The Chronicle*, 'calling on Mr Thomas Francis Meagher, who was in the gallery, to carry out the principles of the confederation'. He was interrupted a second time by a person calling for Thomas Francis Meagher. According to *The Chronicle*, 'Mr Meagher stated that he would be sorry to identify himself with any disturbance there'.[4]

While Thomas Francis believed that he could not support his father in the election, he did not engage in active opposition. Furthermore, the manner in which he disavowed any association with any disturbance suggests that he did not wish to cause him any embarrassment. Thomas Francis's presence in the courthouse on that day appears to have had no political motivation; his reason was personal: he was there out of respect, even affection, for his father on what was a very important day for him.

The divisions apparent in the summer and autumn of 1847 weakened both repeal groups, while showing that the repeal movement was still bitterly divided.[5] The prospects of the Irish Confederation began to improve, however, with the emergence of political clubs affiliated to it during and after the general election. Called 'Confederate Clubs', they were intended to provide the confederation with a network of local support and were regarded by Thomas Francis Meagher and other leaders as forming the basis of a mass party.[6] These clubs were mostly located in cities and towns and had little support in the countryside. In August *The Chronicle* reported on meetings in Waterford of confederate supporters with a view to establishing a club. It was claimed that one meeting was held, in his absence, in the library of the residence of Thomas Meagher on the Mall and was presided over by his son, Thomas Francis. Moreover, it was stated that Thomas Meagher's other son, Henry, while not in attendance, was 'a true believer in the new gospel', though there is no evidence to corroborate this allegation that Henry was a Young Ireland supporter.[7] A Confederate Club, called after Wolfe Tone, was subsequently founded in the city.

WATERFORD BY-ELECTION, 1848

In February 1848 Daniel O'Connell Junior, one of the two MPs for Waterford city, resigned his seat in the House of Commons. On 10 February there was a meeting of a body styling itself a 'committee of citizens' to consider the parliamentary vacancy. Describing themselves as true and uncompromising O'Connellite repealers, they reaffirmed their support for the repeal of the legislative union between Great Britain and Ireland. Resolutions were adopted that any candidate seeking their suffrages should be 'an undoubted repealer'. It was decided to convene a meeting on 14 February to select a candidate who would represent the opinion of the 'true hearted repealers' of the city.[8]

Thomas Francis Meagher was present at the meeting on 14 February, together with a strong contingent of supporters of the Irish Confederation, a fact which caused the O'Connellite repealers some surprise. Divisions between the opposing factions were immediately apparent. When a resolution was proposed expressing regret at the retirement of Daniel

O'Connell, Meagher declared his opposition, stating that it would be 'rank hypocrisy' to associate himself with it. From the moment he began to speak, confusion ensued. The meeting descended into disorder as O'Connellite and confederate supporters attempted to drown each other out. Such was the chaos that the meeting was adjourned.[9]

The reconvened meeting on 16 February proved to be a dramatic event. Thomas Francis was not in attendance due to illness. Roger Hayes, acting as his representative, announced at the outset of proceedings Meagher's intention to be a candidate in the forthcoming by-election and his determination to contest it 'to the last – yes, to the last penny in his possession and, if necessary, with the last drop of his blood'. Confusion immediately ensued between the rival groups of Young Ireland and O'Connellite repealers, with the latter determined to nominate a candidate who reflected their own political views. As the meeting became more heated and ill-tempered, Hayes attempted to read a written message he had received from Meagher, reiterating his resolute determination to be a candidate: 'I protest against any and every arrangement that may be proposed at this meeting. I will abide by the legal and constitutional arrangements of the poll, and by no other on God's earth and I entreat my friends to back me to the last in this determination.'

At this juncture, a Fr Cuddihy, a staunch O'Connellite repealer, interjected with the comment that he had something to say that would surprise those in attendance. He had in his possession a letter from Thomas Meagher, who was in London attending Parliament, to local repeal activist, J. Everard Feehan, which he proceeded to read:

> I have just moved the new writ for Waterford, so prepare and let there be no division in the repeal ranks. Let the electors choose the man they think will serve them best, above all in trying to repeal the Union ... it [the repeal cause] is dreaded [by the government] and nothing has tended more to produce this feeling than the spirited return at the last election of some men who are not to be diverted from the national cause by any influence that can be brought to bear upon them, and there can be no better course to pursue than for every constituency in Ireland, that has its true interests at heart, to labour to increase the number of such men in the House [of

Commons]. I am disposed to think that of all those named for Waterford, Mr [Patrick] Costelloe is the one most likely to prove a faithful representative to the repealers of Waterford.

This was a most significant intervention in the meeting and undoubtedly contributed to the selection of Costelloe as the candidate of the O'Connellites. The contents of the letter were communicated to Thomas Francis Meagher in his sickbed. He recognised at once that they were potentially damaging to his prospective candidacy and he sent an immediate response, which was read to those in attendance by Roger Hayes:

> Gentlemen, I have just learned that the Rev. Mr Cuddihy read you a communication which he states he received from my father to the effect that of any candidate at present before the public, he would desire to see the return of Mr Costelloe secured. In reply to these observations I beg leave to inform you that my father could not possibly know, as yet, that I had determined to stand for this city, since I did not make up my mind to do so until Monday night and therefore my father's opinion could not be quoted against me.[10]

When Thomas Meagher learned of his son's intentions, his reaction was given unequivocal expression in another letter to J. Everard Feehan, dated 18 February 1848, which was published in *The Waterford Mail*:

> When I wrote to you on the subject of the Waterford election, I had no desire or intention to dictate or offer any opinion publicly to the electors. It was merely that as I was on the subject, I felt no hesitation to express what I thought. As it has gone before the public, I have nothing to complain of, more especially as it appears from what you state that its publication has done some good.
>
> When I did so write, I certainly was not aware that my son was to be a candidate. Now that I do know it, I do not see that it can make any difference, for independent of political considerations, I have no wish to see the representation of Waterford entirely engrossed by my family. It is sufficient honour for it that one

member of it should have been chosen. If the other be deemed now, or at any other time, more worthy or more capable of doing service to his native city, I am and shall be, whenever the majority of the electors make known their wishes, ready to resign and give place to him or anyone else.

I entertain no doubt of the present contest, if contest there is to be, that it will result in the success of those principles which I still conceive are still entertained by the majority of the electors.

I have not heard from my son of his intentions and although he wishes to exercise the right to differ on political matters with me – a right I do not wish to dispute – yet I will write to him by this post to inform him that my opinion is adverse to his contesting the city on this occasion, and that if I were in Waterford I would feel bound to support Mr Costelloe, if he should appear to be the best to select in the opinion of those electors with whom I agree, and whom I consider are the majority.[11]

Thomas Meagher had been surprised, if not shocked, by his son's announcement to contest the Waterford by-election. It was the proverbial 'bolt from the blue' and his subsequent reaction was evidently informed by two considerations; one personal, one political. The personal consideration was his decided opinion on the inappropriateness of two members of the same family holding Waterford city's two parliamentary seats. The political consideration was perhaps the more potent: Thomas Meagher's confirmed loyalty to Conciliation Hall and the O'Connellite repeal movement, to which he had dedicated his near three decades of engagement in politics. In fact, as recently as 31 January 1848, he had attended a meeting of the National Repeal Association at Conciliation Hall.[12] He could not, and would not, compromise principles he had advocated with firm conviction; therefore, he could not support his son in the election. Having stated his position on the matter of Thomas Francis's candidacy, he preserved a Trappist-like silence for the remainder of the election campaign. In fact, he was to remain in London for its duration.

Thomas Francis was to make one reference to his father's second letter and thereafter also preserved a perfect silence regarding their political differences. While speaking at a meeting of supporters at Ballybricken on Sunday 20 February, he said that there was one issue to which he had to advert:

> I understand a letter has been received from my father, expressive of disapprobation at my canvassing the city, and that he cannot support me, as I do not represent his principles or opinions. I say I do not. I have differed before and that letter will not deter me. By my own principles I will stand, and by them I will stand or fall.[13]

THOMAS FRANCIS MEAGHER: THE 'UNDUTIFUL' SON

While the Meaghers preserved a silence, others did not. Thomas Francis's opponents readily and enthusiastically presented his determination to contest the election, notwithstanding paternal disapproval, as an act of egregious filial disobedience, in what was a calculated attempt to subvert his campaign. An editorial in *The Chronicle* of 23 February 1848 was devoted to attacking Thomas Francis's character by presenting him as a rebel against the rightful authority of a virtuous father:

> Callous to the advice of the sensible portion of the citizens and deaf to the counsels of his revered father, Thomas Francis Meagher protests that he will contest the coming election on his own merits against the world ... The father of the young 'swordsman' is already our representative – trusted, honoured and regarded – admired for his integrity, revered for his virtues as a representative enjoying the confidence of his fellow citizens ... and receives the deep respect of the entire body of his constituents. He is trusted by all, revered by every class, an honour to his country and sternly devoted to the interests of his native land. Waterford is proud of such a representative. It is only his son, the man of the 'sword' that questions his authority to advise, his right to counsel ... We did not, we candidly confess, anticipate that the son of Alderman Meagher, forgetful in the first place of his duty to his father ... would take the vile course to which he is now committed.

Intoxicated by this torrent of verbal criticism, the writer nearly drowned in words an especially forceful part of the editorial:

> His father's advice was not acceptable – a rebellious son he seeks the representation of this city in opposition to the will of him whom, under God, he is most bound to respect. But he has got into vile hands, and 'tis no wonder that, setting parental authority at defiance, he should claim the liberty of opinion, and broadly assert to speak treason and inculcate insubordination.

The writer was drawing a parallel between Meagher's filial rebellion and his alleged desire to foment chaos and disorder in society by his espousal of the politics of the Irish Confederation (the 'vile hands' of the editorial). The message of the editorial was clear: Thomas Francis Meagher would commit political treason just as he had committed familial treason. His subversion of proper family norms was but a prelude to his subversion of the norms of society.

The Pilot, the official organ of O'Connellite opinion, echoed the sentiments of *The Chronicle*, denouncing 'the infatuation which would cause Mr Meagher to persevere in his course, with his respected father against his proceeding'.[14] Fr Cuddihy, criticising his actions, declared: 'Oh! Mr Meagher, a heavy responsibility will alight on you for making the children of Ireland disobedient to parents.'[15]

The tactic of hallowing Thomas Meagher with a view to denigrating his son was a noteworthy feature of the election. In his address to the electors, Patrick Costelloe stated he was 'perfectly satisfied' that he would best discharge his duties, if elected, 'by acting with that honest and honourable man, Alderman Meagher, who so faithfully represents Waterford at present'.[16] By emphasising his intention to work in cooperation with Meagher, he was highlighting the division between him and his son, with the obvious intention of harming the latter's electoral prospects. In the aftermath of the election, *The Chronicle* continued its onslaught on Thomas Francis, describing him as 'a miserable abortion' and an 'inflated puppy', who 'has only the pure, untarnished, honourable character of his trusted father as a set off against his wild course and infamous procedure'. Warming to its theme, the newspaper continued: 'His father is not only a gentleman, but a true patriot – he has our enduring trust – we are proud of him and shall always give our good word in his favour. He has always been charitable, good and kind; our citizens are grateful to him and we ourselves offer our word in praise of his merits.'[17]

THOMAS FRANCIS MEAGHER: 'REVOLUTIONIST'

Commenting on Thomas Francis Meagher's election campaign, *The Chronicle* accused him of being 'a revolutionist'.[18] A combination of three factors inspired this charge and gave credence to it in the opinion of his opponents. First, Meagher enjoyed a significant measure of popular support, including some of Waterford's poorest inhabitants. *The Freeman's Journal* observed early in the campaign that Meagher 'is manifestly becoming popular with the non-electors'.[19] The Confederate Wolfe Tone Club in the city helped galvanise and organise this support, with the result that, according to *The Nation*, 'ten thousand artisans of Waterford, with banners and music, accompanied him to the hustings'.[20] Second, a body of his supporters seem to have engaged in violent behaviour, attacking the O'Connellite repeal reading room.[21] Third, he was forever associated with the 'Sword Speech', which was transmuted by his critics into an apologia for violent political action. One of Meagher's most strident critics, *The Chronicle,* noted acerbically: 'In truth, the physical force principles … are still dear to Mr Thomas Francis Meagher' – an obvious reference to the 'Sword Speech'.[22]

While Thomas Francis engaged in populist electioneering, he was not a revolutionist. His address to the electors made this manifestly clear. In it he advocated repeal: 'Whilst I live, I shall never rest satisfied until the Kingdom of Ireland has won a parliament, an army and a navy of her own. These institutions are the surest source of prosperity, as they are the sole guarantes of freedom.'[23] In his speech at the nomination of candidates, he reiterated this call for repeal. Patrick Costelloe inquired if parliament, army and navy would be 'under the crown', and *The Freeman's Journal* reported Meagher's reply: 'Yes, under the crown of England and he considered that neither theoretic nor impracticable.'[24] Moreover, his address stated that he would campaign for repeal by politically peaceful and constitutional means: 'I shall go to the English

House of Commons to insist upon the rights of this country to be held, governed and defended by its citizens and by them alone.'[25] Finally, Meagher's decision to contest the election should be viewed in the context of the policy programme of the Irish Confederation, adopted by the members of its council, with his support, in January 1848. This was a statement of objectives founded on unequivocal constitutional principles and included the directive that the confederation concentrate its efforts on the winning of parliamentary seats.[26] Meagher was acting in accordance with the decisions of an organisation that demonstrably was not revolutionary in character.

Perhaps, inevitably, Thomas Francis's stance on the matter of the Queen's Colleges featured in the election campaign and was used to present him as an enemy of the Catholic religion. His father's opposition to them was invoked in a further effort to undermine his son's election campaign. *The Chronicle* reminded its readers of the latter's letter in November 1845 supporting the idea of mixed education. This revealed, according to the newspaper, that he was 'in opposition, on a religious question, to the Right Rev. Dr Foran and his clergy, to his own father and the entire body of his fellow citizens'.[27] At the nomination of candidates, it was alleged by Fr Cuddihy that he sought to subvert the religion of the majority of electors. The priest then declaimed: ''Tis no wonder he would pull down the altar, when he has already pulled down parental authority by going against his father.'[28]

THOMAS FRANCIS MEAGHER DEFEATED

Meagher was defeated in the election. However, so was Patrick Costelloe; the victor was the Whig candidate, Sir Henry Winston Barron. The results were as follows:[29]

Barron	318 votes
Costelloe	301 votes
Meagher	154 votes

As a result, Meagher became even more reviled in the eyes of the O'Connellite repealers: his decision to contest the vacant parliamentary seat had the effect of splitting the repeal vote and facilitating the victory of Barron.[30]

Interestingly, in its editorial denouncing Meagher for his role in the loss of what should have been a repeal seat in Parliament, *The Chronicle* took issue with his supporters' attempts to undermine Costelloe's candidacy by the tactic of highlighting the fact that he had not been born in Waterford and that his Kilkenny antecedents made him a 'stranger' in the constituency. The newspaper's response was to remind Meagher of his family's history: 'Had the people of Newfoundland treated T.F. Meagher's grandfather as a stranger and as such denied him the right of carrying on his legitimate trade in their country, the tongue of his grandson would not now or at any other time be heard in or out of Waterford in the cause of the seceders – or any other cause.'[31]

THE BY-ELECTION: ITS IMPACT ON THE RELATIONSHIP OF MEAGHER AND HIS SON

To state the obvious: the election had implications for the relationship between Thomas Meagher and his son. His letter from London made it perfectly clear that he had no forewarning of his son's intentions to contest the election, nor had there been any prior consultation with him on the matter. These facts displayed a grave lack of consideration on Thomas Francis's side: apart from the personal courtesy his father was due, his decision had implications for his father by virtue of the fact that he was an MP for the same constituency. His father's letter made it clear that his being an MP weighed heavily with him in his reaction to his son's candidacy. While he declared his acceptance of his son's right to differ from him on matters political – he probably felt he had little choice but to accept this fact and make a virtue of the acceptance – he regarded Thomas Francis's candidacy as gravely ill-judged and impulsive, not least the fact that he probably appreciated its potential to split the repeal vote, thus facilitating the election of Barron. This is what transpired and Thomas Meagher would have been dismayed at this loss of what was regarded as a certain repeal seat. Finally, he would not have been human had he not felt (at the very least) some embarrassment and upset at the public enactment of the differences between himself and his son, and the column inches devoted in the newspapers to the publication of them – all because of a decision about which he was kept in the dark and of which he decidedly disapproved.

Ironically, Thomas Francis's candidacy in the election may reveal that his father exercised some degree of influence over him. His decision to seek a seat in Parliament confirmed his commitment to constitutional politics, consistent certainly with the principles of the Irish Confederation, but also with values and beliefs to which he had been exposed by his father. His career in public life was a testimony to constitutionalism; his son learned this at home and witnessed it in his accompaniment of him during his term as Mayor of Waterford. Moreover, when the by-election occurred Thomas Francis was, in Denis Gwynn's words, 'searching earnestly for some opportunity of public service.'[32] The confederation was divided and not advancing its objectives; perhaps he was looking for a sense of greater purpose in his life. The concept of public service was one with which he was familiar in the person of his father, who was an alderman of Waterford Corporation and an MP, and who had served as mayor and a poor law guardian. A seat in the House of Commons definitely chimed with paternal example.

In spite of their acknowledged differences, the two Meaghers retained a silence on them once the election campaign was underway. This suggests that a mutual respect was integral to their relationship. During the nomination of candidates, there was a dramatic – perhaps, more correctly, a melodramatic – moment. Fr Cuddihy was denouncing Thomas Francis Meagher's unfilial behaviour, when a voice shouted: 'He would die for his father.'[33] It was a sentiment which gave expression to a sense that Thomas Francis had real affection, indeed love, for his father, a love the father reciprocated. In his biography of Thomas Francis, Michael Cavanagh, when writing of the 1848 election, gives what is probably the best and most accurate summary of Thomas Meagher's relationship with his son:

> Meagher's father was, at that time, the senior member for Waterford. He was a most indulgent parent and supplied his son liberally with the means of upholding his position in society. But being a confirmed 'Old Irelander', he would not give the young orator any

support or encouragement in his effort to become his colleague in the House of Commons. Eventually, he threw the weight of his influence in favour of the Conciliation Hall candidate. But in thus preferring public principle to private feelings, he was only following his son's example at the time of his own election the year before, when ... the heir of his house and name refrained from voting for him. But these political differences between the father and son never tended towards lessening the mutual affection and esteem which they entertained for one another through life.[34]

Their relationship, tested by the election, was to experience an even greater test in the following months, when Thomas Francis embarked on the road of revolutionary politics, culminating in his role as a leader of an armed insurrection against the English crown.

CHAPTER ELEVEN

A Rebel Son, 1848–1849

The Waterford by-election had not yet reached its conclusion when, on 22 February 1848, Paris was convulsed by political turmoil and within forty-eight hours King Louis Philippe had fled and the Second French Republic was declared. The events in France sent shockwaves throughout Europe. The fact that dramatic political change had been effected with relatively little bloodshed or destruction of property allowed for near-universal welcome for the revolution by disparate groups, including moderates, radicals and nationalists. Repealers of all shades greeted the declaration of the Second Republic with rapturous excitement, as it opened the prospect that political change could be achieved in Ireland by bold and decisive action, but without attendant disorder and chaos.[1] There was to be a remarkable transformation in the temper and language of Irish nationalism in the aftermath of events in Paris; according to Michael Cavanagh, 'The national mind ... was again elevated to a pitch of enthusiasm such as it had not experienced since the summer of 1843.[2] Having endured five excruciatingly fruitless years since the setback at Clontarf, the enthusiasm and energy of the repeal cause were being rekindled.

THOMAS FRANCIS MEAGHER'S 'FIRST UNCONSTITUTIONAL SPEECH'

On 2 March Charles Gavan Duffy proclaimed that the revolution in France had created a historic opportunity; a week later he urged the formation of a national guard, as the power of a people in arms had been shown in Paris.[3] In Waterford city, on 7 March, Thomas Francis Meagher flew a tricolour of green, white and orange at the premises of the Wolfe Tone Confederate Club, at 33 The Mall. This was the first raising of what was later to become Ireland's national flag and was an act of deliberate defiance against the British government, inspired by the French tricolour and its revolutionary associations. Addressing a meeting of the Irish Confederation on 15 March, William Smith O'Brien declared that an Irish parliament could be achieved within twelve months.[4] At this same meeting, Meagher delivered what has been described as his 'first unconstitutional speech.'[5] His rhetoric reveals the extent to which he had absorbed the ecstasy engendered by events on the continent:

> Depute your worthiest citizens to approach the throne and before that throne let the will of the Irish people [in favour of repeal of the Act of Union] be uttered with dignity and decision. If nothing comes of this – if the constitution opens to us no path of freedom – if the Union will be maintained in spite of the will of the Irish people … then up with the barricades and invoke the God of Battles![6]

An 'Address of the Irish Confederation to the Citizens of the French Republic' was adopted and it was resolved that Meagher and Smith O'Brien should lead a deputation to convey it to Paris.[7] Prior to their departure, however, the two men were charged with sedition for their speeches of 15 March. John Mitchel was also charged for printing them in his newspaper, the *United Irishman*. On 22 March the three men presented themselves to the police and were released on bail.[8] Addressing a crowd of supporters afterwards, a defiant Meagher declared: 'The language of sedition is the language of freedom.'[9] On 3 April he and other delegates presented the confederation address to the French Foreign Minister, Alphonse de Lamartine.[10]

THOMAS MEAGHER'S CONCERNS

While en route to Paris, Meagher met with his father in London. In his 'Narrative of 1848', Thomas Francis recorded his recollection of their encounter:

> In the confederate movement ... he [my father] never had the
> slightest faith. More than once – particularly when I met him in
> London on my way ... to present the congratulatory address to its
> Provisional Government of the French Republic in the month of
> April – he warned me against being led away by the success of the
> continental revolutionists ...[11]

Meagher remembered his father's cautious response to the declaration
of the French Republic. Thomas Meagher's attitude put him at variance
with many of his fellow repealers, who were rapturous in their welcome
for it. John O'Connell visited Paris in February 1848 and described the
events there 'as the really sublime spectacle presented to the world'.[12] The
O'Connellite newspaper, The Pilot, advised people to emulate the 'most
glorious revolution recorded and consecrated in history'.[13] A temporary
harmony was restored between O'Connellites and confederates.[14] This
was given expression when John and Maurice O'Connell offered to bail
Meagher and Smith O'Brien, a significant gesture considering the vitriolic campaign that the former had conducted against Young Ireland.[15]

How may Thomas Meagher's attitude to events on the continent be
explained? He was likely viewing them primarily as a parent, and not as a
politician and repealer. His son's increasingly prominent role in the affairs
of the Irish Confederation concerned him – a role which had culminated
in the 'God of Battles' speech. Yes, numerous people in Ireland had been
inspired by the actions of the French, but only three were actually facing
criminal proceedings, and one of them was his son. He was alarmed at
this development. Thomas Meagher appears to have cared deeply for his
elder son, a young man he believed capable of impulsive behaviour, as
evidenced by his candidacy in the by-election. Of course, this decision
had strained their relationship, but it seems to have survived that hiatus.
Thomas Meagher was still supporting his son financially and he resided
in his house whenever he was in Waterford. They were still evidently
talking to one another, and Thomas Francis met with his father while in
London, where, clearly, he felt compelled to voice his reservations about
his son's reaction to the revolutionary events in France. It is ironic that
the words of a socialist republican, James Connolly, perhaps best convey
Thomas Meagher's concerns at this juncture:

> As the progress of the revolutionary movement on the Continent
> … synchronised with the falling apart of the social system in
> Ireland following the Famine, the leaders of the Young Ireland party
> responded to and moved along with the revolutionary current of
> events without ever being able to comprehend the depth and force
> of the stream upon whose surface they were embarked.[16]

The momentum of events was not allowing for realistic reflection by
Thomas Francis and his associates. 'The sense of riding on the tide of
ineluctable epochal change' was further reinforced for them after the visit
to France.[17] Events, as they were to unfold over the next few months,
however, were to confirm for the senior Meagher that his paternal
concerns had not been misplaced.

THOMAS FRANCIS MEAGHER AND THE RISING OF 1848: AN OVERVIEW

On 15 May William Smith O'Brien – and on the following day Thomas
Francis Meagher – stood trial on charges of sedition. Both were acquitted
when the juries failed to convict them. Embarrassed and concerned by
these setbacks, the government was determined to ensure the conviction
of John Mitchel. This it achieved by means of a packed jury, composed
entirely of Protestant anti-repealers. On 27 May he was found guilty
and sentenced to fourteen years' transportation.[18] There was discussion
within the Irish Confederation of attempting a rescue while Mitchel was
being transferred to the convict vessel, with Meagher proclaiming: 'If
the worst befell us, the ship that carried him away should sail upon a sea
of blood.'[19] It was decided, however, that any rescue attempt constituted
too great a risk; Meagher concurred with this decision and it was he
who defended it to frustrated and disillusioned members of Dublin's
Confederate Clubs.[20]

Mitchel's fate shocked Irish nationalists and hardened their resolve
to resist British coercion. On behalf of the confederation, Smith O'Brien
wrote an address to the Irish people after Mitchel's conviction, in which
he declared that 'armed resistance to the oppressors of our country
will become a sacred obligation'.[21] The confederate leadership realised

that it was necessary to develop a coherent response to the actions of the government. To achieve more effective decision-making, it was decided to reorganise the administrative structure of the confederation: its governing council was reduced to twenty-one members, to be elected by the existing and larger council. Meagher and Fr John Kenyon jointly received the highest number of votes.[22] A formal conspiracy was initiated to plan a rising for after the harvest.[23]

The trials of Meagher and Smith O'Brien, together with the transportation of Mitchel, resulted in a dramatic increase in the number of Confederate Clubs throughout Ireland. Confederate leaders became more aggressive and confrontational in their use of language as they toured the country, urging every club member to arm.[24] By early July, there was a widespread sense of anticipation of a rebellion, and by the middle of the month confrontation between Young Ireland and the government seemed inevitable.[25]

The government determined it was time to act. On 8–9 July prominent confederates, including Gavan Duffy, were arrested. On 12 July Meagher was arrested at his father's house in Waterford. It was an incident which caused consternation and tumult in the city.[26] He was conveyed to Dublin and subsequently released on bail. On Sunday 16 July he appeared at a 'monster meeting' at Slievenamon, County Tipperary, declaring defiantly of his arrest by the authorities: 'I am here not only to repent of nothing, but to dare them to do something worse.'[27] That same evening he returned to Waterford city at the head of a 20,000-strong procession.[28]

Events began to move more quickly. The lord lieutenant issued a proclamation making it illegal to carry arms in the cities of Dublin, Cork and Waterford.[29] Meagher, who was in Waterford, issued what *The Waterford Mail* termed a 'counter proclamation' and posted it throughout the city in an act of gross defiance of the government. It described the order of the lord lieutenant as an 'act of despotism' and called on his fellow citizens 'to organise calmly, speedily and fearlessly'.[30] Habeas corpus was suspended on 25 July, a decision which was regarded by Young Ireland as a call to arms.[31]

By its adoption of a policy of repression 'the government had changed the timetable of any revolution and recast the agenda on its terms'.[32] The confederates were forced into an ill-conceived and ill-prepared course

of action. After less than a week of ineffectual campaigning,[33] the Young
Ireland agitation culminated in a confrontation between confederate
supporters and police at Ballingarry, County Tipperary, on 29 July.[34]
After Ballingarry, confederate leaders, including Meagher, went on the
run to evade arrest, but were eventually apprehended. Meagher was tried
for treason and transported to Van Diemen's Land in July 1849.

THOMAS MEAGHER'S ATTITUDE TO THE 1848 RISING

In his 'Personal Narrative of 1848', Thomas Francis Meagher described
his departure from his father's house in Waterford to participate in the
Young Ireland rebellion:

> I ran up to the drawing-room, where my father and aunt were
> sitting at the time to wish them good-bye. I put on my tricolour
> sash – green, white and orange – buckled on my sword-belt,
> cross-belt, cartouche-box – and flourishing a very handsome old
> sword, which belonged to a grand-uncle of mine in the days of the
> Merchant Corps of the Waterford Volunteers, gave myself up to
> the gay illusion of a gallant fight, a triumphal entry, at the head of
> armed thousands, into Dublin, before long!
>
> I was full of liveliness and hope at that moment, and welcomed
> the struggle with a laughing heart. But, I recollect it well, my
> father was far otherwise. He seemed to me mournfully serious,
> and impressed with the saddest anticipations. In the confederate
> movement, however, he never had the slightest faith … to trust
> the fortunes of our cause to the desperate chances of insurrection.
>
> That evening – Thursday, July the 20th 1848 – I saw my home
> for the last time.[35]

The sad anticipation and mournful seriousness of Thomas Meagher
were inspired by the most basic of paternal feelings: love and profound
concern for his elder son and heir, who was about to engage in an act of
rebellion against the British state. Meagher regarded this as a desperate
and hopeless undertaking, and knew that his son, if he was not killed,
would be arrested for treason and suffer the terrible sentence which the

law enjoined on a convicted traitor, that of being hanged, drawn and quartered. There was nothing in any of this to gladden a father's heart.

Thomas Francis's dramatic behaviour prior to his departure from Waterford would have done little to assuage his father's dire anticipation. In a calmer moment, and in later years, Thomas Meagher might have pondered on how the confederates – and especially his own son – had been impelled into action by their own words. The observation of historian James Donnelly, written 150 years later, would likely have resonated with him:

> In the end the principal Young Irelanders or confederates became the prisoners of all their bold talk of action. By calling on the people to arm themselves so that they might be ready if the day for action ever came, the confederate leaders instilled the belief that they meant business, sooner rather than later. They felt wounded when some of their fanatical adherents in effect accused them of being fine talkers rather than courageous men of action. As a result, they themselves drifted aimlessly towards action. They were helped along this path by the widespread notion that the preservation of self-respect, their own and that of a famishing people, required action.[36]

Thomas Francis Meagher's own words confirm this assessment:

> I entertained no hope of success. I knew well the people were unprepared for a struggle; but, at the same time, I felt convinced that the leading men of the confederation were bound to go out, and offer to the country the sword and banner of revolt, whatever consequences might result to themselves for so doing.
>
> The position we stood in; the language we had used; the promises we had made; the defiances we has uttered; our entire career, short as it was, seemed to require from us a step no less daring and defiant than that which the government had taken.[37]

Thomas Meagher's paternal concerns were underpinned by deeply held beliefs which had informed his political, social and personal attitudes for decades: an uncompromising constitutionalism, middle-class values and a fervent Catholicism. During his three decades of involvement in public affairs he revealed himself to be an avowed constitutionalist, in the O'Connellite tradition, who rejected any recourse to violence in pursuit of political goals. Serious incidents of violence in Paris from 22 to 26 June 1848 – the so-called 'June Days' – in which nearly 10,000 were killed, would have confirmed his adherence to constitutionalism.

A member of the bourgeoisie, he shared that class's abhorrence of political and social disorder. On Wednesday 26 July, during the period of the Young Ireland rising, there was a specially convened meeting in Waterford's city hall, principally attended by members of the middle class, to discuss the appointment of special constables. Thomas Meagher was in attendance. The following resolution was adopted: 'That the present circumstances of the city of Waterford demand prompt measures to preserve the peace of the city, and with that view this meeting do resolve to enrol their names as special constables, to give assistance to the constituted authorities for the above purposes.' According to the report in *The Waterford Mail*, 'everyone in the room signed their names to get sworn as special constables, except Lawrence Forristal'.[38] On the basis of this comment, it is clear that Meagher was so sworn: there is no doubt that his failure to do so would have attracted commentary in the same newspaper. In fact, he was reputed to have been the third person sworn in as a constable.[39] Thus, while his son was engaged in rebellious activities, he was helping preserve peace and order in one part of the queen's realm. It was an action consistent with his position as an MP and his bourgeois values.

Thomas Meagher's devout and loyal Catholicism would have recoiled in horror at the murder of the Archbishop of Paris, Denys-Auguste Affré, during the June Days. The incident alarmed the Catholic hierarchy and clergy in Ireland, who became firm in their opposition to the Irish Confederation.[40] Meagher was undoubtedly aware of an address of loyalty presented to Queen Victoria in April by the bishop and priests of the Diocese of Waterford and Lismore,[41] who were concerned at the growth of political activism associated with the Confederate Clubs.[42] He understood that the Catholic Church was erecting, 'a moral bulwark between constitutionalists and revolutionaries' and thus managing 'to sunder from the political purveyors of revolution any pretensions of moral righteousness that might be used to justify their actions'.[43] The effect of all these developments was to confirm and reinforce his early rejection of continental revolution and any Hibernian imitation thereof, a conviction he had relayed to his son on a number of occasions.

THOMAS MEAGHER AND HIS SON: A COMMON PURPOSE

Meagher's participation in the 1848 rising can obscure the extent to which he and his father continued to share common political beliefs. They clearly differed over the matters of O'Connell's leadership of the repeal movement and the use of violence. Thomas Meagher remained an O'Connellite loyalist; Thomas Francis became an opponent of the Liberator. Thomas Meagher rejected the use of violence as an instrument of politics; for his son it was acceptable in certain circumstances. However, they shared a common objective. Thomas Meagher was a confirmed repealer. So were the majority of confederates, including his son. Regardless of their revolutionary rhetoric, they still had as their aim the return of a domestic legislature under the crown.[44] Thomas Francis's rhetoric and involvement in the 1848 rising can obscure this fact. As John Hearne has convincingly argued, 'his political intentions were not separatist'; he wanted Ireland to remain in the British empire, albeit with its own parliament.[45] Indeed, he articulated his continuing commitment to repeal even at moments of great tension between the Irish Confederation and the British government.

Thomas Francis attended a soirée in Waterford city on 7 May, one week before his trial on charges of sedition. In his reply to a toast 'for the prosecuted patriots and repeal of the Union', he declared to his audience: 'You did right to associate the names of the prosecuted patriots with the sentiment of the repeal of the legislative union and you gentlemen [the organisers of the soirée] did right to sanction that association [in the wording of the toast]'. He continued: 'I call upon you to arm. I desire that the public opinion of Ireland, declaring for repeal, may signify a power capable of achieving that measure'.[46] Speaking at Slievenamon, on 16 July, one week before the Young Ireland rising, he spoke to those gathered to hear him in the following terms: '"Forty-three" [the 'Repeal Year'] passed away, but its vows have not passed away. O'Connell, like all great men, had his faults – but he had his virtues – and he had victories. This I will say, that he preached a cause that we are bound to see out.'[47] He was establishing a link between the words of O'Connell and the actions of the Irish Confederation. When the rising broke out, its leaders were not seeking an Irish republic; independence, as encompassed essentially by repeal, was their objective. The Young Irelanders were physical force repealers.

Thomas Francis Meagher's recourse to violence sundered the political relationship between him and his father. However, repeal, as supported and advocated by Thomas Meagher, was at the core of his son's political construct. In that respect, he was his father's son, influenced, perhaps even inspired, by the principles and actions of the older man, who had devoted nearly twenty years of political activism to the repeal cause, in a campaign to achieve greater independence for Ireland. However, circumstances, such as the government's coercive measures and his fiery rhetoric, set Thomas Francis on the path of insurrection. It was not a path he had anticipated or for which he and his associates had planned. In truth, Thomas Francis Meagher was, in Hearne's words, 'a reluctant revolutionary'.[48]

TRIAL AND TRANSPORTATION

While Thomas Meagher deplored the fact of his son's involvement in the 1848 Young Ireland rebellion, he continued to support him in its aftermath. In a letter to Roger Sweetman of Waterford city, dated 31 August 1848 and with the address 'Kilmainham', suggesting that Kilmainham Gaol, where Thomas Francis was detained while awaiting trial, was its place of composition, he wrote: 'Tom is in great health and spirit. In any case, there will not be trials before the end of the month and as a matter of course in Nenagh or Clonmel.'[49] Thomas Francis was eventually to go on trial at Clonmel, County Tipperary, on 16 October.

There was a great sympathy evinced towards the young rebel by those in attendance at the courthouse.[50] In fact, the dashing and handsome man was something of a celebrity, *The Times* of London reporting that he had 'frequent demands for autographs',[51] an observation also made in *The Chronicle*.[52] There is a conflict of evidence in relation to his father's attendance at the trial: according to *The Waterford News,* though Thomas Meagher was in Clonmel, he was not present in the courthouse. This newspaper reported that he had very little hope that his son would be more fortunate than the other prisoners, who had already been convicted and sentenced to death. 'The honourable gentleman is, however, under such distressing circumstances, apparently in very good form.'[53] For its part, *The Chronicle* reported: 'Mr Meagher MP attends the court every day, also his relative, Fr [Patrick Meagher] SJ.'[54] It is more probable than not that he attended at least some part of the court proceedings, given his devotion to his son.

Thomas Meagher also addressed his son's material needs. He paid the costs of his legal defence, which totalled £488,[55] and the debts incurred by him during his incarceration.[56] His father's considerable wealth and influence certainly mitigated the harshness of prison conditions for Thomas Francis, as evident in this description of his cell in Clonmel Jail, as recorded by one of his biographers, Captain W.F. Lyons:

> A warm crimson cloth lined the walls, and at once removed the fever-hospital look of the place. Handsome French prints hung in rich profusion, whose lively colours and fresh gildings were fresh and animating. A pretty sofa bedstead completely filled the farthest end of the cell. Round three sides of it were ranged well-stored book shelves, just within reach of his hand; he thus lay nestled in books, and in the long winter's evenings, deprived of fire, could still read comfortably ... a bright warm carpet, a table, and two or three chairs, all of tasteful form, completed the furniture. An exquisite propriety of cleanliness gave a singular look to this pleasant spot. An atom of dust never seemed ever to have rested on it ... It was utterly impossible to imagine one's self in a condemned cell.[57]

This, in truth, was the easy part for Thomas Meagher, making his son's imprisonment as comfortable as possible. There was no escaping, however, the consequences of his rebellion. He was devastated by the guilty verdict and the inevitable death sentence passed on Thomas Francis; in the words of *The Chronicle*: 'Mr Meagher's affection for his son is extreme and his affliction at the fate to which patriotic enthusiasm hurried him is deep and poignant.'[58] The commutation of the death sentence to transportation was doubtless welcomed by him, though the commuted sentence itself was terrible, and in the words of the biographer of Mary Aikenhead, foundress of the Sisters of Charity, whose endeavours he supported in Waterford, it appeared that 'to the old man was lost forever the son of whom he was so proud.'[59]

Unfortunately, neither father nor son have left any account of their interaction in the months preceding Thomas Francis's transportation. However, the latter was certainly well-prepared for his enforced exile in terms of the acquisition of items, at his father's expense, to make his journey and new life more tolerable. Thomas Francis ordered a rug, new clothing and chests in which to store them. He purchased notebooks, pencils and envelopes. He also bought books, including Shelley's *Essays*, a multi-volume history of Germany, Kohl's *Ireland* and *Coningsby* by Disraeli.[60]

On the day of his transportation, 9 July 1849, Thomas Meagher was not present at Richmond Prison to bid his son farewell. According to *The Waterford Mail*, Rev. Patrick Meagher, Thomas Francis's uncle, and 'several female relations' were there.[61] As his son began his journey to penal exile in Van Diemen's Land, together with William Smith O'Brien, Thomas Bellew McManus and Patrick O'Donoghue, Thomas Meagher must have reflected on how Thomas Francis had forfeited 'everything that gives charm to life – fortune, consideration, family and friends'. After his arrest, *The Pilot* wrote the following of the young rebel; it was reprinted in an editorial in *The Chronicle* and was very likely read by his father:

> Among our regrets for the errors and fate of our young countrymen [the Young Ireland rebels], we feel for none so much, we confess, as for Thomas [Francis] Meagher. He was capable of great things and would, we are convinced, have achieved them had he been the denizen of a country which opened a legitimate field for the ambition which is almost inseparable from true genius ... [had] his powers not been misdirected, he must have triumphed over all difficulties, and been an ornament to his country, his family and name. But there was an inconceivable madness about which, like an epidemic, seized upon age and experience, and how could,

in all cases, the young, the enthusiastic and the bold escape the contagion? That Thomas [Francis] Meagher did not do so, we deem, with the public, a national misfortune.[62]

The sentiments expressed were ones with which his doleful father could identify.

In a personal recollection of his transportation, Thomas Francis wrote: 'July 10 – seven o'clock – off the Waterford coast. A beautiful bright morning. Will no one come out to hail me from Dunmore? I pass by and my own people know nothing of it.'[63] Perhaps his father was in Dunmore? Unlikely: this is but a biographer's (forgivable?) flight of fancy. He was probably in 'Derrynane', his residence on the Mall in Waterford, believing that he would never see his son again. He was effectively bereaved. One thing is certain: Thomas Meagher's grief was intense, even unbearable.

CHAPTER TWELVE

Member of Parliament, 1847–1852: Land and Religion

T homas Meagher served as an MP for Waterford city from 1847 to 1857, during what may be termed a forgotten decade in Irish history. This forgetfulness is primarily due to the preoccupation in the popular historiography with the mythic march of the nation. As R.V. Comerford writes, 'From that perspective the quarter-century after the Famine is fundamentally of little interest apart from the emergence of Fenianism: the "nation" hangs helplessly on the ropes for a few years, then gradually recovers sufficient spirit to put up a splendid fight, under Mr Parnell's coaching, in the next important bout of Irish history.'[1] An examination of Meagher's years as an MP, however, elucidates many of the important developments of the 1850s and allows for a greater understanding and appreciation of the decade's distinctiveness.

EVICTIONS

If nationalist and folk memories regard the Famine years as ones of starvation amidst plenty, these years are also seen as ones of dispossession amidst starvation. There was a huge increase in the rate of evictions between 1846 and 1854. Though it is not possible to give an exact figure for the numbers of people evicted, half a million is not unrealistic.[2] Economists and government inquiries had argued the need for a more streamlined farming structure in the immediate pre-Famine decades, and the consolidation of small holdings was advocated. The economic and social dislocation consequent on the widespread failure of the potato crop gave landlords the opportunity to effect the clearances of unwanted tenants.

In an attempt to protect their interests, tenants began to organise. Throughout 1847, tenant leagues were established in five counties, including Cork and Tipperary.[3] On Sunday, 24 October 1847, a meeting was held at Kilmacthomas, County Waterford, for the purpose of founding such a league 'to secure the reasonable rights of occupying tenants, with due regard to the just rights of the landlord'.[4] The meeting was organised in response to a requisition signed by ninety-one priests and 600 gentlemen.[5] The first name on the requisition was that of Thomas Meagher, an indication of his prominent social and political position.[6]

Meagher was among the speakers who addressed those in attendance, estimated at between 20,000 and 30,000.[7] He declared that he was anxious that 'the landlord should be secured in his rent and that the tenant should be secured in his occupation … Whatever is good for the tenant must be of benefit to the landlord and whatever is good for both landlord and tenant must be beneficial to the country at large.' According to him, it was of the greatest importance that 'tenant farmers should be put in a position to raise themselves from the miserable condition to which the sad calamities of the past years have reduced them. This may be effectively done by an equitable adjustment of the relations between landlord and tenant.' He pledged to support efforts to secure tenants their just rights.[8] The meeting adopted a series of resolutions and a petition to be presented to Parliament.[9]

The Kilmacthomas meeting was characterised by moderation, Meagher's speech capturing the tenor of the occasion. It was not one at which landlordism was denounced. On the contrary, there was a recognition of landlords' rights, and what was demanded was a reciprocal recognition by them of the rights of tenants. The moderate nature of the resolutions – for example, there was none condemning evictions – together with the presence of landlords, made it possible for even a conservative newspaper like *The Waterford Mail* to express its approval of the event.[10] However, there is no evidence that a tenant league was formed as a consequence of the meeting.[11]

Some speakers, in the course of their remarks, associated the rights of tenants with the constitutional objectives of the repeal campaign. Meagher, while pledging himself to promoting the tenants' cause, also declared that 'at the same time, I shall labour, if possible, with redoubled energy, to obtain for you a repeal of the Union which is the source, I maintain, of this and of other evils which afflict this country'. Another speaker asserted that 'there was another tenant right which he wished above all things, namely, the right of everyman to self-government'; while a third speech-maker lamented that 'the present meeting was not called to seek self-government instead of anything else'.[12] Though O'Connell had died in May 1847, the memory of the dead leader, who had inspired three decades of political activism and engagement, cast a shadow over the proceedings, with the (predictable) retailing of the standard nationalist mantra of the Union as the *fons et origio* of all Ireland's misfortunes.

IRISH TENANT LEAGUE, 1850

A few tenant societies were formed in a number of counties in 1847, but none of them proved a success at the time.[13] Meanwhile, the horrors of the Famine continued to expose the problems and evils of the land system, highlighting the fact that 'it was no longer possible to treat the agrarian grievances of the Irish people as an appendage to their constitutional ... complaints'.[14] The first tenant society to secure a permanent following was founded in Callan, County Kilkenny, on 14 October 1849. By mid-1850, at least twenty societies had been formed in ten different counties scattered throughout Munster, Leinster and Connaught.[15] Agitation also began in Ulster, centring, in particular, on the protection of the custom known as tenant right, i.e. the right of outgoing tenants to receive from the incoming tenant a goodwill payment for the farm.[16] Agitation north and south reached its climax at a time when there was no other substantial issue in Irish politics. The timing was right for the launch of an organisation representing the interests of tenants throughout all of Ireland. A national conference was held in Dublin on 6, 7 and 8 August 1850, at which the Irish Tenant League was founded. Its aims were to obtain for all tenants a fair rent fixed by an impartial valuation; fixity of tenure, as long as they paid their rent; and free sale – the right to sell their interest in their holdings.[17]

The newly formed league held its first meeting on 9 August, at which it adopted a resolution that the league should support only 'representatives, who will give a written pledge that they will support, in and out of Parliament, a tenant law based upon, and carrying into effect, the principles adopted by the Irish Tenant League; and that they will withhold all support from any cabinet that will not advance those principles'.[18] Thus, from its inception, the league laid an emphasis on building up a parliamentary party.

STATE OF PARLIAMENTARY POLITICS, 1850

The Irish Tenant League had decided to enter politics at a time when party distinctions in the House of Commons were unusually fluid and confused. The 654 MPs were divided into three parties: Liberals, Conservatives and Peelites, the last having split from the Conservatives in 1846.[19] All parties were politically undisciplined and none had a clear majority.[20] The three dozen or so MPs elected as repealers in the 1847 general election associated themselves in Parliament in 1850 with the Liberal Party.[21] This was not surprising: O'Connell had regarded the repeal movement as being part of the liberal political tradition,[22] and his use of the term 'liberal' was generally in the inclusive sense that identified repealers with the Whigs and radicals as part of a political grouping informed by liberal principles.[23]

Irish Liberal MPs, totalling sixty-four members, were individuals of widely differing points of view, ranging from moderates to more radical parliamentarians.[24] Many of the latter were survivors of the old O'Connellite repeal party and were still animated by a sense of Irish grievances. Notwithstanding the fact that the Liberals had been in government since 1847, according to John Whyte, 'only about one-third of the Irish Liberal MPs could be called consistent followers of the government: the majority had all voted against the ministry at one time or another on an important issue, and scarcely a single ministerial measure in that Parliament escaped being opposed by some at least of the Irish Liberal members'. Whyte continues: 'Indeed, the more extreme members, such as Michael Sullivan, MP for Kilkenny borough or Thomas Meagher, father of the Young Ireland leader and MP for Waterford city, voted against the ministry more often than they supported it; and though they ranked nominally as Liberals they were worse than useless to the party whips.'[25] Such political behaviour was a manifestation of the trenchancy of Meagher's political convictions: he was something of an unredeemed repealer, with a convinced sense of justice for Ireland and of the country's grievances.

However, the newly formed Irish Tenant League received virtually no support from Ireland's Liberal MPs. Only two were in attendance at its inaugural conference and only four sent a letter of excuse for their absence. Meagher neither attended nor excused himself.[26] While he had expressed sympathy with the tenant cause by his presence at the Kilmacthomas meeting in 1847, it is likely that he concurred with the views of his colleagues that the league's demands were too extreme to be practicable: for example, the demand that rents be determined by impartial valuation was regarded as too radical and certain to be rejected by Parliament.[27] Meagher, as the representative of a city constituency, may not have viewed the objectives of the Tenant League as a political priority for him. Moreover, the fact that Waterford was not among the ten counties in which a tenant society had been formed in 1850 may have confirmed him in his attitude.[28] However, the fortunes of the Tenant League and the shape of Irish politics were to be transformed by events in Great Britain in the autumn of that year. And these same events were to have a significant influence on the political career of Thomas Meagher.

RESTORATION OF THE CATHOLIC HIERARCHY IN ENGLAND AND WALES, 1850

On 29 September 1850 Pope Pius IX restored, in England and Wales, the hierarchy of the Catholic Church, which had been abolished at the time of the English Reformation in an assertion of Protestant England's rejection of papal authority. On 7 October Nicholas Wiseman issued a pastoral letter in Rome announcing his elevation to the College of Cardinals and his appointment as Archbishop of Westminster. News of these developments reached England at the end of the second week of

October, causing astonishment, alarm, deep resentment and profound anger. Latent and historic prejudices rose to the surface, 'providing clear evidence of the average Briton's love of Protestantism and hatred of Roman Catholicism'.[29] *The Times* described it as an attempt to restore papal dominion in England, and led the way 'in reasserting the age-old view that Catholicism was backward, disloyal, superstitious and thoroughly out of character with [the] rational, liberal institutions' which characterised Protestant Britain.[30] An intense reaction against what came to be regarded as an act of unprovoked 'papal aggression' ensued.[31] There was an explosion of protest meetings, some sober and dignified, others occasions for the worst kind of anti-popish vituperation.[32] The Liberal prime minister, Lord John Russell, fanned the flames of Protestant outrage. In a letter to the Anglican Bishop of Durham, which was later published in newspapers, he declared that 'the glorious principles and the immortal martyrs of the Reformation shall be held in reverence by the great mass' of the English nation, and he dismissively and insultingly described Catholic beliefs and practices as 'the mummeries of superstition' which 'confine the intellect and enslave the soul'.[33] While this letter has been described as the 'most foolish act of Russell's career',[34] it certainly expressed, albeit clumsily, the views of the Protestant popular mind.[35] Thousands of petitions to Parliament demanded that the government take decisive and firm action against what was widely regarded as an outrageous insult to English Protestantism.

The response of Russell's government was the Ecclesiastical Titles Bill which applied to Ireland as well as Great Britain. The first clause repeated a prohibition of the Emancipation Act of 1829 and made the assumption of territorial titles by Catholic bishops illegal. The contents of the next two clauses, however, were no formulaic repetitions, and they dismayed the Irish bishops. The second clause provided that every deed or writing by a Catholic bishop be void if the name of the see appeared in the document. If enacted, this would dramatically impact on the essential business of the Church; for example, it was by virtue of the title of his see that a bishop ordained priests for his diocese. The third clause declared that any property devised for a bishop or dean by the title of his see or deanery was forfeit to the crown. This would despoil the Church of donations and bequests. This bill was no formality.[36]

In his speech introducing the bill on 14 February 1852, Russell attacked Paul Cullen, Archbishop of Armagh, and the 1850 synod of Thurles, the first national synod of the Catholic Church's hierarchy in Ireland since the Reformation. This occasion was intended to impose discipline and order on the Church, with the objective of strengthening and revitalising it after years of discrimination and Protestant hostility. Clearly, Russell regarded the synod and papal aggression as symptoms of the same threat presented by the Catholic Church to the United Kingdom. The contents of the bill and speech had the effect of bringing a crucial Irish dimension into this divisive matter,[37] with *The Nation* commenting that 'Lord John Russell's fire is directed against Archbishop Cullen and his colleagues. The bill is essentially an Irish one.'[38] And this is how many Irish Catholic MPs came to regard it. On its first reading, thirty-nine Irish Liberal MPs, including Meagher, opposed it. On the second reading, the number increased to forty-eight.[39]

Meagher and the other Irish MPs who voted against the government's proposals were reflecting their disgust, and that of Irish Catholics generally, at the deeply sectarian reaction in Britain to the restoration of the hierarchy and the subsequent titles bill. They believed that the near-frenzied popular response in Britain had forced Parliament into 'a constitutional anachronism: a penal law, a law discriminating against a religious denomination otherwise tolerated and containing many subjects of the queen. For a moment it seemed as though the old union of [Protestant] church and state, as it existed before 1829, was rising out of the mists of past history.'[40] Since 1829, with the enactment of the Catholic Emancipation Act, Parliament had been progressively removing legal disabilities against Catholics. The Ecclesiastical Titles Bill, however, represented a reversal of this trend and the reimposition of restrictions. For Catholics, it proposed to curtail the liberty of their Church and threatened their self-respect by its implications of second-class status. For middle-class Catholics such implications were particularly concerning and reprehensible; their hard-won gains were being eroded.

Thomas Meagher was truly appalled by the bill. He was a devout and convinced Catholic, whose three decades of political activism had been dedicated to the achievement of equality for his co-religionists. A section of an address to the people of Ireland, issued by the Catholic bishops in February 1851 on the subject of the titles bill, would certainly have resonated with him:

> Instructed by you, those who represent you in Parliament will not only assert the independence and freedom of your religion both in England and in Ireland ... but will insist that Catholics shall be put and maintained on a footing of perfect equality with all other subjects of the crown and that every remnant of persecution will be obliterated. We ask for nothing, but what is conceded to others and we cannot be content with less than the full and free right to practise our religion.[41]

These sentiments summarise the essence of Meagher's political credo and engagement since 1820: full equality for Catholics – nothing more, nothing less. Moreover, John Whyte has observed that the strongest opponents of the bill among Irish MPs were those who had been elected as repealers.[42] Justice for Ireland and an acute sense of grievance inspired this cohort. Therefore, it is not surprising that Meagher was unrelenting in his opposition to the proposals of Russell's government.

PROTEST MEETINGS AGAINST THE ECCLESIASTICAL TITLES BILL

Throughout Ireland the outrage felt by Catholics at the Ecclesiastical Titles Bill was given expression at numerous meetings. On Sunday, 2 March 1851, the Catholics of Waterford city gathered in their cathedral to protest against it. According to *The Waterford Chronicle*, it was 'one of the most powerful assemblages that met in this city' since 1826. Resolutions were adopted, one of which described the bill as 'a wanton act of tyranny involving our civil and religious liberty'. In the light of later political developments, a call on Waterford's parliamentary representatives 'to oppose, in every form and on every occasion, any ministry who shall presume to introduce or support such a measure in Parliament' was interesting and significant. Moreover, the assembly resolved to oppose in future elections any candidate who refused to oppose any legislation or ministerial interference in the affairs of the Catholic Church. While Meagher was not present because of his attendance at Westminster, he and the MPs for Waterford county were praised for voting against the bill. Meagher was the recipient of an especially warm commendation from one speaker, because 'he has on all occasions in Parliament done his duty to his religion and his country'. A resolution, lauding the 'small but faithful band' of Irish MPs for their opposition to the titles bill, declared with noteworthy perspicacity (again in the light of later developments) that in that group the meeting recognised 'the nucleus of a party which, with God's blessing and the energetic cooperation of the Irish people, will protect our Church and liberties from future aggression'. A petition opposing the offending item of proposed legislation was adopted for presentation to Parliament. [43]

In late April Meagher was one of the signatories of a requisition calling on the mayor to convene a meeting of citizens to petition against the further progress of the Ecclesiastical Titles Bill and against another recently introduced bill, the Religious Houses Bill.[44] On 23 April a preparatory meeting was held in advance, over which Meagher presided. Addressing the attendees, he stated that while acknowledging that the titles bill was primarily directed at Catholics, he did not want it to be regarded as a purely Catholic issue. Rather, he argued, it was a concern for every lover of civil and religious liberty.

Meagher, however, was more animated on another matter. According to him, another evil had arisen as a consequence of the policy being pursued by the government: MPs felt encouraged to avail of the opportunity to introduce measures he described as 'of a more dangerous kind and more hostile to our religious liberty'. He believed that the Religious Houses Bill, currently before the House of Commons, was one such measure.[45] By its terms, all houses in which ladies resided under religious or monastic vows were to be registered. Magistrates were to be empowered to visit them and should do so without notice. If visiting magistrates found in them any lady who wished to leave, they were to have the authority to remove her.[46]

Meagher was highlighting a legislative proposal that essentially had its origins in the deep suspicion of, and profound distaste for, Catholic convents in some of the more fervid imaginings of English Protestantism. These institutions were common targets in the rich tradition of cheap anti-Catholic literature, where they were often characterised and denigrated as brothels.[47] In the course of the debate on the bill, one MP gave expression to dark Protestant preconceptions: 'How can a poor young girl who is locked up, where she may be either starved or whipped to death, that the priests may clutch her money, ask for protection? ... I assert that nunneries are prisons and I have seen them so used ... They have ever been either prisons or brothels.'[48]

Meagher was especially vocal on this issue because he was a generous benefactor of convents in Waterford, and an admirer and supporter of the work of female religious. Therefore, he denounced the bill as an attempt 'to invade the sacred precincts of religious houses' and he argued that it would be 'monstrous' to allow its enactment without protest. When faced with a proposal 'of so odious a character', it was essential, according to him, to petition against it, thus showing the government that 'we are not to be dealt with in such a manner without experiencing more trouble from us than what they expect at the present moment'.[49]

The meeting of citizens was held on 28 April. In his address, Meagher rejected the charge that the restoration of the English Catholic hierarchy was an act of papal aggression. Rather, it was restored to enable bishops to carry out more effectively the functions of their offices, and it was never intended as an act of interference in the temporal affairs of England. He directed particularly trenchant criticism at the Religious Houses Bill, declaring that he had never seen a proposal that 'contained a greater amount of wickedness'. Having outlined its most objectionable features, he proceeded to defend convents and the good works done by their religious occupants. He referenced the activities of nuns in Waterford city to illustrate the charitable endeavours associated with convents. Meagher highlighted the education provided to poor children: the Ursuline Sisters educated 150 daily, the Presentation Sisters 240, and the Sisters of Charity 300. He concluded his remarks by observing that 'the feelings against Roman Catholics were never so strong as at this moment in England'. Resolutions and petitions against the offending bills were adopted.[50]

On 29 April there was a national meeting of Ireland's Catholics in the Rotundo on Rutland Square, Dublin, to protest against the Ecclesiastical Titles and Religious Houses Bills. The instigators of this event were ten members of the 'Irish Brigade' (see next section), styling themselves the 'Catholic committee'.[51] Meagher was in attendance.[52] The occasion inspired *The Waterford News* to be particularly lyrical in its praise for him: 'The soul cannot yet be said to have left Ireland while she has such men as … Meagher of Waterford to plead the cause of her religious liberty and to defend the honour of her consecrated virgins.'[53] The resolutions adopted decried the titles bill as a 'gross and intolerable violation of our religious liberty', denounced with indignation and disgust the calumnies in the Protestant and English press against nuns, and attacked the Religious Houses Bill for giving 'legal sanction to these calumnies'.[54]

The mass agitation against the bills reached its climax on Sunday, 11 May 1851, when protest meetings were held in parishes throughout Ireland, in accordance with a resolution adopted at the Rotundo gathering.[55] Petitions to Parliament were signed: these were so numerous that it took Irish members nearly two hours to present them.[56] An editorial in *The Freeman's Journal* praised Meagher and six other named MPs for championing these petitions in the House of Commons in the face of government hostility, and not permitting these expressions of the voice of the Irish people 'to be flung contemptuously under the table'.[57]

THE 'IRISH BRIGADE'

Notwithstanding the determined and vigorous opposition of a cohort of Irish Liberal MPs, the titles bill received enormous majorities at every stage of its passage through Parliament, with most Liberal and Conservatives members supporting it. Its Irish opponents soon realised that the only prospect of halting the bill's progress was to strike at the government on other issues. If they were to join with the Conservative opposition in voting against the ministry, there was a possibility that Russell's administration might suffer a defeat. The Irish members' intentions were to exploit the reality of the parliamentary arithmetic, by which there was no great difference in the strength between the usual supporters of the government (and these supporters included Irish Liberals) and the opposition. Should the government be defeated a number of times or on a sufficiently serious matter, it might have to resign, and the titles bill might be lost in the subsequent political confusion.[58] While only about two dozen Irish Liberals adopted these tactics, they acquired a common spirit and sat apart from the rest of their party on the opposition benches. Soon they were being referred to as the 'Irish Brigade'.[59]

Thomas Meagher was a faithful member of this group. For example, in eight reports carried in *The Waterford News* and *The Freeman's Journal* he is recorded as voting against the Liberal government.[60] During the committee stage of the Ecclesiastical Titles bill, he and twenty-two fellow MPs staged a walk-out.[61] Members of the Irish Brigade caused considerable disruption to the business of the House of Commons by their determined opposition to the measure; it was not passed until 4 July.[62] It then had to go to the Lords and did not receive the royal assent until 1 August, six months after its introduction.[63] Moreover, the bill as enacted was an attenuated version of the original: clauses two and three had been removed in an attempt to assuage its opponents.[64] And Meagher had another reason to celebrate: the Religious Houses Bill was defeated at its second reading and he had the pleasure of voting against it.[65] Indeed, Meagher was to comment later that the Catholics of England attributed the bill's defeat to Irish MPs.[66]

TOWARDS THE FOUNDATION OF THE CATHOLIC DEFENCE ASSOCIATION

On 19 May 1851 *The Freeman's Journal* reported that 'arrangements are in progress for the formation of an association for the protection of Catholic freedom'. The arrangements referred to in the newspaper were being undertaken by the Catholic committee that had its origins in the organisation of the Rotundo meeting and which was now ensuring the implementation of the resolutions adopted on that occasion. In a letter to the national meeting in April, Archbishop Cullen had made reference to a Catholic defence association and observed that its institution 'appears to be most desirable', a view endorsed by those in attendance.[67] The Catholic committee began an active correspondence with dignitaries of the Catholic Church and Catholic MPs, with the intention of securing their support for such an organisation.[68]

Thomas Meagher was contacted by the committee and he replied to its secretary, James Burke, on 23 May. As this letter affords an invaluable

insight into his perspective on events as they were unfolding, it deserves
to be quoted extensively:

> I feel there is an imperative duty calling upon everyone who has
> the least regard for those rights and privileges which, after so long a
> struggle, the people of Ireland, under the guidance of their lamented
> leader, O'Connell, obtained, to come forward at the present crisis in
> defence of these rights and by combined vigorous and persevering
> efforts effectively to secure and extend them. I cannot therefore
> resist the call and shall be ready to give my humble cooperation to
> the formation of the association proposed for that purpose.
>
> With the sanction of his Grace, the primate [Archbishop Paul
> Cullen], and the other members of our venerated hierarchy and
> the countenance and support of all orders of our venerated clergy,
> such an association cannot fail to awaken the slumbering energies
> of our people and rouse them to renew those united and noble
> efforts which, in former days, won from a reluctant government
> that religious liberty which a ministry professed to be friendly
> seeks now to violate.
>
> Such an association, too, so formed and working with energy
> cannot fail to encourage the efforts now being made by many Irish
> members to fulfil the wishes of their constituents in resisting, by
> every allowable form, the attempt now being made against their
> religious liberty.[69]

This reply to James Burke encapsulates and reiterates, in so many
respects, the beliefs and values which had inspired, and would continue
to inspire, Meagher's political endeavours. It was a testament to his
determination to resist the erosion of civil and religious rights which had
been hard won after a long struggle – a struggle in which he had played,
and intended to continue playing, an active role. The letter affirmed the
O'Connellite foundations of his political engagement and proclaimed
his loyalty to, and respect for, the hierarchy and clergy of the Catholic
Church, whose support would energise the Irish people in any struggle.

By 20 June, *The Freeman's Journal* was reporting that twenty-two MPs,
including Meagher, had declared themselves in favour of an association

to defend Catholic liberties. Clearly, many of these parliamentarians had decided to take advantage of the enthusiasm generated by the popular agitation against the Ecclesiastical Titles Bill to support the establishment of such an organisation, the foundation of which could be to their political advantage, strengthening their position inside and outside Parliament.

The Catholic committee was very active in its efforts to facilitate the foundation of such a body. The almost daily reportage in *The Freeman's Journal* on its activities attests to this fact.[70] During the summer parliamentary recess, MPs returned to Dublin and became actively involved in the campaign to establish a defence association.[71] On 9 August a sub-committee composed of three MPs and prominent members of the Irish Brigade, John Sadleir, William Keogh and John Reynolds,[72] was appointed to prepare resolutions for a meeting, scheduled for 19 August at the Rotundo, to inaugurate this association.[73] The sub-committee was empowered to add to its membership and very shortly afterwards four other MPs, including Thomas Meagher, were invited to join.[74] The resolutions which they produced certainly bore testimony to Meagher's long-cherished beliefs regarding the rights of Catholics.

These resolutions were presented to a meeting which had certainly generated a considerable degree of public attention and excitement. According to *The Freeman's Journal*:

> From an early hour yesterday morning, the streets leading to the Rotundo were thronged with crowds of our fellow citizens, anxious to catch a glimpse of the distinguished prelates, nobility and gentry whose presence at the great meeting ... was expected. Although the doors were not to be opened to the public until 11 o'clock, for nearly three hours previously considerable groups began to assemble in all localities adjoining the Rotundo.[75]

The imposing gathering was addressed by, among others, the Catholic primate, Archbishop Paul Cullen, and Archbishop John MacHale of Tuam. In a series of speeches, the resolutions, as presented by the sub-committee of MPs, were proposed and seconded, the operative ones being:

That we declare an act lately passed by the imperial Parliament, commonly called the Ecclesiastical Titles Act, to be a violation of the compact contained in the Catholic Relief Act of 1829, and subversive of the great principle of religious liberty, as established in this empire.

That we solemnly pledge ourselves to use every legitimate means within the constitution to obtain a total repeal of that act and of every other statute which imposes upon the Catholics of this empire any civil or religious disability whatever or precludes them from the enjoyment of a perfect equality with every class of their fellow-subjects.

That for the above objects we deem it necessary to establish a Catholic Defence Association, and that the same be and is hereby established.

That as one of the great constitutional and practical means of carrying the objects of this meeting, we pledge ourselves to make every effort to strengthen the hands and increase the power of those faithful representatives who, in the last session of Parliament, so energetically devoted themselves to the formation of an independent party in the legislature, having for its object the maintenance of civil and religious liberty in the British empire ...

It was also resolved to establish a committee composed of prelates and members of the legislature 'to define with accuracy the objects which are to occupy the association, to frame the rules and regulations by which it shall be governed and to submit the same to the next general meeting of the association'. A committee of forty-six was chosen: twenty-nine bishops (nineteen from Ireland and ten from Great Britain) and seventeen MPs, one of whom was Thomas Meagher.[76]

The meeting that established the Catholic Defence Association (CDA) attracted very positive commentary in the newspapers. *The Freeman's Journal*, reflecting on the fact that August was the month of Daniel O'Connell's birth, observed that the country was accustomed to vast displays of popular power: 'Ireland has been the field for the organisation and display of that peculiar force ... On yesterday, the old moral power reappeared.'[77] *The Nation* recalled the emancipation campaign: 'The meeting ... carries back the recollection at a bound of twenty-two years to the great days of the Catholic Association ... Not in the greatest days of that great association was there, we do believe, any so magnificent a public demonstration as this.'[78] A promising beginning was heralded for the new organisation.

And there was good reason to be optimistic about the prospects of the CDA. More than 600 members were already formally enrolled and hundreds more had sent their subscriptions.[79] By December, it was accommodated in what was described as an 'excellent and capacious mansion' at 15 Rutland Square East.[80] It certainly enjoyed a significantly more auspicious launch than that of O'Connell's famed Catholic Association in 1823. During that association's first year it is unlikely that membership exceeded 120.[81] Thomas Meagher had memories of the 1820s, as a young Catholic activist, and the contrast with 1851 would have given him great hopes for the new association's future. These hopes, however, were not to be realised: within five months of its foundation, the CDA was to be seriously weakened by internal divisions.

ARCHBISHOP PAUL CULLEN AND THE CDA

The Archbishop of Armagh, Paul Cullen, wanted the CDA to be, in his own words, 'wholly directed to religious matters'[82] and 'altogether for religious purposes'.[83] Accordingly, the prominent position of Irish Brigade MPs in the association caused him some disquiet.[84] On 20 August the committee of prelates and legislators appointed at the foundation meeting of the CDA to define its objectives and frame its rules convened. A sub-committee, composed of three prelates, eight MPs and one peer, and chaired by Cullen, was nominated to undertake these tasks and to prepare an address to the Catholics of the United Kingdom, its proposals to be considered at a meeting of the full committee in September.[85] The address, which listed the objectives of the association, was approved by the full committee at meetings on 25 and 26 September, for presentation to the membership at a public meeting on 17 October.[86]

Cullen did not like the address: he regarded it as overly political and not sufficiently attentive to his religious concerns.[87] He resolved to act so that the CDA conformed with his ideas. The day before the October public meeting, the full committee of the CDA met, with the archbishop in the chair, to finalise its objectives and rules,[88] which were subsequently to be adopted by its members.[89] What is noteworthy is that there was a very considerable modification in the objectives to those originally contained in the address.[90] Moreover, they were at variance with a key resolution adopted at the founding meeting relating to supporting an independent party in the legislature. While the association continued to seek the repeal of the Ecclesiastical Titles Act and other discriminatory legislation against Catholics, critically there was no reference to an independent Irish party in the objectives endorsed in October. There was a corresponding increase in the emphases on religious objectives: protecting poor Catholics against proselytism; assisting with the provision to all classes of the means to attain a sound Catholic education; and seeking the disestablishment of the Church of Ireland. And consistent with its more religiously assertive agenda, the membership of the association was to be confined exclusively to Catholics.[91]

Cullen also engaged in machinations in the matter of an election of a permanent secretary to the CDA.[92] He favoured the appointment of an Englishman, William Wilberforce. The committee of the CDA met on 17 December to make its selection between Wilberforce and an Irishman, James Burke. Cullen was not in attendance due to illness but was permitted to vote by letter. Wilberforce was appointed. Seven members of the committee, all of them MPs, issued an appeal to the people of Ireland protesting at the choice of Wilberforce. A surprised Cullen was forced to respond. While Wilberforce retained his position, the CDA was damaged by this very public disagreement between members of its leadership. Cullen had ensured that the association would not be transformed into a grass-roots organisation to sustain an independent parliamentary party. However, he paid a price: the association's eventual demise. By December 1851, it was apparent to many Catholic activists that the CDA was no reincarnation of O'Connell's Catholic Association. It was largely unheard of after the fallout over the hiring of Wilberforce, and by the end of 1853 Cullen had phased the organisation out of existence.[93]

MEAGHER AND THE CDA

What were Thomas Meagher's reactions to developments in the CDA? He cannot have been indifferent to them: after all he had played some role in the organisation. It may be remembered that he was one of the MPs who drew up the resolutions for its foundation meeting in August 1851 and was appointed to its committee at that same event. However, he did not attend the September meeting of this committee at which an address to Catholics and the association's objectives were considered. According to a letter of explanation he sent to the sub-committee drafting the address, he was unable to attend due to an illness in his family. In the same letter he stated that he had read the copies of the regulations for the government of the association and the text of the proposed address which had been sent to him for his opinion. He expressed his approval of them, not least because they had been forwarded to the hierarchies of Ireland, England and Wales for their recommendations: 'to my mind they bear so evidently the marks of the authoritative consideration and revision of the high dignitaries of the Church to whom they have been submitted, that nothing remains for me than to express my entire approbation and concurrence.'[94]

Nor did he attend the October committee and public meetings. It appears that only five MPs attended the latter; in fact the attendance of 'gentlemen from the country', as it was described by *The Freeman's Journal*, was 'far from numerous'. At that meeting, he was again nominated to the committee of the association.[95] Meagher would certainly have approved of the objectives, such as the provision of education for Catholics and their protection against proselytism. The latter was an issue of real concern to the Catholic Church, especially with the foundation in 1849 of the Society for Irish Church Missions to the Roman Catholics, an organisation which engaged in aggressive proselytism, especially in the west of Ireland.[96] Even the most casual examination of Irish newspapers for the early years of the 1850s will reveal the alarm caused to Catholics, clerical and lay, by these activities. The Catholic bishops, meeting at the national synod at Thurles in 1850, denounced these proselytising endeavours.[97] In January 1852 Bishop Nicholas Foran of Waterford, addressing a meeting attended by Meagher, criticised 'the mean and disgraceful system of proselytism by which individuals under the guise of religion and charity' were inducing poor Catholics to convert to Protestantism.[98] Meagher's awareness of this issue was almost certainly accentuated by the fact that one of his nearest neighbours on the Mall in Waterford city was the Rt Rev. Robert Daly, Church of Ireland bishop of Cashel and Waterford, a man with a reputation for encouraging and supporting proselytising endeavours.[99] Meagher attended the CDA's committee meeting in November 1851 at which proselytism was discussed and a sub-committee appointed to consider the best means to counteract it and so protect the faith of poor Catholics.[100] There were further meetings on this matter, for example on 29 January and 3 March 1852, but Meagher was absent due to parliamentary commitments.[101]

While there is no record of Meagher's views of the public letter issued by the seven MPs expressing their opposition to William Wilberforce's appointment, it is almost certain that he regarded it as a rash and intemperate response. It was particularly damaging to the CDA because Archbishop Paul Cullen was drawn into the controversy. This would have concerned Meagher because of his profound and oft-repeated respect for the Catholic hierarchy. Moreover, he appreciated the importance of the bishops' support for the association and for the struggle for Catholic equality: quite simply, this support was essential. The words in an editorial in *The Tablet* newspaper would have resonated with him: 'that around which the Catholic public will now rally, that which will engage their sympathies and command their confidence, is not Members of Parliament or any class or description of laymen, but the bishops of the Church'.[102] Any action which compromised this support and, as a consequence, undermined the effectiveness of the CDA was to be avoided.

MEAGHER AND RETIREMENT FROM PARLIAMENT

When Thomas Meagher replied to the invitation of James Burke, secretary of the Catholic committee working to organise a defence association, to participate in this initiative, he began his letter confirming his support with a curious and revealing statement: 'Although I have for some time abstained from taking part in any public movement and am now unwilling to quit the retired position ...'[103] These sentiments suggest that Meagher had decided to quit parliamentary life and consequently not seek re-election. He was only too willing, however, to put aside his preference regarding taking part 'in any public movement' because of the renewed onslaught, as he saw it, on Catholic rights and his resolve to resist government policies eroding religious equality. Events in 1852 were to confirm that he had, in fact, decided to retire from Parliament, but unexpected circumstances were to impact this resolution.

This decision did not mean that Meagher had disengaged from his parliamentary responsibilities. During the last week of January 1852, he travelled to London for the new session of Parliament, which commenced on 3 February with the queen's speech. That afternoon eight Irish Brigade MPs, including Meagher, met to discuss political tactics. The continuation of the strategy employed in 1851 – that of making the brigade's voting strength felt by exploiting the tight numerical balance between the two main English parties – was urged by him and William Keogh. Moreover, Meagher proposed a resolution that the brigade's members should continue to sit together in the House of Commons, on the opposition side of the chamber.[104] One of the first items on the parliamentary agenda was a land bill sponsored by Sharman Crawford, MP, which sought legal recognition of fair rents and free sale for tenants.[105] This was considered by the brigade members and two days later they met Crawford in the apartment of John Sadleir to discuss their support for this bill. They were to personally canvass other Irish MPs to ensure their presence for the bill's first reading.[106] While the bill did secure a first reading, it was to be defeated on the second in May.[107]

By the time of that defeat, the Liberal government of Lord John Russell had fallen, having been defeated on a vote on 20 February. A Conservative prime minister, Lord Derby, took office. However, as he did not command a majority in the Commons, he promised to dissolve Parliament as soon as the essential business of the session was complete.[108] From that moment, the general election campaign began.

THE SEARCH FOR MEAGHER'S REPLACEMENT

In February 1852 *The Waterford Chronicle* reported that it was Meagher's 'desire to retire from Parliament'.[109] In March he confirmed that he had decided not to seek re-election. On 23 March supporters of the Liberal Party in the city met and, after some discussion, it was resolved to write to him requesting that he reconsider his decision,[110] as he was 'of such importance to the cause of Catholicity and of Ireland at the present moment'.[111]

Meagher's letter of reply was read at another meeting of Liberal electors, held on 13 April. He stated that he would 'gladly' have yielded to their wishes, if he had felt himself able to discharge his duties in Parliament in the future:

> But having for some time found that my health did not permit me to give attention or make the exertion the electors might fairly expect, I would have intimated my intention at an earlier period and taken steps to withdraw from Parliament were I willing to put the electors to inconvenience until a dissolution should become inevitable. Now that such an event is impending, I can no longer hesitate to declare my determination.[112]

With Meagher's impending retirement, the search for a replacement candidate began and it soon came to assume the character of a Sisyphean endeavour. From the very start, divisions were apparent among the electors supportive of the Liberal Party.[113] Having noted Meagher's reply, the meeting of 13 April proceeded to nominate a committee to select candidates to contest the city's two seats in Parliament. Alderman James Delahunty argued that it was necessary to form a large committee to accommodate all shades of opinion, an ominous indicator of problems ahead. It was decided to appoint 100 members to it, composed of representatives of Old Ireland, Young Ireland and neutrals.[114] With divisions between Old and Young Irelanders being especially pronounced, the behemoth that was the committee set about its task.[115] At a meeting in late April, nine candidates were proposed. It was resolved to appoint a smaller sub-committee of thirty-one members to expedite the selection process.[116] In the first week of May the sub-committee reported that it was unable to decide on candidates,[117] so it was decided to apply to the CDA and the Tenant League for a list of suitable nominees.[118] This application did not prove fruitful, and by the end of May the sub-committee voted to dissolve itself, having failed to solve the conundrum of finding candidates acceptable to the divided Liberal Party electors.[119]

The inability of Liberal Party supporters to come to an agreement on candidates had the effect of endangering its electoral prospects. *The Waterford Mail*, a journal supportive of the Conservative Party, observed in late April that the increasing divisions among the committee of 100 were offering reasonable grounds that a Tory candidate 'would receive a degree of support which otherwise he would not obtain'.[120] A prospective Conservative candidate began to emerge, William Christmas, and by mid-June he had entered the electoral fray.[121]

It was this very real prospect of the loss of a seat to a Tory which concentrated the attention of Liberals. Calls for unity were translated into action.[122] On 19 June *The Waterford Chronicle* reported that the Roman Catholic clergy of the city had approached Thomas Meagher and Robert Keating (Liberal MP for Waterford county and a member of the Irish Brigade) to stand for election. On 25 June a deputation of electors attended on Meagher at his home on the Mall and presented him with a requisition calling on him to again contest the parliamentary elections, together with Keating.[123] This requisition was signed by Bishop Foran, sixteen priests and 300 electors.[124] A letter dated the same day, 25 June, was published in *The Waterford Chronicle* on the following day. Written by a Catholic priest, Rev. Patrick Kent of Ballybricken parish, it announced an end to all political differences among Liberal voters. The various factions had 'cordially and emphatically' pronounced for Meagher and Keating. 'Be assured these gentlemen will come forward and all are determined to support them.' It is unlikely that such a letter would have been written without the prior knowledge and approval of Bishop Foran, one of Meagher's strongest supporters, whose representations, together with that of his clergy, would have held great sway with Meagher.

All of this persuaded Meagher to run again for Parliament – a decision which almost coincided with its dissolution on 1 July – transforming the fortunes of the Liberal Party in Waterford city. Unity was restored after a long period of recrimination and indecision. *The Freeman's Journal* was of the opinion that his candidacy would also help to facilitate the election of Keating.[125] *The Waterford Chronicle* praised him for agreeing to contest the election and noted that 'dire has been the consternation among the Tories' at the new-found unity among their opponents.[126] The *Mail* could not conceal its resentment at the damage done to Tory election prospects. Directing its fury at Meagher, it accused him of reducing himself to the role of 'puppet' and 'tool' of the Liberal Party. In its frustration, it issued a *cri de coeur*: '... his heart is not in this election; he is tired of the arena of politics. Let Mr Meagher alone.'[127]

RELIGION AND THE 1852 GENERAL ELECTION

In June 1852 the CDA, while weakened, did issue an address to the Catholic electors of Ireland, with the purpose of ensuring that religious concerns were paramount in the exercise of their votes. The association gave a clear and specific description of the type of person Catholics should return to Parliament: advocates of the repeal of the Ecclesiastical Titles Act and other laws directed against the Catholic religion; supporters of denominational education; opponents of the 'godless colleges'; promoters of the rights of tenants; and those who would oppose any government which refused justice to Catholics.[128] In the context of this description, Meagher was an ideal candidate.

When it published this address, the CDA could not have imagined how the issue of religion would dominate the general election campaign. Not long after its publication, the Conservative government of Lord Derby issued, on 15 June, a royal proclamation reminding English Catholics that it was illegal for them, under the law of the land, to participate in public religious processions. This outraged opinion in Ireland, which was still particularly sensitive in the aftermath of the Ecclesiastical Titles Act. The government's action was widely regarded as yet another deliberate insult to the Catholic religion and a crude attempt to win the 'no-popery' vote in the forthcoming general election.[129] Later in the month there was an outbreak of serious sectarian rioting in Stockport, Cheshire. The houses of twenty-four Catholics were sacked and two Catholic chapels were wrecked; in one chapel it was alleged that the tabernacle had been broken open and communion hosts scattered on the ground. This especially appalled Ireland's Catholics, who accused the government of fomenting this disorder by the issuance of the earlier proclamation.[130]

Comerford has observed that, 'Religious tensions put steam into the Irish election of 1852.'[131] Throughout the country, acceptance of the principle of tenant right and religious equality, and promising not to support any government failing to support such policies proved to be a sure and certain means of securing the support of the key middle-class and clerical figures, who in so many constituencies controlled the Liberal Party organisation.[132] Voters, already primed by the earlier campaign in England against the restoration of the Catholic hierarchy, were readily swayed by the avalanche of propaganda produced in reaction to the proclamation and Stockport riots. Probably, never since the Union had there been a general election in which religious passions were so much aroused nationally (the fervour of the 1826 election having been confined to a few constituencies).[133]

THE WATERFORD CITY GENERAL ELECTION, 1852

The election for the Waterford city constituency was held on 12 July. Meagher was proposed by Sir Benjamin Morris Wall, who in his speech made it absolutely clear that Meagher's undoubted preference was to retire from parliamentary politics. However, according to Wall, the Catholic bishop, his clergy and voters generally urged him to stand again, and he had complied with this urgent request to heal the local divisions in the Liberal Party. He outlined the significant proposals Meagher had supported in the last Parliament by his vote: the extension of the franchise; the secret ballot to protect voters against intimidation; shorter Parliaments; and Sharman Crawford's land bill. Alderman James Delahunty seconded the nomination, reiterating that Meagher had been induced to contest the election, voters believing that his name 'is, in itself, a tower of strength'. He asserted that Meagher had by his votes and attendance in Parliament assisted in the organisation of an 'Irish party'.

In a typically brief address, Meagher began with what might have been an allusion to his health, excusing his difficulty in addressing his audience due to his bad lungs. He did not disguise the fact that he was a reluctant candidate, declaring that he had resisted every appeal to him to stand and only changed his mind when political divisions made defeat inevitable for the Liberal Party in the city. He explained that he could not sacrifice what he conceived to be the interests of his country and religion, even if that meant the sacrifice of his own preference for retirement.

Meagher had not issued the traditional address to electors, thus making his speech on the nomination the occasion for outlining the political platform on which he was seeking re-election. It might have been expected that the focus of this speech would have been how the prime minister's actions had inflamed religious tensions. Meagher's principal concern, however, was Lord Derby's attitude to political reforms: his attention was on civil liberty and what he regarded as the right of citizens 'to full participation in the privileges of the constitution'. Hence, he deplored the government's response to proposals to extend the franchise, Meagher highlighting the reality that many of those listening to him could not vote. He was critical of the government's position on the secret ballot, so essential, according to Meagher, to protect voters against landlord intimidation. He urged the necessity of shorter terms for Parliament, to ensure that constituencies were more properly represented by their MPs. Finally, Meagher called on the voters of Waterford to return to Parliament only persons who would always vote against any ministry opposed to civil and religious liberty, tenant rights and political reforms.[134]

This speech gives an interesting insight into Meagher. While he was undoubtedly a reluctant candidate for Parliament, there was nothing diffident or equivocal about his political beliefs and principles. He was on the radical spectrum of politics: he reaffirmed his commitment to civil and religious liberty, justice for Ireland and, on his re-election, opposition to the Derby government.[135] On election day, he topped the poll in the constituency: [136]

Thomas Meagher	465 votes
Robert Keating	446 votes
William Christmas	355 votes
Henry Winston Barron	309 votes

Thus, the reluctant candidate, Thomas Meagher, found himself representing the city of Waterford in Parliament for another five years.

CHAPTER THIRTEEN

Member of Parliament, 1852–1857: Independent Opposition

Thomas Meagher took his seat in the new Parliament as the senior MP for Waterford city. He was a committed advocate of religious equality, rights for tenants and political reform. He was determined to remain independent of any government which failed to adopt these policies. The election results represented a significant success for those associated with the Irish Brigade and the policy of independent opposition. Twenty-eight of the sitting members may be classified as brigade members at the parliamentary dissolution and twenty were re-elected, including Meagher. Among those elected for the first time in 1852 were some influential advocates of an Independent Irish Party (IIP), including Frederick Lucas, editor of *The Tablet*; Charles Gavan Duffy, editor of *The Nation*; and John Francis Maguire, proprietor of *The Cork Examiner*. Seventeen of the new members had specifically pledged themselves to remain independent of all English parties in the House of Commons.[1]

TENANT LEAGUE CONFERENCE, SEPTEMBER 1852

Many of the Irish Liberal MPs had committed themselves to support the cause of tenant rights. The leadership of the Tenant League decided to consolidate the results of the general election and organised a national conference in Dublin on 8 and 9 September, at which the future course of policy would be decided. From early August, a committee was busy sending out invitations.[2] On 12 August *The Freeman's Journal* reported that a large number of MPs had indicated their determination to be present, the newspaper highlighting that five who had already undertaken to attend were old supporters of Sharman Crawford's bill, including Meagher. He was among the forty-five MPs, of the forty-eight invited, who were present at the opening of the conference on 8 September. Resolutions affirming the principles of Crawford's bill were adopted, as was one pertaining to independent opposition:

> That in the unanimous opinion of this conference it is essential to the proper management of this cause that the Members of Parliament who have been returned on tenant-right principles should hold themselves perfectly independent of, and in opposition to, all governments which do not make it a part of their policy and a cabinet question to give to the tenantry of Ireland a measure fully embodying the principles of Mr Sharman Crawford's bill.[3]

RELIGIOUS CONFERENCE, OCTOBER 1852

On 10 September, the day after the conclusion of the Tenant League conference, and inspired by its success, a meeting was held in Dublin to decide on a course of action with regard to the issue of religious equality. The obvious convening body for such a gathering would have been the CDA, but after some activity during the general election campaign, it had practically faded out of existence.[4] Its place on this occasion was taken by a group later to style itself the Friends of Religious Freedom. At the meeting, it was resolved that a committee be appointed to consider how the principle of religious freedom and equality could best be advanced in Parliament and to report its conclusions to a national conference. A committee of sixty-seven was appointed to carry out the objects of the meeting, of which forty-seven members were MPs, including Meagher.[5] Neither he nor the vast majority of MPs nominated to the committee were in attendance at the meeting and were not to play any significant role in the new organisation. However, they were not, in fact, required to do much, if anything. A small group of activists managed its affairs – it was they who decided to convene the planned conference on 28 October in the Rotundo and undertook all the preparatory work in relation to the event.[6]

The national conference attracted an attendance of upwards of 200 gentlemen, including twenty-six MPs.[7] Among the latter was Meagher, and some of the most influential members of the Tenant League, such as Frederick Lucas and Charles Gavan Duffy. The organising committee presented a report outlining the concerns and grievances of Catholics, and this report informed the resolutions which were adopted.[8] One, employing trenchant language, described the established status of the Church of Ireland as 'a badge of conquest and a legalised robbery of the population'. Another resolution declared that the object of the conference was to remove from the country 'the intolerable grievance of religious inequality'. Laws imposing penalties on the ecclesiastics of any church were condemned as being 'inconsistent with the constitution', and the exclusion from public offices of any persons because of their faith conflicted with the principle of religious equality. A crucial resolution was adopted in relation to independent opposition: 'That in the opinion of this conference all Members of Parliament returned by Liberal Irish constituencies should continue independent of, and in opposition to, every government which will not make the concession of perfect religious equality, as explained in the foregoing resolutions, a part of its policy.'[9]

The conference on religious equality was a smaller affair than that convened on the issue of tenants' rights, a circumstance explained by the fact that the Friends of Religious Freedom was a body only recently established and consequently less influential than the Tenant League. Nevertheless, it was an impressive display of the determination to advance the principle of religious equality, particularly in Parliament. And to this end the resolution on independent opposition was of paramount significance. Between the two conferences, a total of forty-two MPs had accepted this pledge.[10] At least another six, who committed to the same policy in election addresses or at adoption meetings, may be added to this figure, making a total of forty-eight,[11] which constituted a significant political grouping in the House of Commons. The cause of independent opposition, therefore, was at the zenith of its political influence in the autumn of 1852, having made spectacular progress since it was first mooted at the Tenant League conference in 1850.

Meagher must have viewed these political developments with mixed emotions. On a personal level, he had little cause for enthusiasm, as he did not want to be an MP. He had wished to retire for health reasons and these were likely to have remained unchanged. However, he had allowed political considerations to trump personal ones. On a strictly political level, he had much to bring him pleasure and satisfaction. His candidacy had secured a victory for the Liberal Party and denied the Tories a seat in Waterford city. Nationally, the cause of religious liberty and equality, which had inspired and informed his involvement in public affairs for over thirty years, was being promoted with some enthusiasm and vigour. Significantly, it had been strategically aligned with a parliamentary policy of independent opposition. And he had been one of the pioneers of this same policy by his association with the Irish Brigade and his votes in Parliament. Perhaps the favourable political situation in the autumn of 1852 might have mitigated somewhat Meagher's reluctance to return to Westminster.

FALL OF THE DERBY GOVERNMENT

The new Parliament assembled on 4 November 1852. Lord Derby's Conservative government did not have a majority; nor did the opposition Liberals and Peelites. This was the ideal situation for the Irish parliamentary supporters of independent opposition, because they held the balance of power.[12] They were to display this power before year's end. Derby reaffirmed his hostility to tenant rights and in the early hours of 17 December, IIP MPs, including Thomas Meagher, joined with the opposition to defeat the government on the budget by 305 votes to 286. This was a significant achievement: the Irish could claim the result was due to them, for without their crucial votes the other parties combined would not have been able to bring the Derby administration down.[13] Certainly, *The Freeman's Journal* felt able to proclaim that 'the fate of the Derby ministry is sealed, and sealed confessedly by the Irish contingent to the House of Commons'.[14]

A new coalition government of Liberals and Peelites was formed under the leadership of Lord Aberdeen, a Peelite. It included Lord John Russell, of Ecclesiastical Titles fame. From Ireland's perspective, interest in the composition of the new administration was dominated by two junior ministerial appointments: those of leaders of the Irish Brigade and the IIP, William Keogh as Solicitor General for Ireland and John Sadleir as a Lord of the Treasury.

Their decision to accept government offices generated a ferocious controversy, because of their pledge not to support any administration that did not make tenant rights and religious equality a cabinet question. To their critics – and they were numerous – Sadleir and Keogh were judged to have violated this pledge of independent opposition. The *Freeman's Journal*, *The Nation* and *The Tablet* unleashed an unrelenting torrent of denunciations.[15] On 11 January the council of the Tenant League adopted a resolution condemning unequivocally their taking office in a government which had not made Sharman Crawford's bill a cabinet question.[16] The next day the Friends of Religious Freedom denounced the two new ministers for violating their pledges in relation to the matter of religious equality, deeming their actions as 'calculated to work the most mischievous consequences to the interests of Ireland, by breaking up the IIP and destroying public confidence in public men'.[17]

MEAGHER'S DEFENCE OF SADLEIR AND KEOGH

On 1 February the Friends of Religious Freedom organised a meeting at Kells, County Meath, for the purpose of adopting a petition to Parliament in pursuit of their objectives. The event attracted a significant attendance.[18] It was also intended that the occasion be used to attack the actions of Sadleir and Keogh. To achieve maximum publicity, the circular issued to invitees requested permission of those unable to attend to publish their approval of the condemnation of the two MPs.[19] Thomas Meagher received an invitation but was unable to be present on the day. In his letter of apology, however, he made it very clear that he did not wish to be associated with any criticism of Sadleir and Keogh.

To associate himself with any condemnation would be for him, in his words, 'a premature conclusion'. Meagher contended that the policy of Lord Aberdeen's government in relation to Ireland was as yet unclear. He was, therefore, 'induced to await until [this] policy ... shall appear to be inimical to our religion, to our people and to our country ... before I take upon myself to join in pronouncing a sentence of unqualified condemnation upon them'. Meagher also referred to the fact that many leading members of the present administration had opposed the Ecclesiastical Titles Bill and he was 'especially' mindful of 'the almost solitary emphatic opposition to it in the Upper House by the head of government'. Moreover, he had witnessed 'the parliamentary exertions' of Sadleir and Keogh 'in defence of our religious liberties when they were assailed and in assertion of Irish tenants' rights'. He obviously felt that their past services to their country entitled them to fair and considered treatment, rather than a rush to judgement.

Meagher was clear in his opinion that if pledges had been broken, he did not approve of such conduct. He had assented to the same pledge and intended to adhere 'strictly' to it. However, he did express, briefly and without elaboration, his reservations about the interpretation of the pledge by an unnamed party member – an interpretation Meagher regarded as rendering it 'valueless as a text of effective parliamentary opposition'. Furthermore, he was concerned about the impact that a condemnation of the two MPs could have on the IIP and how it 'is likely to be bound in more cordial and effective combination by the judgment you [Rev. Nicholas McEvoy, chair of the organising committee] invite me to take a part'. He elaborated on this concern:

> But if I were sure that these gentlemen had not been so faithful, however I might disapprove of their conduct, I would not deem it a sufficient reason for branding them *at once* [my emphasis] as deserters from their party and traitors to their country ... and [thus] doing more to break up the hitherto strong and effective union of the Irish members than their desertion possibly could.[20]

MEAGHER'S LETTER CONSIDERED

Commenting on the controversy surrounding the acceptance of ministerial office by Sadleir and Keogh, the historian of the IIP, John Whyte, has written: 'Some contemporaries – and not only their allies, but men whose own independence was unquestionable, such as Thomas Meagher, MP for Waterford city – considered it unjust to condemn them until the new government had had an opportunity to make clear its policy.'[21] His letter on the occasion of the meeting at Kells highlights the importance

Meagher attached to clarification of the government's Irish policy. His attitude was informed by the sense that the Aberdeen government was, from the perspective of Irish Catholics, an improvement on the Derby administration. Aberdeen's ministers included leading Peelites, members of the only British parliamentary group that had opposed the titles bill and whose presence in government could be regarded as the best guarantee that Catholics would not be subjected to further discriminatory legislation. Therefore, the wisest policy was to keep such a government in office, pending elucidation of its policy.[22]

Meagher also admired the opposition of Sadleir and Keogh to the titles bill, and their advocacy of tenant rights. He had displayed this admiration on other occasions. On 28 October 1851 a banquet was held in Athlone to honour Keogh's leading role in the Irish Brigade. Meagher had been invited; unable to attend, he sent a letter of apology in which he described Keogh as 'an honourable and talented gentleman' and praised 'his value as an Irish representative'.[23] He was in attendance at a dinner in August 1852 honouring Sadleir's re-election.[24] Meagher obviously had a measure of personal and political regard for the two men: he felt they deserved better than what he considered a hasty condemnation.

However, it was the fundamental need to preserve the unity of Irish Liberal MPs elected on the independent opposition ticket that was the principal motivation for the position he was adopting, at this juncture, on the Sadleir and Keogh controversy. His over-arching concern was to avoid division and fragmentation. This outlook was likely inspired by Meagher's experiences of the split in the Repeal Association and the manner in which its political effectiveness had been dissipated by factionalism and internal recriminations. His own recent election in Waterford highlighted for him the enervating consequences of a divided party. He would seek to make his contribution to a resolution whereby the IIP could negotiate the turbulence caused by the actions of Sadleir and Keogh. He got an opportunity at a party meeting in early March.

A DIVISIVE MEETING

This meeting took place at the King's Arms, Palace Yard, Westminster, on Thursday, 3 March 1853, to consider the course of action to be pursued by the IIP 'under present circumstances'.[25] Thirty-seven MPs were in attendance.[26] The meeting, which lasted two hours, was characterised by what *The Tablet* described as 'very considerable differences of opinion'. It continued its report, highlighting a central difficulty facing the participants: 'the language held by all the speakers was uniform as to the absolute necessity of being independent of all governments that will not do *something* for Ireland in regard to land and religion; though what that "something" is or how it shall be defined was a question that presented a good deal of difficulty'.[27] Several proposals were put forward regarding the future course of the party's parliamentary conduct, but no decisions were made. It was in the context of this lack of progress that Meagher made a not insignificant intervention. He proposed the appointment of a committee of seven, representing the different opinions at issue, to consider future policy and to draw up a series of resolutions for the regulation of its future course and on the best means of enabling members to act cordially together.[28] This proposal was clearly inspired by his desire to maintain party unity. It was under consideration when the meeting decided to adjourn to Saturday 5 March.

When the adjourned meeting reconvened, the attendance was smaller: twenty-six MPs were present.[29] It proved to be an acrimonious affair, with *The Freeman's Journal* referring to 'a very protracted ... and rather warm discussion'.[30] There were those who advocated a policy of 'entire independence'.[31] Others argued for giving the government a 'fair trial', pointing to the prospect of a satisfactory land bill. One issue emerged as especially divisive: the seating arrangements to be adopted by IIP MPs in the House of Commons. The conflicting attitudes were emblematic of deeper divisions. Many of the proponents of giving the government a fair trial and who were more disposed to compromise in relation to independent opposition favoured sitting on the government side of the chamber, as Irish Liberal members used do when a Liberal government was in power. It was further argued that such an arrangement simply implied that the present administration approximated more closely to the views of the IIP than the occupants of the opposition benches, namely, the Conservatives.[32] Those in favour of a continued policy of independent opposition insisted that the party's MPs occupy the opposition benches, as the Irish Brigade had done in 1851–2. By this action they were declaring their independence from the government. Amidst all this discussion, Meagher's proposal for a committee to consider policy was eclipsed. Eventually, a motion was put to the twenty-three members still present: 'That the Irish Liberal Party, as constituted in December 1852, will continue to hold themselves independent of the government and to act together in cordial union, irrespective of the position which individual members of the party occupy in the House.' Thirteen members voted in favour, including John Sadleir. Nine opposed it, among whom were Meagher and Charles Gavan Duffy.[33]

Why did Meagher vote as he did? He was still committed to the policy of independent opposition. An agreement whereby it was accepted that IIP MPs could sit anywhere in the chamber – in particular on government benches – represented for him a disposition to dilute this policy, a disposition which might have been all too evident from the contributions of some of his parliamentary colleagues to the discussion. He wanted a party united behind the principle of independent opposition, pursuing agreed policies consistent with this same principle. Of course, party members were supposed to be adherents of independent opposition, a fact which had been given expression in the pledge adopted at the Tenant League and Friends of Religious Freedom conferences. Clearly, however, there were disagreements over the interpretation of this pledge and no agreed definition of what its terms meant. This was a genuine problem and one which leaders of the party were obliged to confront as they sought to clarify its meaning in later years.[34] The urgent need to clarify the meaning and practical application of the pledge in the dynamic world that is politics was critical to the party's viability and future unity. Hence, Meagher made his proposal for a policy committee. While this was a desirable, even necessary initiative, it would not, however, have been sufficient to preserve party unity, as will be seen later in this chapter.

A DIVIDED PARTY

The reality was that the adjourned meeting only deepened the fissures among IIP MPs[35] and their supporters,[36] with partisan press coverage of events exacerbating the situation. *The Freeman's Journal* accused former members of the Irish Brigade (it had Sadleir particularly in mind) of seeking to pull down the whole political fabric by which they had won the confidence of the Irish public and attacked what it termed 'corruptionists' for proposing that MPs sit on the government benches.[37] *The Weekly Telegraph,* a newspaper owned by Sadleir, responded by denouncing those who wanted MPs to sit with the opposition, 'in the heart of the Tory forces, and associate in the House of Commons with those men who are the hereditary enemies of the Catholic religion and the Irish people'.[38]

According to Charles Gavan Duffy, 'a wedge' had been driven right through the party, 'dividing it into two sections',[39] one of which was returning to the loosely knit fellowship of the Liberal Party, and this number was to go on increasing throughout the decade.[40] For the five-year period from 1852 to 1857, Gavan Duffy listed twenty-seven 'deserters' and the IIP, in his words, 'gradually dwindled away'.[41] In August 1855 he presented an even more gloomy picture, writing in *The Nation* that, 'The Irish party is reduced to a handful ... [it] commenced with fifty adherents; to-day more than forty have gone over bodily or in spirit to the enemy'.[42] Notwithstanding a section of MPs who proclaimed continuing allegiance to the principle of independent opposition, including Meagher, Archbishop Cullen wrote in November 1855 that 'the great party ... has melted like snow' and there was 'no trace of it now worth mentioning'.[43]

In fact, the remarkable tide that had swept the independents into Parliament crested over the winter of 1852–53,[44] and the fortunes of the IIP only looked truly bright between July and December 1852,[45] from that year's general election to the defection of Sadleir and Keogh. This defection was to have a devastating impact on the political fortunes of the party, damaging its prestige and credibility. The acceptance of ministerial office by two of its most prominent representatives precipitated a schism[46] and generated bitter internal factionalism, all of which squandered much extra-parliamentary support.[47] However, while undoubtedly the actions of the two defectors were a major factor in the demise of independent opposition, there were other significant reasons.

The defection highlighted and, in a real sense, symbolised a pre-eminent reason: what Whyte has termed 'the distracting power of government patronage'.[48] MPs wanted a share in this to satisfy their personal ambitions – a desire that was intensified by the fact that ordinary (i.e. non-ministerial) parliamentarians were unremunerated.

Independent opposition, however, required its adherents to deny themselves the prospect of advancement. Thus, many were willing to drift back to orthodox Liberalism, which held the prospect of political rewards, when that party was in power.

Moreover, MPs wanted access to patronage for family members and supporters. In the days before competitive examinations for civil service positions, such offices were filled directly by ministerial nomination. The amount of time and care that Victorian politicians had to spend on matters of patronage – seeking and dispensing it – is startling to modern eyes.[49] Ministers, unsurprisingly, favoured representations from supporters; those of opponents were ignored. Quite simply, as long as a party remained in opposition it had no claims to the rewards at the disposal of government; therefore, many IIP MPs were not prepared to endure this political desert.

CONFLICT WITH ARCHBISHOP CULLEN

The matter of patronage was an important factor in what was to be a deterioration in the relationship between the IIP and Archbishop Cullen. For him it was a priority that as many public offices as possible should be filled by Catholics,[50] thus mitigating the Protestant character of the state. This could only be achieved by MPs cooperating with a favourably disposed government and the archbishop was not willing to waste the possible opportunities presented by the Aberdeen administration, the political complexion of which appeared more sympathetic to Catholic concerns than its immediate predecessors. In fact, Cullen wanted to abandon the policy of independent opposition and to work with the Aberdeen ministry, as such an arrangement offered the prospect of being able to influence its policy generally in respect of Catholic demands.[51]

Personal animosities added to already existing tensions. Cullen heartily disapproved of Gavan Duffy's prominent role in the party. Throughout his career, the archbishop 'maintained an almost fanatical hatred of people who had been associated with Young Ireland and the abortive rising of 1848'.[52] As rector of the Irish College, he had been in Rome during the revolutionary events in that city in the same year. He came to equate Young Ireland with Young Italy, and Gavan Duffy with its leader, Mazzini.[53] Cullen began to display an increasingly hostile attitude to independent opposition and, according to Whyte, 'it is beyond question that his obsession with Young Ireland was a major cause of it'.[54]

At a diocesan synod held in Dublin in June 1854, Cullen introduced legislation aimed at regulating the behaviour of priests in relation to political activities. Gavan Duffy and Frederick Lucas viewed this initiative as an attack on the IIP, because without the support of the Catholic Church it was doomed.[55] They mounted a public protest and decided to appeal the synodical decisions to Rome. Not surprisingly, the appeal was unsuccessful, but their action in challenging Cullen in such a manner shocked many Catholics and cost the party valuable support throughout the country.[56] Nor did the appeal do anything to strengthen the party in Parliament. Part of the appeal involved the presentation of a memorial critical of Cullen, signed by six MPs. Unsurprisingly, Meagher was not one of them.[57] His respect for the hierarchy had him eschew any public disagreement with Cullen. Moreover, he would have recognised that such an action was damaging to the party.

For the IIP, by 1855 misfortune was heaped on misfortune. It lost its leading personalities: Lucas died in October and in November Gavan Duffy emigrated to Australia. The party was in disarray.[58]

THOMAS MEAGHER: LOYALTY TO INDEPENDENT OPPOSITION

Despite the declining fortunes of the IIP, Thomas Meagher remained loyal to the policy of independent opposition for the duration of his time in Parliament. The historians of the party have acknowledged this. Knowlton, writing about his defence of Sadleir and Keogh to the organisers of the meeting at Kells, noted Meagher's declaration of his own intention to adhere to his pledge and commented that he was true to his word.[59] Whyte, in an analysis of the political behaviour of Irish Liberal MPs during the Parliament which sat from 1852 to 1857, attempted to show 'how far each was committed to the policy of independence'. His research indicates that Meagher remained committed throughout the life of the Parliament, being one of only ten Irish MPs who acted thus.[60] Contemporary commentary confirms this. His name was included in a list of MPs recognised as advocates of justice for tenant rights compiled by *The Freeman's Journal* in July 1853, a political position consistent with the pledge he took at the Tenant League conference in September 1852.[61] At a Tenant League conference held on 4 October 1853, a report was considered which named MPs who were described as being 'true to the principle of independent opposition' – among the twenty-six named was Meagher.[62]

Why did Meagher remain loyal to the policy of independent opposition? The answer is not a complex one. In his speech at the nomination of candidates in 1852, he called on voters to return to Parliament only persons committed to tenant rights and political reforms – specifically, the extension of the franchise and the adoption of the secret ballot. The governments of Aberdeen and Palmerston did not concede these demands. Accordingly, Meagher's interpretation of his pledge of opposition made to the electors of Waterford precluded him from supporting the government on certain crucial issues.

MEAGHER'S EXPRESSIONS OF SUPPORT FOR
INDEPENDENT OPPOSITION

Meagher expressed his support for independent opposition in three ways. One was the manner in which he voted in Parliament. Whyte has examined the division lists for each of the parliamentary sessions from 1853 to 1857. On the basis of these he sought to identify the Irish members who remained loyal to independent opposition. In his opinion, Meagher was one of them.[63] The Irish independent members were to be found opposing the government on matters of confidence, i.e. ones which would mean resignation of the government or a general election if it were defeated. For example, Meagher opposed the budget introduced by W.E. Gladstone in May 1853, not least because it imposed income tax on Ireland.[64] He later supported an amendment, opposed by Gladstone, to exempt Ireland from this impost.[65] In 1857 he also voted against the budget.[66] On a crucial matter of foreign policy, the government's conduct of the Crimean War (1853–56), he was among those who voted in favour of a motion attributing blame to the ministers for 'the calamities that befell the army'.[67]

Second, where Meagher sat in the chamber of the House of Commons expressed his adherence to independent opposition. Whyte has observed that, 'The main distinction, indeed, between independent opposition and other Irish Liberals was not how it voted, but where it sat, for the independent members remained on the opposition side of the House, and the proof that a member had abandoned the party normally came when he crossed to the ministerial benches.'[68]

Whatever about the manner in which he voted and where he positioned himself in the Commons, the third way in which Meagher supported the policy of independent opposition was perhaps the most significant: he did not seek government patronage. This fact was commented upon by newspapers in Waterford. According to *The Waterford Chronicle*, 'He was not of that pliant, slavish nature which would carry to the feet of the minister every begging letter be received.' However, this 'offended the hungry [place] beggars who would prey on him.'[69] *The Waterford Mail* reported: 'The only complaint we have heard [against Meagher] has been that he has not been so active in looking for places for some of the hungry ones who supported him, as he might have been; this conduct only shows how anxious he was to be independent ...'[70]

INTEGRITY

It may be remembered that at the height of the controversy surrounding the defection of Sadleir and Keogh, Meagher declared that he would be adhering 'strictly' to his pledge. He continued to support independent opposition because he clearly believed that the government was failing to pursue policies which he could conscientiously support. His sense of integrity demanded that he act in a manner consistent with his pledge. And integrity was a characteristic contemporary commentators associated with Meagher. When he first announced that he was not seeking re-election in 1852, *The Freeman's Journal* commented: 'Alderman Meagher withdraws from a representation which he never dishonoured even with a doubtful vote; and at this juncture, when it becomes so important to distinguish between the honest man and the varnished rogue, when the knave puts on a mask of integrity and the rascal simulates patriotism, the loss of men such as Mr Meagher becomes powerfully apparent.'[71]

In faraway Van Diemen's Land, in his exile, William Smith O'Brien was sent Irish newspapers which reported on the 1852 general election. He recorded his reaction to the results in his journal:

> Amongst the Irish representatives there are ten or a dozen
> members whom I believe to be incorruptible defenders of the
> interests of Ireland. Some of them are very able men. These few
> men form the nucleus of a national party ... The national interests
> of Ireland will be supported by several men distinguished for that
> earnestness which is by some called fanaticism. By whatever name
> enthusiasm be called it is the moving power by which great events
> are produced. Amongst these men I place Duffy and Lucas as
> chiefs: and I rely upon the stern integrity of such men as Meagher,
> Potter, Fagan, O'Flaherty and a few others whose independence of
> spirit has been tested and not found wanting.[72]

Commenting on the rejection of the 1853 budget by some Irish
members, the London correspondent of *The Cork Examiner* noted that
this was the position taken by those 'who have no object to gain and
no places to seek for, and who are perfectly independent of the favours
and blandishments of ministers. What ... but a sense of public duty
could influence men such as Thomas Meagher of Waterford and John
Devereux of Wexford ...' The correspondent continued: 'I mention these
men because they are utterly free from personal ambition ... They have
but one object in view, the faithful discharge of their duty, which they
believe they can best accomplish by the preservation of their personal
independence.'[73] When Meagher did retire from Parliament in 1857,
The Waterford News observed in an editorial: 'By men of all parties Mr
Meagher was recognised as a man of integrity.'[74]

Two factors facilitated Meagher's adherence to his pledge. The first
was an attribute rare in an MP: he had no personal political ambitions.
As has been noted on a number of occasions, he was a genuinely reluctant
politician, *The Freeman's Journal* noting: 'He never coveted the prize [of
a seat in Parliament]. It was proffered and accepted at an inconvenience,
because his fellow citizens willed it.'[75] The second factor was his wealth,
which gave him immunity to the lure of lucre in the form of government
patronage. This combination of an absence of personal ambition, ample
financial resources and a strong sense of integrity cloaked him in political
and moral armour impenetrable to any pressures a government might
seek to exert to secure his vote; to quote *The Waterford News*: 'Wanting

no place for himself – independent in fortune as he was in principle – the ministerial whipper-in always looked on Mr Meagher as a member beyond his reach. Hence, he voted as his conscience dictated.'[76]

MEAGHER'S VOTING RECORD IN PARLIAMENT

Meagher certainly appears to have voted with the dictates of his conscience. The matters he supported in Parliament accorded with concerns he had highlighted in his election speeches in 1852: tenant rights, political reforms and civil and religious liberty. He supported the introduction of the secret ballot, a measure which met with deep resistance among a majority of MPs.[77] He favoured the appointment of civil servants by open and competitive examinations, and voted for a motion, which was defeated, that such examinations 'be conducted in public and that the examiners be directed to have due regard to superior qualifications and merits'.[78] He backed efforts (again defeated) to appoint a select committee to inquire into the imposition of the death penalty.[79]

Meagher was a defender of Catholic rights and interests during his ten years as an MP. It has already been noted that he opposed the Ecclesiastical Titles Bill and the Religious Houses Bill. He voted against other efforts to encroach on what he regarded as the religious freedom of convents in 1853 and 1854.[80] Regular parliamentary attempts to withdraw the state grant to Maynooth College were rejected by him.[81] He criticised one of the supporters of this initiative as trying 'in his own fallible opinion to attach the name of idolaters to millions of his fellow creatures'.[82] He favoured the abolition of an impost on Catholics known as ministers' money, by which the householders of eight cities and boroughs (including Waterford) were taxed for the payment of Church of Ireland clergy.[83] Meagher informed the Commons that this issue 'was one of great annoyance to the inhabitants … of towns where the tax was levied, and what the government ought to have done was to introduce a measure for its total abolition at once'.[84] (It was finally abolished in 1857, after Meagher had retired from Parliament.)

Meagher's defence of Catholicism reflected his deep commitment to his faith. It also reflected his deep conviction in the principle of civil and religious liberty for all the queen's subjects. Speaking in the Commons against the removal of the Maynooth grant, he asserted that the votes of Catholic members 'had always been given in favour of civil and religious liberty'.[85] While addressing members on the inequity of minister's money, he commented: 'If dissenters in England felt it a grievance to be called on to contribute towards the performance of [Anglican] divine worship, towards the building and repairing of [Anglican] churches, it must equally be a grievance to the Roman Catholics of Ireland to have to pay this tax.'[86] He was establishing his argument on a universal principle which applied to all non-Anglican denominations. He wanted the tax's abolition 'precisely' because it represented 'a relic of the penal code'.[87] Consistent with his belief in the right of all to equality of religious treatment, he voted in favour of legislation to remove legal disabilities against Jews.[88]

NEWSPAPER COMMENTARY ON THOMAS MEAGHER AS AN MP

As a parliamentarian, Meagher very rarely contributed to debates in the Commons. Moreover, he was a self-declared reluctant politician, whose health was not especially robust. This combination of circumstances probably explains why he was the subject of criticism in the pages of *The Waterford Chronicle*. In November 1850 an article appeared examining the political performance of all of Waterford's MPs. The writer, while praising his honesty, asserted that 'unfortunately in Parliament Mr Meagher does not possess the position which the representative of a commercial community like ours requires'.[89] An editorial the following month concurred with this assessment. It acknowledged him as 'a sagacious and a silent magistrate, an upright and a kindly [poor law] guardian, a virtuous and useful citizen'. However, it continued: 'But his very virtues as a citizen become failings in the representation, and … to some extent incapacitate our worthy member as one of the House of Commons.' He was not 'a bold and strenuous exponent of our grievances and our wrongs'. His 'love of retirement and self-communion' made him temperamentally unsuited to political life at Westminster. His 'very placid tone of mind militates against him when he gets into the national arena'. The editorial concluded on an almost embarrassed note: 'but few constituencies could allege it as their fault against their member that his personal modesty and gentleness of disposition incapacitated him for his public and stirring duties'.[90]

This embarrassment, such as it was, did not alter or moderate *The Waterford Chronicle*'s opinion of Meagher. In February 1852, with a general election approaching, it declared him 'unfit' to be the city's MP. 'His natural reserve places him in the House of Commons in a false light. He appears to be deficient where he is not; to be negligent, when he feels a desire to be active'. The journal was of the definite opinion that 'his temperament, his idiosyncrasies plainly prove that he is not equal [to his role]'.[91] *The Waterford News* also commented editorially in the same month that Meagher 'finds a parliamentary life neither suitable to his health nor habits'.[92]

While *The Waterford Chronicle* was very definitely of the view that Meagher was an inadequate representative of Waterford's interests at Westminster, *The Waterford Mail* expressed a contrary opinion. It praised him for seeking 'perseveringly' to promote the city's interests on every occasion. As an example, it cited his success in June 1855 in securing the appointment of a Commons select committee to inquire into postal arrangements in Waterford city and county, and in adjoining counties.[93] This was a matter of serious public concern and Meagher was to chair the committee.[94]

MEAGHER'S RETIREMENT FROM PARLIAMENTARY POLITICS

In March 1857 Parliament was dissolved and a general election called for the following month. In an address to the electors of Waterford, Meagher stated his intention of not seeking re-election, repeating a, by now, jaded theme: his reluctance as a candidate in the two previous elections.[95] *The Waterford News* reported that he had been approached by the bishop of the diocese, Dominic O'Brien, to allow his name to go forward in nomination, but he had reiterated his determination to retire.[96] The reaction in the local press was muted; interestingly only the Tory-supporting *Waterford Mail* expressed regret, a fact indicative, perhaps, of his good relationship with the city's Protestant community: 'he has not used his position to obtain any personal advantage; but has regarded what he considered to be the interests of his country as of primary importance'.[97] It may be remembered that *The Waterford Chronicle* had not wanted him to contest the 1852 election; its silence, therefore, is understandable. *The Waterford News* made no direct comment: perhaps it regarded Meagher's decision as inevitable and, in effect, stale news not meriting editorial comment. However, it did compliment his integrity in an article discountenancing any notion that he would involve himself in chicanery in the matter of selecting a candidate in his stead.[98]

ASSESSMENT OF MEAGHER AS AN MP

It may be stated with certainty that Meagher was not one of the great parliamentarians of the nineteenth century. This is hardly surprising, not least because he did not particularly want to be an MP. He was most definitely a reluctant representative, who had the misfortune of suffering poor health. He was never, therefore, a forceful presence in the House of Commons. In fact, he rarely spoke, and when he did, his contributions were brief. (The cynic may be inclined to comment that he saw where talking got his son!) Yet, as Charles Gavan Duffy wrote, 'Parliamentary capacity does not necessarily mean the power of talking. Franklin and Jefferson rarely spoke in Congress, and Andrew Marvell never uttered a sentence in the House of Commons.'[99] Noting this comment is not to equate Meagher with these more illustrious historical figures; rather it is to highlight that MPs may decide to use other means to promote their concerns. For Meagher, his vote in a division was his principal method of political expression at Westminster. And many of his votes reveal that while lacking personal ambition, he was a man of ambitious political principles. Civil and religious liberty for him embraced Jews as well as Catholics. Political reform in the shape of the ballot and extension of the franchise envisioned greater participation by a greater number in the parliamentary process, without fear of intimidation, and by extension, more people sharing in the benefits of the constitution. Tenant rights promised a fairer deal for Irish farmers. Though quiet and self-effacing, the senior member for Waterford city was one of the more radical of Ireland's representatives in Parliament. However, it is reasonable to be critical of the fact that he did not make greater use of the right and privilege to speak in Parliament, and to use this forum to highlight those issues which concerned him.

It was because he was a man of conviction and principles that he was willing to enter Parliament at all. He ignored his own genuine sense of reluctance and the personal considerations attendant on his temperamental unsuitability when called upon by his fellow citizens to allow his name to go forward for election. In 1847 the demands of the repeal cause in the aftermath of O'Connell's death, and in 1852 the interests of his country and religion, when faced with the prospect of the loss of a seat in Waterford city to the Tories, prevailed. *The Waterford Chronicle*, in the midst of its criticism of him, acknowledged that he was 'scrupulously anxious to do what he deems as an imperative duty'.[100]

It was because Meagher was a man of principles and convictions that his parliamentary career, while not outstanding, was nevertheless one of some merit. A sense of justice and fairness informed his attitudes to many of the matters he had to consider in Parliament. He was a consistent supporter of the extension of civil and political rights, and an unflinching advocate of religious equality. And at a time when many Irish politicians were accused of dishonesty, he was lauded, almost universally, as a representative of honesty and integrity, a sentiment encapsulated in an editorial comment in *The Waterford Chronicle*: 'NO city in the United Kingdom has a more honest man to represent it'.[101] However, his most significant achievement was his contribution to the cause of independent opposition and the formation of a political party dedicated to this objective.

Whatever may be said about Meagher's career as an MP, it certainly did lack an exciting quality. This fact undoubtedly reflected his temperament. However, it also reflected 'the lack of any widespread political excitement that characterised most of the decade'.[102] The cause of tenant rights and independent opposition did not generate a sustained and vigorous political movement. The initial energy of the tenant cause fizzled out when agricultural prosperity began to return. The interest in the campaign against the Ecclesiastical Titles Bill raised the temperature of politics somewhat more, but was of relatively short duration when it became apparent that it did not herald a return to the days of penal legislation. This act, moreover, was never enforced. The lack of effective leadership compounded the problems of the IIP, as did the fact that the government of Aberdeen, and more so that of Palmerston, lacked enthusiasm for reform. Furthermore, the domination of British politics by foreign and imperial concerns pushed Irish policy down the governmental agenda.[103]

The reason for the quiescent nature of Irish politics, however, was more fundamental. The preceding decade had witnessed the convulsions of the repeal campaign and especially those of the Great Famine. 'In much of rural Ireland the horrors of mass Famine mortality, combined with the scale of depopulation through emigration and land clearance, left a traumatic legacy that was difficult to measure, but qualitatively observable to contemporaries, and lodged in the folk memory of the countryside.'[104] Quite simply, people did not have the psychological and emotional reserves for any cause demanding political engagement of prolonged duration and intensity. Charles Gavan Duffy recognised as much when he wrote of 'a lethargy in the public' and 'a coma in Irish politics'.[105] Announcing his resignation from Parliament in 1855, he declared that 'there seems to me no more hope for the Irish cause than for a corpse on the dissection table'[106] – a recognition that the opportunities and favourable prospects for political campaigning simply did not exist. Fenianism notwithstanding, Ireland was settling as never before, or after, into an accommodation with English power within the United Kingdom, a situation which lasted until the land war of the 1880s.[107] Thus, the undramatic and unexciting character of Meagher's parliamentary career reflected the *zeitgeist* of the 1850s.

CHAPTER FOURTEEN

Faith and Family, 1847–1874

In the midst of an editorial criticising Thomas Meagher in December 1850, *The Waterford Chronicle* noted: 'we can conscientiously, and with pleasure, accord to Mr Meagher all the honour that a man deserves for strong religious feeling; for a life of kind and loving deeds, actuated by those religious sentiments; … and for being a good and committed friend and benefactor to the poor.'[1] This was an accurate summary: in the private and public spheres of his life Meagher's devotion to his Catholic faith remained constant and undimmed. In his characteristically unassuming manner he contributed to the development of the Catholic Church in Waterford and in Ireland in the two decades after the Famine. Complex and powerful cultural forces were operating within Irish society during these years, including the emerging hegemony of the Catholic bourgeoisie.[2] Meagher serves as an example of the role played by a representative of the devout middle class in the shaping of Catholicism in the critical post-Famine years. These were also years in which his son, Thomas Francis Meagher, continued to play – at times unexpectedly – a significant part in his life, during which he was to be gradually, but irreversibly eclipsed in the public mind by the rebel in his family.

PARISH MISSION MOVEMENT

The post-Famine decades were a period of consolidation and change for the Catholic Church. The Great Hunger could have done it great damage;

instead, it emerged stronger and adapted better than any other institution in Ireland.[3] The ecclesiastic most closely associated with this achievement was Paul Cullen (1803–1878). Having served as rector of the Irish College in Rome since 1832, he was appointed Archbishop of Armagh in 1849. In 1852 he was translated to the archdiocese of Dublin and in 1866 was created Ireland's first cardinal. His influence was immense and extensive in all of the institutional and devotional developments in the Irish Church in the third quarter of the nineteenth century. His vision was for a Church that was gloriously and triumphantly Roman in character. This was to be achieved by the wholesale importation of devotional, liturgical and theological norms current in Rome.[4] Devout middle-class Catholics, such as Thomas Meagher, facilitated the achievement of this grand and transformative ambition.

Central to the realisation of Cullen's ambition was the parish mission movement, which he strongly encouraged and enthusiastically supported.[5] The first mission was held in Athy, County Kildare, in November and December 1842. Over the next twenty-five years, virtually all Catholic parishes were visited by missioners of various religious orders, including Vincentians, Jesuits and Redemptorists. These missioners were 'a sort of flying squad of Roman orthodoxy',[6] and they visited a parish, usually, for a period of three to four weeks. The most important exercises during the day were the sermons preached in the morning, at midday and in the evening. Their purpose was to make congregants aware of their sins and encourage them to repentance. The multitudes who flocked to confession bore testimony to the effectiveness of the preaching and the fervour aroused by the sermons. As a consequence of these systematic endeavours, 'the religious face of Ireland was profoundly changed',[7] and the vast majority of the Irish people were transformed into orthodox and publicly practising Catholics.

In March 1863 Redemptorist priests conducted a mission of three weeks' duration in Waterford cathedral.[8] A few days before its conclusion, a public meeting was convened for the purposes of 'testifying appreciation' of the 'indefatigable labour' of the missioners. The first speaker on the occasion was Thomas Meagher. In a characteristically pious and considered address, he stated that while the spiritual benefits of the mission were beyond the assessment of those in attendance, they could publicly acknowledge its 'external blessings'. This ardent advocate of temperance alluded to the absence in recent times of charges relating to drunkenness and the solitary case of assault before the city's magistrates. As an expression of their gratitude to the priests, he proposed the collection of subscriptions towards the erection of a church being undertaken by the Redemptorists in Limerick. The meeting adopted this proposal and selected a committee of eight, including Meagher, to compose an appropriate address. On Sunday 26 March the missioners were presented with the address and the proceeds of the collection for their new church, towards which Meagher donated £2.[9]

His involvement in the meeting and address lauding the missioners testifies to his status in the city's Catholic community: he was regarded as one of its most pre-eminent members. Ten years earlier, in 1853, on the day of the laying of the foundation stone of the Franciscan friary in the city, the principal celebrant concluded his discourse by referring to the 'noble character of the excellent individual, Thomas Meagher, who had taken so prominent a part in the ceremony today'.[10] In 1863 and 1864 he was a principal participant in solemn processions in the cathedral on the feast of Corpus Christi (which honours the Eucharist), when he was one of the six canopy bearers beneath which the Eucharist was carried.[11]

BENEFACTOR OF WATERFORD'S RELIGIOUS ORDERS

A significant reason for his prominence was Meagher's on-going interest in, and support of, the city's religious orders, male and female. As was noted earlier, he was a principal benefactor in the establishment of a convent for the Sisters of Charity in the 1840s. He continued in his support of the nuns: he attended their fundraising bazaars and the laying of the foundation stone of St Martin's Female Orphanage, to be conducted under their auspices, in 1861.[12] He was a speaker at a meeting of friends of the orphanage, prior to its official opening, in November 1863, and hailed the fact that not only were orphans cared for, but adult females received industrial training to fit them as good domestic servants.[13] In February 1864 he was one of the signatories of a requisition calling for a public meeting to discuss the need for building a suitable dwelling house for the Christian Brothers at Mount Sion. At this meeting, he asserted that it was 'one of the most imperative and important' duties of a Christian people to provide a Christian education for its youth. This was being done for the people of Waterford by the brothers; he praised the fact that they had, for sixty years, educated 60,000 youths, thus improving their intellect and giving them, 'best of all', a religious education. Meagher contributed £10 towards the new house.[14]

CATHOLIC UNIVERSITY OF IRELAND

Meagher's conviction in the central importance of religion in Catholic education had caused him to oppose the Queen's Colleges, institutions which were to be non-denominational in character. Two papal rescripts, issued on 9 October 1847 and 11 October 1848, condemned the government's proposals as a threat to the Catholic faith of Ireland's youth and urged the establishment of a Catholic university.[15] In 1850, at the national synod of the Irish bishops convened at Thurles by the newly appointed Archbishop of Armagh, Paul Cullen, it was decided to proceed with the foundation of such a university.[16] Thomas Meagher was to play some role in this endeavour.

The synod appointed a committee, the Catholic University Committee, composed of the four archbishops and one bishop from each of the four ecclesiastical provinces, to oversee this complex project. Each member had the right to co-opt one priest and one layman; and one of the latter was Meagher.[17] He owed his selection to the fact that Nicholas Foran, Bishop of Waterford and Lismore, was the representative of the Cashel province and Meagher was known to him and was admired by him. Doubtless, another advocate of Meagher was Rev. Dr Dominic O'Brien, a priest nominated to the committee. This was the same cleric who proposed Meagher as a suitable candidate for selection in the 1847 general election, on the basis of his opposition to the Queen's Colleges.

Charles Gavan Duffy was dismissive of the eight lay members of the Catholic University Committee: '[it] did not contain one layman of adequate intellect and culture'. He described them as 'mere wooden figures set up for show'. The most notable, according to him, were Meagher and Charles Bianconi; of Meagher he wrote that 'he was a respectable citizen in his proper place'.[18] Clearly, Gavan Duffy did not regard this committee as 'his proper place'. Fergal McGrath, in his study of the university, commented that Meagher 'appears to have played a negligible part in the affairs of the university', like the other lay members, except for Bianconi and Myles O'Reilly.[19]

Regarding Gavan Duffy's caustic criticisms of the lay members of the committee, and Meagher in particular, it should be remembered that he (Gavan Duffy) and Cullen had a fractious relationship, to say the least, and, accordingly, he was not well disposed to the archbishop's endeavours, nor was he disposed to be generous in his comments to those involved in any way with them. McGrath's assessment of Meagher's role is nonetheless essentially accurate. However, it might not have been expected or intended by Foran that he would be, or indeed could be, an active member of the committee. Two factors prevented this. First, he was an MP and this required his absence from Ireland to attend at Westminster. Second, Meagher was not the most robust of men and he did not enjoy rude health. Foran was aware of these circumstances and, in fact, other considerations were the likely determinants in his nomination of Meagher.

It was essential to the success of the scheme that the idea of a newly founded Catholic university was both attractive and credible to members of the Catholic middle class. Therefore, the lay members of the committee had to be persons who were regarded as respectable and responsible representatives of that class in order to appeal to their fellow bourgeois. Meagher satisfied these criteria, possessing, as he did, impeccable middle-class credentials. Foran knew he was a Catholic of stature in Waterford city and would, by extension, be so regarded in the wider Irish Church and society. Perhaps, therefore, in assessing Meagher's role on the committee, it may be more appropriate to regard it as akin to that of a patron of an organisation rather than a committee activist.

A second consideration for Bishop Foran was the practical one that the realisation of the idea of the university required substantial financial support. Meagher was wealthy, with the personal financial capacity to make a decent donation. In that respect he did one thing for the putative university that was of undoubted benefit: he gave £100 to its funds.[20]

Meagher would likely have found his association, however limited, with the efforts to found a Catholic university most gratifying. He was, after all, a convinced believer in what he regarded as the just demand for a separate university for Catholics in order to address the legitimate concerns of his Church in relation to higher education. He viewed the establishment of such an institution as an expression of true religious equality, granting to Catholics what Protestants already enjoyed. The eight prelates, who formed the university committee prior to the appointment of additional members, drew up an *Address to the Irish People*, which was published on 9 September 1850. It contained sentiments which may be considered as an excellent summary of Meagher's attitude to the whole matter of a Catholic university for Ireland and, indeed, of what he regarded as the basis for a proper, equitable and just relationship between members of the different religious denominations in the country:

> We maintain that ... Catholics ... are as entitled, without incurring the charge of bigoted exclusiveness, to have an exclusively Catholic university as to profess the Catholic faith and it alone ... We fear that any attempt to fuse down all religions into one mass would result in an indifferentism more fatal to the interests of true religion ... though men may have been educated apart from one another, some in a Catholic, some in a Protestant Episcopalian, others again in a Presbyterian college, they will all have been taught to cherish brotherly love towards one another; and, when they afterwards enter upon the business of real life, their daily intercourse, mutual relations, reciprocal interests, will necessarily lead to the interchange of good offices and good feeling, provided there be no religious ascendancy, and that odious distinctions on account of religion be totally obliterated.[21]

The Catholic University of Ireland was eventually founded in 1854, under the rectorship of John Henry Newman. Its subsequent history need not concern us; it is sufficient to note that it struggled to survive, lacking, as it did, a charter to grant degrees and sufficient funding.[22]

CHRISTIAN CHARITY

Motivated by his deep religious faith, Meagher's concern for the less advantaged continued to be a central feature of his life. Charitable impulses, first stirred in St John's, Newfoundland, continued unabated. He was an active member of the Society of St Vincent de Paul,[23] serving as vice-president of the St Otteran's conference in 1854.[24] In fact, according to an obituary which appeared in *The Freeman's Journal* after his death in February 1874, he was one of the first members of the society in the country and its founder in Waterford city.[25] He was also actively involved in the Trinitarian Orphan Society, serving as its vice-president in 1853 and 1854; in the latter year the charity housed fifteen girls and thirteen boys.[26] In January 1865 he attended a public meeting called to consider the best means of helping the poor of the city during a period of inclement weather and prevalence of disease. Meagher contributed £2 towards a relief fund.[27]

MEAGHER AND CATHOLICISM: AN OVERVIEW

Thomas Meagher had a profound sense of his Catholicism, and a real and deep awareness of his identity as a Catholic: his religious creed was part of his DNA. He was exposed to its formative influence while in Newfoundland. His sense of Catholic identity was confirmed and strengthened during his first decade in Waterford, when he was a leading activist in the campaign for Catholic emancipation. It was during this struggle that politics became closely associated with the institutional Catholic Church. The granting of emancipation in 1829 did not herald an era of equality for Catholics; rather, a deep-rooted Protestant establishment thwarted its practical implementation and denied Catholics access to positions to which they were legally entitled. Informal sectarianism proved almost as effective a bar to Catholics in the public life of the United Kingdom, as had the penal laws.[28] Being a Catholic remained a significant disadvantage in terms both of access to public employment and of opportunity within large parts of the public sector.[29] Thus, Catholics continued to have a mighty arsenal of grievances, which denied them 'the measure of dignity, power and influence in the land to which they felt entitled'.[30]

For Meagher, therefore, his four decades in politics were consumed by his involvement in an ongoing campaign to achieve what he believed to be the entitlement of Catholics: religious and civil equality, which meant in practical terms the right to receive the exact same treatment as Protestants. The highlights of this campaign may be summarised, its duration underscoring the range of discrimination and the level of resistance faced at all stages. In the 1820s he was active in the emancipation struggle. The following decade was dominated by demands for a system of municipal governance which recognised the claims of middle-class Catholics to representation on the country's corporations. In the 1840s he was a repealer, motivated by the belief that only the restoration of an Irish parliament could bring justice to his co-religionists. He was also an advocate for a denominational Catholic university, demanding for Catholics what Protestants had enjoyed for centuries. In the 1850s he opposed the Ecclesiastical Titles Act. As a consequence of four decades of campaigning by Catholics for their rights, a nationalist Catholic identity, in which Meagher shared, was the most significant feature of Irish political life in the mid-nineteenth century.[31]

Meagher's activism in the campaign for Catholic rights coincided with a period when his Church was under assault by Protestant proselytisers. Their efforts have been given the general title 'Second Reformation' and lasted, with varying degrees of intensity, for nearly five decades, from the 1820s through to the 1860s. While there is a tendency in some historiography to ignore or underplay its significance,[32] it has been mentioned on a number of occasions in this book as a very real and ongoing concern for the Catholic Church. Indeed, Archbishop Cullen believed it to be one of the greatest challenges facing the institution.

Furthermore, as an MP, Meagher witnessed, at first hand, the realities of a 'tradition of anti-Catholicism whose wide acceptance and long endurance, among all classes in [English] society, secured it an important place in Victorian civilisation'.[33] This anti-Catholicism found vehement expression in the early 1850s: the general outrage at the act of 'papal aggression' in restoring the Catholic hierarchy in England; the Durham letter of the prime minister, Lord John Russell; the anti-Catholic Stockport riots; the Ecclesiastical Titles Act; the introduction of bills to regulate Catholic convents; and regular parliamentary attempts to withdraw the state grant to Maynooth College. Roman Catholicism was assailed in Westminster, the press, popular literature and at public meetings. Its beliefs in the sacerdotal nature of the Christian ministry, the primacy of the See of Peter, the invocation of the saints, the veneration of the Virgin Mary and transubstantiation 'seemed to some Protestants mildly derisory, to others downright weird and to some even perverted.[34] For Meagher, however, these were central tenets of his revered religious faith and the faith of the majority of the Irish people.

The combined effects of determined Protestant resistance to the notion of Catholic equality, proselytism and anti-Catholicism in England created in Meagher a sense of his religion under siege, contending with assaults on its spiritual integrity and civil, social and political status. The essentially Protestant character of the state was revealed in the hostility of the ruling elite in England and the entrenched Protestant establishment in Ireland towards the Church of Rome. Meagher's sense of a Catholic nationalist identity must, therefore, 'be set against the effective Protestantism (or perhaps Anglicanism) so central to contemporary Britishness'.[35] The cumulative experience of four decades of political activism confirmed Meagher in the belief that throughout the whole of the United Kingdom Catholics were still regarded as second-class citizens.

This circumstance prevailed for most of Meagher's lifetime, despite the efforts of the Church of Rome, in alliance with its middle-class membership, to advance its status. As has been noted, the middle class provided the local and parliamentary leadership in the political campaigns. It was also the middle class that helped re-energise the Church. Under Cullen there was a 'progressive and more general *embourgeoisement* of the culture of Catholic devotional life and practice'.[36] This development, however, was more the intensification of trends which had begun in the Irish Church before the Famine; it was not a sudden *démarche* which coincided with Cullen's arrival in Ireland. Meagher is an example of the middle-class Catholic who was a leader in his community since the 1820s. His career highlights the critical and pivotal role this alliance between the institutional Church and its bourgeois members played in the progress made by Catholics over many decades, before and after Cullen's appointment. In 1863 Meagher proclaimed: 'Ireland was fast returning to the good, old, happy, glorious time when God covered this land with convents and monasteries.'[37] If there is any truth in this assertion, it was due, to a significant degree, to lay Catholics such as him.

As was noted earlier, before the Famine Meagher was a benefactor of the Presentation and Ursuline religious communities, and, in particular, of the Irish Sisters of Charity. He was also active in the Society of St Vincent de Paul, the Trinitarian Orphan Society and the Magdalen asylum before and after the Great Hunger. After the Famine, he supported the building of a Christian Brothers' monastery at Mount Sion. Clearly, he spent a great deal of his time and wealth in support of the Catholic Church and on the poor and marginalised. Meagher saw himself as a Christian of the Roman Catholic variety, loyal and devoted to the teachings of the Church and its ministers, especially the bishops. He believed that his faith obligated him to help those less fortunate than himself. His social actions and his philanthropic deeds were predicated on what he perceived as transcendental realities. Oliver Rafferty has commented that 'given the social and cultural environment of the twenty-first century, it is at times difficult to appreciate how, in the not very remote past, religion played a decisive role in the way in which individuals and nations saw themselves.'[38] A consideration of the life of Thomas Meagher bears testimony to the central role religion played in it and how he regarded it as a vital element in the life of the Ireland in which he lived.

Religion, however, was the cause of deep divisions between Catholics and Protestants. As a consequence of the emancipation campaign, there were unbreakable links between nationalism and Catholicism. Catholics continued the struggle for equality by espousing the repeal cause; Protestants were deeply hostile to this. Alarmed at these developments, Protestants adopted a defensive posture, founded on a communal solidarity buttressed by a sense of their religious identity.[39] Meagher would have been aware of increasing religious divisions in Ireland, but as a champion of equality between religions, he regarded the political activities in which he and his co-religionists engaged as necessary to advance their objectives. He would not have seen such activities as constituting a threat to Protestants. It is not possible to judge to what extent he appreciated the deep-rooted Protestant fears that Catholic triumph would come at the expense of the Protestant sense of security in the land. It seems unlikely that he had worked out in his own mind a scheme to effect a reconciliation between Catholic nationalism and Protestant apprehensions and concerns.

At local level, Meagher did appear to enjoy good relations with the members of the minority religious community in Waterford city. Reference has already been made to the address presented to him in

1845 by a committee of citizens, composed of many Protestants, on the completion of his term as mayor, and to the fact that Protestants voted for him in the general election of 1847. Most significant, perhaps, was the reported comment of the Conservative Party candidate and Church of Ireland member, William Christmas, at the nomination of candidates in the 1852 general election: 'He had every respect for Mr Meagher, so much so that had he come forward at an earlier date, it is not likely that he (Mr Christmas) would have entered the lists at all.'[40]

THOMAS MEAGHER AND HIS EXILED SON

Though Meagher was heavily involved in political and religious concerns, his exiled son still loomed large in his life. After a journey of 112 days and 14,000 miles, on board HMS *Swift*, Thomas Francis Meagher and his fellow prisoners, William Smith O'Brien, Thomas Bellew McManus and Patrick O'Donoghue, arrived in Van Diemen's Land in late October 1849. The island was the size of Ireland and in 1851 had a population of 69,000. A penal colony since 1803, it was regarded by the government as a dumping ground for the 'undesirables' of English society – its 'robbers and pickpockets, forgers and whores'.[41] The Young Ireland rebels were offered tickets-of-leave due to their good conduct on the outward journey and their status as gentlemen. For a promise not to make any attempt at escape, the prisoners enjoyed relatively unrestricted liberty within an area to which each was assigned. Meagher was sent to Campbell Town, but finding it uncongenial, he was granted permission to move to Ross.

On the outward journey, the *Swift* stopped at Capetown, South Africa, on 12 September 1849, to take on supplies. Meagher used the opportunity to send a letter to his family in Waterford. He gave some details of the voyage, commenting, for example, on the food, which he found 'not composed of the most soft and savoury ingredients', though this did not bother him unduly. He sounded an upbeat note which must have gladdened his father: 'Besides, a cheerful heart can sweeten all things – can make the best of everything, and bless even darker days than ours with the richest fragrance and the softest sunshine.'[42]

The optimism Meagher had expressed in this letter proved to be premature and misplaced. He was never to accept his exile, nor did he ever embrace the felonious society in which he was compelled to live,[43] describing it as 'coarse, wool-brained and mutton-headed'.[44] The British government had intended that the Irish prisoners 'be officially lost in gentlemanly oblivion' on the other side of the world.[45] While, to the great irritation of ministers, they continued to receive publicity in Ireland, their experiences in the penal colony tested their spirits and endurance. The reality was that the Young Irelanders were out of place in Van Diemen's Land. Gone were their political and professional activities, and the status they had heretofore enjoyed by virtue of their abilities and birth into social privilege. John Mitchel wrote that 'the glowing and fiery life of Meagher is plunged into eclipse … morally and intellectually he collapses, as we all do'.[46] As early as December 1849, in a letter to William Smith O'Brien, Meagher expressed the realisation that his life had become 'devoid of all high and enabling pursuits' and his existence 'thus harassed, deadened, drained, ceases to be a blessing – it becomes a penalty'.[47] He had to contend with a 'Goliath of boredom',[48] writing to a friend in Van Diemen's Land that 'I am compelled to a life of uselessness and can do little or nothing to realise the dream that gave light and music to my early days'.[49] By 2 January 1851, he was telling another Young Ireland exile, Kevin O'Doherty, that 'I felt, day by day, the impulses, which prompted me to act a generous part at home, withering and dying fast, and felt, with equal pain, despondency and remorse, a spirit of indifference, inertness and self-abandonment seizing on my heart'.[50]

In May 1850 *The Waterford News* reported that Thomas Meagher had received a letter from his son and printed the text. Dated 1 December 1849, it gave a detailed account of his life in Van Diemen's Land. The last paragraph contained an early hint of the trials of exile: 'My life is very lonesome. Were it not for occasional companionship, it would be as lonesome as that of the most secluded hermit'.[51] His father got a further insight into his circumstances in a letter published in the same newspaper in January 1851. Written by an unidentified correspondent, and dated Hobart, 30 September 1850, the writer claimed that he had seen Thomas Francis and had frequent letters from him. He described him as being 'in excellent health, but not spirits'.[52] Such information undoubtedly distressed the elder Meagher. Notwithstanding the constraints imposed by the great distance between them, he did the one thing he could: he sent Thomas Francis generous financial assistance, and this certainly contributed to making the exile's plight more bearable.

With the help of his father's money, Thomas Francis leased land on the edge of Lake Sorell and built a cottage for himself, an activity which helped absorb his energy and gave him some sense of purpose, for a time at least. He also leased sixty acres on an island in the middle of the lake and employed a farm servant to cultivate crops.[53] He ordered a boat from Hobart, which was hauled the seventy-mile distance to the lake by a team of oxen. This he converted into a yacht that was launched on St Patrick's Day, 1850. It helped greatly in sustaining his spirits and that of his fellow exiles.[54] His father's money also allowed him indulge in some luxuries, such as cigars.[55]

Meagher and others were involved in organising an attempted escape by William Smith O'Brien. It was a failure and the expenses incurred fell on Meagher. He sent the bill to his father. On 17 June 1851 he received a letter of reply from London, dated 5 February:

> When your bill of £550 was presented to me, with only your note of advice pinned to it, I was at a loss to know what it was for, and in that state of doubt, I declined to accept the bill, reserving to myself, however, the alternative of paying it when due, should I hear from you in the meantime. Your letter of explanation arrived a few days before the bill became payable. It gave me a full statement of the circumstances which induced you to make so large a call, and I therefore (though deeply sensible that the adventure in which you risked so much had been excessively improvident and fruitless) determined upon relieving you from any further disagreeable result. I have done so. The bill is now paid.[56]

A relieved Thomas Francis wrote to Kevin O'Doherty that 'there is the horrid business quietly and honourably settled'.[57]

Thomas Meagher's letter to his son sheds an interesting and revealing light on its author. This pillar of the establishment was willing to pay his son's debt, notwithstanding the manner in which it had been incurred. It was a simple case of his looking out for his son's best interests and welfare, even though he was engaged in what was an illegal activity. This incident puts a different complexion on rumours which were circulating around the time of Meagher's transportation, that while he 'greatly deplored Tom's rebellious politics', he had 'employed four brigantines to cruise off the southern and western coasts to facilitate his escape'.[58] Even though these rumours and the payment of the £550 debt were inconsistent with Thomas Meagher as a model of probity, they were not with that of a man heartbroken at the plight of his son and willing to do all he could to mitigate his sufferings.

CATHERINE BENNETT

On 22 February 1851 the twenty-seven-year-old Thomas Francis Meagher married Catherine Bennett ('Bennie' as Meagher called her), who was aged nineteen. She was the daughter of Bryan and Mary Bennett, her father having been transported to Van Diemen's Land for holding up a mail coach in Ireland in 1818. On completion of his sentence, he became a free settler and built up a farm of over 100 acres.[59] The marriage was generally disapproved of by Meagher's fellow Young Ireland exiles because of the disparity in social standing between the bride and groom: he was a gentleman, she the daughter of a felon. The critics of the marriage may have been the avowed political enemies of the British queen, 'but in their social dealings their manners were those of English gentlemen',[60] whose values were shaped by a rigid class system. John Martin , a fellow Young Ireland exile, was distressed at the prospect of the 'social degradation to which the origin and present condition of his wife's family must subject him'.[61] Smith O'Brien confided to his journal that, 'She is a person of manner very pleasing, but in a worldly point of view the connexion cannot be considered advantageous to him.'[62] Some of the critics were especially concerned about the reaction of his father, a figure they knew to be of significant social stature. Martin wrote of 'the vexation and disappointment of his father ...' and Jenny Mitchel, wife of John Mitchel, commented in a letter to a friend: 'I fear his father will be very wroth with him.'[63] Maybe they were worried lest he would cease his financial support of his son in protest at the marital alliance. They need not have had such concerns at the possible reaction of Thomas Meagher. Perhaps the most significant support he offered his son was the kindness he showed Catherine Bennett in her times of greatest need.

In early January 1852 Thomas Francis escaped from Van Diemen's Land, arriving in New York on 27 May of that year. He and Catherine had agreed that she, who was now pregnant, would follow him into freedom. A month later, on 7 February, she gave birth to a boy, Henry Emmet Fitzgerald O'Meagher. (The child's surname reflected the fact that during the voyage to Van Diemen's Land, Thomas Francis announced that he would be known as O'Meagher while in exile.) Sadly, the child died four months later, on 8 June.[64] Shortly afterwards, Catherine received a letter from Thomas and Henry Meagher, her first communication with her husband's family and 'a bond of friendship was created between them'.[65]

It was decided that Catherine would travel to Ireland before proceeding to New York to be reunited with her husband. She left Hobart on 5 February 1853 and arrived in Dublin in late June, where she was welcomed by Thomas and Henry Meagher and Miss Quan. On Monday 27 June they travelled together to Waterford, and Catherine stayed in the Meagher home on the Mall. Her presence in the city occasioned great excitement. On Wednesday she appeared in public and one senses that the arrangements for the morning and afternoon were orchestrated by her father-in-law. They attended mass together in the Franciscan Church, where a large crowd gathered to catch a glimpse of her. They then visited the various convents in the city. That same evening a very large crowd of 20,000 gathered on the Mall to extend her a welcome.[66] On Wednesday 6 July a delegation of sixty prominent citizens called on her at Meagher's residence to present an address to her, which had been adopted at a public meeting on the previous Monday. This document extolled Thomas Francis's virtues. An address was also presented to Meagher, congratulating him on the arrival of his daughter-in-law in the city and expressing the hope that the queen would extend an amnesty to his son and his fellow political exiles.[67]

Of Catherine Bennett's visit to Waterford, Timothy Egan has written: 'The elder Meagher welcomed Bennie as a lost daughter. And in the sixty-four-year-old patriarch she found a comforting hand and a steady soul. Together they sailed for America.'[68]

Thomas Meagher and Catherine Bennett arrived in New York on 23 July 1853. The *Irish American* newspaper extended a warm welcome to the wife of the 'glorious young tribune' and to her father-in-law, to whom was expressed gratitude and respect for his integrity and patriotism as a public servant. They joined Thomas Francis in his residence at the Metropolitan Hotel, where they received visitors wishing to pay their respects, the first being Archbishop of New York John Hughes. A deputation arrived from Boston to invite Meagher to a banquet to be given on 3 August in honour of his son's thirtieth birthday.[69] He declined the invitation, pleading his 'infirm health', which had not been improved by his Atlantic voyage and the very warm weather of the city.[70]

A delegation of gentlemen from Cincinnati presented Thomas Meagher with a cane cut from the grave of the 'illustrious Washington', as a mark of their esteem and respect for him as the father of 'one of Ireland's most beloved exiles' and as an 'upright and faithful representative in the British Parliament'. The accompanying address, dated 1 August, made reference to his character as an 'Irish gentleman' and member of the House of Commons, where, 'in the midst of treachery and corruption, you are always found the earnest friend of the people'. His association with the Irish Brigade and IIP had won him transatlantic accolades. In his reply, Meagher acknowledged the exceptionally warm and generous welcome extended to his son in America.[71]

Thomas Francis began a series of lectures, travelling through the north-east of the United States, accompanied by his wife and father. Around this time he was offered a lecture tour in California and it was decided that Catherine, who was once again pregnant, would return to Waterford to be delivered of her child. Both she and the child were then to rejoin Meagher in America.[72] Whether Meagher's decision to embark on this tour presented him with the opportunity to escape the 'awkward intimacy' of his life with Catherine,[73] reflecting the fact that he was tired of their relationship, is not central to the narrative of this book. Whatever the circumstances, she and her father-in-law arrived in Liverpool on 22 October 1853 and then journeyed to Ireland.[74]

At the beginning of May 1854, Catherine Bennett gave birth to another boy, Thomas Bennett Meagher. She was, however, in a very weakened state after the birth and, having contracted typhoid fever, died on 9 May. This tragic event caused genuine and widespread sorrow in Waterford. Thomas Meagher was, according to *The Waterford News*, deeply affected by her death at the age of just twenty-two:

> With all the devoted fondness of a widowed parent did Thomas
> Meagher love this girl – with all the enthusiastic affection of an only
> brother did Henry Meagher's undying attention accompany her.
> Cold and cheerless is the house which her presence illuminated for
> the past few months, and many a pang of bitter sorrow wrings the
> hearts that loved her with such intensity.[75]

Bennie's demise at such a young age likely reminded him of the death of his young wife, Alicia Quan, thus intensifying his grief. Both women are buried in the Meagher family vault, in Faithlegg church, outside Waterford city.

Meagher, together with his sister-in-law, Miss Quan, undertook the care of his grandson. After his mother's death, what Thomas Keneally calls 'an uneasy compact' was arrived at between the Meaghers, father and son. The young boy was to be reared in Waterford, educated at Clongowes and perhaps, in time, would join his father in America.[76] In November 1855 Thomas Francis married Elizabeth Townsend, and she visited Waterford in 1858 to meet with her father-in-law and her husband's three-year-old son. The boy's family believed that the time was not right for him to relocate to New York: he was doing well with his doting grandfather.[77] Thus, 'the elder Meagher retained care of his grandson, both in the name of the child's education and of his own fondness'.[78]

Whatever their hopes and plans, Thomas Meagher and his son were never to meet again. Thomas Francis began to establish a new life for himself in the United States, the details of which need not concern us. His father was well informed of his activities through the medium of newspapers, which published extensive reports on his early years in America, and during the civil war in particular. Reading about the latter cannot have been without its moments of great anxiety for his concerned father. How much contact there was between them is difficult to gauge, but they appear to have maintained some degree of correspondence. For example, on the eve of his departure for Montana as territorial secretary in August 1865, Thomas Francis wrote to his father: 'I leave this evening for the far west, one of our richer new territories … I entertain the liveliest hopes that this enterprise will prove a profitable one to me and that it will enable me to pay you a visit in France next summer.'[79] (France was mentioned as Thomas Francis could not set foot on any part of the United Kingdom.)

THOMAS MEAGHER AND HIS SON: AN OVERVIEW OF THEIR PERSONAL AND POLITICAL RELATIONSHIP

Thomas Meagher loved his son, but his paternal care and generosity were often exercised across 'a gulf of incomprehension',[80] in support of a child of whose actions he was deeply disapproving. This disapproval and incomprehension were the products of very different personalities and conflicting political attitudes. The elder Meagher was cautious, reflective, serious and naturally retiring: his public persona was reserved and laconic. By contrast, his son was impulsive, extrovert and vain; in public he was flamboyant and verbose. In Waterford and Dublin the young man cut a dandy image, handsome and fashionably groomed and attired. He had a most engaging personality and was popular and well liked:[81] he was, in Egan's words, 'the Prince of Waterford'.[82] Though his father was widely respected and himself a popular figure in his home city, he never attracted the adulation engendered by his son.

Mitchel, in his short memoir of Thomas Francis Meagher, succeeded in conveying how many contemporaries must have regarded the distinctive and contrasting characters of father and son. On the day after he first met the young Meagher, he came into the offices of *The Nation* to see Mitchel. They spent some time in one another's company and Mitchel recorded his impressions:

> What eloquence of talk was his! ... What wealth of imagination and princely generosity of feeling! To me it was the revelation of a great nature and I revelled in it, plunged into it, as into a crystal lake ... We arrived at my home, and he stayed to dinner. Before he left he was a favourite with all our household ... [83]

Sometime afterwards he visited Meagher in Waterford and met his father. 'In a quiet street of the town, and in a large gloomy mansion ... dwells in strict domestic privacy a retired merchant, the father of Meagher; ... Mr Meagher the elder is small and meagre, of aspect and manner somewhat dry and cold, but not austere. The furniture of the dwelling suits its proportions and character, being dark and massive ...' He remembered the house as being one of 'sombre rooms'. The memoir continues:

I had visited him on my way to Cork; had been received with kind hospitality by the elders of the house [Thomas Meagher and Miss Quan]; but it was at night, when we retired to [Thomas Francis's] study, that we felt truly at home. In the arrangements of his room he had followed his own taste, and therefore there was a predominance of red colour; … he always in his heart loved the scarlet. His eye sought and craved it, for 'the colour of red is like the sound of a trumpet'.[84]

The reader can sense Mitchel's relief when he and Thomas Francis retired to the latter's study – the charms, such as they were, of the elder Meagher's company had begun to wane for the visitor. And the style of that room, with its vibrant colour, contrasted with the more sober aspect of the rest of the house: in this private space Thomas Francis gave expression to his personality, just as the other rooms suggested the more serious nature of its owner.

Political differences, concentrated within a relatively short time frame, came in battalions to put severe stresses on the paternal–filial relationship of the Meaghers: a split in the Repeal Association (1846); a general election (1847); a by-election (1848); and the Young Ireland rising (1848). Throughout these crises, Thomas Meagher's reactions were informed by two overarching considerations: his loyalty to O'Connell and by extension to constitutional politics, and an increasing concern at his son's drift to militancy. Even when Thomas Francis was exiled in Van Diemen's Land, his father was to be reminded of matters which were a serious source of conflict between them. Thomas Francis wrote an account of his personal experiences of the 1848 rebellion and this was serialised in some of Waterford's newspapers in 1851.[85] In April of the same year the following appeared in *The Waterford News*: 'A report being, to some extent, in circulation, that Thomas Meagher, Esq., MP for this city, was a party to the publication of his son's memoirs, we are authorised to contradict the report, and to state that he knew nothing whatever of it, until he read it in the newspaper; and moreover, that its publication gave him considerable pain.'[86] He had never approved of his son's rebellious actions; he most certainly did not want to be reminded of them in this very public fashion. He very likely viewed these articles as detrimental to any prospects of a royal pardon and, therefore, represented an egregious lack of judgement on the part of his son.

The editorial reaction in the same newspaper contrasted dramatically with that of the elder Meagher. This reaction confirms that his son was progressing towards the attainment of an iconic status in the popular memory and imagination: 'his country should only look at him through the brilliancy of his intellect, emblazoned on the records as glorious a talent and as splendid a genius as any country in Europe could boast of: and the generosity of future ages will gladly award that merit which was so justly due.'[87] And it was these same 'future ages' that admitted Thomas Francis to the pantheon of nationalism. With the growth of militant nationalist sentiment in the first two decades of the twentieth century, his oratory was appropriated by the advocates of separatism seeking to establish an unbroken chain of violent resistance to Britain. In 1917 Arthur Griffith edited a collection of his speeches, in the introduction to which he wrote: 'But he was the most picturesque and gallant figure of Young Ireland and stands above all his colleagues, and indeed above all Irishmen of his century as the National Orator. In the speeches he delivered in Ireland from 1846 to 1848 he will live forever. They are the authoritative and eloquent voice of Irish Nationalism.'[88]

Such appropriation, however, misrepresented Thomas Francis Meagher's political views. Roy Foster has commented that 'his basic beliefs may have been closer to his father's constitutionalism than was seen at the time, or remembered since.'[89] It was noted earlier that the younger Meagher was a reluctant revolutionary. Moreover, he was not a separatist: 'His Ireland would be an independent nation within the British empire.'[90] In fact, as John Hearne has observed, it could be argued that among the Young Irelanders he was 'the closest ideologically to the Liberator'.[91] Meagher's participation in the 1848 rebellion, however, has obscured this reality, at the time and subsequently. Thomas Francis Meagher's ideological closeness to the Liberator reflected the influence of his father on him: the older man was a dedicated supporter and admirer during his long involvement in politics.

Meagher's father had another significant influence on him: he reared and educated him to be a gentleman and Thomas Francis was conscious of this. In public he had the bearing and exuded the qualities and confidence of a gentleman. One of his biographers, Captain W.F. Lyons, who knew him personally, wrote: 'Meagher was a gentleman – an Irish gentleman – and no flattery could add to the consciousness which he already possessed that he represented and that he was always ready to represent that class the world over.'[92] It was this awareness of his status that spurred his ambition for social success in America. The death of Catherine Bennett in 1854 focused his attention on a respectable career and the desirability of transforming his public standing into a more lasting social position.[93] This was one of the considerations in his acceptance of a government position in Montana: he was presented with possibilities for personal achievement which reflected his political and social ambitions.[94] The man who had given up the life of privilege, status and comfort in Waterford when he turned rebel, brought with him to America that sense of social and personal worth that had been instilled in him in his homes on the Quay and the Mall, and in the Jesuit education at Clongowes and Stonyhurst secured for him by family wealth, to fulfil the ambitions a father had for his beloved elder son.

O'CONNELLITES AND THE MAKING OF THE MODERN IRISH STATE

Militant separatism's lionisation and valorisation of Thomas Francis's rhetoric and rebel deeds, and the words and actions of other Young Irelanders, resulted in an emphasis on violence in the progress towards Irish independence. One consequence of this was that constitutionalism was denigrated as a contradiction in terms, since Irish and British interests were inherently opposed to each other.[95] A result of such denigration was the rejection of Daniel O'Connell's views on political violence. For some of the more extreme separatists, he became a figure of particular revulsion and singled out as a symbol of Britain's malevolent influence in Ireland; the Liberator came to be regarded as a collaborator with English rule.[96] They readily accepted Mitchel's description of him as 'the worst enemy that Ireland ever had'.[97] By extension, there was an ideological condemnation of Irish politicians of the nineteenth century who supported him and Thomas Meagher was included in this general denunciation. Thus, the significant constitutional and parliamentary political tradition which they represented, whose 'major actors have not been legendary heroes and villains cast in an epic mould, but everyday men of affairs', came to be obscured with this emphasis on militancy.[98] However, in the subsequent struggle for independence in the aftermath of 1916, it was to reassert itself; the majority of those involved in this struggle believed in parliamentary democracy.[99] The newly independent Irish state established such a system of government: 'in its origins and throughout its development the modern Irish state of the twentieth century has preserved a parliamentary form and operated parliamentary norms'.[100] Peaceful, democratic and constitutional politics became the foundations of the Irish Free State, contributing to its stability. Thus, the political values and beliefs of O'Connellites, such as Thomas Meagher, found a central place in an independent Ireland.

'A QUIETER SPHERE OF LIFE'

In his address to the electors of Waterford city in March 1857, in which he announced his intention of not seeking re-election, Meagher declared that he was retiring to 'a quieter sphere of life'.[101] For a number of years he continued to play a part in the life of the city: he served as a poor law guardian, for example, from 1861 to 1863.[102] He also maintained a profile as an active member of the Catholic Church, as was noted earlier in this chapter. However, after the autumn of 1865 his name ceases to appear in the pages of local newspapers. One of the last entries was in August of that year, when he was reported as being a subscriber to a fund to assist three orphaned children.[103]

In July 1867 newspapers began carrying reports of the death by drowning of his son, Thomas Francis, in the Missouri river, near Fort Benton, Montana, on 1 July. On the occasion of the 'melancholy and unexpected termination of the eventful life of our gifted fellow-citizen', *The Waterford News* expressed its condolences to Thomas Meagher: 'The deepest sympathy is felt for his respected father, who has lived to have his declining years shadowed by the remembrance of such mournful tidings as are revealed in the sad news of so sudden a termination to the life of a beloved son'.[104]

There is no known record of Meagher's reaction to his son's death, but his grief was certainly intense. The circumstances of the younger man's demise were especially sad; to quote *The Freeman's Journal*: 'In the very prime of life – not yet forty-five years of age – and on the threshold of a career of usefulness, the thread of life has been broken.' There was something particularly lamentable in a death by drowning 'for one, who with signal distinction and brilliant heroism, had passed through some of the most desperate engagements of the late American civil war'. In the midst of his mourning, the elder Meagher would probably have identified with the sentiments expressed in *The Freeman's Journal* when it spoke of his beloved son as 'gifted with great intellectual powers and possessed of a matchless eloquence when yet a young man', but 'the unfortunate events of '48 sadly dissipated the hopes which his admitted genius had created'. But no historian or editor can hope to convey the desolation of a man whose handsome, brilliant and patriotic son, lost to him by exile in 1849, was now lost to him forever. This desolation was undoubtedly intensified by the fact that the body of Thomas Francis was never found. For the intensely religious elder Meagher, this meant that his son never enjoyed the dignity and consolation of Christian burial. The unfound body meant that Thomas Meagher never experienced closure when it came to his grief and mourning.

MEAGHER'S SURVIVING CHILDREN

Meagher had two living children after the death of Thomas Francis. The older was his eldest daughter, Christina Mary. Little is known about her: she became a Benedictine nun at Taunton, Devon.[105] His other surviving child was Henry, who probably lived his life more in accord with his father's hopes and expectations than his elder brother. He attended Clongowes Wood College with Thomas Francis, with both boys entering it in 1833. When Daniel O'Connell visited the college in 1841, Henry read an address from the students 'in a loud and distinctive voice'.[106] Henry pursued a military career and appears to have served for a period in the late 1840s in the Pope's Noble Guard.[107] In 1854 he was appointed to hold a commission in one of Waterford's regiments, and was serving at the rank of captain in the Waterford Artillery Regiment in 1863.[108] He obtained the honorary rank of lieutenant colonel in 1867.[109]

As a gentleman and Meagher's son, he was considered in 1852, albeit briefly, as a possible general election candidate for the local Liberal Party, following his father's decision not to seek nomination for another term in Parliament. His name was put before the committee charged with seeking a suitable replacement for Meagher. *The Waterford Mail* reported that 'when the name of Henry Meagher was announced there was a tremendous burst of applause'.[110] A little over a week later, the same journal informed its readers that he would not be standing, 'nor is it his father's wish he should do so'.[111] Henry was again mentioned in the local press as a possible candidate in 1857, following his father's retirement, with the latter's supporters being 'desirous of bringing forward his younger son'.[112] In accordance with his social position, he served as High Sheriff of Waterford city in 1867.[113]

Like his father, Henry was a devout Catholic and a benefactor of causes and charities associated with his Church. In 1848 he presented an address to the pope on behalf of the Catholics of Waterford and was accorded the privilege of an interview with the pontiff, who presented him with two gold medals, one for himself and one for his father.[114] He contributed to the fund for the completion of the Presentation convent chapel[115] and towards the erection of a residence for the Christian Brothers at Mount Sion.[116] He supported the Sisters of Charity female orphanage.[117] In February 1863 he attended a special meeting convened by the Society of St Vincent de Paul to consider the issue of distress in the city and contributed to a special fund to alleviate it.[118] He served on the board of governors of a local charity, the Fanning Institute, and was one of its life governors in 1902.[119]

Henry was a person who appears to have largely avoided engaging in public controversy. However, he did so in the local press in December 1854. He prefaced a letter of his which appeared in *The Waterford News* with the following statement: 'I have much disinclination to place my name before the public and feel still a stronger objection to engage in correspondence which may have the slightest bearing on religious controversy'. However, he felt compelled to write a letter refuting allegations of proselytism levelled against the Sisters of Charity and the Society of St Vincent de Paul in the pages of *The Waterford Mail*. He rejected, utterly and forcefully, these charges. The sisters, he wrote, 'do not intrude on the consciences of others; they do not tamper with religious convictions'. His refutation of the allegations against the Society of St Vincent de Paul was based, he asserted, 'on his personal experience of sharing its labour in the city'.[120]

Henry married Marian Murphy, daughter of Francis Murphy, a wealthy landowner from Kilcairn, County Meath, in 1867.[121] The couple lived in Bray, County Wicklow, to where Henry's father relocated. This explains the absence of Thomas Meagher's name in the local Waterford press from the late 1860s onwards. Henry and Marian had three children: a daughter and two sons. Henry Meagher died in 1906.

DEATH OF MEAGHER

Thomas Meagher died on 27 February 1874 at his residence, 10 Duncairn Terrace, Bray,[122] where, in the words of *The Waterford News*, 'he had been sojourning for some time'.[123] His funeral, to Glasnevin Cemetery, took place the following Tuesday, 3 March.

The news of his death had little impact in Waterford. This is hardly surprising: he was long retired from public life and had quit the city in the late 1860s. An obituary appeared in *The Waterford News* highlighting his steadfast adherence to the leadership of Daniel O'Connell during his political career and his charity to the less fortunate.[124] A short obituary in *The Freeman's Journal* described him as being 'remarkable for his genuine spirit of religion and his unostentatious charity to the poor'.[125]

At a meeting of Waterford Corporation, tributes were paid to him: with the passage of time, few members knew him personally. Captain Johnson referred to the fact that he had been the first mayor elected by the reformed corporation in 1842. Alderman Jacob recounted how he remembered when Meagher came to Waterford as a young man from Newfoundland and how, in a short time, he achieved prominence in the life of the city, making himself 'highly useful by his intelligence and energy'. Mr Fisher commented that 'his high personal character and innate dignity obtained the respect of all members of all classes and politics'. He continued: 'I admired Mr Meagher for the simplicity and dignity of his conduct, for the manly intelligence which guided his public life, for the sedulous attention he paid to any duty he undertook and for the honesty and honour which invariably characterised his public life.'[126]

Thomas Meagher:
A Life Considered

Thomas Meagher lived during a time of great social, economic and political change. He sought to influence that change by active political involvement, especially as Mayor of Waterford and the city's MP for ten years. Throughout his career he was a constitutional nationalist in the mould of Daniel O'Connell. A distinguished civic figure in his adopted city, he gave his fellow citizens leadership during the momentous events of the repeal campaign. His years of public service were characterised by integrity, honesty and loyalty. Such attributes were especially evident, and of special significance, while he was a member of the IIP, as central to the concept of independent opposition was adherence to pledges by elected representatives. Meagher was faithful to his pledges; had others acted likewise the party might have enjoyed a greater measure of success. However, he was ever the reluctant MP, who did not enjoy good health. His sense of duty trumped personal considerations and he endured ten years at Westminster. Though lacking personal ambitions, he never lacked political ones and was a supporter of progressive causes, such as rights for tenants; the secret ballot; and the extension of the franchise. It was his support for such causes, combined with his intrinsic decency, which ensured that his parliamentary career was not otherwise one of sterile futility.

Equality for Catholics was the paramount objective of his forty years of political activism. He campaigned tirelessly for civil and religious equality for his co-religionists. He rejected, utterly and definitively, the treatment of Catholics as second-class citizens: they were entitled to the same regard under the law and constitution as Protestants – nothing more, nothing less. His own Catholic faith was an integral part of his life, informing his thoughts, words and deeds. Most especially, it inspired his many acts of charity and philanthropy.

This generosity which was a distinguishing feature of so much of his life was no less evident in his treatment of his son, Thomas Francis, with whom he is forever associated in the historical remembrance. He stood by his elder son, notwithstanding Thomas Francis's espousal of violent rebellion, which he deeply deplored. However, the younger Meagher's involvement in the 1848 Young Ireland rebellion has served to obscure the extent to which he shared his father's political views, and the fact that he was not so far removed from his constitutional nationalist beliefs as is often thought.

For a reluctant politician and a man who did not enjoy robust health, Thomas Meagher had an active public career, characterised by deeply held principles and involvement in many causes. His personal life, however, was essentially a sad one. He was a widower after only six years of marriage. Of his seven children, only two were alive at the time of his death, four of them having died at a very young age. His elder son drowned aged only forty-four. The only surviving photograph of him is of a man who appears to have known the pain of grief and loss.

Thomas Meagher was never a politician or leader of the first order, not least because of his temperament and personal disposition. It was inevitable that this reserved and serious, even sombre, man was always going to be overshadowed in the historical record by a son who was part of greater and more dramatic events, and who is now remembered and honoured, as one of Ireland's iconic patriots. And the older man will always be remembered primarily as his father. However, Thomas Meagher was also a patriot, in the O'Connellite mould, who lived a life of service to Ireland and to Waterford. The campaign for religious liberty and equality, embracing all the queen's subjects, dominated his years of political activism. He promoted the cause of greater independence for Ireland for two decades by his involvement in the repeal movement. Advocacy and support of reforms to extend the benefits of the constitution to a greater number of his fellow citizens informed his parliamentary career. He was clearly a man of high ambitions for his country and those who lived in it. Generous acts of charity and philanthropy characterised his lifelong attitudes towards the less advantaged in society. In his family life he supported his son, daughter-in-law and grandson in their times of need. This essentially decent man deserves remembrance for being more than *just* the father of Thomas Francis Meagher.

Endnotes

INTRODUCTION

1   *The Waterford News*, 8 November 1929.

2   Patrick Egan, *Guide to City and County of Waterford* (Kilkenny: P.M. Egan, 1893), p. 323.

3   Roy Foster, 'Foreword', in John M. Hearne and Rory T. Cornish (eds), *Thomas Francis Meagher: The Making of an Irish American* (Dublin: Irish Academic Press, 2006), p. xv.

4   Alan Downey, *The Complete Young Irelander: Thomas Francis Meagher* (Waterford: Carthage Press, 1945), p. 29.

5   John Mannion, 'Genealogy, Geography and Social Mobility: The Family Background of Thomas Francis Meagher', in Hearne and Cornish (eds), *Thomas Francis Meagher*, p. 31.

6   Thomas Francis Meagher, 'Recollections of Waterford', in Arthur Griffith (ed.), *Meagher of the Sword: Speeches of Thomas Francis Meagher in Ireland, 1846-1848* (Dublin: M.H. Gill and Son, Ltd, 1917), pp. 280-307, see pp. 284-5.

7   Thomas Francis Meagher, 'A Personal Narrative of 1848', in ibid., pp. 173-234, see p. 174.

8   Mannion, 'Genealogy, Geography and Social Mobility', p. 31.

9   W.F. Lyons, *Brigadier-General Thomas Francis Meagher: His Political and Military Career* (London: Burns Oates & Washbourne Ltd, 1869), p. vi.

10 Griffith, *Meagher of the Sword*, p. xviii.

11 Foster, 'Foreword', p. xvi.

12 Fergus O'Ferrall, *Catholic Emancipation: Daniel O'Connell and the Birth of Irish Democracy, 1820-30* (Dublin: Gill & Macmillan, 1985), pp. 120-33.

13 Quoted in Colin Reed, *The Lost World of Stephen Gwynn: Irish Constitutional Nationalism and Cultural Politics, 1864-1950* (Manchester: Manchester University Press, 2011), p. 5.

14 Ibid.

15 Oliver P. Rafferty, *The Catholic Church and the Protestant State: Nineteenth-Century Irish Realities* (Dublin: Four Courts Press, 2008), p. 11.

16 Theresa Reidy, 'Same-Sex Marriage and the Liberal Transformation of Ireland', *Georgetown Journal of International Affairs* (15 January 2020), http://gjia. georgetown.edu/2020/01/15/same-sex-marriage-and-the-liberal-transformation-of-ireland/, accessed 18 October 2021.

17 Senia Paseta, *Before the Revolution: Nationalism, Social Change and Ireland's Catholic Elite, 1879–1922* (Cork: Cork University Press, 1999), p. 4.

CHAPTER ONE: THE MEAGHERS OF NEWFOUNDLAND, *c.*1780–1819

1 Cyril Byrne, 'The Waterford Colony in Newfoundland, 1700–1850', in William Nolan and Thomas Power (eds), *Waterford History and Society: Interdisciplinary Essays on the History of an Irish County* (Dublin: Geography Publications, 1992), p. 369.

2 Mark Kurlansky, *Cod: A Biography of the Fish that Changed the World* (London: Vintage Books, 1999), p. 49.

3 Ibid., p. 51.

4 Ibid., pp. 33–4.

5 Ibid., p. 73.

6 Byrne, 'The Waterford Colony in Newfoundland', pp. 351 and 353.

7 Timothy Egan, *The Immortal Irishman: The Irish Revolutionary Who Became an American Hero* (New York: Houghton Mifflin Harcourt, 2016), p. 13.

8 Eamonn McEneaney, 'Waterford and Newfoundland', in *The Newfoundland Emigrant Trail: The Story of Emigration from the South East Coast of Ireland to Newfoundland during the 18th and 19th Centuries* (Waterford: no publication details, 2010), p. 11.

9 Quoted in John Mannion, 'Migrants and Emigrants of Waterford to Newfoundland 1700–1850: A Geographical Guide', in ibid., p. 4.

10 From Arthur Young, *A Tour in Ireland, 1776–1779*; quoted in T.N. Fewer, *I Was a Day in Waterford: An Anthology of Writing about Waterford City and County from the Eighteenth to the Twentieth Century* (Waterford: Ballylough Books, 2001), p. 39.

11 John Mannion, 'The Maritime Trade of Waterford in the Eighteenth Century', in William J. Smyth and Kevin Whelan (eds), *Common Ground: Essays on the Historical Geography of Ireland* (Cork: Cork University Press, 1998), p. 216.

12 Mannion, 'Genealogy, Geography and Social Mobility', p. 15; John Mannion, 'Migration and Upward Mobility: The Meagher Family in Ireland and Newfoundland, 1780–1830', *Irish Economic and Social History*, 15 (1980), p. 55.

13 See John Mannion Papers for his correspondence with various persons in Ireland on this matter.

14 John Mannion, 'From Comfortable Farms to Mercantile Commerce and Cultural Politics: The Social Origins and Family Connections of Thomas Francis Meagher', *Decies: Journal of the Waterford Archaeological and Historical Society*, 59 (2003), p. 5.

15 John Mannion Papers.

16 John Mannion and Fidelma Maddock, 'Old World Antecedents, New World Adaptations: Inistioge Immigrants in Newfoundland', in William Nolan and Kevin Whelan (eds), *Kilkenny: History and Society: Interdisciplinary Essays on the History of an Irish County* (Dublin: Geography Publications, 1990), p. 353.

17   John Mannion, 'A Transatlantic Merchant Fishery: Richard Welsh of New Ross and the Sweetmans of Newbawn and Newfoundland, 1734–1862', in Kevin Whelan (ed.), *Wexford History and Society: Interdisciplinary Essays on the History of an Irish County* (Dublin: Geography Publications, 1987), p. 373.

18   Egan, *The Immortal Irishman*, p. 13.

19   M.F. Howley, 'How Meagher Became a Millionaire: A True Story of Old St John's', *The Newfoundland Quarterly*, December 1904, p. 2.

20   Mannion, 'From Comfortable Farms to Mercantile Commerce', pp. 6–7.

21   Ibid., p. 7.

22   Ibid., p. 8.

23   Mannion, 'Migration and Upward Mobility', p. 57.

24   Mannion, 'From Comfortable Farms to Mercantile Commerce', p. 11.

25   John Mannion Papers, Auction notice, 2 July 1818.

26   John Mannion Papers, passim.

27   'List of the Original Members of the Newfoundland Irish Society' in Anon., *Centenary Volume: Benevolent Irish Society, St John's, Newfoundland* (Cork: Guy and Co. Ltd, 1906), p. 196.

28   Ibid., p. 18.

29   Ibid.

30   'Committee of Review and Correspondence', in ibid., p. 195.

31   Ibid., p. 28.

32   Ibid., p. 26.

33   Ibid., p. 30.

34   Olaf U. Janzen, 'The "Long" Eighteenth Century, 1697–1815, in Anon., *A Short History of Newfoundland and Labrador* (Newfoundland: Newfoundland Historical Society, 2008), p. 70.

35   Ibid., p. 55.

36   John Mannion, 'O'Donel's Mission: Catholics in Newfoundland in the Eighteenth Century', in *Ktaqamkuk, Across the Water, Thar Muir: Irish Journal of Newfoundland and Labrador Research* (Waterford: Waterford Institute of Technology, 2009), p. 68, n27.

37   Collier, Keith, 'St John's, 1500–1815', Newfoundland and Labrador Heritage (2011), http//www.heritage.nf.ca.>articles>society?st-john's-1815, accessed 7 November 2019.

38   Janzen, '"Long" Eighteenth Century', p. 71.

39   John Mannion, 'Vessels, Masters and Seafaring: Patterns in Waterford Voyages, 1766–1771', in William Nolan and Thomas Power (eds), *Waterford History and Society: Interdisciplinary Essays on the History of an Irish County* (Dublin: Geography Publications, 1992), pp. 387–8.

40   Mannion, 'Migrants and Emigrants', p. 3.

41   For an account of O'Donel's endeavours, see Mannion, 'O'Donel's Mission', pp. 51–90.

42   Ibid., p. 53.

43   Ibid.

44   Janzen, '"Long" Eighteenth Century', p. 65.

45   Cyril Byrne (ed.), *Gentlemen-Bishops and Faction Fighters: The Letters of Bishops O'Donel, Lambert, Scallan and Other Irish Missionaries* (St John's Newfoundland: Jesperson Press, 1984), p. 8.

46   Mannion, 'O'Donel's Mission', p. 74.

47   Byrne, *Gentlemen-Bishops*, p. 11.

48   John P. Greene, *Between Damnation and Starvation: Priests and Merchants in Newfoundland Politics, 1745–1855* (Montreal and Kingston: McGill-Queen's University Press, 1999), p. 17.

49   Colin Barr, *Ireland's Empire: The Roman Catholic Church in the English-Speaking World, 1829–1914* (Cambridge: Cambridge University Press, 2020), p. 79.

50   Mannion, 'O'Donel's Mission', p. 58.

51   Janzen, '"Long" Eighteenth Century', p. 63.

52   Mannion, 'O'Donel's Mission', pp. 78–9.

53   For a survey of Lambert's period as bishop, see Byrne, *Gentlemen-Bishops*, pp. 20–5.

54   Mannion, 'Genealogy, Geography and Social Mobility', p. 21; John Mannion Papers.

55   *Centenary Volume: Benevolent Irish Society*, p. 18.

56   John Mannion Papers.

57   Ibid.

58   Mannion, 'From Comfortable Farms to Mercantile Commerce', p. 20.

59   Mannion and Maddock, 'Old World Antecedents', p. 395. While concerned with Inistioge, County Kilkenny, the observations are relevant to all settlers.

60   Greene, *Between Damnation and Starvation*, p. 7.

61   Mannion and Maddock, 'Old World Antecedents', p. 396.

62   Mannion, 'From Comfortable Farms and Mercantile Commerce', p. 13.

63   John Mannion Papers.

64   Mannion, 'Genealogy, Geography and Social Mobility', p. 21.

65   Byrne, *Gentlemen-Bishops*, pp. 13–14.

66   John Mannion Papers.

67   See the genealogical chart of the Meagher family in Mannion, 'From Comfortable Farms to Mercantile Commerce', p. 4.

68   See, for example, pp. 13–16.

69   Information contained in email from John Mannion to author, 23 January 2020.

70   Ibid. See also John Mannion Papers.

71   John Mannion Papers: Rev. F.J. Turner, SJ, archivist, Stonyhurst, to John Mannion, 15 April 1988.

72   Howley, 'How Meagher Became a Millionaire', p. 3.

73   John Mannion Papers.

74   Mannion, 'From Comfortable Farm to Mercantile Commerce', p. 10.

75   Mannion, 'Genealogy, Geography and Social Mobility', pp. 22–5.

76   Ibid., p. 24.

77 John Mannion, 'Thomas Meagher', *Dictionary of Canadian Biography*, http://www.biographi.ca/en/bio/meagher_thomas_7E.html, accessed 7 November 2019.
78 *Merchant's Journal*, 25 February 1819, John Mannion Papers.
79 Mannion, 'Genealogy, Geography and Social Mobility', p. 22.

CHAPTER TWO: WATERFORD: THE EARLY YEARS 1819–1825
1 John Mannion Papers, 'Meagher, Waterford and St John's', article in an unidentified newspaper.
2 Mannion, 'Migration and Upward Mobility', p. 70.
3 Mannion, 'Genealogy, Geography and Social Mobility', p. 24.
4 Ibid.
5 Ibid., pp. 24–5.
6 Ibid., p. 27.
7 Mannion, 'Migration and Upward Mobility', pp. 66–7.
8 W.P. Burke, 'Newport's Waterford Bank', *Journal of the Cork Historical and Archaeological Society'*, 4 (1898), pp. 279–80.
9 Mannion, 'Genealogy, Geography and Social Mobility', p. 25.
10 Burke, 'Newport's Waterford Bank', p. 284.
11 Mannion, 'Genealogy, Geography and Social Mobility', p. 25.
12 *The Waterford Mirror*, 9 December 1822.
13 *The Waterford Mail*, 17 March 1824; 27 July 1825.
14 John Mannion Papers.
15 See entries entitled 'Catholic Convention' and 'Catholic Relief Acts', in Seán Connolly (ed.), *The Oxford Companion to Irish History'* (Oxford: Oxford University Press, 1998), pp. 75, 77–8.
16 John Mannion Papers.
17 Ibid.
18 Mannion, 'From Comfortable Farms to Mercantile Commerce', pp. 3–4.
19 Mannion, 'Genealogy, Geography and Social Mobility', p. 25.
20 Eugene Broderick, 'Protestants and the 1826 Waterford Election', *Decies: Journal of the Waterford Archaeological and Historical Society*, 53 (1997), pp. 45–6.
21 *The Waterford Mirror*, 4 April 1821.
22 Ibid.
23 *The Waterford Mirror*, 3, 5 December 1821.
24 Ibid., 17 December 1821.
25 *Ramsey's Waterford Chronicle*, 18 December 1821.
26 Ibid., 18, 20 December 1821.
27 Eugene Broderick, *Waterford's Anglicans: Religion and Politics, 1819–1842* (Newcastle upon Tyne: Cambridge Scholars Publishing, 2009), pp. 205–6.
28 Maureen Wall, 'The Rise of the Catholic Middle Class in Eighteenth-Century Ireland', in Gerard O'Brien (ed.), *Catholic Ireland in the Eighteenth-Century: Collected Essays of Maureen Wall* (Dublin: Geography Publications, 1989), pp. 73–84.
29 O'Ferrall, *Catholic Emancipation*, p. 281.

30 For an examination of the experience of the Catholic middle class in Cork, whose experience had many parallels in Waterford, see John B. O'Brien, *The Catholic Middle Classes in Pre-Famine Cork* (Dublin: National University of Ireland, 1980).

31 See Brian M. Walker (ed.), *Parliamentary Election Results in Ireland, 1801–1922* (Dublin: Royal Irish Academy, 1978), p. 241.

32 See, for example, *The Waterford Mail*, 13, 27 March, 17 April 1824.

33 *The Waterford Mirror*, 27 March 1824.

34 Thomas Wyse, *Historical Sketch of the Late Catholic Association of Ireland*, 2 vols. (London: Henry Colburn, 1829), vol. I, p. 199.

35 Seán Connolly, 'Mass Politics and Sectarian Conflict, 1823–30', in W.E. Vaughan (ed.), *A New History of Ireland*, vol. V: *Ireland under the Union, 1801–70* (Oxford: Clarendon Press, 1989), p. 85.

36 Wyse, *Historical Sketch*, vol. I, p. 224.

37 D. George Boyce, *Nationalism in Ireland* (London: Routledge, second edition, 1991), p. 140.

38 *The Waterford Mail*, 6 March 1824.

39 O'Ferrall, *Catholic Emancipation*, p. 122.

40 Pierce A. Grace, *The Middle Class of Callan, Co. Kilkenny, 1825–45* (Dublin: Four Courts Press, 2015), p. 10.

41 Ibid., p. 46.

42 An observation made by O'Brien regarding the Catholic middle class in Cork, but which may be applied to the middle class of Waterford. See O'Brien, *Catholic Middle Classes*, p. 9.

43 *The Waterford Mirror*, 20 March 1824.

44 Connolly, 'Mass Politics and Sectarian Conflict', p. 74.

45 Donald H. Akenson, *Discovering the End of Time: Irish Evangelicals in the Age of Daniel O'Connell* (Montreal and Kingston: McGill-Queen's University Press, 2016), p. 179.

46 Broderick, *Waterford's Anglicans*, pp. 76–8.

47 *The Waterford Mail*, 30 December 1826.

48 Eugene Broderick, 'The Famine and Religious Controversy in Waterford, 1847–1850', *Decies: Journal of the Waterford Archaeological and Historical Society*, 51 (1995), p. 12.

49 Irene Whelan, *The Bible War in Ireland: The 'Second Reformation' and the Polarisation of Protestant–Catholic Relations, 1800–1840* (Dublin: Lilliput Press, 2005), pp. 85–123. This book is an excellent account of an often ignored, but critical episode in Irish history.

50 Broderick, *Waterford's Anglicans*, p. 84.

51 Whelan, *Bible War*, p. 137.

52 Ibid., p. 149.

53 Wyse, *Historical Sketch*, vol. I, p. 236.

54 Whelan, *Bible War*, p. 203.

55 See Broderick, *Waterford's Anglicans*, pp. 82–94.

56 *The Waterford Mail*, 10 January 1827.

57 Broderick, *Waterford's Anglicans*, p. 86.

58 Waterford and Lismore Roman Catholic Diocesan Archives, Rev. Dr Thomas Hearn, PP, to the Secretaries of the Kildare Place Societies, 8 May 1822.

59 *Second Report of the Commissioners of Irish Education Inquiry 1826*, H.C. 1826–7 (12), xii, pp. 164–5; quote from Wyse, *Historical Sketch*, vol. I, p. 234.

60 *The Waterford Mail*, 25, 29 September 1824.

61 Donald Akenson, *The Irish Education Experiment: The National School System in the Nineteenth Century* (London: Routledge and Kegan Paul, 1970), p. 82.

62 The account of this meeting is based on *The Waterford Mirror*, 30 October 1824.

63 Broderick, *Waterford's Anglicans*, p. 86.

64 *The Waterford Mail*, 30 October 1824.

65 *The Waterford Mirror*, 20 March 1824.

66 O'Ferrall, *Catholic Emancipation*, p. 61.

67 Wyse, *Historical Sketch*, vol. I, p. 209.

68 *The Waterford Mail*, 14 August 1824.

69 O'Ferrall, *Catholic Emancipation*, p. 60.

70 Based on information in ibid., p. 67.

71 Ibid., p. 77.

72 Ibid., p. 58.

73 Wyse, *Historical Sketch*, vol. I, pp. 209–10. The italics are those of Wyse.

74 Thomas Meagher to Sir John Newport, 12 March 1825, reproduced in *The Waterford Mirror*, 23 March 1825.

75 James Reynolds, *The Catholic Emancipation Crisis in Ireland, 1823–1829* (Newport, CT: Greenwood Press, 1970), p. 13.

76 O'Ferrall, *Catholic Emancipation*, p. 86.

77 *The Waterford Mirror*, 12 February 1825.

78 Ibid., 16 February 1825.

79 For an account of the debate in Parliament, see O'Ferrall, *Catholic Emancipation*, pp. 86–90.

80 *The Waterford Mirror*, 23 March 1825. For the text of Meagher's letter and Newport's reply, see ibid.

81 Gearóid Ó Tuathaigh, *Ireland before the Famine, 1798–1848* (Dublin: Gill & Macmillan, 1972), p. 69.

82 For an excellent summary of the situation facing O'Connell, see Connolly, 'Mass Politics and Sectarian Conflict', p. 97.

83 *The Waterford Mirror*, 28 December 1825.

84 Ibid., 7 January 1826.

85 Ibid., 6 April 1825.

86 *The Waterford Mail*, 9 November 1825.

CHAPTER THREE: TOWARDS CATHOLIC EMANCIPATION, 1826–1829

1 *The Waterford Mail*, 10 August 1825.

2 Oliver MacDonagh, *The Hereditary Bondsman: Daniel O'Connell, 1775–1829* (London, Weidenfeld & Nicholson, 1988), p. 223.

3   Beresford voted against Catholic claims on 1 June 1811; 2 March, 11 and 24 May 1813; 21 May 1816; 9 May 1817 and 3 May 1819. See R.G. Thorne, *The House of Commons, 1790–1820*, vol. III (London: Secher and Warburg, 1986), p. 187.

4   J.J. Auchmuty, *Sir Thomas Wyse, 1791–1862: The Life and Career of an Educator and Diplomat* (London: P.S. King, 1939), p. 81.

5   Donal McCartney, 'Electoral Politics in Waterford in the Early 19th Century', *Decies: Journal of the Waterford Archaeological and Historical Society*, 20 (May 1982), p. 41.

6   Ibid., p. 40.

7   Wyse, *Historical Sketch*, vol. I, p. 287.

8   *Return of the Numbers of Freeholders in each County in Ireland* H.C. 1825 (312), pp. xxii, 12.

9   Wyse, *Historical Sketch*, vol. I, p. 267. The italics are those of Wyse.

10 Ibid., p. 270.

11 Ibid., p. 280.

12 Ibid., p. 285.

13 Auchmuty, *Wyse*, p. 85.

14 O'Ferrall, *Catholic Emancipation*, p. 122.

15 Quoted in ibid., p. 130.

16 R.F. Foster, *Modern Ireland, 1600–1972* (London: Allen Lane, The Penguin Press, 1988), p. 299.

17 Broderick, *Waterford's Anglicans*, pp. 148–59; Broderick, 'Protestants and the 1826 County Election', *Decies: Journal of the Waterford Archaeological and Historical Society*, 53 (1997), pp. 45–66.

18 Quoted in Reynolds, *Catholic Emancipation Crisis*, pp. 95–6.

19 O'Ferrall, *Catholic Emancipation*, p. 133.

20 Henry Villiers Stuart to Daniel O'Connell, 9 June 1826, letter 1308 in Maurice O'Connell (ed.), *The Correspondence of Daniel O'Connell*, vol. III: *1824–1828* (Shannon: Irish University Press, 1972), pp. 246–7.

21 See, for example, Daniel O'Connell to Mary O'Connell, 19 June 1826, letter 1312; and Daniel O'Connell to Mary O'Connell, 21 June 1826, letter 1314, in ibid., pp. 248–51.

22 O'Ferrall, *Catholic Emancipation*, p. 145.

23 *The Waterford Mail*, 15 July 1826.

24 *The Waterford Chronicle*, 1 July 1826.

25 *The Waterford Mail*, 23 September 1826.

26 For example, see ibid., 27 September; 30 September; 4 October; 18 October; 1 and 8 November 1826.

27 *The Waterford Mirror*, 21 August 1826.

28 *The Waterford Mail*, 23 August 1826; *The Waterford Mirror*, 30 August 1826.

29 *The Waterford Mail*, 15 July 1826.

30 So identified in *The Waterford Mirror*, 6 September 1826.

31 For these amounts, see ibid., 15, 23 and 30 August 1826 respectively.

32 Ibid., 6 September 1826.

33   *The Waterford Mail*, 29 November 1826.

34   Ibid., 23 September 1826.

35   *The Waterford Mirror*, 4 October 1826.

36   Fr John Sheehan to Daniel O'Connell, 3 November 1826, letter 1349, *Correspondence of Daniel O'Connell*, vol. III, p. 279.

37   Cited in O'Ferrall, *Catholic Emancipation*, p. 146.

38   *The Waterford Mirror*, 12 August 1826.

39   O'Ferrall, *Catholic Emancipation*, p. 146.

40   *The Waterford Mirror*, 6 January 1827.

41   Ibid., 6 September and 4 October 1826 respectively.

42   Ibid., 23 August 1826.

43   Ibid., 6 September 1826.

44   Ibid., 13 February 1828.

45   Ibid., 9 April 1827.

46   *The Waterford Mirror*, 15 August 1826.

47   Ibid., 9 April 1827.

48   'Written Pedigree of the Meagher Family', *Waterford History*, http://waterfordireland. tripod.com/written_pedigree_of_the_meagher_family.htm, accessed 5 May 2020.

49   Erin I. Bishop, *The World of Mary O'Connell, 1778–1836* (Dublin: Lilliput Press, 1999), p. 3.

50   Maria Luddy and Mary O'Dowd, *Marriage in Ireland, 1660–1925* (Cambridge: Cambridge University Press, 2020), p. 122.

51   Seán Connolly, 'Marriage in pre-Famine Ireland', in Art Cosgrove (ed.), *Marriage in Ireland* (Dublin: College Press, 1985), p. 81. Paula Bartley, *The Changing Role of Women, 1815–1914* (London: Hodder & Stoughton, 1996), p. 9.

52   Connolly, 'Marriage in pre-Famine Ireland', p. 95.

53   Ciarán O'Neill, 'Bourgeois Ireland, or, on the Benefits of Keeping One's Hands Clean', in J. Kelly (ed.), *The Cambridge History of Ireland*, vol. III: *1730–1880* (Cambridge: Cambridge University Press, 2018), p. 526.

54   Connolly, 'Marriage in pre-Famine Ireland', p. 87.

55   'Written Pedigree of the Meagher Family', *Waterford History*, http://waterfordireland. tripod.com/written_pedigree_of_the_meagher_family.htm, accessed 5 May 2020, for details of the children of Alicia and Thomas Meagher.

56   Bishop, *Mary O'Connell*, p. 68.

57   Lindsey Earner-Byrne and Diane Urquhart, 'Gender Roles in Ireland since 1740', in Eugenio Biagini and Mary E. Daly (eds), *The Cambridge Social History of Modern Ireland* (Cambridge: Cambridge University Press, 2017), p. 314.

58   Ibid., p. 312. See Bishop, *Mary O'Connell*, pp. 88–107, for an interesting treatment of Daniel O'Connell's wife's experience of this sphere.

59   Wyse, *Historical Sketch*, vol. II, Appendix XXV, 'Letter from Mr Wyse on the Organisation of Liberal Club', 30 July 1828, pp. cxlv–clvi.

60   O'Ferrall, *Catholic Emancipation*, p. 170.

61   Fergus O'Ferrall, *Daniel O'Connell* (Dublin: Gill & Macmillan, 1981), p. 62.

62 *The Waterford Mirror*, 9 April 1827.

63 *The Waterford Mail*, 9 April 1828.

64 Ibid., 12 July 1828.

65 See ibid., 16 July, 26 July, 30 July, 17 September 1828.

66 O'Ferrall, *Catholic Emancipation*, p. 188.

67 Ibid., pp. 188–200.

68 Ibid., pp. 206–57.

69 D. George Boyce, *Ireland, 1828–1923: From Ascendancy to Democracy* (Oxford: Blackwell, 1992), p. 15.

70 A reading of the report on the meeting which appeared in *The Waterford Chronicle*, 24 March 1829, would suggest this.

71 MacDonagh, *Hereditary Bondsman*, pp. 274–5.

72 *The Waterford Mirror*, 29 April 1829.

73 O'Ferrall, *Catholic Emancipation*, pp. 262–4.

74 Quoted in ibid., p. 264.

75 Ibid., p. 281.

76 Foster, *Modern Ireland*, p. 302.

77 Gustave de Beaumount, *Ireland: Social, Political and Religious,* translated by W.C. Taylor (Cambridge, Mass: Belknap Press of Harvard University Press, 2006), p. 225.

78 O'Ferrall, *Catholic Emancipation*, p. 264.

79 Ibid., p. 244.

80 Wyse, *Historical Sketch*, vol. I, p. 282.

81 Patrick Power, *Parochial History of Waterford and Lismore during the Eighteenth and Nineteenth Centuries* (Waterford: N. Harvey, 1912), p. 128.

82 *The Waterford Chronicle*, 13 October 1829.

83 Wyse, *Historic Sketch*, vol. II, p. cxlix.

CHAPTER FOUR: POLITICS, PHILANTHROPY AND PUBLIC OFFICE, 1830–1842

1 Ó Tuathaigh, *Ireland before the* Famine, p. 160.

2 Ibid.

3 *The Waterford Chronicle*, 19 October 1830.

4 Ibid., 18 December 1830.

5 Ibid., 20 January 1831.

6 Donal McCartney, *The Dawning of Democracy: Ireland, 1800–1870* (Dublin: Helicon Limited, 1987), p. 124.

7 Walker, *Parliamentary Election Results in Ireland*, p. 55.

8 Foster, *Modern Ireland*, pp. 307–8.

9 O'Ferrall, *Catholic Emancipation*, pp. 276–7.

10 Patrick Geoghegan, *Liberator: The Life and Death of Daniel O'Connell, 1830–1847* (Dublin: Gill & Macmillan, 2010), p. 55.

11 Oliver MacDonagh, *The Emancipist: Daniel O'Connell, 1830–1847* (London: Weidenfeld and Nicolson, 1989), p. 122.

12 Ó Tuathaigh, *Ireland before the Famine*, p. 165.

13 Ibid., p. 181. See MacDonagh, *The Emancipist*, pp. 106–38, for a more detailed treatment of the period under consideration.

14 William J. Smyth, 'The Creation of the Workhouse System', in John Crowley, William J. Smyth and Mike Murphy (eds), *Atlas of the Great Irish Famine* (Cork: Cork University Press, 2012), p. 121.

15 Fergus O'Ferrall, *John Ferrall: Master of Sligo Workhouse, 1852–66* (Dublin: Four Courts Press, 2019), p. 7.

16 Peter Gray, *The Making of the Irish Poor Law* (Manchester: Manchester University Press, 2009), pp. 92–129.

17 Ibid., p. 118.

18 Quoted in Emmet O'Connor, *A Labour History of Waterford* (Waterford: Waterford Trades Council, 1989), pp. 41–2.

19 This account is based on Gray, *Irish Poor Law*, pp. 281–331.

20 *The Waterford Chronicle*, 9 May 1839.

21 O'Ferrall, *Catholic Emancipation*, p. 122.

22 See Maurice O'Connell (ed.), *The Correspondence of Daniel O'Connell*, vol. VI: *1837–1840* (Shannon: Irish University Press, 1972), Rev. J. Sheehan to Daniel O'Connell, 19 December 1837, letter 2482, pp. 109–11; ibid., 18 January 1839, letter 2582, pp. 208–9.

23 *The Waterford Chronicle*, 28 May 1839.

24 Ibid., 11 June 1839.

25 Gray, *Irish Poor Law*, p. 297.

26 Broderick, *Waterford's Anglicans*, pp. 186–9.

27 *The Waterford Chronicle*, 11 June 1839.

28 Ibid.

29 Ibid., 25 June 1839.

30 Ibid., 2 July 1839.

31 Christine Kinealy, *This Great Calamity: The Irish Famine, 1845–1852* (Dublin: Gill & Macmillan, 1994), p. 25.

32 Rita Byrne, 'The Workhouse in Waterford City, 1847–49', in Des Cowman and Donald Brady (eds), *Teacht na bPrátaí Dubha: The Famine in Waterford, 1845–1850* (Dublin: Geography Publications and Waterford County Council, 1995), p. 119.

33 Gray, *Irish Poor Law*, p. 293.

34 Matthew Potter, *The Municipal Revolution in Ireland: A Handbook of Urban Government in Ireland since 1800* (Dublin: Irish Academic Press, 2011), p. 84.

35 Bob Cullen, *Thomas L. Synnott: The Career of a Dublin Catholic* (Dublin: Irish Academic Press, 1997), p. 9.

36 *The Waterford Chronicle*, 11 May 1839.

37 Ibid., 28 November 1843.

38 Mannion, 'From Comfortable Farms to Mercantile Commerce', p. 25.

39 *The Waterford Mirror*, 9 January 1830.

40 Ibid., 'Statement of the Number of Children Received in the Establishment since its Commencement and the Manner in which they have been Disposed of'.

41 *The Waterford Mirror*, 1 October 1823.

42   *The Waterford Chronicle*, 9 January 1830.

43   Niall Byrne, *The Waterford Leper Hospital of St. Stephen & the Waterford County and City Infirmary: a History of Institutional Medicine in Waterford* (Dublin: Linden Publishing Services, 2011), p. 24.

44   *The Waterford Mirror*, 12 November 1827.

45   *The Waterford Chronicle*, 24 January 1839.

46   Richard Ryland, *The History, Topography and Antiquities of the County and City of Waterford* (first published, 1824; reprinted Kilkenny: Wellbrook Press, 1982), p. 197.

47   Anon., *Report of the Fanning Institute, Waterford, for the First Ten Years with the History of its Origins* (Waterford: Thomas Harvey, 1853), p. 47.

48   Ciarán McCabe, *Begging, Charity and Religion in Pre-Famine Ireland* (Liverpool: Liverpool University Press, 2018), p. 100.

49   Ibid., p. 96.

50   Ibid., p. 148.

51   Ibid., p. 159.

52   Ibid., p. 164.

53   Ibid., p. 161.

54   *The Waterford Mirror*, 26 November 1825.

55   Ibid., 26 May 1826.

56   *The Waterford Chronicle*, 10 January 1839.

57   Ibid., 12 January 1839.

58   Ibid., 21 September 1839.

59   McCabe, *Begging, Charity and Religion*, p. 171.

60   Anon., *History of the Ursuline Waterford: From the Annals, 1816–2016* (no publication details, 2016), p. 8.

61   Anon., *Waterford's Presentation Community: A Bicentenary Record, 1798–1998* (no publication details, 1998), pp. 22–3.

62   Sara Atkinson, *Mary Aikenhead: Her Life, Her Work and Her Friends* (Dublin: Gill, 1879), pp. 286–93.

63   Mother Mary Aikenhead to Mother Mary de Chantal, 9 June 1842, in Anon., *Letters of Mary Aikenhead* (Dublin: M.H. Gill & Sons Ltd, 1914), p. 137. Mother Mary Aikenhead to Mother Mary de Chantal, 20 June 1842, in ibid.

64   Eamonn McEneaney with Rosemary Ryan, *Waterford Treasures: A Guide to the Historical and Archaeological Treasures of Waterford City* (Waterford: Waterford Museum of Treasures, 2004), pp. 198–9.

65   *The Waterford Chronicle*, 22 January 1848.

66   Frances Finnegan, *Do Penance or Perish: A Study of Magdalen Asylums in Ireland* (Kilkenny: Congreve Press, 2001), p. 84.

67   Ibid., pp. 85–6.

68   Ibid., pp. 84–5.

69   McCabe, *Begging, Charity and Religion*, p. 196.

70   Ibid., p. 103.

71   Ibid., p. 149.

72 See ibid., pp. 203–7 for a discussion of the Sisters of Charity. Ibid., p. 204.

73 Ibid., p. 205.

74 Ibid., p. 206.

75 McCartney, *Dawning of Democracy*, p. 151.

76 *The Waterford Chronicle*, 29 May 1838.

77 Ibid., 12 January 1839.

78 Ibid.

79 See ibid., 2, 26 February 1839 for criticism of the society.

80 Ibid., 23 November 1839.

81 Ibid., 27 April 1839.

82 Ibid., 4 May 1839.

83 Broderick, *Waterford's Anglicans*, pp. 194–5.

84 *The Waterford Chronicle*, 20 July 1841.

85 Quoted in Virginia Crossman, *Local Government in Nineteenth-Century Ireland* (Belfast: Institute of Irish Studies, 1994), p. 78.

86 *First Report of the Commissioners Appointed to Inquire into Municipal Corporations in Ireland*, H.C. (23), xxvii, Appendix 1, p. 39.

87 Ibid., p. 23.

88 For an account of this Corporation, see Eugene Broderick, 'Privilege and Exclusiveness: the Unreformed Corporation of Waterford, 1818–1840', *Decies: Journal of the Waterford Archaeological and Historical Society*, 63 (2007), pp. 165–76.

89 Ibid., pp. 166–9.

90 Waterford City and County Archives (hereafter WCCA), Corporation Minutes, 24 June and 3 November 1829.

91 *First Report of the Commissioners*, p. 617.

92 For example, the offices of recorder and town clerk attracted salaries of £200 and £120 respectively, while the mayor's clerk and the porter of the town hall earned £40 and £30 respectively. See ibid., pp. 588–91, for a full list of officers' duties and salaries.

93 *The Waterford Mail*, 16 July 1828.

94 Ibid., 19 July 1828.

95 WCCA, TNC 1/3.

96 *First Report of the Commissioners*, p. 617.

97 *The Waterford Mirror*, 14 and 18 December 1833.

98 Ibid., 28 December 1833.

99 WCCA, Corporation Minutes, 18 February 1831.

100 D. George Boyce, *Nineteenth-Century Ireland: The Search for Stability* (Dublin: Gill & Macmillan, 1990), p. 69. Boyce is describing the debate at parliamentary level; his comments apply equally to the debate at local level in Waterford.

101 *The Waterford Mail*, 25 October 1828.

102 Potter, *Municipal Revolution*, p. 86.

103 Ibid., 2 March 1839.

104 Ibid., 3 August 1839.

105 Ibid., 15 February 1840.

106 Boyce, *Nineteenth-Century Ireland*, pp. 68–9.
107 Quoted in Crossman, *Local Government*, p. 78.
108 WCCA, Corporation Minutes, 24 August 1835.
109 *The Waterford Mail*, 5 January 1839.
110 WCCA, Corporation Minutes, 13 May 1840.
111 Potter, *Municipal Revolution*, p. 86
112 Ibid., p. 101.
113 *The Waterford Chronicle*, 31 May 1842.
114 Ibid., 2 June 1842.
115 Ibid., 8 October 1842.
116 Ibid., 15 October 1842.
117 Potter, *Municipal Revolution*, p. 93.
118 Ibid.
119 Ibid., p. 101.
120 O'Connor, *Labour History of Waterford*, p. 53.
121 Potter, *Municipal Revolution*, p. 88.
122 O'Connor, *Labour History of Waterford*, p. 53.
123 W.E. Vaughan and A.J. Fitzpatrick (eds), *Irish Historical Statistics: Population, 1821–1971* (Dublin: Royal Irish Academy, 1978), p. 34.
124 O'Brien, *Catholic Middle Classes*, p. 20.
125 WCCA, Corporation Minutes, LA1/1/A/16, 26 October 1842.

CHAPTER FIVE: MAYOR OF WATERFORD, 1843, 1844
1 *The Waterford Chronicle*, 3 November 1842.
2 Eugene Broderick, 'From the Shadow of his Son: "Honest Thomas Meagher" – the Father of an Irish Patriot', in Hearne and Cornish (eds), *Thomas Francis Meagher*, p. 40.
3 WCCA, Minute Book, Waterford Corporation, 1 November 1842, LA/1/A/16.
4 *The Waterford Chronicle*, 3 November 1842.
5 Eamonn McEneaney, *Discover Waterford* (Dublin: O'Brien Press, 2001), p. 54.
6 *The Waterford Chronicle*, 8 November 1842.
7 WCCA, Minute Book, Waterford Corporation, 29 November 1842, LA1/1/A/16.
8 WCCA, Minute Book, Waterford Corporation, 29 November 1842, LA1/1/A/16.
9 WCCA, Minute Book, Waterford Corporation, 10 January 1843, LA1/1/A/16.
10 WCCA, Minute Book, Waterford Corporation, 21 February 1843, LA1/1/A/16.
11 WCCA, Minute Book, Waterford Corporation, 10 January 1843, LA1/1/A/16.
12 WCCA, Minute Book, Waterford Corporation, 13 December 1842, LA1/1/A/16.
13 WCCA, Minute Book, Waterford Corporation, 13 December 1842, LA1/1/A/16.
14 WCCA, Minute Book, Waterford Corporation, 1 December 1843, LA1/1/A/16.
15 See, for example, WCCA, Minute Book, Waterford Corporation, 7 May 1844, LA1/1/A/16.
16 See, for example, WCCA, Minute Book, Waterford Corporation, 8 October 1844, LA1/1/A/16.

17   WCCA, Minute Book, Waterford Corporation, 29 November 1842, LA1/1/A/16.

18   WCCA, Minute Book, Waterford Corporation, 29 November 1842, LA1/1/A/16.

19   Eugene Broderick, 'A Decade of Agitation and Strife: Thomas Meagher, Mayor – 1843, 1844', in Eamonn McEneaney (ed.), *A History of Waterford and its Mayors from the 12th to the 20th Century* (Waterford: Waterford Corporation, 1995), p. 188.

20   WCCA, Minute Book, Waterford Corporation, 6 February 1844, LA1/1/A/16.

21   WCCA, Minute Book, Waterford Corporation, 2 December 1844, LA1/1/A/16.

22   *The Waterford Chronicle*, 12 November 1842.

23   Geoghegan, *Liberator*, pp. 127–30.

24   Ibid., pp. 129–30.

25   WCCA, Minute Book, Waterford Corporation, 1 November 1842, LA1/1/A/16.

26   Daniel O'Connell to Thomas Meagher, 3 November 1842, published in *The Waterford Chronicle*, 8 November 1842.

27   *The Waterford Chronicle*, 12 November 1842.

28   WCCA, Minute Book, Waterford Corporation, 21 March 1843, LA1/1/A/16.

29   *The Waterford Chronicle*, 23 March 1843.

30   Matthew Kelly, 'Nationalisms', in Richard Bourke and Ian McBride (eds), *The Princeton History of Modern Ireland* (Princeton and Oxford: Princeton University Press, 2016), p. 451.

31   *The Waterford Chronicle*, 23 April 1843.

32   Geoghegan, *Liberator*, p. 134.

33   Ibid., p. 133.

34   Gary Owens, 'Nationalism without Words: Symbolism and Ritual Behaviour in the Repeal "Monster Meetings" of 1843–5', in J.S. Donnelly and Kerby A. Miller (eds), *Irish Popular Culture, 1650–1850* (Dublin: Irish Academic Press, 1998), p. 244.

35   Ibid.

36   McCartney, *Dawning of Democracy*, p. 153.

37   Geoghegan, *Liberator*, p. 135.

38   *The Waterford Chronicle*, 11 July 1843.

39   Ibid., 19 October 1843.

40   WCCA, Minute Book, Waterford Corporation, 20 October 1843, LA1/1A/16.

41   *The Waterford Chronicle*, 25 November 1843.

42   WCCA, Minute Book, Waterford Corporation, 22 November 1843, LA1/1/A/16.

43   WCCA, Minute Book, Waterford Corporation, 25 March 1844, LA1/1/A/16.

44   *The Waterford Chronicle*, 10 April 1845.

45   WCCA, Minute Book, Waterford Corporation, 31 May 1844, LA1/1/A/16.

46   *The Waterford Chronicle*, 5 June 1844.

47   WCCA, Minute Book, Waterford Corporation, 4 June 1844, LA1/1/A/16.

48   *The Waterford Chronicle*, 8 and 15 June 1844.

49   WCCA, Minute Book, Waterford Corporation, 11 September 1844, LA1/1/A/16.

50   *The Waterford Chronicle*, 14 September 1844.

51   Ibid.

52   Ibid., 25 September 1844.

53   Ibid., 12 November 1842.

54   Ibid., 7 February 1843.

55   Ibid., 1 July 1843.

56   Ibid., 19 October 1843.

57   Ibid., 5 June 1844.

58   Ibid., 8 June 1844.

59   Ibid., 14 September 1844.

60   Quoted in James H. Murphy, *Abject Loyalty: Nationalism and Monarchy in Ireland during the Reign of Queen Victoria* (Cork: Cork University Press, 2001), p. 32.

61   Ibid.

62   Ibid.

63   Oliver MacDonagh, 'O'Connell's Ideology', in Laurence Brockliss and David Eastwood (eds), *A Union of Multiple Identities: The British Isles, c.1750–c.1850* (Manchester: Manchester University Press, 1997), p. 155.

64   WCCA, Minute Book, Waterford Corporation, 21 March 1843, LA1/1/A/16.

65   *The Waterford Chronicle*, 23 March 1843.

66   Ibid., 12 November 1842.

67   Murphy, *Abject Loyalty*, p. xxxii.

68   WCCA, Minute Book, Waterford Corporation, 2 May 1843, LA1/1/A/16.

69   James Loughlin, *British Monarchy and Ireland: 1800 to the Present* (Cambridge: Cambridge University Press, 2007), p. 48.

70   For example, see *The Waterford Chronicle*, 3, 7 July 1838.

71   Ibid., 11 February 1840.

72   Loughlin, *British Monarchy and Ireland*, p. 54.

73   Murphy, *Abject Loyalty*, p. xix.

74   Paul A. Townend, *Father Mathew, Temperance and Irish Identity* (Dublin: Irish Academic Press, 2002), p. 209.

75   McCartney, *Dawning of Democracy*, p. 153.

76   Townend, *Father Mathew*, pp. 33–42.

77   Ibid., p. 226.

78   *The Waterford Chronicle*, 19 October 1843.

79   Ibid., 8 June 1844.

80   Townend, *Father Mathew*, p. 1.

81   *The Waterford Chronicle*, 19 March 1840.

82   Townend, *Father Mathew*, p. 1.

83   Ibid., p. 53.

84   Ibid., p. 5.

85   Ibid., p. 11.

86   Ibid., p. 78.

87   *The Waterford Chronicle*, 3 November 1842.

88   *The Waterford Mirror*, 14 December 1833.

89   Cited in Donnchadh Ó Ceallacháin, 'The Temperance Movements in Waterford, 1839–1841', *Decies: Journal of the Waterford Archaeological and Historical Society*, 52 (1996), p. 59.

90 John M. Hearne, 'The Cost of Living and Standard of Living of Urban Workers in Waterford, 1834–56', *Saothar: Journal of the Irish Labour History Society*, 26 (2000), p. 39.

91 Des Cowman, 'Trade and Society in Waterford City, 1800–1840', in William Nolan and Thomas Power (eds), *Waterford History and Society: Interdisciplinary Essays on the History of an Irish County* (Dublin: Geography Publications, 1992), p. 444.

92 Ibid.

93 Hearne, 'Cost of Living', p. 39.

94 Colm Kerrigan, *Father Mathew and the Irish Temperance Movement, 1838–1849* (Cork: Cork University Press, 1992), p. 78.

95 Townend, *Father Mathew*, p. 4.

96 Ibid., p. 42.

97 *The Waterford Chronicle*, 7 January 1843.

98 Quoted in Broderick, 'Thomas Meagher, Mayor', p. 191.

99 *The Waterford Chronicle*, 6 May 1843.

100 Ibid., 14 September 1843. Meagher was on pilgrimage to Rome in 1839 and 1840.

101 Ibid., 19 October 1843.

102 Ibid., 8 June 1844.

103 Ibid., 6 May 1843.

104 Townend, *Father Mathew*, pp. 56–9.

105 Ibid., p. 59.

106 Ibid., pp. 59–67.

107 Kerrigan, *Father Mathew*, pp. 65–6.

108 Townend, *Father Mathew*, pp. 235–60; see ibid., p. 246.

109 *The Waterford Chronicle*, 14 September 1843.

110 Ibid., 14 July 1847.

111 Geoghegan, *Liberator*, p. 195.

112 *The Chronicle and Munster Advertiser*, 13 November 1844.

113 Ibid., 5 November 1845.

114 Ibid., 8 November 1845.

115 Ibid., 31 December 1845.

116 Ibid., 14 December 1844.

117 MacDonagh, *The Emancipist*, p. 253

118 Ibid., p. 252.

119 Ibid., Appendix II, 'Assessment by Dr B.J. O'Neil of the Cause of O'Connell's Death', pp. 338–9.

CHAPTER SIX: THOMAS MEAGHER: 'OLD IRELANDER', 1845–1847

1 James S. Donnelly, 'A Famine in Irish Politics', in W.E. Vaughan (ed.), *A New History of Ireland*, vol. V: *Ireland under the Union, 1801–70* (Oxford: Clarendon Press, 1989), p. 357.

2 Kevin B. Nowlan, *The Politics of Repeal: A Study in the Relations between Great Britain and Ireland, 1841–50* (London: Routledge and Kegan Paul, 1965), p. 45.

3   Ibid., pp. 37–58.

4   MacDonagh, *The Emancipist*, pp. 244–70.

5   Donal A. Kerr, *Peel, Priests and Politics: Sir Robert Peel's Administration and the Roman Catholic Church in Ireland, 1841–1846* (Oxford: Clarendon Press, 1982), pp. 110–23.

6   Ibid., pp. 123–51.

7   Ibid., pp. 224–89.

8   Ibid., pp. 290–351.

9   Geoghegan, *Liberator*, pp. 212–27.

10   Patrick Geoghegan, 'The Impact of O'Connell', in J. Kelly (ed.), *The Cambridge History of Ireland*, vol. III: *1730–1880* (Cambridge: Cambridge University Press, 2018), p. 122.

11   Kerr, *Peel, Priests and Politics*, pp. 123–5.

12   Ibid., p. 124.

13   Ibid., p. 130.

14   Ibid., p. 133.

15   Ibid., p. 185.

16   *The Chronicle and Munster Advertiser*, 18 December 1844.

17   Ibid.

18   Kerr, *Peel, Priests and Politics*, p. 121.

19   Quoted in ibid., p. 129.

20   *The Chronicle and Munster Advertiser*, 18 December 1844.

21   Kerr, *Peel, Priests and Politics*, pp. 300–1.

22   Ibid., p. 312.

23   Helen Mulvey, *Thomas Davis and Ireland: A Biographical Study* (Washington, DC: Catholic University Press of America, 2003), pp. 178–9.

24   Kerr, *Peel, Priests and Politics*, p. 312.

25   Quoted in MacDonagh, *The Emancipist*, p. 269.

26   Kerr, *Peel, Priests and Politics*, p. 313.

27   *The Chronicle and Munster Advertiser*, 8 November 1845.

28   *The Waterford Chronicle*, 3 November 1842.

29   Ibid., 14 September 1843.

30   Ibid., 19 October 1843.

31   *The Chronicle and Munster Advertiser*, 14 December 1844.

32   Ibid., 11 January 1845.

33   Kerr, *Peel, Priests and Politics*, p. 304.

34   Ibid., p. 291.

35   Ibid., n4.

36   Michael Kavanagh, *Memoirs of Gen. Thomas Francis Meagher* (Worcester, Mass.: Messenger Press, 1892), p. 35.

37   For an examination of proselytism during the Great Famine, see Desmond Bowen, *Souperism: Myth or Reality?* (Cork: Mercier Press, 1971). For the situation in Waterford, see Broderick, *Waterford's Anglicans*, pp. 240–82.

38 *The Chronicle and Munster Advertiser*, 9 July 1845.

39 Ibid., 22 October 1845.

40 Quoted in Kerr, *Peel, Priests and Politics*, p. 312.

41 *The Chronicle and Munster Advertiser*, 8 April 1846.

42 Kerr, *Peel, Priests and Politics*, p. 302.

43 Ibid.

44 Quoted in ibid., p. 301.

45 Ibid., pp. 224–89.

46 Quoted in ibid., p. 234.

47 MacDonagh, *The Emancipist*, p. 274.

48 Ibid., pp. 274–6.

49 Ibid., pp. 274–5.

50 *The Nation*, 20, 27 December 1845.

51 Ibid., 20 December 1845.

52 Ibid., 27 December 1845.

53 Ibid., 20 December 1845.

54 Ibid., 27 December 1845.

55 *The Chronicle and Munster Advertiser*, 5 June 1847.

56 Quoted in Oliver MacDonagh, 'The Contribution of O'Connell', in Brian Farrell (ed.), *The Irish Parliamentary Tradition* (Dublin: Gill & Macmillan, 1973), pp. 167–8.

57 J.J. Lee, 'Daniel O'Connell', in Maurice R. O'Connell (ed.), *Daniel O'Connell: Political Pioneer* (Dublin: Institute of Public Administration, 1991), p. 5.

58 Oliver MacDonagh, 'The Age of O'Connell, 1830–45', in W.E. Vaughan (ed.), *A New History of Ireland*, vol. V: *Ireland under the Union, 1801–70* (Oxford: Clarendon Press, 1989), p. 167.

59 *The Chronicle and Munster Advertiser*, 19 June 1847.

60 Ibid., 23 June 1847.

61 Ibid., 10 July 1847.

62 Brian Walker, 'The Great Famine General Election, 1847', in John Gibney (ed.), *The Great Famine: Irish Perspectives* (Barnsley: Pen & Sword Books, 2018), p. 38.

63 Nowlan, *The Politics of Repeal*, p. 143.

64 *The Chronicle and Munster Advertiser*, 14 July 1847.

65 Ibid., 4 August 1847.

66 Ibid., 7 August 1847.

67 Ibid.

68 Walker, *Parliamentary Election Results in Ireland*, p. 79. The total number of eligible voters in the constituency was 1,696.

69 *The Chronicle and Munster Advertiser*, 4 August 1847.

70 Ó Tuathaigh, *Ireland before the Famine*, p. 197. Some of those elected were only nominal repealers.

71 Kevin Nowlan, 'The Political Background', in R. Dudley Edwards and T. Desmond Williams (eds), *The Great Famine: Studies in Irish History, 1845–52* (Dublin: Lilliput Press, 1994), p. 168.

72   *The Chronicle and Munster Advertiser*, 14 July 1847.

73   Ibid., 4 August 1847.

74   For a consideration of Protestant attitudes to repeal, see Broderick, *Waterford's Anglicans*, pp. 171–201.

75   *The Waterford Chronicle*, 3 November 1842.

76   MacDonagh, *The Emancipist*, p. 268.

77   Ibid., p. 266.

78   Donnelly, 'A Famine in Irish Politics', p. 358.

79   MacDonagh, *The Emancipist*, p. 267; Thomas Bartlett, 'The Emergence of the Irish Catholic Nation, 1750–1850', in Alvin Jackson (ed.), *The Oxford Handbook of Modern Irish History* (Oxford: Oxford University Press, 2014), p. 541.

80   From 'Celts and Saxons', https://celt.ucc.ie//published/E850004-003/text001.html, accessed on 3 July 2020.

81   MacDonagh, *The Emancipist*, p. 267.

82   *The Waterford Mail*, 25 November 1843.

83   *The Chronicle and Munster Advertiser*, 15 January 1845.

84   Ibid.

85   Ibid., 29 January 1845.

86   Ibid., 5 March 1845.

87   'Address of the Citizens of Waterford to Thomas Meagher, Esq., Late Mayor of Waterford, 28 February 1845', Waterford Museum of Treasures.

88   Captain Thomas Roberts to William Roberts, 26 February 1845, Roberts' Letters, Waterford Museum of Treasures. The underlined text is that of Captain Roberts.

89   Captain Thomas Roberts to William Roberts, 28 February 1845, Roberts' Letters, Waterford Museum of Treasures. My thanks to Cliona Purcell for the references to the Roberts Letters.

90   *The Chronicle and Munster Advertiser*, 7 August 1847.

CHAPTER SEVEN: FAMINE, 1845–1848

1   William J. Smyth, 'The Role of Cities and Towns during the Great Famine', in John Crowley, William J. Smyth and Mike Murphy (eds), *Atlas of the Great Irish Famine* (Cork: Cork University Press, 2012), p. 242.

2   Ibid.

3   Mary E. Daly, *The Famine in Ireland* (Dundalk: Dundalgan Press, 1986), p. 55.

4   Ibid., p. 53.

5   *The Waterford Mail*, 25 October 1845.

6   *The Waterford Freeman*, 12 November 1845.

7   Thomas P. O'Neill, 'The Organisation and Administration of Relief, 1842–52', in R. Dudley Edwards and T. Desmond Williams (eds), *The Great Famine: Studies in Irish History, 1845–52* (Dublin: Lilliput Press, 1994), pp. 212–22.

8   Mary Daly, 'The Operations of Famine Relief, 1845–47', in Cathal Póirtéir (ed.), *The Great Irish Famine* (Cork: Mercier Press, 1995), pp. 127–8.

9   Kinealy, *This Great Calamity*, pp. 44–5.

10   O'Neill, 'Organisation and Administration of Relief', p. 216.

11   *The Chronicle and Munster Advertiser*, 8 April 1846.

12   Ciarán Ó Murchadha, *The Great Famine: Ireland's Agony, 1845–1852* (London: Continuum, 2011), p. 37.

13   *The Waterford Mail*, 8 April 1846.

14   *The Chronicle and Munster Advertiser*, 15 April 1846.

15   *The Waterford Mail*, 16 May 1846.

16   O'Neill, 'Organisation and Administration of Relief', p. 217.

17   *The Waterford Mail*, 16 May 1846.

18   Ibid., 25 April 1846.

19   Ibid., 16 May 1846.

20   *The Chronicle and Munster Advertiser*, 29 April 1846.

21   Ibid., 20 June 1846.

22   Ibid., 23 September 1846.

23   Ibid., 15 April 1846.

24   Ibid., 2 May 1846.

25   *The Waterford Mail*, 26 August 1846.

26   Eugene Broderick, 'The Famine in Waterford as Reported in the Local Newspapers', in Des Cowman and Donald Brady (eds), *Teacht na bPrátaí Dubha: The Famine in Waterford, 1845–1850* (Dublin: Geography Publications and Waterford County Council, 1995), p. 159.

27   Ibid., pp. 159–66.

28   James S. Donnelly, 'The Administration of Relief, 1846–7', in W.E. Vaughan (ed.), *A New History of Ireland*, vol. V: *Ireland under the Union, 1801–70* (Oxford: Clarendon Press, 1989), p. 276.

29   For an account of the influences of various ideologies on the Famine policy of the Whigs, see Peter Gray, 'Ideology and the Famine', in Cathal Póirtéir (ed.), *The Great Irish Famine* (Cork: Mercier Press, 1995), pp. 86–103.

30   Donnelly, 'Administration of Relief', pp. 294–306.

31   *The Waterford Mail*, 23 September 1846.

32   Donnelly, 'Administration of Relief', p. 298.

33   *The Waterford Freeman*, 7 October 1846.

34   *The Waterford Mail*, 21 October 1846.

35   John M. Hearne, 'The Official View of the Famine: Waterford, a Regional Dimension', in Des Cowman and Donald Brady (eds), *Teacht na bPrátaí Dubha: The Famine in Waterford, 1845–1850* (Dublin: Geography Publications and Waterford County Council, 1995), p. 49.

36   Broderick, 'Famine in Waterford', pp. 170–1.

37   *The Chronicle and Munster Advertiser*, 5 December 1846.

38   Peter Gray, 'The Great Famine, 1845–1850', in J. Kelly (ed.), *The Cambridge History of Ireland*, vol. III: *1730–1880* (Cambridge: Cambridge University Press, 2018), p. 652.

39   *The Waterford Mail*, 16 December 1846.

40   Broderick, 'Famine in Waterford', pp. 171–2.

41   Donnelly, 'Administration of Relief', p. 300.

42   Ibid., p. 303.

43   Waterford's newspapers did convey a sense of these miserable conditions; see Broderick, 'Famine in Waterford', pp. 174–5.

44   Gray, 'Great Famine', p. 652.

45   *The Waterford Freeman*, 9 January 1847.

46   Gray, 'Great Famine', p. 652.

47   Hearne, 'Official View of the Famine', p. 53.

48   Ó Tuathaigh, *Ireland before the Famine*, p. 214.

49   Ibid.

50   *The Waterford Mail*, 10 April 1847.

51   Ibid., 14 April 1847.

52   James S. Donnelly, 'The Soup Kitchens', in W.E. Vaughan (ed.), *A New History of Ireland*, vol. V: *Ireland under the Union, 1801–70* (Oxford: Clarendon Press, 1989), pp. 307–15.

53   Circular from the Relief Commission Office, Dublin, 6 August 1847; reprinted in *The Waterford Mail*, 14 August 1847.

54   Ó Murchadha, *Great Famine*, pp. 37–8.

55   Ó Tuathaigh, *Ireland before the Famine*, pp. 215–16. See also Donnelly, 'Administration of Relief', p. 317, for a more detailed overview.

56   *The Chronicle and Munster Advertiser*, 2 April 1847.

57   Christine Kinealy, 'The Operation of the Poor Law during the Famine', in John Crowley, William J. Smyth and Mike Murphy (eds), *Atlas of the Great Irish Famine* (Cork: Cork University Press, 2012), p. 90.

58   Byrne, 'The Workhouse in Waterford City', p. 119.

59   For the figures pertaining to each month, see the following editions of *The Waterford Mail*: 7 April, 26 June, 21 August, 29 September, 30 October, 27 November 1847.

60   *The Chronicle and Munster Advertiser*, 1 May 1847.

61   Ibid.

62   *The Waterford Mail*, 15 May 1847.

63   *Report of the Commissioners of Health, Ireland, on the Epidemics of 1846 to 1850* (Dublin: Alexander Thom, 1852), p. 12.

64   Ibid., p. 1.

65   William P. MacArthur, 'Medical History of the Famine', in R. Dudley Edwards and T. Desmond Williams (eds), *The Great Famine: Studies in Irish History, 1845–52* (Dublin: Lilliput Press, 1994), p. 265. For a description of the various diseases, see ibid., pp. 265–70.

66   Laurence Geary, 'Famine, Fever and Bloody Flux', in Cathal Póirtéir (ed.), *The Great Irish Famine* (Cork: Mercier Press, 1995), p. 76.

67   MacArthur, 'Medical History of the Famine', p. 271.

68   *Report of the Commissioners of Health*, Appendix A, No. 15, 'Summary Returns, showing the Number of Patients treated under the Temporary Fevers Acts in the principal towns of Ireland', p. 66.

69 *The Waterford Chronicle*, 30 October 1874.

70 John O'Connor, *The Workhouses of Ireland: The Fate of Ireland's Poor* (Dublin: Anvil Books, 1995), p. 145.

71 Smyth, 'The Creation of the Workhouse System', p. 127.

72 Kinealy, *This Great Calamity*, pp. 113–14.

73 'Meetings of Guardians, Number of Attendances, &c., from the 25th of March 1847 to the 17th March 1848', in *Papers Relating to Proceedings for the Relief of Distress and the State of the Unions and Workhouses in Ireland* [Sixth Series] 1847–48 (Shannon: Irish University Press, 1968) (Famine 3), p. 681.

74 Ibid., 2 December 1847, p. 687.

75 Ibid., 27 December 1847, p. 688.

76 *The Waterford Mail*, 5 February 1848.

77 Byrne, 'The Workhouse in Waterford City', p. 121.

78 *Report of the Commissioners of Health*, Appendix No. 14, 'Table showing the date at which Requisitions were issued for the provision of Temporary Fever Hospitals and Dispensaries', p. 60, and Appendix No. 1, 'Plan and Section of Temporary Fever Wards of Economical Construction for Fifty Patients proposed for the Central Board of Health, Ireland', pp. 43–4.

79 Byrne, 'The Workhouse in Waterford City', p. 121.

80 MacArthur, 'Medical History of the Famine', p. 292.

81 Waterford Central Library, 'State of the Fever Hospital from 1 January to 31 December 1846', Item 30/29.

82 Ibid.

83 *The Chronicle and Munster Advertiser*, 22 May 1847.

84 Ibid., 11 September 1847.

85 *The Waterford Mail*, 29 December 1847.

86 *The Chronicle and Munster Advertiser*, 15 January 1848.

87 *Papers Relating to Proceedings for the Relief of Distress*, p. 682.

88 Waterford Central Library, Report of the Committee of the Fever Hospital, Item 30/29.

89 Waterford Central Library, 'State of the Fever Hospital', Item 30/29.

90 *The Chronicle and Munster Advertiser*, 17 April 1847.

91 Ibid., 8 May 1847.

92 *The Waterford Mail*, 15 May 1847.

93 Ibid., 10 July 1847.

94 Ibid., 21 August 1847.

95 Ibid., 27 November 1847.

96 Ibid., 27 October 1847.

97 Ibid., 30 October 1847.

98 Ibid., 29 January 1848.

99 'Mr Burke to the Commissioners – Dissolution of the Board of Guardians, March 17, 1847', in *Papers Relating to Proceedings for the Relief of Distress*, p. 681.

100 Ibid.

101 Ibid.
102 Matthew 22:21.
103 *The Chronicle and Munster Advertiser*, 17 April 1847.
104 Kinealy, *This Great Calamity*, p. 186.
105 *The Chronicle and Munster Advertiser*, 17 April 1847.
106 Kinealy, *This Great Calamity*, pp. 185–94.
107 *Papers Relating to Proceedings for the Relief of Distress*, p. 681.
108 'Return of the Names etc. of the 100 of the Highest Rate Payers who have not yet Paid their Respective Rates in the Waterford Electoral Division', in ibid., p. 685.
109 *The Chronicle and Munster Advertiser*, 17 April 1847.
110 *The Waterford Mail*, 7 April 1847.
111 Kieran Foley, 'The Killarney Poor Law Guardians and the Great Famine', in Maurice J. Bric (ed.), *Kerry: History and Society: Interdisciplinary Essays on the History of an Irish County* (Dublin: Geography Publications, 2020), p. 362.
112 Ibid.
113 Byrne, 'The Workhouse in Waterford City', p. 124.
114 Letter of Sir Henry Winston Barron in *Papers Relating to Proceedings for Relief of Distress*, p. 683.
115 Mr. Burke to the Commissioners, 17 March 1848, in ibid., pp. 681–2.
116 'Medical Officer's Report', 16 March 1848, in ibid., p. 684.
117 Commissioners to the Clerk of the Guardians, 22 March 1848, in ibid., pp. 691–2.
118 Kinealy, *This Great Calamity*, p. 211. For an overview of the dissolution of boards by the Poor Law Commissioners, see ibid., pp. 210–16.
119 Quoted in Foley, 'Killarney Poor Law Guardians', p. 349.
120 William J. Smyth, 'Classify, Confine, Discipline and Punish: the Roscrea Union: A Microgeography of the Workhouse System during the Famine', in John Crowley, William J. Smyth and Mike Murphy (eds), *Atlas of the Great Irish Famine* (Cork: Cork University Press, 2012), p. 131. Smyth is quoting Professor Cormac Ó Gráda.
121 Kinealy, *This Great Calamity*, p. 24.
122 Kinealy, 'Operation of the Poor Law', p. 91.
123 Gray, *The Making of the Irish Poor Law*, p. 334.
124 'Fifth Report of the Irish Relief Commissioners to the Lords of the Treasury', 17 August 1847, published in *The Waterford Mail*, 18 August 1847.
125 Peter Gray, 'British Relief Measures', in John Crowley, William J. Smyth and Mike Murphy (eds), *Atlas of the Great Irish Famine* (Cork: Cork University Press, 2012), p. 84.
126 Kinealy, 'Operation of the Poor Law', p. 95.
127 'Return of Attendance of Guardians from 26 March 1847 to 16 March 1848', in *Papers Relating to Proceedings for Relief of Distress*, pp. 687–8.
128 Mr Burke to the Commissioners in ibid., p. 682.
129 Commissioners to the Clerk of the Guardians, 22 March 1848, in ibid., p. 692.
130 'Return of Attendance of Guardians from 26 March 1847 to 16 March 1848', in ibid., p. 686.

131 *The Waterford Mail*, 31 July; 7, 14, 21 August 1847.
132 See 'Return of Attendance of Guardians from 26 March 1847 to 16 March 1848', in *Papers Relating to Proceedings for Relief of Distress*, p. 688 for the number of meetings. This time period coincided with the 1848 by-election contested by Thomas Francis Meagher and, as was noted earlier, Thomas Meagher was in London during this event.
133 Broderick, 'Famine in Waterford', p. 207.
134 Ibid., pp. 161–2.

CHAPTER EIGHT: FATHER AND SON, 1823–1844: A COMMON PURPOSE
1 Mannion, 'Genealogy, Geography and Social Mobility', pp. 31–2.
2 Michael Cavanagh, *Memoirs of Gen. Thomas Francis Meagher* (Worcester, Mass.: Messenger Press, 1892), pp. 13–14.
3 Ibid., p. 14.
4 Lyons, *Brigadier-General Thomas Francis Meagher*, p. 25.
5 Mannion, 'Genealogy, Geography and Social Mobility', p. 28.
6 Mannion, 'From Comfortable Farms to Mercantile Commerce', pp. 26–7.
7 Sarah-Anne Buckley and Susannah Riordan, 'Childhood since 1740', in Eugenio Biagini and Mary E. Daly (eds), *The Cambridge Social History of Modern Ireland* (Cambridge: Cambridge University Press, 2017), p. 330.
8 Ibid., p. 328.
9 Ibid., p. 329.
10 Ibid.
11 See *The Waterford Mirror*, 30 December 1826, for an advertisement for 'The Misses Quan Academy'.
12 Tony Pierce, 'The "Clongowes" of Thomas Francis Meagher', *Decies: Journal of the Waterford Archaeological and Historical Society*, 59 (2003), pp. 31–9.
13 Ibid., p. 33.
14 Thomas Keneally, *The Great Shame: The Story of the Irish in the Old World and the New* (London: Vintage, 1999), p. 61.
15 Quoted in Erin I. Bishop, *'My Darling Danny': Letters from Mary O'Connell to her Son Daniel, 1830–1832* (Cork: Cork University Press, 1998), p. 2. Mary O'Connell, wife of Daniel O'Connell, was familiar with the curriculum offered at Clongowes, where her son, Daniel, became a boarder in 1830.
16 Ibid.
17 Cavanagh, *Memoirs*, p. 20.
18 Griffith, *Meagher of the Sword*, p. 271.
19 Ibid., p. 272.
20 Cavanagh, *Memoirs*, p. 25.
21 Ibid., p. 17.
22 For an account of Meagher's years at Stonyhurst, see David Knight, 'Thomas Francis Meagher: His Stonyhurst Years', in *Decies: Journal of the Waterford Archaeological and Historical Society*, 59 (2003), pp. 40–52.

23   Denis Gwynn, *Thomas Francis Meagher* (Dublin: National University of Ireland, 1966), p. 7.

24   Cavanagh, *Memoirs*, p. 35.

25   Quoted in Knight, 'Meagher: His Stonyhurst Years', p. 49.

26   Quoted in ibid.

27   Griffith, *Meagher of the Sword*, pp. 280–6.

28   Ibid., p. 282.

29   Ibid., pp. 284–5.

30   Ibid., p. 283.

31   Ibid.

32   Ibid., pp. 299–307.

33   Ibid., p. 299.

34   Ibid., pp. 299–300.

35   Ibid., p. 307.

36   *The Waterford Chronicle*, 6 May 1843.

37   Ibid. The newspaper report reproduced the text of the address.

38   Cavanagh, *Memoirs*, p. 24.

39   *The Waterford Chronicle*, 14 September 1843.

40   E. West, 'Thomas Francis Meagher's Bar Bill', *Decies: Journal of the Waterford Archaeological and Historical Society*, 59 (2003), pp. 113–18.

41   Cavanagh, *Memoirs*, p. 35.

42   Christine Kinealy, *Repeal and Revolution: 1848 in Ireland* (Manchester: Manchester University Press, 2009), p. 31.

43   Cavanagh, *Memoirs*, p. 35.

44   Griffith, *Meagher of the Sword*, pp. 36–7.

45   For an account and discussion of the 'Grand Tour' see Rachel Knowles, 'The Grand Tour', www.regencyhistory.net/2013/04/the-grand-tour.html, accessed 6 August 2020; and Janet Simmonds, 'History of the Grand Tour', *The Educated Traveller* (23 November 2017), www.educated-traveller.com/2017/11/23/history-of-the-grand-tour, accessed 6 August 2020.

46   Robert G. Athearn, *Thomas Francis Meagher: An Irish Revolutionary in America* (New York: Arno Press, 1976), p. 1.

47   Gwynn, *Meagher*, p. 7.

48   Griffith, *Meagher of the Sword*, p. 280.

49   *The Waterford Chronicle*, 11 July 1843.

50   *The Nation*, 30 September 1843.

51   *The Waterford Chronicle*, 19 October 1843.

52   Gwynn, *Meagher*, p. 14.

53   *The Waterford Chronicle*, 19 October 1843.

54   Egan, *The Immortal Irishman*, p. 24.

55   Cavanagh, *Memoirs*, pp. 37–8.

56   Ibid., p. 38.

57   Athearn, *Thomas Francis Meagher*, p. 3.

58   Griffith, *Meagher of the Sword*, p. 289.
59   *The Chronicle and Munster Advertiser*, 10 April 1844.
60   Ibid., 8 June 1844.
61   Ibid., 14 September 1844.
62   Ibid., 21 September 1844.
63   Ibid., 12 October 1844.
64   Ibid., 14 December 1844.
65   Ibid., 18 December 1844.
66   Ibid., 8 June 1844.
67   Ibid., 11 September 1844.
68   Ibid.
69   Ibid.
70   Ibid., 18 December 1844.

CHAPTER NINE: FATHER AND SON, 1845–1847: POLITICAL DIVISIONS
1   McCartney, *Dawning of Democracy*, p. 158.
2   Ibid.
3   James Quinn, *Young Ireland and the Writing of Irish History* (Dublin: UCD Press, 2015), p. 81.
4   Ibid.
5   Bartlett, 'The Emergence of the Irish Catholic Nation', p. 540.
6   Ó Tuathaigh, *Ireland before the Famine*, p. 186.
7   William Sloan, *William Smith O'Brien and the Young Ireland Rebellion of 1848* (Dublin: Four Courts Press, 2000), p. 118.
8   Cavanagh, *Memoirs*, p. 53.
9   Foster, *Modern Ireland*, p. 314.
10   Matthew Kelly, 'Nationalisms', p. 452.
11   MacDonagh, 'The Age of O'Connell, 1830–45', p. 161.
12   These observations are based on comments made by Micheál Martin, TD, on criticisms of Éamon de Valera. See Eoghan Harris, *The Sunday Independent*, 20 September 2020.
13   Geoghegan, 'The Impact of O'Connell', p. 122.
14   Cavanagh, *Memoirs*, p. 43.
15   R.V. Comerford, *Ireland* (London: Hodder Arnold, 2003), p. 37.
16   John Mitchel, 'Mitchel on Meagher', in M.J. MacManus (ed.), *Thomas Davis and Young Ireland* (Dublin: Stationery Office, 1945), p. 72.
17   Egan, *The Immortal Irishman*, p. 28.
18   Thomas Francis Meagher, *Speeches on the Legislative Independence of Ireland* (New York: Redfield, 1853), p. xxii.
19   Cavanagh, *Memoirs*, p. 46.
20   *The Nation*, 27 September 1845.
21   *The Chronicle and Munster Advertiser*, 26 November 1845.
22   Kinealy, *Repeal and Revolution*, p. 65.
23   *The Chronicle and Munster Advertiser*, 8 November 1845.

24   Ibid., 12 November 1845.

25   Ibid., 23 February 1848.

26   Ibid., 15 November 1845.

27   *The Nation*, 20, 27 December 1845.

28   Kinealy, *Repeal and Revolution*, p. 70.

29   *The Chronicle and Munster Advertiser*, 21 March 1846.

30   Griffith, *Meagher of the Sword*, p. 5.

31   Ibid., p. 13.

32   Ibid., p. 19. This speech was delivered on 22 June 1846.

33   Ibid., p. 25. This speech was delivered on 13 July 1846.

34   *The Chronicle and Munster Advertiser*, 10 April 1844.

35   Quoted in Cavanagh, *Memoirs*, p. 43.

36   Gwynn, *Meagher*, p. 10.

37   Quoted in ibid., p. 11.

38   Mitchel, 'Meagher', p. 72.

39   Griffith, 'Preface', *Meagher of the Sword*, p. v.

40   Quoted in Gwynn, *Meagher*, p. 11.

41   Griffith, 'Preface', *Meagher of the Sword*, p. v–vi.

42   *The Chronicle and Munster Advertiser*, 10 June 1846.

43   Griffith, *Meagher of the Sword*, p. 15.

44   Sloan, *William Smith O'Brien*, p. 157.

45   Quoted in MacDonagh, *The Emancipist*, p. 293.

46   Sloan, *William Smith O'Brien*, p. 158.

47   Kinealy, *Repeal and Revolution*, p. 63.

48   Donnelly, 'A Famine in Irish Politics', p. 360.

49   For a general overview of the events leading to the peace resolutions, see John M. Hearne, 'Thomas Francis Meagher: Reluctant Revolutionary', in Hearne and Cornish (eds), *Thomas Francis Meagher*, pp. 66–91, especially pp. 67–76.

50   For the text of this speech, see Griffith, *Meagher of the Sword*, pp. 27–37.

51   Ibid., pp. 35–6.

52   Sloan, *William Smith O'Brien*, pp. 133–64.

53   Michael Doheny, *The Felon's Track* (Dublin: M.H. Gill & Son, Ltd, 1943), p. 107.

54   Cavanagh, *Memoirs*, p. 70.

55   Sloan, *William Smith O'Brien*, pp. 165–96.

56   Ibid., p. 165.

57   Mitchel, 'Meagher', p. 86.

58   Griffith, *Meagher of the Sword*, p. 42.

59   Sloan, *William Smith O'Brien*, p. 165.

60   Cavanagh, *Memoirs*, pp. 76–81.

61   Kinealy, *Repeal and Revolution*, p. 93.

62   Hearne, 'Reluctant Revolutionary', p. 79.

63   Sloan, *William Smith O'Brien*, pp. 197–208, for an account of the events leading to this split.

64   Griffith, *Meagher of the Sword*, p. 46.

65   Cavanagh, *Memoirs*, p. 77.

66   Kinealy, *Repeal and Revolution*, p. 95.

67   Griffith, *Meagher of the Sword*, p. 43.

68   Kinealy, *Repeal and Revolution*, p. 81.

69   Cavanagh, *Memoirs*, p. 77.

70   Kinealy, *Repeal and Revolution*, p. 95.

71   Ibid.

72   Quoted in Sloan, *William Smith O'Brien*, p. 204.

73   Hearne, 'Reluctant Revolutionary', p. 79.

74   Ibid., p. 80.

75   Sloan, *William Smith O'Brien*, pp. 175, 199.

76   Griffith, *Meagher of the Sword*, pp. 136–7.

77   Nowlan, *The Politics of* Repeal, p. 128.

78   Kinealy, *Repeal and Revolution*, p. 95.

79   Thomas F. Meagher (ed.), *Letters of a Protestant on Repeal by the Late Thomas Davis* (Dublin: Irish Confederation, 1847), p. iv.

80   Quoted in Ó Tuathaigh, *Ireland before the Famine*, p. 162.

81   Sloan, *William Smith O'Brien*, pp. 160–70.

82   Cavanagh, *Memoirs*, p. 78.

83   Griffith, *Meagher of the Sword*, p. 61.

84   MacDonagh, *The Emancipist*, p. 84.

85   Foster, *Modern Ireland*, p. 308.

86   Quoted in Ó Tuathaigh, *Ireland before the Famine*, p. 162.

87   MacDonagh, 'O'Connell's Ideology', pp. 154–8, for a fascinating insight into O'Connell's political thinking on the matter of repeal.

88   Ibid., p. 153.

89   MacDonagh, 'The Age of O'Connell, 1830–45', p. 167.

90   Donnelly, 'A Famine in Irish Politics', p. 363.

91   Geoghegan, 'The Impact of O'Connell', p. 114.

92   K. Theodore Hoppen, *Ireland since 1800: Conflict and Conformity* (London and New York: Longman, 1989), p. 22.

93   Griffith, *Meagher of the Sword*, p. 19.

94   Gwynn, *Meagher*, p. 16.

95   Quinn, *Young Ireland and the Writing of Irish History*, p. 91.

96   *The Chronicle and Munster Advertiser*, 19 May 1847.

97   Donnelly, 'The Soup Kitchens', p. 309.

98   Smyth, 'The Creation of the Workhouse System', p. 127.

99   R. V. Comerford, *The Fenians in Context: Irish Politics and Society, 1848–82* (Dublin: Wolfhound Press, 1998), p. 21.

100 *The Waterford Freeman*, 24 February 1847.

101 Daly, 'The Operations of Famine Relief, 1845–47', p. 134.

CHAPTER TEN: TWO ELECTIONS, 1847, 1848

1　Griffith, *Meagher of the Sword*, p. 14.

2　*The Chronicle and Munster Advertiser*, 19 May 1847.

3　Ibid., 10 July 1847.

4　Ibid., 7 August 1847.

5　Kinealy, *Repeal and Revolution*, p. 111.

6　Sloan, *William Smith O'Brien*, p. 193.

7　*The Chronicle and Munster Advertiser*, 25 August 1847.

8　Ibid., 12 February 1848.

9　Ibid., 16 February 1848.

10　Ibid., 19 February 1848.

11　*The Waterford Mail*, 23 February 1848.

12　*The Pilot*, 2 February 1848.

13　*The Freeman's Journal*, 25 February 1848.

14　*The Pilot*, 25 February 1848.

15　*The Chronicle and Munster Advertiser*, 1 March 1848.

16　Ibid., 23 February 1848.

17　Ibid., 4 March 1848.

18　Ibid.

19　*The Freeman's Journal*, 23 February 1848.

20　*The Nation*, 4 March 1848.

21　*The Cork Examiner*, 23 February 1848.

22　*The Chronicle and Munster Advertiser*, 23 February 1848.

23　Ibid.

24　*The Freeman's Journal*, 28 February 1848.

25　*The Chronicle and Munster Advertiser*, 23 February 1848.

26　Sloan, *William Smith O'Brien*, p. 204.

27　*The Chronicle and Munster Advertiser*, 23 February 1848.

28　Ibid., 1 March 1848.

29　Walker, *Parliamentary Election Results in Ireland*, p. 317.

30　*The Chronicle and Munster Advertiser*, 4 March 1848.

31　Ibid.

32　Gwynn, *Meagher*, p. 20.

33　*The Chronicle and Munster Advertiser*, 1 March 1848.

34　Cavanagh, *Memoirs*, pp. 89–90.

CHAPTER ELEVEN: A REBEL SON, 1848–1849

1　For an overview of the impact of the 1848 French Revolution in Ireland, see Kinealy, *Repeal and Revolution*, pp. 136–40.

2　Cavanagh, *Memoirs*, p. 97.

3　Sloan, *William Smith O'Brien*, p. 210.

4　Ibid., pp. 213–14.

5　Cavanagh, *Memoirs*, p. 104.

6   Griffith, *Meagher of the Sword*, p. 156. See ibid., pp. 149–56 for the full text of the speech.

7   See Cavanagh, *Memoirs*, pp. 102–4, for the text of this address. Ibid., p. 109.

8   Ibid., pp. 116–19.

9   Ibid., p. 119.

10 For an account of Meagher's visit to Paris, see ibid., pp. 119–27.

11 Griffith, *Meagher of the Sword*, p. 174.

12 Nowlan, *The Politics of Repeal*, p. 182.

13 Quoted in ibid., p. 183.

14 Ó Tuathaigh, *Ireland before the Famine*, p. 200.

15 Sloan, *William Smith O'Brien*, p. 217.

16 James Connolly, *Labour in Irish History* (Dublin: New Books Publications, 1973), p. 101.

17 Comerford, *The Fenians in Context*, p. 15.

18 Kinealy, *Repeal and Revolution*, pp. 160–6.

19 Quoted in ibid., p. 163.

20 Cavanagh, *Memoirs*, pp. 207–9.

21 Quoted in Sloan, *William Smith O'Brien*, p. 233.

22 Cavanagh, *Memoirs*, p. 206.

23 Ibid., p. 211.

24 Kinealy, *Repeal and Revolution*, p. 188.

25 Hearne, 'Reluctant Revolutionary', p. 85 and Kinealy, *Repeal and Revolution*, p. 189.

26 *The Chronicle and Munster Advertiser*, 12 July 1848.

27 Cavanagh, *Memoirs*, p. 238. For an account of the meeting at Slievenamon, see ibid., pp. 236–40.

28 Hearne, 'Reluctant Revolutionary', p. 85.

29 Cavanagh, *Memoirs*, p. 241.

30 *The Waterford Mail*, 22 July 1848.

31 Kinealy, *Repeal and Revolution*, p. 195.

32 Ibid., p. 188.

33 Hearne, 'Reluctant Revolutionary', p. 87.

34 See Kinealy, *Repeal and Revolution*, pp. 195–201, for an account of the rising. See also William Nolan, 'The Final Days of Meagher's Irish Uprising', in Hearne and Cornish (eds), *Thomas Francis Meagher*, pp. 92–105.

35 Griffith, *Meagher of the Sword*, p. 174.

36 Donnelly, 'A Famine in Irish Politics', p. 368.

37 Meagher, 'A Personal Narrative of 1848', p. 194.

38 *The Waterford Mail*, 29 July 1848.

39 David Smith, 'Thomas Francis Meagher in Love and War: A Narrative History', in Hearne and Cornish (eds), *Thomas Francis Meagher*, p. 203.

40 Kinealy, *Repeal and Revolution*, pp. 146–7.

41 Georgina Flynn, 'The Young Ireland Movement in Waterford 1848', part 1, *Decies: Journal of the Waterford Archaeological and Historical Society*, 18 (September 1981), p. 48.

42   Dermot Power, 'The Politicisation of the People? Strange Episodes in 1848-9', in Des Cowman and Donald Brady (eds), *Teacht na bPrátaí Dubha: The Famine in Waterford, 1845-1850* (Dublin: Geography Publications and Waterford County Council, 1995), pp. 291-310.

43   Hearne, 'Reluctant Revolutionary', pp. 84-5.

44   Christine Kinealy, *The Great Irish Famine: Impact, Ideology and Rebellion* (London: Palgrave Press, 2002), p. 203.

45   Hearne, 'Reluctant Revolutionary', p. 88.

46   *The Nation*, 13 May 1848.

47   Cavanagh, *Memoirs*, pp. 238-9.

48   Hearne, 'Reluctant Revolutionary', pp. 88-9.

49   Thomas Meagher to Roger Sweetman, 31 August 1848. My thanks to Mr Kieran Cronin, Deputy Librarian, Waterford Institute of Technology, for providing me with a copy of this letter.

50   *The Chronicle and Munster Advertiser*, 18 October 1848.

51   *The Times*, 20 October 1848.

52   *The Chronicle and Munster Advertiser*, 25 October 1848.

53   *The Waterford News*, 20 October 1848.

54   *The Chronicle and Munster Advertiser*, 25 October 1848.

55   *The Waterford News* (Supplement), 23 February 1895.

56   Mannion, 'From Comfortable Farms to Mercantile Commerce', p. 28.

57   Lyons, *Brigadier-General Thomas Francis Meagher*, pp. 35-6. Lyons was quoting from an account which had appeared in a publication entitled *Dublin Nation*.

58   *The Chronicle and Munster Advertiser*, 1 November 1848.

59   Atkinson, *Mary Aikenhead*, p. 355.

60   Keneally, *The Great Shame*, p. 195.

61   *The Waterford Mail*, 14 July 1849.

62   *The Chronicle and Munster Advertiser*, 16 August 1848.

63   Quoted in Cavanagh, *Memoirs*, p. 299.

CHAPTER TWELVE: MEMBER OF PARLIAMENT, 1847–1852: LAND AND RELIGION

1   R.V. Comerford, 'Ireland, 1850–70: Post-Famine and Mid-Victorian', in W.E. Vaughan (ed.), *A New History of Ireland*, vol. V: *Ireland under the Union, 1801–70* (Oxford: Clarendon Press, 1989), p. 372.

2   James S. Donnelly, 'Mass Evictions and the Great Famine: the Clearances Revisited', in Cathal Póirtéir (ed.), *The Great Irish Famine* (Cork: Mercier Press, 1995), p. 155.

3   J.H. Whyte, *The Independent Irish Party, 1850-9* (Oxford: Oxford University Press, 1959), p. 5.

4   *The Chronicle and Munster Advertiser*, 23 October 1847.

5   Broderick, 'The Famine in Waterford as Reported in the Local Newspapers', p. 185.

6   *The Chronicle and Munster Advertiser*, 23 October 1847.

7   *The Cork Examiner*, 25 October 1847.

8   *The Chronicle and Munster Advertiser*, 27 October 1847.

9   *The Nation*, 30 October 1847.

10 Broderick, 'The Famine in Waterford as Reported in the Local Newspapers', p. 186.

11 Ibid.

12 *The Chronicle and Munster Advertiser*, 27 October 1847.

13 Whyte, *Independent Irish Party*, p. 5.

14 J.H. Whyte, *The Tenant League in the Eighteen-Fifties* (Dundalk: Dundalgan Press, 1972), p. 6.

15 Whyte, *Independent Irish Party*, pp. 5–6.

16 Ibid., pp. 8–11.

17 See *The Freeman's Journal*, 7, 8, 9 August 1850, for a detailed account of the conference.

18 Ibid., 10 August 1850.

19 Whyte, *Tenant League*, p. 3.

20 J.H. Whyte, 'Political Problems, 1850–1860', in Patrick J. Corish (ed.), *A History of Irish Catholicism*, vol. V (Dublin: M.H. Gill and Son Ltd, 1967), p. 14.

21 R.V. Comerford, 'Churchmen, Tenants and Independent Opposition', in W.E. Vaughan (ed.), *A New History of Ireland*, vol. V: *Ireland under the Union, 1801–70* (Oxford: Clarendon Press, 1989), p. 399.

22 George L. Bernstein, 'British Liberal Politics and Irish Liberalism after O'Connell', in Stewart J. Brown and David W. Miller (eds), *Piety and Power in Ireland, 1760–1960: Essays in Honour of Emmet Larkin* (Belfast: Institute of Irish Studies), pp. 44–5.

23 Ibid., p. 45.

24 Whyte, *Independent Irish Party*, p. 14.

25 Ibid., p. 16.

26 Whyte, *Independent Irish Party*, p. 17. See p. 17, n2.

27 Ibid.

28 Ibid., p. 6, n3, for a list of tenant societies formed in 1850.

29 Donald MacRaild, *The Irish Diaspora in Britain, 1750–1939* (Basingstoke: Palgrave Macmillan, second edition, 2011), p. 175.

30 Ibid., p. 176.

31 For an excellent overview of the 'papal aggression' episode in British history, see Owen Chadwick, *The Victorian Church*, part 1 (London: Adam & Charles Black, third edition, 1971), pp. 271–309.

32 Ibid., p. 294.

33 See *The Freeman's Journal*, 8 November 1850, for the text of the letter.

34 Chadwick, *Victorian Church*, p. 296.

35 Ibid., p. 298.

36 Donal A. Kerr, *'A Nation of Beggars'? Priests, People and Politics in Famine Ireland, 1846–1852* (Oxford: Clarendon Press, 1994), p. 265.

37 Ibid., p. 262.

38 *The Nation*, 22 February 1851.

39 Whyte, *Independent Irish Party*, p. 21.

40 Ibid., p. 304.

41 *The Freeman's Journal*, 28 February 1851.

42 Whyte, *Independent Irish Party*, p. 23.

43 *The Waterford Chronicle*, 8 March 1851.

44 *The Waterford News*, 25 April 1851.

45 Ibid.

46 'Religious Houses Bill', *Hansard 1803–2005*, https://api.parliament.uk/historic-hansard/commons/1851/may/14/religious-houses-bill, accessed 17 March 2021.

47 MacRaild, *Irish Diaspora in Britain*, pp. 174–5.

48 Quoted in James O'Shea, *Prince of Swindlers: John Sadleir MP, 1813–1856* (Dublin: Geography Publications, 1999), p. 146.

49 *The Waterford News*, 25 April 1851.

50 Ibid., 2 May 1851.

51 O'Shea, *Prince of Swindlers*, p. 164.

52 *The Freeman's Journal*, 30 April 1851.

53 *The Waterford News*, 2 May 1851.

54 *The Freeman's Journal*, 30 April 1851.

55 Ciarán O'Carroll, *Paul Cardinal Cullen: Portrait of a Practical Nationalist* (Dublin: Veritas Publications, 2008), p. 39.

56 Ibid.

57 *The Freeman's Journal*, 17 May 1851.

58 Whyte, *Independent Irish Party*, p. 21.

59 Ibid., p. 24.

60 *The Waterford News*, 16, 23 May 1851; *The Freeman's Journal*, 12, 19, 22 May 1851 and 2, 5, 9 June 1851.

61 Whyte, *Independent Irish Party*, p. 23.

62 O'Shea, *Prince of Swindlers*, pp. 172–3.

63 Kerr, 'Nation of Beggars', p. 279.

64 Ibid., p. 273.

65 *The Freeman's Journal*, 17 May 1851.

66 Thomas Meagher to James Burke, secretary to the Catholic Committee, 23 May 1851; published in *The Waterford News*, 6 June 1851.

67 *The Freeman's Journal*, 30 April 1851.

68 Ibid., 24 May 1851.

69 Thomas Meagher to James Burke, secretary to the Catholic Committee, London 23 May 1851; published in *The Waterford News*, 6 June 1851.

70 See, for example, the reports for July: *The Freeman's Journal*, 2, 3, 4, 7, 8, 9, 10, 17, 18, 19, 22, 23, 24, 25, 28, 30 July 1851.

71 O'Shea, *Prince of Swindlers*, p. 187.

72 Whyte, *Independent Irish Party*, pp. 25–7.

73 *The Freeman's Journal*, 11 August 1851.

74 Ibid., 14 August 1851.

75 Ibid., 20 August 1851. *The Freeman's Journal* produced a supplement to its edition on that day, such was the extensive nature of its coverage.

76 Emmet Larkin, *The Making of the Roman Catholic Church in Ireland, 1850–1860* (Chapel Hill: University of North Carolina Press, 1980), pp. 99–100.

77 *The Freeman's Journal*, 20 August 1851.

78 Quoted in Kerr, *'Nation of Beggars'*, p. 294.

79 O'Shea, *Prince of Swindlers*, p. 202.

80 *The Freeman's Journal*, 1 December 1851.

81 MacDonagh, *Hereditary Bondsman*, p. 207.

82 Paul Cullen to Bernard Smith, vice rector, Irish College, Rome, 22 August 1851; quoted in Larkin, *Making of the Roman Catholic Church*, p. 105.

83 Paul Cullen to Bernard Smith, vice rector, Irish College, Rome, 15 September 1851, quoted in ibid., p. 106.

84 O'Carroll, *Paul Cardinal Cullen*, p. 43.

85 *The Freeman's Journal*, 21 August 1851.

86 Ibid., 26, 27 September 1851.

87 Larkin, *Making of the Roman Catholic Church*, p. 107.

88 *The Freeman's Journal*, 18 October 1851.

89 *The Tablet*, 18 October 1851.

90 Larkin, *Making of the Roman Catholic Church*, p. 103.

91 *The Freeman's Journal*, 18 October 1851.

92 See Larkin, *Making of the Roman Catholic Church*, pp. 108–13, and O'Shea, *Prince of Swindlers*, pp. 213–17, for overviews of this complex episode.

93 Steven R. Knowlton, *Popular Politics and the Irish Catholic Church: The Rise and Fall of the Independent Irish Party, 1850–1859* (New York and London: Garland Publishing, 1991), p. 84.

94 Letter of Thomas Meagher to the secretaries, Catholic Defence Association, 17 September 1851, and published in *The Tablet*, 4 October 1851.

95 *The Freeman's Journal*, 18 October 1851.

96 Miriam Moffitt, *The Society for Irish Church Missions to the Roman Catholics, 1849–1950* (Manchester: Manchester University Press, 2010).

97 'The Synodical Address of the Fathers of the National Council of Thurles, 1850', in *Decreta Synodi Plenariae Thurlesianae Episcoporum Hiberniae, Habitae Anno 1850* (Dublin: J.M. O'Toole, 1873), pp. 102–3.

98 *The Waterford News*, 2 January 1852.

99 Broderick, *Waterford's Anglican*, pp. 255–82. See also idem., 'Robert Daly: Ireland's 'Protestant Pope'', *History Ireland*, November/December 2006, pp. 23–8.

100 *The Tablet*, 15 November 1851.

101 *The Freeman's Journal*, 30 January, 4 March 1852.

102 *The Tablet*, 18 October 1851.

103 Thomas Meagher to James Burke, secretary to the Catholic Committee, London 23 May 1851; published in *The Waterford News*, 6 June 1851.

104 *The Weekly Telegraph*, 7 February 1852.

105 Whyte, *Independent Irish Party*, p. 32.

106 O'Shea, *Prince of Swindlers*, p. 228.

107 *The Freeman's Journal*, 14 February 1852; *The Weekly Telegraph*, 8 May 1852.

108 Whyte, *Independent Irish Party*, p. 39.

109 *The Waterford Chronicle*, 14 February 1852.

110 *The Waterford News*, 26 March 1852.

111 *The Weekly Telegraph*, 17 April 1852.

112 Thomas Meagher, London, to J.E. Feehan, 27 March 1852; published in ibid.

113 *The Waterford News*, 16 April 1852.

114 *The Waterford Chronicle*, 17 April 1852.

115 *The Waterford Mail*, 24 April 1852.

116 Ibid., 28 April 1852.

117 Ibid., 8 May 1852.

118 *The Freeman's Journal*, 13 May 1852.

119 *The Waterford News*, 28 May 1852.

120 *The Waterford Mail*, 24 April 1852.

121 Ibid., 19 June 1852.

122 *The Waterford News*, 28 May, 4 June 1852.

123 Ibid., 25 June 1852.

124 *The Weekly Telegraph*, 3 July 1852.

125 *The Freeman's Journal*, 6 July 1852.

126 *The Waterford Chronicle*, 3 July 1852.

127 *The Waterford Mail*, 30 June 1852.

128 *The Freeman's Journal*, 12 June 1852.

129 Whyte, *Independent Irish Party*, pp. 57–9.

130 Ibid., pp. 59–60.

131 Comerford, 'Churchmen, Tenants and Independent Opposition', p. 402.

132 Ibid.

133 Whyte, *Independent Irish Party*, p. 81.

134 This account is based on *The Waterford News*, 13 July 1852 and *The Waterford Chronicle*, 17 July 1852.

135 *The Waterford News*, 16 July 1852; *The Waterford Chronicle*, 17 July 1852.

136 *The Waterford News*, 16 July 1852.

CHAPTER THIRTEEN: MEMBER OF PARLIAMENT, 1852–1857: INDEPENDENT OPPOSITION

1 Whyte, *Independent Irish Party*', pp. 85–6.

2 Ibid., p. 86.

3 For an account of the conference, see *The Freeman's Journal*, 9, 10 September 1852. See Whyte, *Independent Irish Party*, pp. 86–8, for an excellent summary of the occasion.

4 Whyte, *Independent Irish Party*, p. 88.

5 *The Freeman's Journal*, 11 September 1852.

6   See editions of ibid. through September and October 1852 for details of the activities of the Friends of Religious Freedom and Equality.

7   The account of the conference is based on ibid., 29 October 1852.

8   See ibid. for the text of the report.

9   See ibid. for the full text of all resolutions.

10   Whyte, *Independent Irish Party*, p. 89.

11   Ibid.

12   Ibid., p. 93.

13   For an account of the defeat of Lord Derby's government, see ibid., pp. 94–7.

14   *The Freeman's Journal*, 23 December 1852.

15   See *The Freeman's Journal*, 3, 6 January 1853; *The Nation*, 1, 8 January 1853; *The Tablet*, 1, 8, 15 January 1853.

16   *The Freeman's Journal*, 12 January 1853.

17   Ibid., 13 January 1853.

18   Ibid., 2 February 1853.

19   O'Shea, *Prince of Swindlers*, p. 341.

20   Thomas Meagher to Rev. Nicholas McEvoy, PP, Kells, printed in *The Freeman's Journal*, 2 February 1853.

21   Whyte, *Independent Irish Party*, p. 102.

22   This point is considered in ibid., p. 98.

23   *Westmeath Independent*, 1 November 1851.

24   *The Freeman's Journal*, 25 August 1852.

25   Ibid., 5 March 1853.

26   See ibid. for a list of those in attendance.

27   *The Tablet*, 12 March 1853.

28   Ibid. and *The Nation*, 12 March 1853.

29   *The Weekly Telegraph*, 19 March 1853.

30   *The Freeman's Journal*, 7 March 1853.

31   This phrase was used in ibid.

32   *The Weekly Telegraph*, 19 March 1853.

33   Ibid.

34   See Whyte, *Independent Irish Party*, pp. 148–51, for a consideration of this point.

35   O'Shea, *Prince of Swindlers*, p. 343.

36   For example, see James O'Shea, *Priests, Politics and Society in Post-Famine Ireland: A Study of County Tipperary, 1850–1891* (Dublin: Wolfhound Press, 1983), pp. 78–83, for an account of tensions among supporters of the IIP in County Tipperary.

37   *The Freeman's Journal*, 7 March 1853.

38   *The Weekly Telegraph*, 19 March 1853.

39   Charles Gavan Duffy, *The League of North and South: An Episode in Irish History, 1850–1854* (London: Chapman and Hall, 1886), p. 249.

40   Comerford, 'Churchmen, Tenants and Independent Opposition', p. 407.

41   Duffy, *League of North and South*, pp. 322–3.

42   *The Nation*, 18 August 1855.

43   Knowlton, *Popular Politics*, p. 200.

44   Ibid., p. 133.

45   Ibid., p. 255.

46   Douglas Kanter, 'Post-Famine Politics, 1845–1850', in J. Kelly (ed.), *The Cambridge History of Ireland*, vol. III: *1730–1880* (Cambridge: Cambridge University Press, 2018), p. 696.

47   See O'Shea, *Prince of Swindlers*, pp. 307–77.

48   Whyte, *Independent Irish Party*, p. 45.

49   Ibid.

50   Comerford, 'Churchmen, Tenants and Independent Opposition', p. 408.

51   O'Carroll, *Paul Cardinal Cullen*, p. 76.

52   Ibid., p. 48.

53   Knowlton, *Popular Politics*, pp. 158–61.

54   Whyte, *Independent Irish Party*, p. 116.

55   Kanter, 'Post-Famine Politics', p. 697.

56   Knowlton, *Popular Politics*, pp. 176–80.

57   Ibid., pp. 179–80.

58   Kanter, 'Post-Famine Politics', p. 697.

59   Knowlton, *Popular Politics*, p. 125.

60   Whyte, *Independent Irish Party*, 'Appendix B: Irish Liberal MPs 1852–7', pp. 180–81.

61   *The Freeman's Journal*, 14 July 1853.

62   Ibid., 5 October 1853.

63   Whyte, *Independent Irish Party*, 'Appendix B: Irish Liberal MPs, 1852–7', pp. 180–81.

64   *The Freeman's Journal*, 5 May 1853.

65   Ibid., 9 May 1853.

66   Whyte, *Independent Irish Party*, p. 145.

67   'The Army in the Crimea, Sebastopol Committee, Adjourned Debate, 19 July 1855', *Hansard 1803–2005*, https://api.parliament.uk/historic-hansard/commons/1855/jul/19, 1051, 1186, accessed 5 July 2021.

68   Whyte, *Independent Irish Party*, p. 145.

69   *The Waterford Chronicle*, 21 March 1857.

70   *The Waterford Mail*, 19 March 1857.

71   *The Freeman's Journal*, 25 May 1852.

72   Richard Davis (ed.), *'To Solitude Confined': The Tasmanian Journal of William Smith O'Brien* (Sydney: Crossing Press, 1995), p. 378. The entry is dated 16 November 1852.

73   Quoted in *The Waterford News*, 6 May 1853.

74   Ibid., 18 March 1857.

75   *The Freeman's Journal*, 25 May 1852.

76   *The Waterford News*, 18 March 1857.

77   'The Ballot, 22 May 1855', *Hansard 1803–2005*, www.api.parliament.uk/historic-hansard/commons/1855/may/22/the-ballot, 920–47, accessed 5 July 2021; www.api.

parliament.uk/historic-hansard/commons/1856/may/20/the-ballot, 430–50, accessed 5 July 2021.

78 'Administrative Reform, 10 July 1855', *Hansard 1803–2005*, https://api.parliament.uk/historic-hansard/commons/1855/jul/10/administrative-reform, 675–745, accessed 5 July 2021.

79 'Punishment of Death, 10 June 1856', *Hansard 1803–2005*, https://api.parliament.uk/historic-hansard/commons/1856/jun/10/punishment-of-death, 1231–62, accessed 5 July 2021.

80 'Inspection of Nunneries, 10 May 1853', *Hansard 1803–2005*, https://api.parliament.uk/historic-hansard/commons/1853/may/10/inspection-of-nunneries-bill, 79–133, accessed 5 July 2021; ibid., 'Conventual and Monastic Institutions, 28 February 1854', https://api.parliament.uk/historic-hansard/commons/1854/feb/28/conventual-and-monastic-institutions, 53–135, accessed 5 July 2021.

81 See, for example, 'Maynooth College Committee, 15 April 1856', *Hansard 1803–2005*, https://api.parliament.uk/historic-hansard/commons/1856/apr/15/maynooth-college-committee, 1049–104, accessed 5 July 2021; ibid., 'Maynooth College Committee, 19 February 1857', https://api.parliament.uk/historic-hansard/commons/1857/feb/19/motion-for-committee, 874–919, accessed 5 July 2021.

82 *Hansard's Parliamentary Debates*, Third Series, CXLI, 15 April 1856, 1081.

83 Donald H. Akenson, *The Church of Ireland: Ecclesiastical Reform and Revolution 1800–1885* (New Haven and London: Yale University Press, 1971), pp. 199–201.

84 *Hansard's Parliamentary Debates*, Third Series, CXL, 19 February 1856, 1004.

85 Ibid., 15 April 1856, 1081.

86 Ibid., 16 April 1856, 1115.

87 Ibid.

88 'Jewish Disabilities Bill, 11 March 1853', *Hansard 1803–2005*, https://api.parliament.uk/historic-hansard/commons/1853/mar/11/jewish-disability-bill, 71–122, accessed 5 July 2021; and ibid., 'Jewish Disabilities Bill, 15 April 1853', https://api.parliament.uk/historic-hansard/commons/1853/apr/15/jewish-disability-bill, 1217–91, accessed 5 July 2021.

89 *The Waterford Chronicle*, 30 November 1850.

90 Ibid., 14 December 1850.

91 Ibid., 14 February 1852.

92 *The Waterford News*, 26 March 1852.

93 *Hansard's Parliamentary Debates*, Third Series, CXXXVIII, 19 June 1855, 2251–3.

94 *The Waterford News*, 13 July 1855. Ibid., 13, 20 July 1855.

95 *The Waterford Chronicle*, 21 March 1857.

96 *The Waterford News*, 20 March 1857.

97 *The Waterford Mail*, 19 March 1857.

98 *The Waterford News*, 20 March 1857.

99 Duffy, *League of North and South*, p. 224.

100 *The Waterford Chronicle*, 14 February 1852.

101 Ibid.

102 Comerford, 'Churchmen, Tenants and Independent Opposition', p. 411.

103 Kanter, 'Post-Famine Politics', p. 698.

104 Peter Gray, 'Famine and Land, 1845–80', in Alvin Jackson (ed.), *The Oxford Handbook of Modern Irish History* (Oxford: Oxford University Press, 2014), p. 555.

105 *The Nation*, 11 August 1855.

106 Ibid., 18 August 1855.

107 Comerford, 'Ireland, 1850–70: Post-Famine and Mid-Victorian', p. 373.

CHAPTER FOURTEEN: FAITH AND FAMILY, 1847–1874

1 *The Waterford Chronicle*, 14 December 1850.

2 Gearóid Ó Tuathaigh, 'Reassessing Paul Cullen: an Afterword', in Dáire Keogh and Albert McDonnell (eds), *Paul Cullen and his World* (Dublin: Four Courts Press, 2011), pp. 436–7.

3 Gerard Moran, 'The Catholic Church after the Famine', in Brendan Bradshaw and Dáire Keogh (eds), *Christianity in Ireland: Revisiting the Story* (Dublin: The Columba Press, 2002), p. 186.

4 Colin Barr, 'The Re-energising of Catholicism, 1790–1880', in J. Kelly (ed.), *The Cambridge History of Ireland*, vol. III: *1730–1880* (Cambridge: Cambridge University Press, 2018), p. 293.

5 Emmet Larkin, 'The Parish Mission Movement, 1850–1880', in Brendan Bradshaw and Dáire Keogh (eds), *Christianity in Ireland: Revisiting the Story* (Dublin: The Columba Press, 2002), pp. 195–204.

6 Barr, 'Re-energising of Catholicism', p. 298.

7 Larkin, 'Parish Mission Movement', p. 200.

8 *The Waterford News*, 27 March 1863.

9 Ibid., 3 April 1863.

10 Ibid., 20 May 1853.

11 Ibid., 5 June 1863; 27 May 1864.

12 Ibid., 5 January 1855 and 30 December 1864; 16 August 1861.

13 Ibid., 13 November 1863.

14 Ibid., 19 February 1864.

15 Colin Barr, *Paul Cullen, John Henry Newman and the Catholic University of Ireland, 1845–1865* (Notre Dame: University of Notre Dame Press, 2003), pp. 39–44.

16 'Synodical Address of the Fathers of the National Council of Thurles', p. 96.

17 Fergal McGrath, *Newman's University: Idea and Reality* (London: Longman's, Green and Co., 1951), p. 97.

18 Duffy, *League of North and South*, p. 306.

19 McGrath, *Newman's University*, p. 98.

20 Catholic University of Ireland, *Report of the Committee and List of Subscriptions* (Dublin: J.M. O'Toole, 1852), p. 43.

21 McGrath, *Newman's University*, pp. 101–2.

22 Barr, *Paul Cullen*, pp. 133–225.

23 *The Waterford News*, 9 January 1852.

24 Ibid., 3 February 1854.

25 *The Freeman's Journal*, 2 March 1874.

26 Ibid., 14 January 1853; 10 February 1854.

27 Ibid., 3 February 1865.

28 Rafferty, *The Catholic Church and the Protestant State*, p. 14. For consideration of the Protestant character of the state and its implications for Catholics, see ibid., pp. 11–34.

29 Seán Connolly, 'Patriotism and Nationalism', in Alvin Jackson (ed.), *The Oxford Handbook of Modern Irish History* (Oxford: Oxford University Press, 2014), p. 37.

30 Comerford, 'Ireland, 1850–70: Post-Famine and Mid-Victorian', p. 385.

31 Comerford, *The Fenians in Context*, p. 31.

32 Rafferty, *The Catholic Church and the Protestant State*, p. 28.

33 E.R. Norman, *Anti-Catholicism in Victorian England* (Oxford: Routledge, 2016), p. 13.

34 Ibid., p. 14.

35 Richard English, *Irish Freedom: The History of Nationalism in Ireland* (London: Macmillan, 2006), p. 137.

36 Ó Tuathaigh, 'Reassessing Paul Cullen', p. 437.

37 *The Waterford News*, 27 March 1863.

38 Rafferty, *The Catholic Church and the Protestant State*, p. 28.

39 Broderick, *Waterford's Anglicans*, pp. 238–40.

40 *The Waterford News*, 13 July 1852.

41 Egan, *The Immortal Irishman*, p. 85.

42 Meagher to his family, 3 September 1849; published in *The Nation* (New York), 26 January 1850. Quoted in Blanche M. Touhill, *William Smith O'Brien and His Revolutionary Companions in Penal Exile* (Columbia and London: University of Missouri Press, 1981), p. 26.

43 Elaine Sullivan, 'O'Meagher in Australia', in Hearne and Cornish (eds), *Thomas Francis Meagher*, p. 111.

44 Thomas Meagher to Kevin O'Doherty, Lake Sorell, postmarked 2 January 1851, quoted in T.J. Kiernan, *The Irish Exiles in Australia* (Dublin: Clonmore & Reynolds Ltd, 1954), p. 97.

45 Touhill, *William Smith O'Brien*, p. 35.

46 Mitchel, 'Meagher', p. 99.

47 Quoted in Touhill, *William Smith O'Brien*, p. 40.

48 Egan, *The Immortal Irishman*, p. 84.

49 Quoted in ibid., p. 113.

50 Quoted in Kiernan, *Irish Exiles*, p. 97.

51 *The Waterford News*, 3, 10 May 1850.

52 Ibid., 31 January 1851.

53 Sullivan, 'O'Meagher in Australia', p. 111.

54 Gwynn, *Meagher*, p. 35. For Mitchel's description of sailing on this boat, see Mitchel, 'Meagher', pp. 100–1.

55 Thomas Francis Meagher to Kevin O'Doherty, 18 June 1851; quoted in Kiernan, *Irish Exiles*, p. 100.

56 Meagher transcribed this section of his father's letter in one he wrote to Kevin O'Doherty, dated 18 June 1851. See Kiernan, *Irish Exiles*, pp. 99–100 for the text of this letter.

57 Ibid., p. 100.

58 Atkinson, *Mary Aikenhead*, p. 355, n1.

59 See Smith, 'Meagher in Love and War', pp. 198–201, for particulars of Catherine Bennett and her marriage to Meagher.

60 Keneally, *The Great Shame*, p. 234.

61 Gwynn, *Meagher*, p. 36.

62 Davis, '*To Solitude Confined*', p. 212.

63 Egan, *The Immortal Irishman*, pp. 112–13.

64 Smith, 'Meagher in Love and War', pp. 200–1.

65 Sullivan, 'O'Meagher in Australia', p. 116.

66 *The Waterford Chronicle*, 2 July 1853.

67 Ibid., 9 July 1853.

68 Egan, *The Immortal Irishman*, p. 144.

69 Report from the *Irish American*, reprinted in *The Waterford News*, 12 August 1853.

70 *The Waterford News*, 19 August 1853

71 Eugene Broderick, 'Thomas Meagher', in McEneaney and Rosemary Ryan, *Waterford Treasures*, p. 198.

72 Smith, 'Meagher in Love and War', pp. 203–4.

73 Keneally, *The Great Shame*, p. 279.

74 *The Waterford News*, 28 October 1853.

75 Ibid., 12 May 1854.

76 Keneally, *The Great Shame*, p. 280.

77 Egan, *The Immortal Irishman*, p. 159.

78 Keneally, *The Great Shame*, p. 311.

79 Quoted in Eugene Broderick, 'From the Shadow of his Son', p. 59.

80 Keneally, *The Great Shame*, p. 61.

81 Touhill, *William Smith O'Brien*, p. 17.

82 Egan, *The Immortal Irishman*, p. 23.

83 Mitchel, 'Meagher', pp. 72–3.

84 Ibid., p. 73.

85 See *The Waterford News*, 14, 21, 28 February and 14 March 1851.

86 Ibid., 26 April 1851.

87 Ibid., 15 February 1851.

88 Griffith, *Meagher of the Sword*, p. xviii.

89 Foster, 'Foreword', p. xvi.

90 Hearne, 'Reluctant Revolutionary', p. 88.

91 Ibid., p. 89.

92 Lyons, *Brigadier-General Thomas Francis Meagher*, p. 27.

93 Rory T. Cornish, 'An Irish Republican Abroad: Thomas Francis Meagher in the United States, 1852–65', in Hearne and Cornish (eds), *Thomas Francis Meagher*, p. 143.

94 Jon Axline, '"With Courage and Undaunted Obstinacy": Meagher in Montana, 1865–1867', in Hearne and Cornish (eds), *Thomas Francis Meagher*, p. 176.

95 Patrick Maume (ed.), 'Introduction' in John Mitchel, *The Last Conquest of Ireland (Perhaps)* (Dublin: University College Dublin Press, 2005), p. xxii.

96 Brian Farrell, 'The Paradox of Irish Politics', in Brian Farrell (ed.), *The Irish Parliamentary Tradition* (Dublin: Gill & Macmillan, 1973), p. 23.

97 Mitchel, *Last Conquest*, p. 136.

98 Farrell, 'Paradox', p. 21.

99 Basil Chubb, *The Politics of the Irish Constitution* (Dublin: Institute of Public Administration, 1991), p. 11.

100 Farrell, 'Paradox', p. 21.

101 *The Waterford Mail*, 19 March 1857.

102 See *The Waterford News*, 1861, 1862, 1863 passim.

103 Ibid., 25 August 1865.

104 Ibid., 26 July 1867.

105 There is a brief reference to her in the obituary of Thomas Meagher, which appeared in *The Waterford News*, 6 March 1874.

106 *The Cork Examiner*, 29 November 1841. My thanks to Donnchadh Ó Ceallacháin, Waterford Museum of Treasures, for information on Henry Meagher.

107 *Leinster Express*, 25 October 1851; *The Waterford News*, 24 November 1854.

108 *The Waterford News*, 24 November 1854. Ibid., 26 June 1863.

109 *The Freeman's Journal*, 6 January 1876.

110 *The Waterford Mail*, 28 April 1852.

111 Ibid., 8 May 1852.

112 *The Waterford News*, 14 March 1857.

113 P.M. Egan, *History, Guide and Directory of the County and City of Waterford* (Kilkenny: P.M. Egan, 1893), p. 230.

114 *The Nation*, 1 January 1848.

115 *The Waterford News*, 21 June 1861.

116 Ibid., 5 December 1862; 19 February 1864.

117 Ibid., 16 August 1861.

118 Ibid., 6 February 1863.

119 Ibid., 21 March 1862 and 17 January 1902.

120 Ibid., 29 December 1854.

121 Ibid., 22 September 1867.

122 *The Freeman's Journal*, 2 March 1874.

123 *The Waterford News*, 6 March 1874.

124 Ibid.

125 *The Freeman's Journal*, 2 March 1874.
126 *The Munster Express*, 7 March 1874.

Bibliography

PRIMARY SOURCES

John Mannion Papers, St John's, Newfoundland
Papers relating to the Meagher and Quan families

National Library of Ireland
Wyse Papers, Ms. 15,023

Waterford Central Library
Report of the Committee of the Fever Hospital, Item 30/29
'State of the Fever Hospital from 1 January to 31 December 1846', Item 30/29
Subscription List, Waterford Fever Hospital, Item 30/29

Waterford City and County Archives (WCCA)
Minutes of Waterford Corporation
Applications for Freedom, 1824, TNC 1/3

Waterford Museum of Treasures
Captain Roberts's Letters
Address to Thomas Meagher
Will of Thomas Meagher

Roman Catholic Diocese of Waterford and Lismore Archives
Letter of the Rev. Dr Thomas Hearn, PP, to the Secretaries of the Kildare Place Societies,
    8 May 1822.

Newspapers
Ramsey's Waterford Chronicle
The Chronicle and Munster Advertiser
The Cork Examiner
The Freeman's Journal

The Munster Express
The Nation
The Pilot
The Tablet
The Waterford Chronicle
The Waterford Freeman
The Waterford Mail
The Waterford Mirror
The Waterford News
The Weekly Telegraph

Parliamentary papers

Report from the Select Committee appointed to inquire into the State of Ireland, more particularly with reference to the Circumstances which may have led to Disturbances in that part of the United Kingdom, H.C. 1852 (129), viii.

Minutes of Evidence taken before the Select Committee of the House of Lords appointed to inquire into the State of Ireland, more particularly with reference to the Circumstances which may have led to Disturbances in that part of the United Kingdom, H.C. 1825 (181), ix.

Return of the Numbers of Freeholders in each County in Ireland, H.C. 1825 (312), xxii.

Second Report of the Commissioners of Irish Education Inquiry 1826, H.C. 1826–7 (12), xii.

First Report of the Commissioners appointed to Inquire into Municipal Corporations in Ireland, H.C. 1835 (23), xxvii.

Appendix to the First Report of the Commissioners (Southern, Midland and Western Circuit), H.C. 1835 (27), xxvii.

Official publications

British Parliamentary Debates (Hansard)

Papers Relating to Proceedings for the Relief of Distress and the State of the Unions and Workhouses in Ireland [Sixth Series] 1847–48 (Shannon: Irish University Press, 1968) (Famine 3).

Report of the Commissioners of Health, Ireland, on the Epidemics of 1846 to 1850 (Dublin: Alexander Thom, 1852).

SECONDARY SOURCES

Akenson, Donald H., *Discovering the End of Time: Irish Evangelicals in the Age of Daniel O'Connell* (Montreal and Kingston: McGill-Queen's University Press, 2016).

Anon., *Centenary Volume: Benevolent Irish Society, St. John's, Newfoundland* (Cork: Guy and Co. Ltd, 1906).

Anon., *Waterford's Presentation Community: A Bicentenary Record, 1798–1998* (no publication details, 1998).

Anon., *History of the Ursuline Waterford: From the Annals, 1816–2016* (no publication details, 2016).

Anon., *A Short History of Newfoundland and Labrador* (Newfoundland: Newfoundland Historical Society, 2008).

Athearn, Robert G., *Thomas Francis Meagher: An Irish Revolutionary in America* (New York: Arno Press, 1976).

Atkinson, Sara, *Mary Aikenhead: Her Life, Her Work and Her Friends* (Dublin: Gill, 1879).

Axline, Jon, '"With Courage and Undaunted Obstinacy": Meagher in Montana, 1865–1867', in John M. Hearne and Rory T. Cornish (eds), *Thomas Francis Meagher: The Making of an Irish American* (Dublin: Irish Academic Press, 2006), pp. 176–94.

Barr, Colin, *Paul Cullen, John Henry Newman and the Catholic University of Ireland, 1845–1865* (Notre Dame: University of Notre Dame Press, 2003).

—, 'The Re-energising of Catholicism, 1790–1880', in J. Kelly (ed.), *The Cambridge History of Ireland*, vol. III: *1730–1880* (Cambridge: Cambridge University Press, 2018), pp. 280–304.

—, *Ireland's Empire: The Roman Catholic Church in the English-Speaking World, 1829–1914* (Cambridge: Cambridge University Press, 2020).

Bartlett, Thomas, 'The Emergence of the Irish Catholic Nation, 1750–1850', in Alvin Jackson (ed.), *The Oxford Handbook of Modern Irish History* (Oxford: Oxford University Press, 2014), pp. 517–43.

Bernstein, George L., 'British Liberal Politics and Irish Liberalism after O'Connell', in Stewart J. Brown and David W. Miller (eds), *Piety and Power in Ireland, 1760–1960: Essays in Honour of Emmet Larkin* (Belfast: Institute of Irish Studies, 2000), pp. 43–64.

Bishop, Erin I. (ed.), *'My Darling Danny': Letters from Mary O'Connell to her Son Daniel, 1830–1832* (Cork: Cork University Press, 1998).

—, *The World of Mary O'Connell, 1778–1836* (Dublin: Lilliput Press, 1999).

Boyce, D. George, *Nineteenth-Century Ireland: The Search for Stability* (Dublin: Gill & Macmillan, 1990).

—, *Nationalism in Ireland* (London: Routledge, second edition, 1991).

—, *Ireland, 1828–1923: From Ascendancy to Democracy* (Oxford: Blackwell, 1992).

Breen, Mary, *Waterford Port and Harbour, 1815–42* (Dublin: Four Courts Press, 2019).

Broderick, Eugene, 'The Famine in Waterford as Reported in the Local Newspapers', in Des Cowman and Donald Brady (eds), *Teacht na bPrátaí Dubha: The Famine in Waterford, 1845–1850* (Dublin: Geography Publications and Waterford County Council, 1995), pp. 153–213.

—, 'The Famine and Religious Controversy in Waterford, 1847–1850', in *Decies: Journal of the Waterford Archaeological and Historical Society*, 51 (1995), pp. 11–24.

—, 'A Decade of Agitation and Strife: Thomas Meagher, Mayor – 1843, 1844', in Eamonn McEneaney (ed.), *A History of Waterford and its Mayors from the 12th to the 20th Century* (Waterford: Waterford Corporation, 1995), pp. 182–200.

—, 'From the Shadow of his Son: "Honest Thomas Meagher" – the Father of an Irish Patriot', in John M. Hearne and Rory T. Cornish (eds), *Thomas Francis Meagher: The Making of an Irish American* (Dublin: Irish Academic Press, 2006), pp. 37–66.

—, 'Privilege and Exclusiveness: the Unreformed Corporation of Waterford, 1818–1840', in *Decies: Journal of the Waterford Archaeological and Historical Society*, 63 (2007), pp. 165–76.

—, *Waterford's Anglicans: Religion and Politics 1819–1872* (Newcastle upon Tyne: Cambridge Scholars Publishing, 2009).

Buckley, Sarah-Anne and Riordan, Susannah, 'Childhood since 1740', in Eugenio Biagini and Mary E. Daly (eds), *The Cambridge Social History of Modern Ireland* (Cambridge: Cambridge University Press, 2017), pp. 327–43.

Burke, W.P., 'Newport's Waterford Bank', *Journal of the Cork Historical and Archaeological Society*, 4 (1898), pp. 278–86.

Byrne, Cyril (ed.), *Gentlemen-Bishops and Faction Fighters: The Letters of Bishops O'Donel, Lambert, Scallan and Other Irish Missionaries* (St John's Newfoundland: Jesperson Press, 1984).

—, 'The Waterford Colony in Newfoundland, 1700–1850', in William Nolan and Thomas Power (eds), *Waterford History and Society: Interdisciplinary Essays on the History of an Irish County* (Dublin: Geography Publications, 1992), pp. 351–72.

Byrne, Niall, *The Waterford Leper Hospital of St. Stephen & the Waterford County and City Infirmary: a History of Institutional Medicine in Waterford* (Dublin: Linden Publishing Services, 2011).

Byrne, Rita, 'The Workhouse in Waterford City, 1847–49', in Des Cowman and Donald Brady (eds), *Teacht na bPrátaí Dubha: The Famine in Waterford, 1845–1850* (Dublin: Geography Publications and Waterford County Council, 1995), pp. 119–36.

Cavanagh, Michael, *Memoirs of Gen. Thomas Francis Meagher* (Worcester, Mass.: Messenger Press, 1892).

Comerford, R.V., 'Churchmen, Tenants and Independent Opposition', in W.E. Vaughan (ed.), *A New History of Ireland*, vol. V: *Ireland under the Union, 1801–70* (Oxford: Clarendon Press, 1989), pp. 396–414.

—, 'Ireland 1850–70: Post-Famine and Mid-Victorian', in W.E. Vaughan (ed.), *A New History of Ireland*, vol. V: *Ireland under the Union, 1801–70* (Oxford: Clarendon Press, 1989), pp. 372–95.

—, *The Fenians in Context: Irish Politics and Society, 1848–82* (Dublin: Wolfhound Press, 1998).

Connolly, Seán J., 'The Catholic Question, 1801–12', in W.E. Vaughan (ed.), *A New History of Ireland*, vol. V: *Ireland under the Union, 1801–70* (Oxford: Clarendon Press, 1989), pp. 24–47.

—, 'Mass Politics and Sectarian Conflict, 1823–30', in W.E. Vaughan (ed.), *A New History of Ireland*, vol. V: *Ireland under the Union, 1801–70* (Oxford: Clarendon Press, 1989), pp. 74–107.

—, 'The Great Famine and Irish Politics', in Cathal Póirtéir (ed.), *The Great Irish Famine* (Cork: Mercier Press, 1995), pp. 34–49.

Cornish, Rory T., 'An Irish Republican Abroad: Thomas Francis Meagher in the United States, 1852–65', in John M. Hearne and Rory T. Cornish (eds), *Thomas Francis*

Meagher: The Making of an Irish American (Dublin: Irish Academic Press, 2006), pp. 139–62.

Cowman, Des, 'Trade and Society in Waterford City, 1800–1840', in William Nolan and Thomas Power (eds), *Waterford History and Society: Interdisciplinary Essays on the History of an Irish County* (Dublin: Geography Publications, 1992), pp. 427–58.

Cullen, Bob, *Thomas L. Synnott: The Career of a Dublin Catholic* (Dublin: Irish Academic Press, 1997).

Daly, Mary, 'The Operations of Famine Relief, 1845–47', in Cathal Póirtéir (ed.), *The Great Irish Famine* (Cork: Mercier Press, 1995), pp. 123–34.

Davis, Richard, *The Young Ireland Movement* (Dublin: Gill & Macmillan, 1988).

— (ed.), *'To Solitude Confined': The Tasmanian Journal of William Smith O'Brien* (Sydney: Crossing Press, 1995).

Donnelly, James S., 'Famine and Government Response, 1845–6', in W.E. Vaughan (ed.), *A New History of Ireland*, vol. V: *Ireland under the Union, 1801–70* (Oxford: Clarendon Press, 1989), pp. 272–85.

—, 'The Administration of Relief, 1846–7', in W.E. Vaughan (ed.), *A New History of Ireland*, vol. V: *Ireland under the Union, 1801–70* (Oxford: Clarendon Press, 1989), pp. 294–306.

—, 'The Soup Kitchens', in W.E. Vaughan (ed.), *A New History of Ireland*, vol. V: *Ireland under the Union, 1801–70* (Oxford: Clarendon Press, 1989), pp. 307–15.

—, 'The Administration of Relief, 1847–51', in W.E. Vaughan (ed.), *A New History of Ireland*, vol. V: *Ireland under the Union, 1801–70* (Oxford: Clarendon Press, 1989), pp. 316–31.

—, 'A Famine in Irish Politics', in W.E. Vaughan (ed.), *A New History of Ireland*, vol. V: *Ireland under the Union, 1801–70* (Oxford: Clarendon Press, 1989), pp. 357–71.

Downey, Alan, *The Complete Young Irelander: Thomas Francis Meagher* (Waterford: Carthage Press, 1945).

Duffy, Charles Gavan, *The League of North and South: An Episode in Irish History, 1850–1854* (London: Chapman and Hall, 1886).

Earner-Byrne, Lindsey and Urquhart, Diane, 'Gender Roles in Ireland since 1740', in Eugenio Biagini and Mary E. Daly (eds), *The Cambridge Social History of Modern Ireland* (Cambridge: Cambridge University Press, 2017), pp. 312–26.

Egan, Timothy, *The Immortal Irishman: The Irish Revolutionary Who Became an American Hero* (New York: Houghton Mifflin Harcourt, 2016).

English, Richard, *Irish Freedom: The History of Nationalism in Ireland* (London: Macmillan, 2006).

Farrell, Brian, 'The Paradox of Irish Politics', in Brian Farrell (ed.), *The Irish Parliamentary Tradition* (Dublin: Gill & Macmillan, 1973), pp. 13–25.

Finnegan, Frances, *Do Penance or Perish: A Study of Magdalen Asylums in Ireland* (Kilkenny: Congreve Press, 2001).

Foster, R.F., *Modern Ireland, 1600–1972* (London: Allen Lane, The Penguin Press, 1988).

Geary, Laurence, 'Famine, Fever and Bloody Flux', in Cathal Póirtéir (ed.), *The Great Irish Famine* (Cork: Mercier Press, 1995), pp. 74–85.

Geoghegan, Patrick, *King Dan: The Rise of Daniel O'Connell, 1775–1829* (Dublin: Gill & Macmillan, 2008).

—, *Liberator: The Life and Death of Daniel O'Connell, 1830–1847* (Dublin: Gill & Macmillan, 2010).

—, 'The Impact of O'Connell', in J. Kelly (ed.), *The Cambridge History of Ireland*, vol. III: *1730–1880* (Cambridge: Cambridge University Press, 2018), pp. 102–27.

Grace, Pierce A., *The Middle Class of Callan, Co. Kilkenny, 1825–45* (Dublin: Four Courts Press, 2015).

Gray, Peter, 'Ideology and the Famine', in Cathal Póirtéir (ed.), *The Great Irish Famine* (Cork: Mercier Press, 1995), pp. 86–103.

—, *The Making of the Irish Poor Law* (Manchester: Manchester University Press, 2009).

—, 'British Relief Measures', in John Crowley, William J. Smyth and Mike Murphy (eds), *Atlas of the Great Irish Famine* (Cork: Cork University Press, 2012), pp. 75–84.

—, 'Famine and Land, 1845–80', in Alvin Jackson (ed.), *The Oxford Handbook of Modern Irish History* (Oxford: Oxford University Press, 2014), pp. 544–61.

—, 'The Great Famine, 1845–1850', in J. Kelly (ed.), *The Cambridge History of Ireland*, vol. III: *1730–1880* (Cambridge: Cambridge University Press, 2018), pp. 639–65.

Greene, John P., *Between Damnation and Starvation: Priests and Merchants in Newfoundland Politics, 1745–1855* (Montreal and Kingston: McGill-Queen's University Press, 1999).

Griffith, Arthur (ed.), *Meagher of the Sword: Speeches of Thomas Francis Meagher, 1846–1848* (Dublin: M.H. Gill and Son, Ltd, 1917).

Gwynn, Denis, *Thomas Francis Meagher* (Dublin: National University of Ireland, 1966).

Hearne, John M., 'The Official View of the Famine: Waterford, a Regional Dimension', in Des Cowman and Donald Brady (eds), *Teacht na bPrátaí Dubha: The Famine in Waterford, 1845–1850* (Dublin: Geography Publications and Waterford County Council, 1995), pp. 41–67.

—, 'The "Sword" Speech in Context', *Decies: Journal of the Waterford Archaeological and Historical Society*, 59 (2003), pp. 53–8.

—, 'Thomas Francis Meagher: Reluctant Revolutionary', in John M. Hearne and Rory T. Cornish (eds), *Thomas Francis Meagher: The Making of an Irish American* (Dublin: Irish Academic Press, 2006), pp. 66–91.

Hoppen, K. Theodore, *Ireland since 1800: Conflict and Conformity* (London and New York: Longman, 1989).

Kanter, Douglas, 'Post-Famine Politics, 1845–1850', in J. Kelly (ed.), *The Cambridge History of Ireland*, vol. III: *1730–1880* (Cambridge: Cambridge University Press, 2018), pp. 688–715.

Kelly, Matthew, 'Nationalisms', in Richard Bourke and Ian McBride (eds), *The Princeton History of Modern Ireland* (Princeton and Oxford: Princeton University Press, 2016), pp. 447–69.

Keneally, Thomas, *The Great Shame: The Story of the Irish in the Old World and the New* (London: Vintage, 1999).

Kerr, Donal A., *Peel, Priests and Politics: Sir Robert Peel's Administration and the Roman Catholic Church in Ireland, 1841–1846* (Oxford: Clarendon Press, 1982).

Kerrigan, Colm, *Father Mathew and the Irish Temperance Movement, 1838–1849* (Cork: Cork University Press, 1992).

Kiely, Brendan, *The Waterford Rebels of 1849: The Last Young Irelanders and their Lives in America, Bermuda and Van Diemen's Land* (Dublin: Geography Publications, 1999).

Kiernan, T.J., *The Irish Exiles in Australia* (Dublin: Clonmore & Reynolds Ltd, 1954).

Kinealy, Christine, 'The Workhouse System in County Waterford, 1838–1923', in William Nolan and Thomas Power (eds), *Waterford History and Society: Interdisciplinary Essays on the History of an Irish County* (Dublin: Geography Publications, 1992), pp. 579–96.

—, *This Great Calamity: The Irish Famine, 1845–1852* (Dublin: Gill & Macmillan, 1994).

—, *The Great Irish Famine: Impact, Ideology and Rebellion* (London: Palgrave Press, 2002).

—, *Repeal and Revolution: 1848 in Ireland* (Manchester: Manchester University Press, 2009).

—, 'The Operation of the Poor Law during the Famine', in John Crowley, William J. Smyth and Mike Murphy (eds), *Atlas of the Great Irish Famine* (Cork: Cork University Press, 2012), pp. 87–95.

Knight, David, 'Thomas Francis Meagher: His Stonyhurst Years', in *Decies: Journal of the Waterford Archaeological and Historical Society*, 59 (2003), pp. 40–52.

Knowlton, Steven R., *Popular Politics and the Irish Catholic Church: The Rise and Fall of the Independent Irish Party, 1850–1859* (New York and London: Garland Publishing, 1991).

Kurlansky, Mark, *Cod: A Biography of the Fish that Changed the World* (London: Vintage Books, 1999).

Larkin, Emmet, *The Making of the Roman Catholic Church in Ireland, 1850–1860* (Chapel Hill: University of North Carolina Press, 1980).

—, 'The Parish Mission Movement, 1850–1880', in Brendan Bradshaw and Dáire Keogh (eds), *Christianity in Ireland: Revisiting the Story* (Dublin: The Columba Press, 2002), pp. 195–204.

Lee, J.J., 'Daniel O'Connell', in Maurice R. O'Connell (ed.), *Daniel O'Connell: Political Pioneer* (Dublin: Institute of Public Administration, 1991), pp. 1–6.

Loughlin, James, *British Monarchy and Ireland: 1800 to the Present* (Cambridge: Cambridge University Press, 2007).

Lyons, W.F., *Brigadier-General Thomas Francis Meagher: His Political and Military Career* (London: Burns Oates & Washbourne Ltd, 1869).

MacArthur, William P., 'Medical History of the Famine', in R. Dudley Edwards and T. Desmond Williams (eds), *The Great Famine: Studies in Irish History, 1845–52* (Dublin: Lilliput Press, 1994), pp. 260–315.

MacDonagh, Oliver, *The Hereditary Bondsman: Daniel O'Connell, 1775–1829* (London: Weidenfeld and Nicolson, 1988).

—, 'The Age of O'Connell, 1830–45', in W.E. Vaughan (ed.), *A New History of Ireland*, vol. V: *Ireland under the Union, 1801–70* (Oxford: Clarendon Press, 1989), pp. 158–68.

—, 'Politics, 1830–45', in W.E. Vaughan (ed.), *A New History of Ireland*, vol. V: *Ireland under the Union, 1801–70* (Oxford: Clarendon Press, 1989), pp. 169–92.

—, 'Ideas and Institutions, 1830–45', in W.E. Vaughan (ed.), *A New History of Ireland*, vol. V: *Ireland under the Union, 1801–70* (Oxford: Clarendon Press, 1989), pp. 193–217.

—, *The Emancipist: Daniel O'Connell, 1830–1847* (London: Weidenfeld and Nicolson, 1989).

—, 'O'Connell's Ideology', in Laurence Brockliss and David Eastwood (eds), *A Union of Multiple Identities: The British Isles, c.1750–c.1850* (Manchester: Manchester University Press, 1997), pp. 147–61.

MacManus, M.J., (ed.), *Thomas Davis and Young Ireland* (Dublin: Stationery Office, 1945).

MacRaild, Donald, *The Irish Diaspora in Britain, 1750–1939* (Basingstoke: Palgrave Macmillan, second edition, 2011).

McCabe, Ciarán, *Begging, Charity and Religion in Pre-Famine Ireland* (Liverpool: Liverpool University Press, 2018).

McCarthy, Pat, 'The Lost Leader? Thomas Francis Meagher and the Fenian Brotherhood', in John M. Hearne and Rory T. Cornish (eds), *Thomas Francis Meagher: The Making of an Irish American* (Dublin: Irish Academic Press, 2006), pp. 163–75.

McCartney, Donal, 'Electoral Politics in Waterford in the Early 19th Century', *Decies: Journal of the Waterford Archaeological and Historical Society*, 20 (May 1982), pp. 39–50.

—, *The Dawning of Democracy: Ireland, 1800–1870* (Dublin: Helicon Limited, 1987).

McEneaney, Eamonn, 'Waterford and Newfoundland', in *The Newfoundland Emigrant Trail: The Story of Emigration from the South East Coast of Ireland to Newfoundland during the 18th and 19th Centuries* (Waterford: no publication details, 2010), pp. 16–17.

McEneaney, Eamonn, with Ryan, Rosemary, *Waterford Treasures: A Guide to the Historical and Archaeological Treasures of Waterford City* (Waterford: Waterford Museum of Treasures, 2004).

McGrath, Fergal, *Newman's University: Idea and Reality* (London: Longman's, Green and Co., 1951).

Mannion, John, 'Migration and Upward Mobility: The Meagher Family in Ireland and Newfoundland, 1780–1830', *Irish Economic and Social History*, 15 (1980), pp. 54–70.

—, 'A Transatlantic Merchant Fishery: Richard Welsh of New Ross and the Sweetmans of Newbawn and Newfoundland, 1734–1862', in Kevin Whelan (ed.), *Wexford History and Society: Interdisciplinary Essays on the History of an Irish County* (Dublin: Geography Publications, 1987), pp. 373–421.

—, 'Vessels, Masters and Seafaring: Patterns in Waterford Voyages, 1766–1771', in William Nolan and Thomas Power (eds), *Waterford History and Society: Interdisciplinary Essays on the History of an Irish County* (Dublin: Geography Publications, 1992), pp. 373–402.

—, 'From Comfortable Farms to Mercantile Commerce and Cultural Politics: The Social Origins and Family Connections of Thomas Francis Meagher', *Decies: Journal of the Waterford Archaeological and Historical Society*, 59 (2003), pp. 1–29.

—, 'Genealogy, Geography and Social Mobility: The Family Background of Thomas Francis Meagher', in John M. Hearne and Rory T. Cornish (eds), *Thomas Francis Meagher: The Making of an Irish American* (Dublin: Irish Academic Press, 2006), pp. 11–36.

—, 'O'Donel's Mission: Catholics in Newfoundland in the Eighteenth Century', in *Ktaqamkuk, Across the Water, Thar Muir: Irish Journal of Newfoundland and Labrador Research* (Waterford: Waterford Institute of Technology, 2009), pp. 51–90.

—, 'Migrants and Emigrants, Waterford to Newfoundland, 1700–1850: A Geographical Guide', in *The Newfoundland Emigrant Trail: The Story of Emigration from the South East Coast of Ireland to Newfoundland during the 18th and 19th Centuries* (Waterford: no publication details, 2010), pp. 3–6.

Mannion, John, and Maddock, Fidelma, 'Old World Antecedents, New World Adaptations: Inistioge Immigrants in Newfoundland', in William Nolan and Kevin Whelan (eds), *Kilkenny History and Society: Interdisciplinary Essays on the History of an Irish County* (Dublin: Geography Publications, 1990), pp. 345–404.

Meagher, Thomas Francis, *Speeches on the Legislative Independence of Ireland* (New York: Redfield, 1853).

Mitchel, John, 'Mitchel on Meagher', in M.J. MacManus (ed.), *Thomas Davis and Young Ireland* (Dublin: Stationery Office, 1945), pp. 71–104.

Moran, Gerard, 'The Catholic Church after the Famine', in Brendan Bradshaw and Dáire Keogh (eds), *Christianity in Ireland: Revisiting the Story* (Dublin: The Columba Press, 2002), pp. 186–94.

Mulvey, Helen, *Thomas Davis and Ireland: A Biographical Study* (Washington, DC: Catholic University Press of America, 2003).

Murphy, James H., *Abject Loyalty: Nationalism and Monarchy in Ireland during the Reign of Queen Victoria* (Cork: Cork University Press, 2001).

Nolan, William, 'The Final Days of Meagher's Irish Uprising', in John M. Hearne and Rory T. Cornish (eds), *Thomas Francis Meagher: The Making of an Irish American* (Dublin: Irish Academic Press, 2006), pp. 92–105.

Norman, E.R., *Anti-Catholicism in Victorian England* (Oxford: Routledge, 2016).

Nowlan, Kevin B., *The Politics of Repeal: A Study in the Relations between Great Britain and Ireland, 1841–50* (London: Routledge and Kegan Paul, 1965).

O'Brien, John B., *The Catholic Middle Classes in Pre-Famine Cork* (Dublin: National University of Ireland, 1980).

O'Carroll, Ciarán, *Paul Cardinal Cullen: Portrait of a Practical Nationalist* (Dublin: Veritas Publications, 2008).

Ó Ceallacháin, Donnchadh, 'The Temperance Movements in Waterford, 1839–1841', in *Decies: Journal of the Waterford Archaeological and Historical Society*, 52 (1996), pp. 57–91.

O'Connell, Maurice (ed.), *The Correspondence of Daniel O'Connell*, 8 vols (Shannon: Irish University Press, 1972).

O'Connor, Emmet, *A Labour History of Waterford* (Waterford: Waterford Trades Council, 1989).

O'Ferrall, Fergus, *Catholic Emancipation: Daniel O'Connell and the Birth of Irish Democracy, 1820–30* (Dublin: Gill & Macmillan, 1985).

—, *John Ferrall: Master of Sligo Workhouse, 1852–66* (Dublin: Four Courts Press, 2019).

O'Neill, Thomas P., 'The Organisation and Administration of Relief, 1842–52', in R. Dudley Edwards and T. Desmond Williams (eds), *The Great Famine: Studies in Irish History, 1845–52* (Dublin: Lilliput Press, 1994), pp. 207–59.

O'Shea, James, *Priest, Politics and Society in Post-Famine Ireland: A Study of County Tipperary, 1850–1891* (Dublin: Wolfhound Press, 1983).

—, *Prince of Swindlers: John Sadleir MP, 1813–1856* (Dublin: Geography Publications, 1999).

Ó Tuathaigh, Gearóid, *Ireland before the Famine, 1798–1848* (Dublin: Gill & Macmillan, 1972).

—, 'Reassessing Paul Cullen: an Afterword', in Dáire Keogh and Albert McDonnell (eds), *Paul Cullen and his World* (Dublin: Four Courts Press, 2011), pp. 435–43.

Owens, G., 'Constructing the Repeal Spectacle: Monster Meetings and People Power in Pre-Famine Ireland', in M. O'Connell (ed.), *People Power: Proceedings of the Third Annual Daniel O'Connell Workshop* (Dublin: Institute of Public Administration, 1993), pp. 80–93.

Pierce, Tony, 'The "Clongowes" of Thomas Francis Meagher', in *Decies: Journal of the Waterford Archaeological and Historical Society*, 59 (2003), pp. 31–9.

Potter, Matthew, *The Municipal Revolution in Ireland: A Handbook of Urban Government in Ireland since 1800* (Dublin: Irish Academic Press, 2011).

Power, Dermot, 'The Politicisation of the People? Strange Episodes in 1848–9', in Des Cowman and Donald Brady (eds), *Teacht na bPrátaí Dubha: The Famine in Waterford, 1845–1850* (Dublin: Geography Publications and Waterford County Council, 1995), pp. 291–310.

Quinn, James, *John Mitchel* (Dublin: UCD Press, 2008).

—, *Young Ireland and the Writing of Irish History* (Dublin: UCD Press, 2015).

Rafferty, Oliver P., *The Catholic Church and the Protestant State: Nineteenth-Century Irish Realities* (Dublin: Four Courts Press, 2008).

Sloan, Robert, *William Smith O'Brien and the Young Ireland Rebellion of 1848* (Dublin: Four Courts Press, 2000).

Smith, David, 'Thomas Francis Meagher in Love and War: A Narrative History', in John M. Hearne and Rory T. Cornish (eds), *Thomas Francis Meagher: The Making of an Irish American* (Dublin: Irish Academic Press, 2006), pp. 195–222.

Smyth, William J., 'The Creation of the Workhouse System', in John Crowley, William J. Smyth and Mike Murphy (eds), *Atlas of the Great Irish Famine* (Cork: Cork University Press, 2012), pp. 120–7.

—, 'Classify, Confine, Discipline and Punish: the Roscrea Union: A Microgeography of the Workhouse System during the Famine', in John Crowley, William J. Smyth and Mike Murphy (eds), *Atlas of the Great Irish Famine* (Cork: Cork University Press, 2012), pp. 128–44.

—, 'The Role of Cities and Towns during the Great Famine', in John Crowley, William J. Smyth and Mike Murphy (eds), *Atlas of the Great Irish Famine* (Cork: Cork University Press, 2012), pp. 228–39.

Sullivan, Elaine, 'O'Meagher in Australia', in John M. Hearne and Rory T. Cornish (eds), *Thomas Francis Meagher: The Making of an Irish American* (Dublin: Irish Academic Press, 2006), pp. 106–22.

Touhill, Blanche M., *William Smith O'Brien and His Revolutionary Companions in Penal Exile* (Columbia and London: University of Missouri Press, 1981).

Townend, Paul A., *Father Mathew, Temperance and Irish Identity* (Dublin: Irish Academic Press, 2002).

Walker, Brian M. (ed.), *Parliamentary Election Results in Ireland, 1801–1922* (Dublin: Royal Irish Academy, 1978).

Whelan, Irene, *The Bible War in Ireland: The 'Second Reformation' and the Polarisation of Protestant–Catholic Relations, 1800–1840* (Dublin: Lilliput Press, 2005).

Whyte, J.H., *The Independent Irish Party, 1850–9* (Oxford: Oxford University Press, 1959).

—, *The Tenant League in the Eighteen-Fifties* (Dundalk: Dundalgan Press, 1972).

Wyse, Thomas, *Historical Sketch of the Late Catholic Association of Ireland*, 2 vols (London: Henry Colburn, 1829).

Acknowledgements

In writing this book, I accumulated many debts and I am delighted to have this opportunity to acknowledge the assistance of many people. The archivists and library staffs of a number of institutions were generous with their time and expertise: Boole Library, University College Cork; National Library of Ireland; Queen Elizabeth II Library, Memorial University Newfoundland; State Library and Archives Service, Tasmania; and Glasnevin Cemetery Trust. Particular mention must be made of Jane Cantwell, Waterford City and County Librarian and the staff of Waterford Central Library. Over a number of years, I worked my way through newspapers and other material which were to prove invaluable in my account of Thomas Meagher's life. This publication is testimony to the importance of local libraries in historical research. A very special word of thanks to Joanne Rothwell, Waterford City and County Archivist, who was most helpful in facilitating access to various documents. Kieran Cronin, Deputy Librarian, Luke Wadding Library, Waterford Institute of Technology, obtained copies of books which were of special significance in my research and for this I am most grateful. Truly, without good librarians and archivists the work of the historian would be difficult, if not impossible.

Professor John Mannion, the doyen of scholars of the links between Waterford and Newfoundland, was very generous in allowing me access to his extensive collection of primary sources. He and his wife, Maura, were most welcoming when my wife, Miriam, and I visited St John's in September 2019. I am also deeply indebted to Dr Christina Henri, Tasmania, for her kind assistance in facilitating access to material deposited in that state's archives.

I wish to thank Daniel Mulhall, Irish Ambassador to the United States, for his ready willingness to write the foreword, despite the many demands being made on his time.

I express my appreciation to Noel Browne for taking some of the photographs used in this book. I also happily acknowledge the photographic skills of my friend and neighbour, Ray Leahy.

The professionalism and commitment of Irish Academic Press to the production of this book were exemplary. Conor Graham, managing director, Wendy Logue, production manager and Maeve Convery, marketing manager, embraced this project with energy and enthusiasm. It was a pleasure working with them. It is with pleasure and gratitude that I acknowledge the consummate editing skills of Wendy Logue and Caroline Pegum, whose advice and guidance contributed so much to the improvement of the final text.

I wish to acknowledge and thank Waterford City and County Council for their generous financial assistance towards the publication of this book. I would like to especially thank Jane Cantwell, Waterford City and County Librarian, for securing the funding. I happily thank Eamonn McEneaney, Director, Waterford Museum of Treasures, for his support of my application.

Donnchadh Ó Ceallacháin, Rosemary Ryan, Cliona Purcell and John Butler, Waterford Museum of Treasures, have been, as ever, sources of much support and practical help. I owe them much, and not just for their assistance in the writing of this book, but in my other endeavours over many years. It has been my real pleasure to have been associated with them in the work of Waterford Museum of Treasures.

My brother-in-law, Paul Leamy and my good friend, Ann McEneaney, undertook the difficult and time-consuming task of proofreading the text. I thank them most sincerely for undertaking this in such a positive, patient and good-humoured way: their advice and observations made an invaluable contribution towards ensuring a more readable and polished text.

Three people, in particular, made the writing and publication of this book possible: Miriam Broderick, Eamonn McEneaney and Ann Cusack. The Cusack family are the proprietors of the Granville Hotel, formerly the family home of Thomas Meagher for a number of years. Ann has always had a great interest in this Meagher connection with the Granville and has done much over the years to foster an interest in the life and achievements of Thomas Francis Meagher. From the first time I mentioned this book to her, she has been enthusiastic about it. Ann has been most generous in her practical and financial assistance towards its publication, and for this I am very grateful. In thanking her, I also, of course, thank all the Cusack family for their support.

Eamonn McEneaney, Director, Waterford Museum of Treasures, whose constant friendship I have enjoyed over many years, offered much help and counsel in seeing this book to completion. I thank him and the Museum for all the support I have received. More importantly, Eamonn's unquenchable and infectious enthusiasm and energy for the preservation and promotion of Waterford's rich history have always been a source of inspiration and encouragement for my own endeavours. I owe him a great debt of gratitude which I will never be able to repay.

Finally, and most importantly, a sincere word of thanks to my wife, Miriam. She took a particular interest in this book, Thomas Meagher's life appealing to her. Without her unfailing and generous encouragement, this story would never have been told. On a practical level, she read the various drafts, proving herself a gentle, but most perceptive critic. Her comments and observations greatly enhanced the text. It is with much love and gratitude that I acknowledge her vital contribution to this book.

Finally, any errors or deficiencies in this book are entirely my responsibility.

Eugene Broderick
Waterford,
January 2022

Index